Mental Models and Human-Computer Interaction 1

Human Factors in Information Technology *3*

Series Editors:

Hans-Jörg Bullinger
FhG-IAO
Stuttgart
FRG

Peter G. Polson
Institute of Cognitive Science
University of Colorado
Boulder, Colorado, USA

Assistant Series Editors:

Klaus-Peter Fähnrich
Jürgen Ziegler

FhG-IAO, Stuttgart, FRG

NORTH-HOLLAND
AMSTERDAM · NEW YORK · OXFORD · TOKYO

Mental Models and Human-Computer Interaction 1

Edited by

D. ACKERMANN
ETH-Zentrum
Zürich, Switzerland

M. J. TAUBER
Universität Paderborn
Paderborn, FRG

1990

NORTH-HOLLAND
AMSTERDAM · NEW YORK · OXFORD · TOKYO

NORTH-HOLLAND
ELSEVIER SCIENCE PUBLISHERS B.V.
Sara Burgerhartstraat 25
P.O. Box 211
1000 AE Amsterdam
The Netherlands

Distributors for the U.S.A. and Canada:
ELSEVIER SCIENCE PUBLISHING COMPANY, INC.
655 Avenue of the Americas
New York, N.Y. 10010
U.S.A.

Library of Congress Cataloging-in-Publication Data

Mental models and human-computer interaction 1 / edited by D. Ackermann, M.J. Tauber.
p. cm. -- (Human factors in information technology ; 3)
"Selected papers of the 6th Interdisciplinary Workshop in Informatics and Psychology, which was held in Schärding, Austria, in June 1987.
ISBN 0-444-88453-X
1. Human-computer interaction--Congresses. I. Ackermann, D. (David) II. Tauber, Michael J. III. Interdisciplinary Workshop in Informatics and Psychology (6th : 1987 : Schärding, Austria)
IV. Series.
QA76.9.H85M46 1990
004'.01'9--dc20 89-70977
CIP

ISBN: 0 444 88453 X

PRINTED IN THE NETHERLANDS

PREFACE

This book presents selected papers of the "6th Interdisciplinary Workshop in Informatics and Psychology" which was held in Schärding, Austria, in June 1987. Aim of this series of international workshops is to discuss the state of the art of interdisciplinary work between Informatics and Psychology. A central field with this respect is Human-Computer Interaction. The particular workshop presented by this book discussed the concept of mental models and its importance for Human-Computer Interaction research.

Mental model research is based on the assumption that knowledge of how users represent systems and how users should represent systems will lead to a better understanding of usable systems. The hopes are that insights in a user's cognitive processes when using a system could successfully change the current style of designing user interfaces. Current user-interface design is still based more on beliefs and taste rather than on a deep and precise understanding of the user. The mental model approach was introduced by a paper of Norman (Norman, 1983) on the role of mental models and conceptual models for the design of systems.

Mental model research must be interdisciplinary per se. To understand HCI as a new discipline, we need a consistent theoretical framework in which the mental model concept has its central place. Psychology as one major discipline involved in HCI is challenged to extend the scope of research to the study of people using those complex tools and environments provided by computers. This in fact, is a new dimension in psychology and affects model building as well as empirical methods. Informatics or Computer Science as the other major discipline involved in HCI needs for the designing task psychological insights into a user's behaviour and cognitive processes. To consider systems from a user's point of view is a rather new challenge for the designer. HCI research can not be done by simply exchanging problems and results between the two disciplines. To export a problem to the other side and to wait for an answer will not lead to reasonable results. Rather psychologists are asked to become also designers and designers are asked to become also psychologists without loosing the main focus and main methods of their own discipline. Mental model based approaches can only be successful in such a research environment.

The papers presented in the book must be seen from this point of view. They all are an attempt to establish mental model based research in both Informatics and Psychology and to relate it to the joint research on Human-Computer Interaction. The contributors come from both disciplines. Some of the papers can not be assigned clearly to one of the disciplines and they are on the theoretical foundations of HCI. Other can be classified as being a paper of a psychologist or a designer but each of this papers relates the concrete work either to a designing issue if it is mainly a psychological paper or to a psychological issue if it is mainly directed to design. As Green points out in its introductory chapter, HCI at the moment is a very scrappy and disintegrated field. So the reader should not expect that this book can provide any consistent and already solved view to the mental model approach. On the other side, it is the hope of the editors that this book can contribute to a better understanding and promotion of the role of mental models in HCI.

The Content of the Book

The book is organised into 6 parts: Theory, Mental Models and Psychology, Empirical Investigations, Learning, Interdisciplinary Design, and Formal Modelling.

The first part of the book addresses theoretical issues. In his invited opening lecture, Thomas Green analyses the current state of HCI research in a remarkable way. At the moment, there is no fundamental understanding of HCI as a discipline and the field presents itself as "scrappy and disintegrated". On the one side, the mental model approach in HCI is theoretically promising on the way to designing user interfaces guided by theory. On the other side, it is even the theory of mental representation which is not resolved yet in Cognitive Psychology and Cognitive Science. So the question arises whether HCI as the discipline of the design of "usable systems" should wait until these basic sciences have completely solved all the issues on mental models which HCI needs for a theory-guided design. In order to avoid the dilemma that designers either must wait and wait or they have to do their designs without any theoretical foundations, Green suggests to "construe HCI as a progress towards a 'requirements structure' linking many limited theories". By discussing the concept of mental models as a basic problem of Cognitive Psychology and sketching a task-action grammar as a limited theory which has its origin in the mental model approach and which also is useful for designers, Green gives an example how HCI research can escape from that dilemma.

After reviewing several common understandings of the mental model concept as restricted and singular views to the cognitive control of actions, Rasmussen presents a theory of different levels of action control. He distinguishes control of actions at the skill level, the rule level and the knowledge level. Each of these level is another kind of mental representation. Rasmussen discusses how the mental representations are developed during learning and adaptation to the task's requirements. Rasmussen also discusses the importance of means-end considerations for problem solving and understanding.

The second part of the book gives examples for mental model considerations in psychology. Waern's paper on the dynamics of mental models continues the theoretical discussions of the first two papers and determines intention / attention, evocation of prior knowledge, forming a plan, action, evaluation, memorization and interpretation as the main stages in building up a mental model. Supported by an experimental study, Waern works out a concept for providing helps based on the insights about how mental models are developing.

Gumm and Hagendorf discuss relationships between the classical field of problem solving (in psychology) and the new field of HCI. This paper demonstrates how the new questions of HCI influence psychological research and empirical work.

Individual differences in how people use their cognitive system are reflected in the kind of mental models users employ in learning and using a system. Hockey discusses the problem of individual differences in general and the concept of cognitive style in particular. The paper reviews the traditional measures of cognitive style and tests of general abilities as discussed in psychology. Then he proposes an alternative approach based on a analysis of individual differences in information processing skills. This analysis leads to a framework in which individual differences in cognition are conceptualised in terms of skill in the management of competence.

The third part of the book presents some empirical work on a user's mental model. The paper of Ackermann and Greutmann suggests an approach to identifying individual differences in mental models and to reconstruct a user's mental model experimentally. In this approach, cognitive modelling is the key method for representing mental models. Ackermann and Greutmann represent a user's knowledge by a production system and use computer simulations on these representations to identify individual differences. With this method, the authors can explain individual differences in learning and using a system by different mental models.

The paper of Ringelband and Kluwe reports case studies in the domain of complex system control. The main focus of their investigations is on the question how far a user's mental model must match the system's conceptual model in order to ensure a competent interaction with the system. Based on their empirical findings with their particular system, they assume that in contrast to common claims a complete accurate mental model is not always necessary for successfully operating a complex system. In order to evaluate this hypothesis they also constructed a knowledge based system which does not perfectly mimic the conceptual model and used computer simulation on it to see how successfully this knowledge base is operating the system.

The next two papers of part 3 are empirical investigations on using databases. Linde and Bergström report an experimental study to investigate whether pretraining on textual information, pertaining to database content, has any effect on the ability to learn search principles in a database system. Pretraining on textual information that was identical with the content in the database was found to facilitate the learning of search principles. The subjets were also classified as Visualisers or Nonvisualisers. Visualizers tended to have a better search performance. Specific properties of the text that was identical with the content in the database were assumed to account for the larger proportion of "Visualizers", which in turn gave a better search performance. Linde and Bergström discuss their empirical findings in the light of the well known theoretical framework on mental models suggested by Johnson-Laird (1983).

Wettler and Glöckner-Rist employ empirical investigations to find rules for the design of an end-user interface to online bibliographic information systems. The central problem in using those systems is the translation of end-user requests into expressions of the query language. This problem was studied through interviews between professional searchers and end-users. The feasibility and usefulness of this methodological approach is demonstrated.

The two contributions of part 4 are mainly focused to learning of how to use a system. Briggs makes a distinction into learning as an internally versus an externally driven process. The role of a user's mental model differs with respect to these different learning processes. In the case of externally directed learning (being taught or instructed) the mental model plays a role in the communication between a personal or computer-based teacher and the user. Prior expectations are considered as either aids or obstacles in the process of knowledge acquisition. The influence of both, externally directed learning and internally directed learning is discussed based on a field study with real computer novices.

Schindler and Schuster address the problem of how a user might be assisted when learning a system more or less by himself. With the help of experiments, they explore users who teach themselves with respect to their behaviour in exploring and using the system. Then they study two particular learning procedures- learning by examples and learning by rules - and their usefulness in self-directed learning. The analysis brought up a number of unsolved theoretical and practical problems in designing efficient tutorials or online assistance. Therefore the authors propose an iterative designing and prototyping approach to user assistance which is determined by empirical investigations on a user's self-teaching process.

Part 5 has its main focus to a design based on mental model considerations. Wetzenstein-Ollenschläger and Wandke present a framework which discusses design as seen from a cognitive psychologist's viewpoint. By an example, they show how knowledge of cognitive psychology can be used to design interface components through the analysis of human knowledge and task performance. In this framework, the use of empirical investigations plays a central role. The authors argue that methods for the analysis of a user's knowledge and tasks and their results should be incorporated in the design and architecture of User Interface Management Systems. Such an approach would allow design of interfaces being flexible or adaptive with respect to tasks and user characteristics.

Van der Veer et al report the current state of an interdisciplinary research project which has as main goal the development of reference models and representational languages to ensure designs based on an explicit conceptual model of the system and a user's mental model of the application. Although the paper presents an early phase of the project, it shows how an existing application is analysed by the framework. Also some representational issues with respect to prototyping designs based on conceptual models are presented.

Begeman presents a visual interface to an existing message system. He demonstrates that a visual interface which reinforces a user's mental model of the task can aid the user to effectively express that model via the visual supported man-machine communication.

Rohr as a psychologist, discusses some preliminaries to be considered when a graphical query language is to be designed. She addresses the need to find out rules of what should be represented graphically and in which form and discusses the different task characteristics to be taken into consideration. This design phase of the language is supported by empirical analysis and ends up in a first draft to a direct manipulation interface for a database.

Rupietta presents a framework how mental model considerations can lead to structured and better design of user manuals. Manuals should be based on explicit considerations of the conceptual model of a system.

Part 6 contains two papers which are mainly based on a formal modelling approach which can be used to run models of users and tasks on a machine. Desmarais et al. present how the user module of an advice-giving system (coach) can be represented. They describe a formalism for the representation and the inference of a user's state of knowledge which serves as a basis for the user module of a text-editing coach. They show that with a knowledge structure defined with this formalism it is possible to infer user knowledge from the analysis of behaviour in terms of goals, methods, and primitive actions. Moreover, a method is proposed to automatically construct the knowledge structure from data on a number of individual's knowledge state.

Hoppe presents a method called task oriented parsing which inverts the process of task-action mapping. Task-action mapping is a very common model of a user activity in Human-Computer Interaction.

Task oriented parsing works on a formal grammar representing a task structure provided by the system. Such an explicit representation of tasks on the system's side could be helpful for task monitoring, intelligent tutoring, context dependent helps and others. With a bidirectional Prolog program, Hoppe shows how task-oriented parsing and task-action mapping can be realised.

David Ackermann, Michael J. Tauber

Zürich, Paderborn, June 1989

CONTENTS

THEORY

Mental Models and Human-Computer Interaction 1
D. Ackermann and M.J. Tauber (Editors)

LIMITED THEORIES AS A FRAMEWORK FOR HUMAN-COMPUTER INTERACTION

Thomas R.G. Green

Rank Xerox EuroPARC, Cambridge, UK and
MRC Applied Psychology Unit, Cambridge, UK

Must we solve cognitive psychology before doing HCI?

I need hardly say that I am delighted to have been asked to deliver the opening address to this meeting. The high status of this series of workshops has once again been demonstrated by the large number of participants from foreign countries and by the wide variety of papers.

Many opening addresses are designed to tell the audience why the topic of the meeting is important and challenging. I shall not tell you why our topic, "Mental Models in Human-Computer Interaction", is important, because I expect you know. Otherwise you would be somewhere else. Some opening addresses present a review of the state of the art, but I am not sure that our field is ready for a serious review. In fact, our field is remarkably scrappy and disintegrated at present. And it is that very fact, the scrappy nature of the field of human-computer interaction (HCI), that has led me to take a more ambitious theme: to suggest a way in which this field might be structured, and to show how the particular topic of mental models in HCI fits into the structure that I shall propose.

This theme was suggested to me while ruminating on the problems raised by mental models. Mental models are a very convincing idea, well supported by intuition and to some degree supported by research. The difficulty is that mental model research quickly leads us to face some of the central questions of cognitive science and cognitive psychology, to do with the nature of imagery and the mental representations of objects, of causal relations, of temporal phenomena, and the like. These are intractable issues on which huge amounts of research effort has already been spent. It is most unlikely that the issues will be resolved in, say, the next decade. On the other hand, understanding more about mental models is vital for the progress of HCI. So we have a dilemma - if we HCI workers wait for the purer disciplines, cognitive science and cognitive psychology, to resolve the issues raised by mental models, we shall wait literally for years. During that time, the designers and evaluators of computer-based devices will have no option but to continue their present practice, which is to design devices with little or no reference to the mental models created by the user.

Indeed, mental models are not unusual in this respect. The same is true of other topics in HCI. Do we wish to look at errors in using systems? Then we must consider theories of the control of action, theories of working memory, theories of knowledge representation. Do we wish to . . . ? And so on.

On the face of these things, therefore, making generalisations and theoretical statements in HCI will be impossible for many years to come. Yet the alternative horn of this dilemma is just as painful. If HCI workers cannot make adequate theoretical statements, they will be reduced to performing simple user acceptance tests on every new device that is designed. That would be intolerable. Remember that testing any one design can take months. There really is no possibility that every individual design could be satisfactorily tested, especially during the present torrent of innovation.

If HCI is going to get anywhere reasonably soon, we must find a resolution to this dilemma. It is obviously not true that we need to solve the whole of cognitive psychology before we can make a single useful statement about HCI!

The purpose of my talk, therefore, is to propose a resolution to this dilemma. What I propose is this: we should construe HCI as a progress towards a 'requirements structure' linking many limited theories. Briefly, my argument is this:

- we cannot 'solve' even a simple case completely without 'solving' cognitive psychology, which is not yet possible.
- we cannot proceed without generalisations at the theoretical level; but they must be 'limited', so that they are not tied to the whole of cognitive psychology.

- we cannot proceed using large numbers of unlinked generalisations (which is what we are trying to do), because we do not know when to use which.
- so we must find a way to link these limited generalisations.
- a suitable link is a 'requirements structure', which attempts to describe what is required of a satisfactory interface in order to support a desired mode of behaviour.

In the next two sections, after reminding ourselves of some background ideas in this area I shall explore some simple cases, and show how ideas about mental models in HCI burst their wrappings and leak back into the rest of cognitive psychology. In the concluding two sections I shall sketch how the problem might be resolved.

What and why are mental models?

Before starting to consider how well the mental model notion stands up to real life examples, we should perhaps remind ourselves of some of the fundamental ideas.

One structure models another, as Professor Rasmussen (this volume) reminds us in a later chapter, when the elements of the two structures are different but the relations between the elements are substantially the same - although usually, the model contains only a carefully chosen subset of the relations in the target structure. In the case of mental models in HCI, various target structures might be modelled in various ways. Tauber (1988) lists some of the distinctions that can be found in the literature, such as the user's model of the system, the system's model of the user, the designer's model of the user's model of the system, etc. I shall concentrate particularly on the user's model of the system. It is important to recognise that such models are created for a purpose - they do not merely exist as some sort of optional extra in the user's head. And that purpose, according to Rasmussen, is to assist the user in finding appropriate actions to achieve his or her goals. Rasmussen expounds his 'SRK' (skill-rules-knowledge) framework, showing how action may take place at the skill level, at the rule level, or at the knowledge level. It is at the knowledge level, he argues, that mental models are used. In contingencies which have forced the user to appeal to reasoning, rather than acting by learnt rules or well-practised skills, it is easier to reason about a simplified model than about the real world in all its complexity.

The conventional wisdom decrees that the designers of systems and applications programs should try to ensure that program entities and functions support and agree with the hypothesized mental models brought by new users when they first meet the system. A common example is the spreadsheet, an applications program type where the program entities (rows and columns of figures related by simple formulae) are very similar to the 'external' domain entities (since those are likewise rows and columns of figures related by simple formulae). Spreadsheets have been received with great acclaim and are now very widely used, and this is often seen as convincing support for the dogma that program entities should match mental model entities.

What is the nature of these mental entities? Young (1983) has distinguished between two important types of mental models. One is the surrogate. "A surrogate model S of a device D is essentially just the familiar notion of a 'working model' ... Typically S presents a highly simplified account of D ... S is called a surrogate because it can be used instead of D for answering questions about D's behaviour." (Young, 1983, p. 40). The other type is the task/action mapping, which "describes the structure of the task and action domains in such a way that there is a simple and direct mapping between their corresponding parts." Since it will not normally be possible to achieve this over the whole domain, one or more central core tasks and their core action sequences are chosen which can be put into close correspondence" and other tasks are mapped by expressing them as variants of the core tasks. (Op. cit. p. 45).

Payne (1987a) takes the surrogate concept further and shows how it can be amalgamated with the mental models proposed by Johnson-Laird (1983) for a rather different purpose, to produce "concrete analogical representations that are 'run' rather than reasoned about" (Payne, op. cit.). This distinction, between mappings and runnable analogies, may never have been intended to be a sharp division, but that is what it has tended to become in the literature; and, at the same time, the actual complexities of using these hypothetical models seem to have been somewhat ignored.

We are all familiar with some of the research findings in this area. For instance, a well-known paper by Halasz and Moran (1983) showed that novice users of a simple device, in this case a calculator, learnt more or less equally well whether they were given ordinary instructions or a mental model on which to base their learning, as long as the performance measure was based on mastery of what they had been taught; however, the 'mental models' group performed better on a test which required reasoning about novel, untaught, aspects of the calculator's behaviour. These and similar findings have helped to establish the 'mental models' notion as an important contribution to HCI.

Moran (1983) distinguished between two different conceptual worlds: the "external" world of goals and subgoals, and the "internal" world of the system. Setting out to write a sonnet is an external goal. So is the goal of replacing a word because you cannot find a rhyme. On the other hand, making the actual text-editing device delete the word in question is an internal task, solved perhaps by crossing the word out with a pen (and regarding that sign as a communication comprehensible to subsequent readers), or perhaps by issuing the EMACS command "escape-D", or perhaps by the vi command "dw", or perhaps by the typical Macintosh actions "point to word, drag, press Backspace", etc. These are different 'methods', in the sense established by Card et al. (1983) in their GOMS model, where one or more methods were associated with each user goal, and each method was eventually representable as a sequence of operators usable on the particular device being described. Following the Moran-Young approach I shall refer to Device Methods, meaning the way that a particular goal is achieved when using a particular device. Different methods will be appropriate for different devices, even when the external goal remains the same. In the following section I shall explore some aspects of methods.

Mental models and real tasks

The previous section somewhat cursorily revisited some analyses of what mental models are. Now we must think about how they are used. Two ways to use them are figuring out actions to perform, and interpreting the state of the environment. They are also used for repairing mistakes in performance of intended actions, and for learning how to do tasks. No doubt they have other uses, but as the last verse of an old song goes, "if I knew any more / it'd be too long." I shall give a brief illustration of how they have been applied in each of these four ways, and in each case my aim is to show how the study of mental models 'leaks' back into the rest of psychology.

My first example is intended to demonstrate the weakness of the dogma that program entities should match mental model entities. An important need - perhaps even the primary need - for mental models is that they should help users get their tasks done. Given that mental entities are related to program entities, then they should support task requirements. This need may conflict with the ideal of making the entities in the application program match the entities in the outside world of the application domain, and if a solution is found, the effect may be to create unwelcome complexity in the Device Model. Again, the simple contrast given above between types of mental model (surrogates versus mappings) is inadequate: I shall use my second example to argue that mental models contain components as needed, and that the contrast breaks down even in cases that appear quite innocuous at first. This example will focus particularly on the problems of repairing live performance. Finally, turning to the use of mental models in learning, I shall describe an analysis showing how users can exercise a certain degree of choice over what they have to learn about a system by choosing to build a simple mental model or an elaborate one.

Example 1

My first example describes a graphics construction package written for the Macintosh, and originally designed to support the construction of comic strips and similar material. In the past, assembling documents containing both text and graphics has been extremely cumbersome, because the fundamental storage mechanisms are quite different. One method has been to prepare the graphics in a separate program, and then to insert them into the running text. This approach is adequate for documents which consist mainly of text, like this one, and where the graphical parts are separate entities from the text. Comic strips, of course, freely combine text and graphics, with the text sometimes overlaid on top of the graphics or sometimes fitted in to blank spaces in the graphics. Nobody can prepare graphics in one program and text in another program and hope to make them fit! The package I shall describe attempted to provide a method for achieving this goal which would combine the freedom of the artist's usual tools, pencil, pen, and airbrush, with the facilities made available by the use of the computer. It is reasonably successful, but not entirely.

Figure 1. A typical comic strip design. Note close fitting of text and graphics.

The program in question, which I shall call "Comic Opera" (not its real name), identifies four entities which appear in the application domain (figure 1): pages, panels, easels, and balloons. Pages contain panels (the boxes containing successive episodes of the strip). Panels can contain any number of easels, on which artwork is placed, and balloons, which contain text. As in the 'real world' (can comics be said to be part of the real world?), each easel and balloon is recognisably part of a particular panel, and normally lies entirely within the panel - although methods are provided to allow exceptions in which bits of artwork or text can stick out of a panel.

So much for the entities. The tasks of the user will include making first drafts; jiggling bits around to improve the spatial relationship; rewriting text; redrawing artwork; re-ordering panels; etc. To support these, each easel and balloon in Comic Opera is owned by a particular panel, so that when the panel is moved all its easels and balloons move with it. Each panel can possess any number of easels, so that different components of the picture can be separately drawn on different easels and can then be touched up without destroying each other; the same for balloons. Each easel and balloon is displayed superimposed on the ones 'behind' it, and as they are successively created they are placed 'in front'; naturally, there are methods for re-ordering them, as well as provision for 'transparent paper' so that an easel need not obscure the background.

Without elaborating on Comic Opera any further, I think it will be clear that what we have here is a relatively complex Device Model. The original devices that we listed above, the pens, pencils, and airbrushes of the artist's trade, require a great deal of skill to use them properly, but are not complex in themselves. To support the same tasks in a different setting, the designers of Comic Opera have been forced to create a rich ontology and provide for operations such as 'change superimposition order' which have no analogues in the original devices. These various entities, and how they relate, are hard to learn. It may be hard to realise just how hard to learn, without looking more closely at what has to be learnt, so let's compare the Device Model for pencil and for Comic Opera, with reference to the task of adding a caption to a panel. The method for the Pencil Device will be something like:

To add a caption to a panel:

write the caption, draw a balloon around it.

The method for the Comic Opera Device will be something like:

To add a caption to a panel:

select the panel; choose the desired balloon shape; select the balloon tool; place a balloon in the right place; click on the balloon to get the re-shaping handles; drag its handles to the right place (so that the words come out of someone's mouth, for instance); select the text tool; mark the start of the text; start typing the text; if the final balloon obscures something important, change its superimposition order (or use various other techniques).

The comparison is not entirely fair, because the Pencil Device does not support easy revision, while the Comic Opera Device allows balloons to be reshaped with ease. So users of the Pencil Device must be able to envision exactly what size to make their balloon, and will probably therefore need to construct at least one rough draft as well as carefully scheduling their tasks so that the balloons are constructed at the right point in the sequence of building up the picture. Nevertheless, it is clear that the Task Models for the two devices are pretty different. And we can add a different kind of complexity to that. The program has to distinguish on the screen between four different types of 'bounded graphic entity', namely the pages, panels, easels, and balloons already mentioned. Each must be distinguished in some way to show what kind of entity it is, where its boundaries are, what it is 'on top' of, whether it has been selected or not, and (for an easel or a balloon) which panel owns it. Comic Opera makes a valiant try, but this is a tall order and not surprisingly users take some time to learn the distinguishing features. Waern (this volume) draws attention to the difficulties learners have in forming the correct conceptual model of even a simple word-processing system, so that they treat a space as a particular sign rather than as part of a blank background; the problems with Comic Opera are much greater.

The conclusion I want to offer from this example is very simple. Although the analysis of mental models can easily be seen as a mission to make the system model exactly fit the user's conceptual model, such an attempt should not be made lightly. As applications more nearly approach this aim, they may introduce too much complexity in the Device Model for users to be able to use them. A 'fit' between mental model and system model is not necessarily always a good thing.

Example 2

I shall use my second example to argue that the simple contrast between types of mental model (surrogates versus mappings) is inadequate: mental models contains components as needed, and the contrast breaks down even in cases that appear quite innocuous at first. Worse, their use demonstrates that some of the most difficult problems in cognitive psychology need to be resolved before we can fully understand the mental processes involved.

I shall consider here a very different, and very much simpler, type of device, one that is not connected with the world of HCI in any direct way: the three-hole tabor pipe, used in England to accompany morris dancing, which is a type of elaborate folk dance. Such a device should be considered first in the context of use, so I ask you to consider yourselves to be pipers at the end of an exhausting day. You have played a good many tunes and they are beginning to get jumbled in your head. You may well have imbibed a certain amount of alcoholic refreshment (morris dancing takes place near pubs, for technical reasons we need not consider here). Out there stand six people with large sticks, who have not thought to tell you what tune they are going to require next. The leader of the group chaffs the audience in traditional style and finishes by announcing the next dance. You are expected to recall the tune and play it, instantly and correctly. If you go wrong you must quickly recover yourself and repair your performance well enough to keep the dancers going without missing beats or phrases. Breaking down irretrievably will probably bring you seven years' bad luck - beginning with the wrath of six people wielding large sticks.

What goes on in the piper's head?

At first sight, playing a simple tune by rote memory is a skill based on a very simple mental model of the device, in which each available note of the instrument is mapped onto a particular fingering to obtain that note. This would lead us to suppose that the relevant type of mental model would be a mapping, in the sense of Young. The skilled player would then use what appears, at first, to be a very simple algorithm:

Pipe Algorithm 1:

> Listen to the tune 'in the head', by scanning successive notes in the mental representation. Translate each note into the appropriate fingering by consulting the mental model of the device.

However, the three-hole pipe uses a fingering system that is rather like the fingering of the trumpet. There are only four effectively distinct finger combinations, which are: all holes open, thumb hole closed, thumb and first finger holes closed, all three holes closed. ('Upper' holes dominate 'lower' holes, so if the thumb hole is open it makes no difference whether the finger holes are open or closed.) These four combinations are re-used several times to cover the compass of twelve or thirteen notes usually employed, and - again like on the trumpet - the breath pressure determines which note is sounded.

Now, a design like this has interesting properties, considered from the perspective of the mental processes in the player. First, there is no single perceptual dimension on to which the different note-fingerings can be mapped. Contrast the multiplicity of fingerings with the 'fingering' of a piano, where there is a very salient perceptual dimension, because the notes are spread out in space. The space-based piano algorithm, for playing by ear with one finger, really is very simple (especially if we ignore black notes!):

Piano Algorithm:

> to play a high note, move to the right: to play a note that is, say, an octave higher than the note just played, move your finger approximately 16 cm to the right.

The piano algorithm is based on relative pitches of successive notes of the tune, whereas our first pipe algorithm is based on absolute pitches. This makes it clear that the pipe player who uses Algorithm 1 has to solve a different problem from the pianist using our Piano Algorithm, because of having no strong spatial dimension to utilise. It is well-known that absolute pitch (the ability to name a single note heard in isolation) is much rarer and harder to learn than relative pitch, which suggests that Algorithm 1 is unlikely to be a good algorithm for most players. A further problem is that Algorithm 1 demands that the piper stores the tune as a succession of distinct and unrelated notes.

Moreover, there is some suggestion that handling a device on which the same action is required to achieve several rather different goals can be difficult (Norman, 1981); the user cannot examine the most recently-performed action to repair a lapse in concentration and obtain unambiguous information from it. Many musicians report 'waking up' during performance and asking themselves "Hey, which bit am I playing?", and indeed this switch from unconscious or automatic processing to conscious processing is a moment when many slips of action can occur. The piper who is using Algorithm 1 will get little information by examining the state of his fingers, since the same fingering can be used for many notes. Even if he knew what note he had just played, little information is conveyed by that one note, just as little information is conveyed by observing that one has just typed the letter 'r' while writing a paper.

A more likely suggestion is that the experienced piper codes the tune not as successive and unrelated notes, but as a series of phrases which are mostly familiar. (This would tie in with the observation that sight-reading random notes is much harder than sight-reading music in, say, the style of the classical tradition.) The piper has now formed a better conceptual model of the domain, one which includes scalic passages (C-D-E-F-G), arpeggios (C-E-G), leaps from dominant to tonic (G-C), such cadential clichés as C-B-C, and so on. The amount to be remembered about each tune would be much less, and the piper could generate a pattern of finger movements from each phrase, perhaps using a dictionary of 'motor programs'. On 'waking up', observing the pattern of finger movements would give one much more information than observing a single fingering, both about the particular cliché and also about where one had got to in the tune, since clichés are repeated less often than notes.

These clichés are not entirely sufficient to describe a tune, however. Other material that the player must need to recall will include 'landmarks', such as what note the tune starts on, what is its highest point, which notes are difficult to play, etc; and structural aspects of the tune, such as sequences and 'musical rhymes' (repetition or near-repetition of phrases). (For a more scholarly analysis of this topic, see West et al., 1985, and other papers in that volume.) All this information, some of which is shown in figure 2 must be combined while the piper is playing, so it must be used in real time to generate the next individual fingering for the next note of the tune.

Pipe Algorithm 2:

> Recall a variety of different types of information about the tune and combine it to compute the next note or sequence of notes.

Advantages:

> reduces translation load; solves 'waking up' problem.

Disadvantages:

> gets trapped by capture errors and has no way to predict them nor to recover from them.

Algorithm 2 is much more likely to succeed, but it still has a problem: it easily gets trapped on certain unexpected phrases, such as the point marked in figure 2 where the expected note is a G (because the cliché E-C-G is very familiar) but the correct note is an A. These 'capture errors' are very familiar in other contexts (Norman, 1981) and can readily be observed in musical performance. What is the piper to do now? The answer is that the truly experienced piper, the one who is not for the first time playing at the end of an exhausting day during which more than one beer went its way, has also learnt about himself (or herself). The piper has a self-model which predicts enough of the mistakes to have provided a body of repair points. "This will be a difficult bit, if I go wrong under pressure where shall I pick the tune up from?" At this point, I would maintain, we have moved from the Skill level of Rasmussen's Skill-Rules-Knowledge framework, which characterised Algorithm 1, to the Knowledge level, where a mental model is being used.

Pipe Algorithm 3:

> As Algorithm 2 but also use a simple self-model to add extra information to the representation of the tune, showing (a) traps, where performance might easily go wrong, and (b) repair points - where to start again after a crash.

What have we now achieved by considering this task in some detail?

First, the distinction between a mapping and a surrogate has broken down. The pipe algorithm probably uses some components of each. Secondly, the importance of perceptual support for mappings has been remarked on; this is what differentiates between the pipe and the piano. Thirdly, the need for a self-model has been noticed, showing how in real tasks it seems likely that the user incorporates such fragments as are needed, with no respect for differentiations between one thing and another that might worry the theorist. Finally, and very importantly, we have left our piper casually combining "all available information" to translate a tune into a fingering pattern.

The theoretical psychology of information combination is not in a strong condition at present. One can readily point to areas, such as word recognition or phoneme production, which closely resemble our pipe example, in that a wide variety of different types of information at various levels (syntactic, semantic, pragmatic) can be shown to be relevant to performance, and it seems that these sources of information are combined, in real time, not in some rigid top-down way but as a flexible control mechanism. Many different models of, say, word recognition have been proposed to account for the effects. The underlying mechanisms of these models are remarkably diverse - file-access models, logogen models, cohort models, horse race models, etc. have

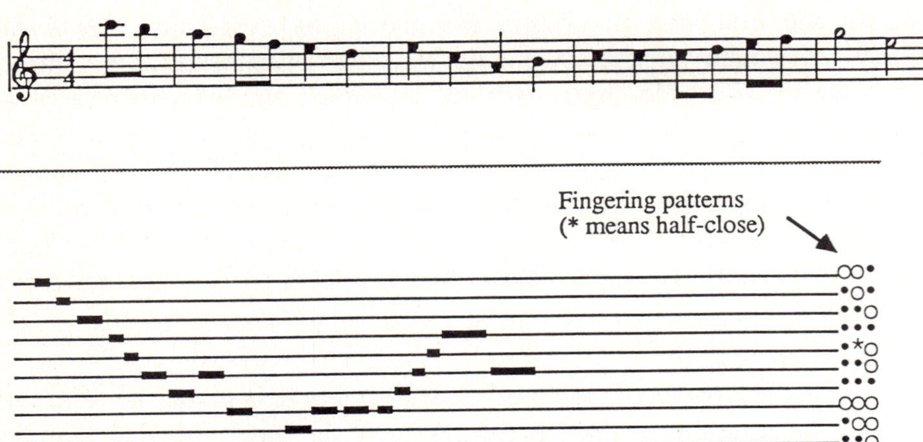

a) In this view, the piper has a simple representation of time (horizontal axis) and pitch (vertical axis). Pitches are translated one by one into fingerings for notes, as the tune is played.

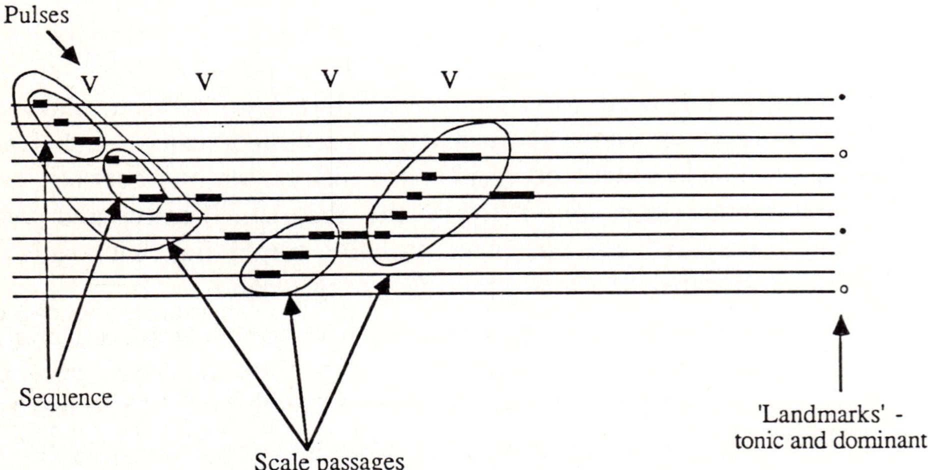

b) This view shows some of the higher-order knowledge about the tune and about the structure of the musical scale. Scaling passages can be run off as a familiar sequence of movements, as can chord patterns (no example shown). A sequence is a repetition of a phrase at a different pitch.

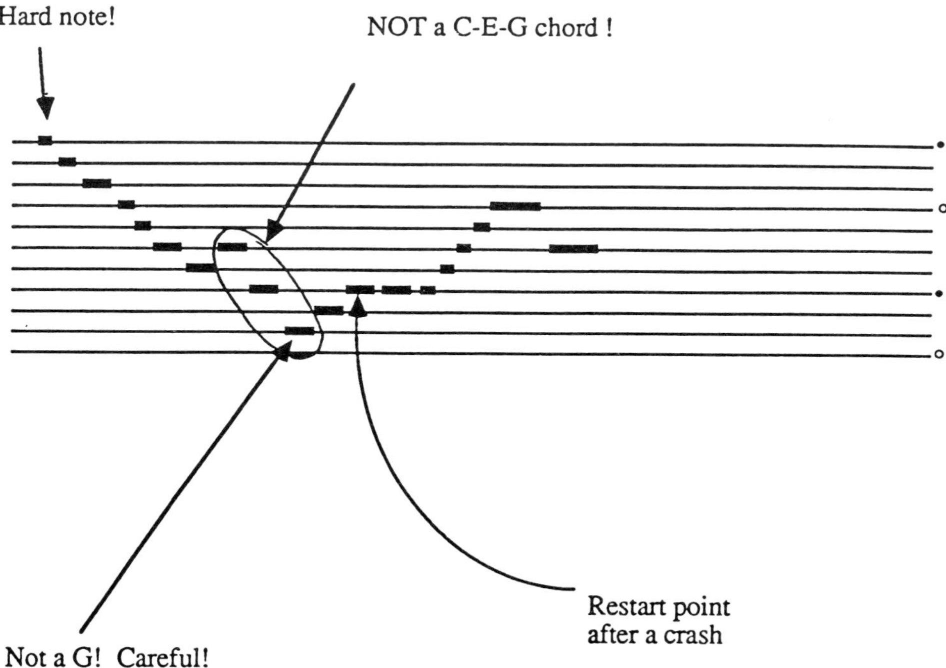

c) This view shows additional information based on the piper's self knowledge. The passage labelled 'NOT a C-E-G chord' is likely to be the site of a capture error, because the C-E-G pattern is very familiar and starts with the same two notes; the representation shown not only carries a warning about that but also shows a point to restart playing if a capture error occurs and disturbs the performance.

Figure 2. The start of the morris tune 'Brighton Camp' (shown above in conventional music notation). Three successively fuller representations of the tune and the knowledge about it. The performer combines information from the low-level representations (a), the musical structure (b), and the 'difficult-bits' representation (c). How ?

all been put forward to explain the facts of word recognition and priming (Forster, 1976; Morton, 1979; Marslen-Wilson and Tyler, 1980; Norris, 1982); some of these attempts seem extraordinarily artificial. Presumably their proponents were struggling more with the difficulties of devising a flexible control mechanism than with the details of the psychological phenomena, so that virtually any mechanism that came to mind which could react flexibly enough was seized upon to become the basis of a model. Inescapably one must conclude that at present researchers are still searching for a good framework with enough generality to model the facts of real-time combination of information from different sources.

The conclusion from this example is, therefore, that when we consider real-life tasks, even the most simple of devices leads us into areas of cognitive psychology where serious unsolved problems are to be found. How are we going to avoid these difficulties?

Example 3: mental models in learning

Needless to say a mental model exists for a reason. It is something that the user relies upon in handling certain tasks. Rasmussen's work within the Skill-Rules-Knowledge framework has shown how the mental models can be used in two kinds of tasks - to help users interpret signals from the environment, and to help in working out appropriate actions. The previous section illustrated how mental models, especially reflexive models, might be used to help in repairing performance errors.

This section is devoted to the role of mental models in learning a system. In particular, we shall look at the analysis made by Payne (1987a, 1987b) of how a learner might choose to deliberately create different kinds of mental model in order to allow different styles of learning. Such an analysis goes some way to explain the large individual variation among mental models that has been demonstrated by the work of Ackermann and his co-workers (Ackermann and Stelovsky, 1988; Ackermann and Greutmann, this volume).

Payne's very detailed analysis is applied to the text editor TEdit, marketed by Xerox as part of its Interlisp-D operating system. At the cost of dispensing with some of his ideas, I shall simplify the analysis and apply it to the much better-known application program MacDraw, an 'object-oriented' graphics program marketed by Apple for the Apple Macintosh. The interface language to this program has already received a certain amount of formal analysis from various angles (Payne and Green, 1986; Schiele and Green, in preparation).

Interface languages are frequently described by manufacturers in terms of their features, but an alternative mode is to analyse how the user's tasks can be achieved by applying those features. The skilled user of, say, MacDraw, can be seen as one who knows how to perform a large repertoire of tasks by invoking familiar methods. This view of 'skill as knowledge' is very familiar in such areas as cognitive science (Anderson, 1983), student learning models (Young and O'Shea, 1981), and human-computer interaction (Card et al., 1983); with regard to the latter's GOMS model, the authors say explicitly that 'what distinguishes cognitive skill from problem solving is the packaging of operator sequences into integrated methods' (p. 367). Without wishing to detract from the very real achievements of the authors cited, Payne lists some weaknesses in the approach. His most profound criticism is that their concentration on procedural knowledge overlooks the readily-demonstrable presence of a great deal of conceptual knowledge. It is here, of course, that mental models come into their own, as a form of representation of the user's conceptual knowledge.

Now, individual variation in mental models is very great. The work of Ackermann and his team has documented several examples. But it is not clear why this individual variation should exist; is it merely random, or does it fit into some larger pattern? Payne's analysis suggests how it might fit into a larger pattern. He describes how individuals might choose to elaborate their mental model in order to reduce the amount of purely procedural learning they need to acquire. Let us look at the use of MacDraw.

Among the tasks that the experienced user of MacDraw might wish to perform is that of moving a graphic object from one place to another. This is readily performed by the following sequence:

To move an object:

locate cursor on object
depress mouse button
move mouse to new position, keeping button depressed
release button.

The actions involved occur frequently enough for them to be characterised by most users, we imagine, as a single operation, 'dragging', applied to the relevant object, so the sequence can be simplified to the form:

drag object to new position.

Although this is a simplification it only requires the creation of a macro-operator, 'drag', which is no more than a repackaging of the primitive actions. To invent a macro-operator is to create an integrated method, in the sense of Card et al. cited above; it does not require any substantive change in the user's conceptual model, so it can readily be analysed by the skill-as-method approach.

Now consider the task of moving an object to a new position while constraining the movement to be either horizontal or vertical - a useful facility when one wishes to preserve an existing alignment. The action sequence for this is:

To perform constrained motion:

locate cursor on object
depress mouse button
depress SHIFT key
move mouse to new position, keeping button depressed
release button
release SHIFT key.

This action sequence is considerably longer than the previous one; moreover, it is not susceptible to being simplified by creating macro-operators. Still worse, the order of pressing the mouse button and the Shift key is important. Pressing them in the opposite order produces a different action (a multiple selection, for those familiar with the Macintosh).

The point that Payne makes is that users have a choice. They can indeed learn the long and arbitrary sequence of operators, but they have the choice of revising their conceptual model. If they take the latter course, they can create for themselves a model of the MacDraw device which has an 'object selected' state and a 'constrained action' state. They can then represent their 'how-to-do-it' knowledge in a different way. Instead of representing it solely as actions required in order to achieve external goals, some of their knowledge becomes knowledge of how to change the state of the MacDraw device. Eg:

To enter 'constrained action' state:

depress SHIFT key.

Thus, users can accept a more elaborate mental model of the device, in order to simplify their representation of methods for achieving goals; or, if preferred, they can do the opposite. The context which Payne analyses shows that a good deal of variation is possible even in a quite simple case.

Presently available research on the mental models constructed by users certainly shows wide variation from user to user. It would be extremely interesting to see whether there was any degree of systematic connection between the users' conceptual models of their devices, and the how-to-do-it knowledge that they internalise. The implication of Payne's analysis, of course, is that there should be a relationship such that complex action sequences are linked with simple conceptual models and vice versa. This is, once again, unexplored territory, where the notion of a mental model has led us into looking at cognitive styles in learning, a whole literature of research to be imported and digested. Once again we have to ask: does HCI have to wait for this research activity to be completed?

Limited and unlimited theories

The examples given in the last section demonstrated how the idea of a mental model led us, unwillingly but irresistibly, into areas where cognitive psychology has no solutions. One way to resolve the difficulty is to insist on developing theories and models for limited purposes. In this section I shall discuss an example of a limited theory, Task-Action Grammar (Payne and Green, 1986).

What do I mean by a 'limited theory'? I certainly do not mean "any familiar topic within HCI". The present scrappy and unsatisfactory state of the field is largely created by doing research on "any familiar topic within HCI" while ignoring the relationships between topics and the fact that different topics may be drawn from fundamentally differing categories. Thanks to such an approach to research strategy, we find that in conferences and journals there are unexpected neighbours: research on something like the usability of menus (essentially ergonomic) jostles against research on the nature of Unix expertise (essentially a problem of knowledge representation) or research on how to improve speech recognition (essentially a problem in technology).

An important requirement is to distinguish between a limited theory in HCI, and a typical theory or model in standard cognitive psychology. To explain this, let me picture a user wondering how to make a particular device do a particular thing. A description of the process by which the user remembers or constructs a suitable method would qualify as an HCI theory. On the other hand, a description of the faculty of working memory would not qualify. Working memory is undoubtedly a resource that is employed by the user, but it forms part of the domain of cognitive psychology, not of HCI. Existing knowledge of working memory should be imported into HCI but it should not be considered part of HCI's own domain of study. Deciding precisely where to draw the boundaries is not easy and it may not be possible to define strict boundaries, nor even desirable to attempt to do so.

One should not, by the way, try to distinguish between HCI and straight psychology by pointing to the presence or absence of a computer system in front of the subject. Cognitive psychology may employ computers for its experiments, and HCI is only fortuitously concerned with the computer: its real aim, as I see things, is to explain the General Theory of the Artefact. Computers happen to be an extremely interesting class of artefact, that's all.

A limited theory: Task-Action Grammar

Task-Action Grammar (Payne and Green, 1986) is a theory (or better, model) developed for a single purpose, to explicate the notion of consistency in an interface. Consistency is the property of 'family resemblance' between different parts of a system - so that deleting a word is more or less like deleting a character, or drawing a square is more or less like drawing a circle. Taking again the MacDraw program mentioned above, we find that the method for drawing an ellipse (rather than a circle) is this:

Draw an ellipse:

Select the 'ellipse' tool, place mouse in appropriate place on graphics plane, drag to other place, release.

To adapt this for drawing a circle, all that is needed is to hold the Shift key down while doing it.

Draw a circle:

Hold Shift key down and proceed as though drawing an ellipse.

The intelligent user can perhaps figure out in advance the following method for drawing rectangles and squares. Even if the method is not figured out in advance, its family resemblance with the circle method makes it easy to remember and easy to recall when needed:

Draw a rectangle:

Select the 'rectangle' tool, place mouse in appropriate place on graphics plane, drag to other place, release.

Draw a square:

Hold Shift key down and proceed as though drawing a rectangle.

The characteristic of consistency, as modelled by TAG, is that similar tasks, as seen by the user, are performed by similar action sequences. Drawing ellipses and rectangles are rather similar tasks, and in MacDraw, a notably consistent system, they are achieved by rather similar methods.

It is essential to keep it clear that TAG models the tasks as seen by the user. The presentation above assumed that circles were seen as special cases of ellipses, and that squares were seen as special cases of rectangles. The interface language captures this conceptualisation by assigning the Shift key to the special cases. But many children become familiar with squares, rectangles, and circles well before they become familiar with ellipses, and they might see the ellipse as a special kind of circle rather than seeing the circle as a special kind of ellipse. In that event the structure above would not work so well for them. Possibly it would be better to use a standard command for drawing a circle, and to put the Shift key down to mean a 'special' circle - i.e. an ellipse.

In order to capture this relationship between the tasks and the actions, we need some method to describe the tasks. Presumably the user has a concept of the task to be performed, and TAG accordingly views the tasks as concepts. Many psychological models of concepts have been proposed, and TAG uses the very simplest, in which concepts are defined by features. Continuing to use MacDraw as our example, typical features and their possible values are:

effect :	insert/delete/move
type of entity :	rectangle, ellipse, line, ...
special case :	Yes/No

Thus, the task 'draw a square' (conceptualised as a special case of a rectangle) is defined by the following feature-values:

effect = insert
type of entity = rectangle
special case = Yes

Now we come to the representation of actions. Most formalisms for describing 'how-to-do-it' knowledge are built around 'methods' for accomplishing tasks; they assign a hierarchical structure to these methods, so that one method can invoke several sub-methods, such as 'drag the mouse from A to B'. TAG does likewise except that to relate the tasks to the required actions it uses a 'feature grammar'. This grammar determines which set of feature values invokes which method, in the following manner. Any particular grammar rule is applicable when, and only when, a specified set of features is present in the task. For drawing a square, the features are those just listed above:

Draw a square:
task [effect = insert, type of entity = rectangle, special case = Yes]
-> press SHIFT + draw-object [type of entity = rectangle]

This rule will be invoked whenever the user is trying to perform a task that has the specified feature values; since those values define the task of drawing a square, the rule will only be invoked when the user is trying to draw a square. The rule calls for one direct action, 'press SHIFT', and invokes a sub-method. The sub-method for 'draw an object' has various different forms depending on what type of object is to be drawn. Using a hierarchical representation like this is one way to model the user's knowledge, based on the assumption that users try to avoid forming multiple, independent representations of methods, and instead use a subroutine-like structure in which 'draw an object' has a single representation that can be invoked whenever desired.

Let's take this a step farther. The user, we have supposed, sees squares as special rectangles, and the system supports this view. How can we represent this fact? What we certainly do not want to do is to have one task rule specifically for squares, and to introduce another task rule specifically for rectangles - i.e., we don't want to have the following pair of rules:

```
**task [effect = insert, type of entity = rectangle, special case = Yes]
      -> press SHIFT + draw-object [type of entity = rectangle]
**task [effect = insert, type of entity = rectangle, special case = No]
        -> draw-object [type of entity = rectangle]
```

That representation would lose the very considerable similarity between the two rules.

Instead, the representation we shall use is a generalised one where the special action, pressing Shift, is only performed when a special result is wanted, like this:

```
task [effect = insert, type of entity = rectangle, special case = ANY]
     -> special-action [special case] +
         draw-object [type of entity = rectangle]
special-action [Yes] -> press SHIFT
special-action [No]  -> NIL            {i.e. take no action}
```

(Note: in these last rules, the feature 'Special case' is used essentially as a parameter to a subroutine to determine whether a special action is needed. In a Pascal-like language, we would see a construction like "if special-case = Yes then press SHIFT".)

The importance of using the feature values becomes apparent when we consider how to represent knowledge of how to draw circles and ellipses. The similarity between drawing rectangles and drawing ellipses will be readily apparent to most users. This is a statement of faith, made by the designer or the analyst when constructing a Task-Action Grammar: it is readily testable, since it predicts that most users, once shown how to draw a rectangle, will be able to generalise to drawing ellipses. Moreover, if these users already know how to draw a square (as a special case of a rectangle), and if they conceptualise circles as special cases of ellipses, they will also be able to generalise to drawing circles. That is precisely what we mean by consistency. TAG describes this state of affairs by allowing a single generalised rule which draws many kinds of graphic objects:

```
task [effect = insert, type of entity = ANY, special case = ANY]
     -> special-action [special case] + draw-object [type of entity]
draw-object [type of entity]  ->  select-tool [type of entity] +
                                   move-mouse ...
```

In this manner, a single expression becomes a generalised statement applying to several types of action sequence. The important thing is that such a compact representation is only possible when two conditions are fulfilled:

- the interface language has a consistent structure,
- and that structure fits the user's mental representation.

To see what happens when these conditions are not fulfilled, consider the TAG representation of a system where a special shortcut is provided for drawing a square. The shortcut could be anything, e.g. 'press Control-S', and the idea is that the designer has provided it because it is such a frequently used action that it is better to accept the inconsistent interface structure than to force users to adopt a longwinded method each time they need to draw a square. What we want to verify is that, when a totally inconsistent shortcut of this type is provided, TAG will show that the user has more to learn. And indeed, that is what we see. (We cannot, of course, provide any way to demonstrate that the designer has, or has not, made the correct choice.) The earlier representation now has to be expanded to include a special case for the square:

task [effect = insert, type of entity = rectangle, special case = Yes]
-> press 'CONTROL-S'

That means that at least one more top-level rule must be learnt. Perhaps worse, the special case must be defined out of the features of the other rules, so that we know not to apply them:

task [effect = insert, type of entity = ellipse, special case = ANY]
-> ..... as before

task [effect = insert, type of entity = rectangle, special case = No]
-> ..... as before

So we find here that a system which contains an inconsistent command (that is, a command which cannot be figured out by thinking about the other commands) requires more rules. This gives us a metric of consistency which can be applied to a design for a system. Not a very well-normalised metric, it is true, yet it serves to predict relative learnability between different, but related, designs.

Of course, the exact formalism that would most aptly describe the cognitive representation is a matter for conjecture. Maybe the last two rules would be better presented as a single general rule, the same one as before but with an exception condition stating "This rule must not be applied when type of entity = rectangle AND special case = Yes". Variations in the details of representation would alter the value of a consistency metric.

Conjecture of this sort is fruitless in the present state of knowledge and indicates that we have reached the limit of reasonable application of TAG; it can give a general account of sources of difficulties, but when predictions become heavily dependent on particular details of the formalism, we need to turn to the literature on retrieval from long-term memory and the uses of formal techniques of knowledge representation to model the retrieval phenomena. This is a level of sophistication which has not been attempted in the HCI context as yet. If we push TAG any harder to answer questions it was not intended to handle, it will start to 'leak' into the broader areas of psychology. Any limited theory will do the same.

Some of the other aspects of TAG, such as the way in which it handles mnemonics, are explained in Payne and Green (1986). We have established enough here to serve our purpose of showing firstly how it handles consistency; secondly, that it makes no attempt to handle the many other aspects of interface design, including the visual feedback given by the system in response to commands; and thirdly, that it makes no claim to describe how the user performs tasks, the actual processes of cognition. In this sense it is a limited theory, and will remain limited unless we push it too hard.

A structure of linked theories

The final problem is this. If we are to conceive of HCI as dealing in limited theories, instead of holistic models, how will we know which such theory to apply at any given time? We have seen how the notion of mental models has leaked into the rest of psychology as soon as we started to apply it to a realistic situation. The same will happen with Task-Action Grammar if thoroughly applied. As we have just seen, it leads into questions of long-term memory and of knowledge representation. There is a tendency for every good theoretical idea to turn into yet another way to look at the rest of the field. The problem is to prevent that.

The solution, I suggest, is motivate theoretical ideas in a different way. The normal approach to theorising in cognitive psychology is to propose a theory and then to see how much can be predicted from it, squeezing as much juice as possible from whatever fruit it bears. This approach is widely, and I think correctly, accepted as the proper way to proceed in pure psychology. But in a strictly applied area, it seems to me that a more useful approach is to pose well-considered questions and then to apply whatever theoretical apparatus is available to obtain an answer to those questions. No theory or model is to be extended outside the questions it was designed to answer.

Theoretical ideas will then be motivated strictly by the questions they were meant to answer. Any time we find ourselves addressing a different question, we can choose to abandon that theory and turn to a different theoretical idea. No single theory need attempt to define the whole of relevant knowledge.

Such an approach can only work if a satisfactory framework of questions can be formulated. This section proposes a framework based on 'requirements'. I shall take a common type of task, the design task, and briefly examine some of the relevant literature describing how people behave. The present evidence indicates that a particular mode of behaviour, 'serendipitous planning', is preferred; systems and interfaces which allow this style are apparently easier than ones which impose different constraints. If we accept this evidence, then we can ask what requirements are necessary to support serendipitous planning. And it is at this point that we can at last see the notion of 'mental model' in context, as one theoretical notion amongst many, a theory which can answer questions about one type of requirement.

Planning and performance

Careful studies of user activity have now been reported in a number of different situations. Among these, Whitefield (1985) has studied computer-assisted design activity by professional designers using their normal working system. Whitefield separated time spent in activity that was directly related to the task set to the designers from time spent in activity that was not directly productive - essentially this means that the time was spent in getting CAD tool to do right thing or in cleaning up after a small change which made other small changes necessary. Whitefield formed the conclusion that the designers were willing, within the limit of the tools they were using, to work on whatever goal came to mind, as long as it could be approached without undue difficulty.

They did not pursue the strategy of taking one task goal, breaking it into subgoals, solving each subgoal in turn, and then taking the next task goal. Such a strategy is implied by simple theories of performance, but a more realistic view appears to be that users keep an agenda of unsolved subgoals, and can proceed with any one of them at any time.

As Whitefield points out, the nearest approach to such behaviour in the literature on computational models of planning is the 'opportunistic' planning model proposed by Hayes-Roth and Hayes-Roth (1979). This model contains a variety of special mechanisms to achieve its effects; but I shall not detail these mechanisms here. The mode of behaviour is more relevant to our present concerns than the computational means by which it is accomplished. One of the features that characterises this approach is sudden shifts of level, from high level activity to detailed activity and back again, as required.

Studies of design by other researchers have led to similar conclusions. Hoc (1981, 1988) reports on studies of program design using different types of system, which lead to the suggestion that the preferred strategy is opportunistic but that the details of the interface can determine the strategy. Siddiqi and Sumiga (1986) have proposed a model of program design based on opportunistic planning and have shown how it applies to data on the construction of Pascal programs. Flower and Hayes (1980) have shown similar behaviour in designing documents. Ullman et al. (1987, cited by Guindon et al.) have documented similar behaviour in the area of mechanical design. Carroll and Rosson (1985) have analyzed cases of system design and lay great stress on the designer's willingness to change the level of abstraction, to make small changes often and occasionally to make very large changes and start redesign almost from scratch, because, they argue, a new understanding of the 'real' problem has been achieved.

Finally, in a particularly ambitious study, Guindon et al. (1987) made detailed studies of professional designers solving a difficult problem. They write: "Our observations ... show that designers use a wide variety of design strategies, both within and between designers, in addition to the top-down refinement approach described in software engineering. We also found that our designers were able to work at different levels of abstraction and detail and not just follow a balanced development strategy. We also observed serendipitous problem-solving, not reported in previous studies of software design by individuals" (p. 80), where by 'serendipitous' design they mean a process similar to opportunistic design but where the process is "controlled by recognition of partial solutions, at different levels of detail or abstraction"; and add "we speculate that exploration of the problem environment induces serendipitous design, as opposed to balanced development. However, in the absence of specialized design schemas [familiar methods] we believe serendipitous design is advantageous." (p. 79). 'Serendipity', defined as "the faculty of making chance discoveries of pleasing or valuable things" (Longman, 1984), was coined to describe the heroes of a Persian fairy tale called "The Three Princes of Serendip" (Serendip being an ancient name for Sri Lanka), and its adoption by Guindon and her colleagues at MCC in Texas introduces pleasing images of magic brass bottles and flying carpets enlivening to our somewhat monotonous VDU screens.

It must not be forgotten that design is not always an activity in which unconstrained behaviour is desirable. In the cases cited above it was reasonable, even desirable, that the designer should make high-level changes to the design, or even modify the original goals. This is not always the case. Certain tasks, such as the development of program code to meet very precise specifications, do not encourage high-level design activity. (Indeed, such tasks may, in their most extreme form, be considered more as tasks of translation than of design.)

Nevertheless, we shall accept the evidence that the strategy of serendipitous planning is one that is often desirable. In the next section, therefore, we can ask how to achieve it, and how that relates to our conceptions of HCI.

Requirements for serendipitous planning

In this section I shall sketch out some of the requirements that must be met by any system that is intended to support serendipitous planning. Each of these requirements, it is suggested, should be the subject of limited theorising. The requirements structure is only the most preliminary of sketches, but my claim is that it helps us to develop theories about topics without having to solve the whole of cognitive psychology first. Mental models can be assigned a particular place in the structure, allowing them to be seen in the context of other notions about interfaces.

Generation

If users are to be enabled to take advantage of unexpected opportunities and to behave serendipitously, they must be able to put most of their mental effort into thinking about what they are producing. Correspondingly, not much effort must be taken up in driving the system they are using. Therefore, the instruction language must be easy to generate; harking back to Whitefield's work mentioned above, it is important that users should be able to spend their time in activity that is directly productive, rather than in getting their tool into the right mode, etc.

At the same time, users must be enabled to generate the items of their structure in the order that comes most naturally. Hoc (1988) and Green et al. (1987) have reported on the problems of systems which constrain the order of producing items, or which force users to make premature decisions about the structure they are building. I call this the requirement of linear generation.

Evaluation

A clear characteristic of serendipitous design is that the user will frequently review what has been done so far, to check it against the goals or to see what can be done next. It must therefore be possible to obtain the requisite information easily. A frequent difficulty, and one that can surely be avoided very simply, is the 'one-way pointer' or 'hidden dependency'; for instance, in spreadsheets, where the formula in cell A may refer to cell B, there will be a pointer in cell A, showing that A depends on B, but there will be nothing in cell B showing that it is depended-on by A. Under these conditions the user cannot freely change an arbitrary cell in the spreadsheet because there is no direct way to establish that that cell is not depended-on by some other cell. Where pointers exist and form a 'trail', it must be easy to follow the trail without requiring difficult mental operations (see Green et al., 1981, for a discussion of the mental operations involved in trail-following) .

Users must also be able to see very clearly what they have produced in the appropriate form - i.e. they must be able to comprehend it without having to translate it out of the form presented by the system and into some more appropriate form. That sounds simple and obvious, but it is not always. The structure that is presented by the system may not correspond to the mental representations held by users, for example. This has been demonstrated in the context of programming by Gilmore and Green (1988, in press), who showed that the performance of Pascal programmers in locating planted bugs was better when the structure presented by the system corresponded to the hypothesized mental representation. To describe this effect we introduced the term 'role-expressiveness'. Ideally, an interface would present an appearance whose perceptual structure matched the user's internal structure of the task, showing not only the existence of various components but also their role, the reason or purpose for their existence. Little is known about how to achieve this goal at present!

Modification

Users must also be able to change and rebuild their work. Continual change is part of the essence of serendipitous planning, as we saw in the previous section. Too often, however, systems that are very capable in many respects make it difficult to change one item without dealing with many other details. These details may be linked in the most mechanical and shallow ways to the original item, but they must still be attended to. Resistance to local change has been called 'viscosity' (Green et al., 1987).

Each of these requirements may create further requirements. For example, how can we satisfy the requirement of 'easy generation'? One method is to design a system that is highly consistent, in the sense that we discussed above and that has been modelled by Task-Action Grammar: namely, that knowing how to perform one task with the system allows the user to infer how to perform a related task. So here we have a secondary requirement. Moreover, the requirements may interact, as linear generability and role-expressiveness appear to do. Green et al. (1987) argue that when a structure cannot be built up linearly, but must instead be built from interleaved fragments, the user has to parse existing fragments before interleaving new fragments in with them. Thus role-expressiveness becomes more important when linear generation is prevented.

A requirements structure as a basis for HCI theorising

Having suggested in the last section that we can find a way to limit theoretical ideas to their proper context, the next task was to seek a context where users showed a preferred strategy of behaviour and to offer at least a sketch of the requirements that had to be satisfied for that strategy to be supported by an interactive device. The context chosen was design activity, where several studies have reported strategies resembling serendipitous planning; and a broad analysis was made of the requirements. We do not have space to pursue the analysis of requirements down to fine so we shall have to be satisfied with an armchair analysis.

Figure 3 shows an approximation of such a requirements structure for serendipitous planning. It should not be taken too seriously; it is a suggestion for how a structure of linked theories could be built, if we follow the ideas presented here. This particular complex of requirements, it must be noted, deals only with the activity of an experienced user performing one kind of task, and not with, say, how novices achieve learning, nor even how experienced users perform different tasks, such as comprehending an information structure built by someone else.

Within the structure, the role of mental models now becomes more evident. As shown here, their main role is that suggested by Rasmussen (this volume), in the finding of methods to achieve particular goals. Nothing new has been added to Rasmussen's account. But then, the purpose of this approach is not to create new hypotheses about mental models and the other notions of HCI, but to simplify the problem that we described above, namely that it is very hard to study one notion without it leaking into many others.

Ideally, there would be a body of knowledge relevant to each of the terms (and the terms themselves would have been better researched, instead of being produced from my armchair, as these have been). Some of the terms used here have been the subject of a certain degree of research, as noted above, but many of them have been thoroughly neglected. For example, to achieve predictable effects of operations, it must be possible to predict what happens when several operations are combined; in practice, certain operations, such as the use of indirect pointers or repeated negation, become very hard to handle when they

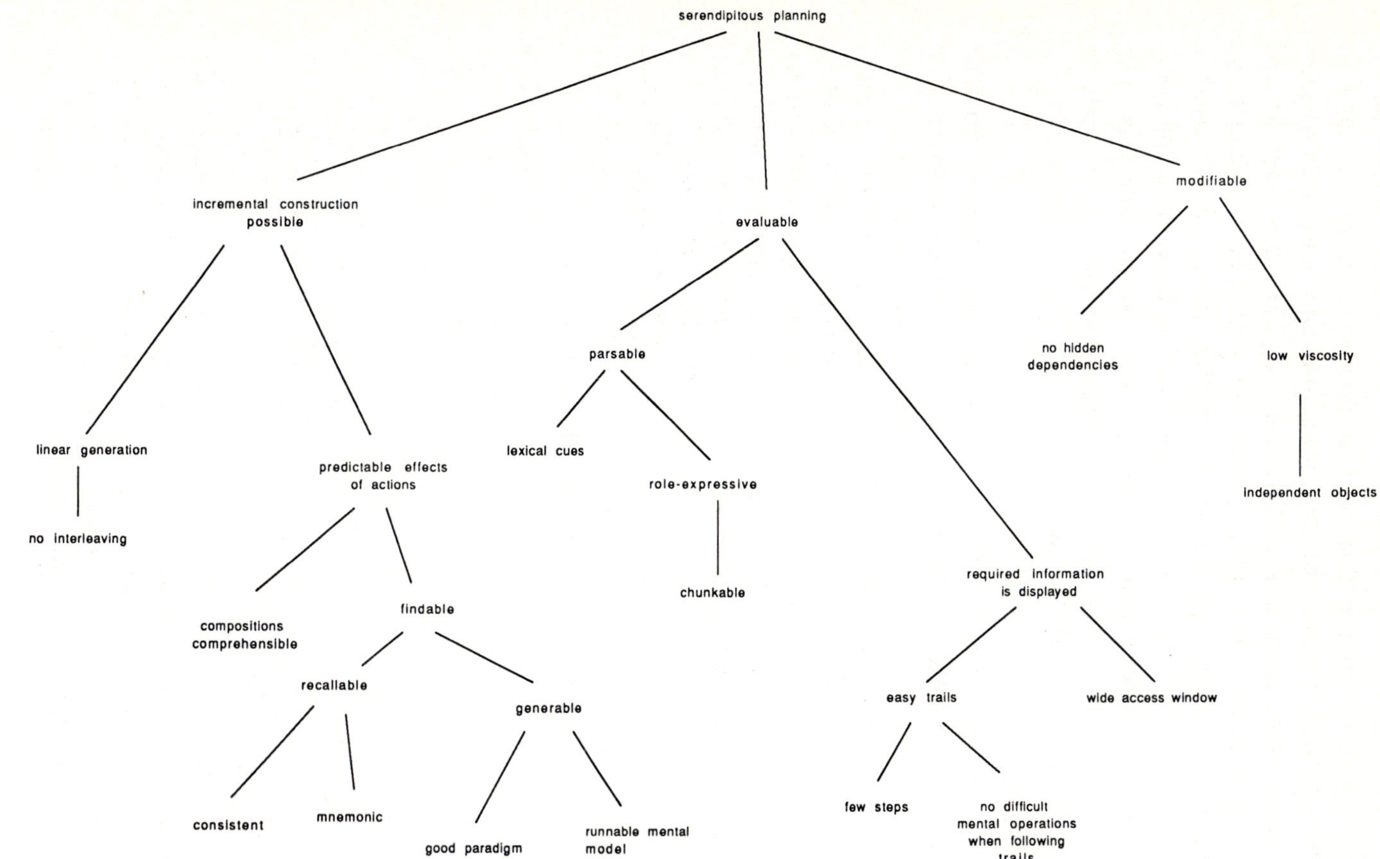

Figure 3. A 'requirements structure' for concepts in HCI. Lower items are requirements for higher ones - e.g. 'incremental construction' requires linear generation. To achieve 'serendipitous planning', the preferred mode of planning for design tasks, all components are required. The diagram can also be read as showing the purpose of an HCI concept - e.g. the purpose of a 'runnable mental model' is to allow easy generation of actions. No HCI theory is to be quizzed outside its intended purpose.

are combined with themselves. What is the common factor of such operations?

One role of such a structure, then, is to indicate gaps in our existing knowledge. There is a second role that is more important to my argument. Viewing this structure as a linking of fragments of theory, its role is to determine the question that shall be put to each fragment. The question to ask about mental models is not: what can they explain? but instead: what can they explain about how required operations are generated by users? In this way, the question is confined to the original purpose for which the notion was invented.

Time to conclude. I have argued that the problem of HCI is that it is an extremely scrappy field, and that one reason for the scrappiness is that explanatory concepts tend to be intertwined with each other or else to become investigations of the whole of cognitive psychology. My suggestion is that we should recognise that fact, and we should attempt to unify the field by linking together the questions we wish to answer. Each explanatory concept can then be kept within its proper bounds by using it only when we are addressing the type of question for which it is intended. This is what I have called 'limited theorising'. The device of a requirements structure, as a form of linkage, is not the only one that could be proposed, nor is my attempt at creating such a structure by any means to be regarded as the last word; it is an illustration of how one might go about such a proceeding.

References

Ackermann, D. & Stelovsky, J. (1987). The role of mental models in programming. In P. Gorny & M.J. Tauber (Eds.), *Visualization in Programming*. Lecture Notes in Computer Science, Vol. 282. Berlin-Heidelberg: Springer Verlag.

Ackermann, D. & Greutmann, T. (1989). Experimental reconstruction and simulation of mental models. In M.J. Tauber & D. Ackermann (Eds.), *Mental Models and Human-Computer Interaction.* Proceedings of the 6th Interdisciplinary Workshop on "Informatics and Psychology", Schärding, Austria, 1987. Amsterdam: North-Holland.

Anderson, J. (1983). *The Architecture of Cognition.* Cambridge, Mass.: Harvard University Press.

Card, S.K., Moran, T.P., & Newell, A. (1983). *The Psychology of Human-Computer Interaction.* Hillsdale, New Jersey: Erlbaum.

Carroll, J.M. & Rosson, M.B. (1985). Usability specifications as a tool in iterative development. In H.R. Hartson (Ed.), *Advances in Human-Computer Interaction.* Norwood: Ablex.

Flower, L.S. & Hayes, J.R. (1980). The dynamics of composing: making plans and juggling constraints. In L.W. Gregg & E. Steinberg (Eds.), *Cognitive Processes in Writing.* Hillsdale, New Jersey: Erlbaum.

Forster, K.I. (1976). Accessing the mental lexicon. In R.J. Wales (Ed.), *New Approaches to Language Mechanisms.* Amsterdam: North-Holland.

Gilmore, D.J. & Green, T.R.G. (1988). Programming plans and programming expertise. *Quarterly Journal of Experimental Psychology,* in press.

Green, T.R.G., Bellamy, R.K.E. & Parker, J.M. (1987). Parsing and gnisrap: a model of device use. In G.M. Olson, S. Sheppard, & E. Soloway (Eds.), *Empirical Studies of Programmers: Second Workshop.* Norwood: Ablex.

Green, T.R.G., Sime, M.E. & Fitter, M.J. (1981). The art of notation. In M.J. Coombs & J.L. Alty (Eds.), *Computing Skills and the User Interface.* London: Academic Press.

Guindon, R., Krasner, H. & Curtis, B. (1987). Breakdowns and processes during the early activities of software design by professionals. In G.M. Olson, S. Sheppard, & E. Soloway (Eds.), *Empirical Studies of Programmers: Second Workshop.* Norwood: Ablex.

Halasz, F.G. & Moran, T.P. (1983). Mental models and problem solving in using a calculator. In A. Janda (Ed.), *Proceedings of CHI '83 Conference on Human Factors in Computing Systems.* New York: ACM.

Hayes-Roth, B. & Hayes-Roth, F. (1979). A cognitive model of planning. *Cognitive Science,* 3, pp. 275-310.

Hoc, J-M. (1981). Planning and direction of problem-solving in structured programming: an empirical comparison between two methods. *Int. J. Man-Machine Studies,* 15, pp. 563-583.

Hoc, J-M. (1988). Assessment of computer aids in designing programs. In G.C. van der Veer, T.R.G. Green, J-M. Hoc & D. Murray (Eds.), *Working with Computers: Theory versus Outcome.* London: Academic Press.

Johnson-Laird, P.N. (1983). *Mental Models.* Cambridge: Cambridge University Press.

Longman (1984). *Longman Dictionary of the English Language.* Harlow, Essex: Longman.

Marslen-Wilson, W.D. & Tyler, L.K. (1980). The temporal structure of spoken language understanding. *Cognition,* 8, pp. 1-71.

Moran, T.P. (1983). Getting into a system: external-internal task mapping analysis. In A. Janda (Ed.), *Proceedings of CHI '83 Conference on Human Factors in Computing Systems.* New York: ACM.

Morton, J. (1979). Word recognition. In J. Morton & J.C. Marshall (Eds.), *Psycholinguistics Series 2: Structures and Processes.* London: Elek.

Norman, D.A. (1981). Categorization of action slips. *Psychological Review,* 88, pp. 1-15.

Norris, D.G. (1982). Autonomous processes in comprehension: a reply to Marslen-Wilson and Tyler. *Cognition,* 11, pp. 97-101.

Payne, S. J. (1987a). Methods and mental models in theories of cognitive skill. In J. Self (Ed.), *Intelligent Computer-Aided Instruction.* Chapman and Hall.

Payne, S. J. (1987b). Using models of users' knowledge to analyse learnability. To appear in J. Long & A. Whitefield (Eds.), *Cognitive Ergonomics and Human-Computer Interaction.*

Payne, S.J. & Green, T.R.G. (1986). Task-action grammars: a model of the mental representation of task languages. *Human Computer Interaction,* 2, pp. 93-133.

Rasmussen, J. (1989). Mental models and the control of action in complex environments. In M.J. Tauber & D. Ackermann (Eds.), *Mental Models and Human-Computer Interaction.* Proceedings of the 6th Interdisciplinary Workshop on "Informatics and Psychology", Schärding, Austria, 1987. Amsterdam: North-Holland.

Schiele, F. & Green, T.R.G. (in preparation). Using task-action grammars to analyze 'the Macintosh style'. To appear in H. Thimbleby (Ed.), *Formal Methods in HCI.* Cambridge: Cambridge University Press.

Siddiqi, J.I.A. & Sumiga, J.H. (1986). Empirical evaluation of a proposed model of the program design process. *4th Symposium on Empirical Foundations of Information and Software Sciences,* Atlanta, Georgia.

Tauber, M.J. (1988). On mental models and the user interface. In G.C. van der Veer, T.R.G. Green, J-M. Hoc, & D. Murray (Eds.), *Working with Computers: Theory versus Outcome.* London: Academic Press.

Ullman, D.G., Stauffer, L.A., & Dietterich, T.G. (1987). Preliminary results of an empirical study of the mechanical design process. *Proceedings of the Workshop on the Study of the Design Process.* Oakland, California.

Waern, Y. (1989). On the dynamics of mental models. In M.J. Tauber & D. Ackermann (Eds.), *Mental Models and Human-Computer Interaction.* Proceedings of the 6th Interdisciplinary Workshop on "Informatics and Psychology", Schärding, Austria, 1987. Amsterdam: North-Holland.

West, R., Howell, P. & Cross, I. (1985). Modelling perceived musical structure. In P. Howell, I. Cross & R. West (Eds.), *Musical Structure and Cognition.* London: Academic Press.

Whitefield, A. (1985). *Constructing and Applying a Model of the User for Computer System Development: the Case for Computer-Aided Design.* PhD thesis, University College, London.

Young, R.M. (1983). Surrogates and mappings: two kinds of conceptual models for interactive devices. In D. Gentner and A.L. Stevens (Eds.), *Mental Models.* Hillsdale, New Jersey: Erlbaum.

Young, R.M. and O'Shea, T. (1981). Errors in children's subtraction. *Cognitive Science,* 5, pp. 153-177.

Mental Models and Human-Computer Interaction 1
D. Ackermann and M.J. Tauber (Editors)

MENTAL MODELS AND THE CONTROL OF ACTION IN COMPLEX ENVIRONMENTS

Jens Rasmussen

Technical University Copenhagen and
Riso National Laboratory Roskilde, Denmark

ABSTRACT

The concept of mental models has become an important ingredient in models of the cognitive control of human behaviour. The paper reviews different approaches to the definition of mental models taken in psychology and cognitive sciences, which typically have been considering selected aspects of human activities. The need for analysis of complex work scenarios is discussed, together with the necessity of considering several levels of cognitive control depending upon different kinds of internal representations. The development of mental representations during learning and adaptation to the requirements of a task is discussed. Finally, the role of means-end considerations in problem solving and in understanding of the functioning of purposive mechanisms is illustrated.

Introduction

The concept of a mental model is widely discussed in studies of the interaction of humans with their environment. Unfortunately, the concept has become very ambiguous, having been adopted by researchers approaching human cognitive functions from very different points of view. The aim of the present paper is to discuss the concept as seen from the point of view of analysis and design of interfaces between humans and their work based on advanced information technology. What is the nature of humans' conception of their work content, and how can computer-based information systems be made transparent and support the proper mental models?

The concept

In general, the concept of mental model is used to characterise features of the resident knowledge base, representing properties of the task environment which can serve the planning of activities and the control of acts when instantiated and activated by observation of the actual state of affairs.

Craik's mental models

An early attempt to characterise the notion of a 'mental model' was Craik's discussion (1943) of a mental model as a basis for explanation and understanding. Craik mentions three essential processes of reasoning: "(1) 'Translation' of external process into words, numbers or other symbols, (2) Arrival at other symbols by a process of 'reasoning', deduction, inference, etc., and (3) 'Retranslation' of these symbols into external processes (as building a bridge to a design) or at least recognition of the correspondence between these symbols and the external events (as in realising that a prediction is fulfilled)." He then argues: "A calculating machine, an anti-aircraft 'predictor' and a Kelvin's tidal predictor all show the same ability. In all these cases, the physical process which it is desired to predict is imitated by some mechanical device or model which is cheaper, or quicker, or more convenient in operation. .... By a model we thus mean any physical or chemical system which has a similar relation-structure to that of the process it imitates. By 'relation-structure' I do not mean some obscure non-physical entity which attends the model, but the fact that it is a physical working model which works in the same way as the process it parallels, in the aspects under consideration." He continues: "... in the case of our own nervous systems, the reason why I regard them as modelling the real process is that they permit trial of alternatives, in, e.g. bridge design, to proceed on a cheaper and smaller scale than if each bridge in turn were built and tried by sending a train over it, to see whether it was sufficiently strong." Craik also emphasises the fact that models only represent a selected set of relations: "Any kind of a working model is, in a sense, an analogy. Being different it is bound to break down by showing properties not found in the process it imitates or by not possessing properties possessed by the process it imitates." (p. 51-53). The implications of the latter statement will be that for the representation of human knowledge in a complex working context more than one 'mental model' should be considered. In general, Craik's conception of a model is very close to that of the engineering profession.

Two recent approaches to 'mental models'

After Craik's early use of the term 'model' for cognitive representations, the theme has been considered from two different points of view. Mental models are the bridge between the work environment to be controlled and the mental processes underlying this control. Consequently, a study can be approached by a study of human mental processes as well as by a study of work requirements, and these approaches result in different concepts. The approach from the psychological point of view quite naturally focuses on the explanation of human performance, which often will be influenced by the AI related cognitive science. The focus of this research will be on the nature and form of the mental model together with its role in human reasoning and its relations to the 'mind'. Consequently, the criterion of success will often be whether a theory can be phrased explicitly in procedural form for simulation on computer (Johnson-Laird, 1983).

In contrast, the approach based on studies of actual work performance and systems analysis will typically be looking for the content of the possible mental models which will be effective for a given task repertoire in a specific work domain. The criterion of validity of the theories in this case will be whether they are useful, i.e., whether functionality of human-machine systems can be adequately predicted.

The two approaches are supplementary rather than competing and interaction between them is important for the development of modern information technology. The psychologically oriented approach serves to identify human reasoning mechanisms and resource profiles, while the approach from analysis of work requirements is necessary so as to interrelate the different human mechanisms in a complex work situation. Together, such studies may add up to be a response to Brunswik's request for an ecological psychology as a basis for system design (Brunswik, 1957).

The cognitive science approach

A typical representative of the cognitive science approach is Johnson-Laird (1983). He distinguishes "at least three types of mental representations: propositional representations which are strings of symbols that correspond to natural language, mental models which are structural analogues of the world, and images which are perceptual correlates of models from a particular point of view." Basically, he categorises the form of representations rather than their content - which is in correspondence with his discussion from the point of view of modelling the reasoning mechanisms. He distinguishes "at least two levels of representation: a representation of the sense of discourse, and a representation of its significance (including what it refers to). This distinction is precisely what is captured in the theory of propositional representations and mental models." (p. 395)

Johnson-Laird derives his concepts of mental models from a discussion of basic reasoning procedures, e.g., syllogistic or propositional reasoning, hence the requirement of procedural, computational tests. He takes the position that "a natural mental model of discourse has a structure that corresponds directly to the structure of the state of affairs that the discourse describes". The structure Johnson-Laird has in mind appears to be the physical anatomy of the environment. He states on the nature of mental models: "Mental models owe their evolution to the perceptual ability in organisms with nervous systems." Referring to David Marr's (1982) work he concludes: "It is therefore safe to assume that a primary source of mental models - three-dimensional kinematic models of the world - is perception." This formulation brings Johnson-Laird's concepts close to the concept of the "dynamic world model" discussed in a subsequent section. Thus, Johnson-Laird's mental models basically are representations of the context of reasoning, the "background" (Searle, 1983). Johnson-Laird says: "The meaning of a sentence, according to the principle of compositionality, is a function of the meanings of its words and the syntactic relations between them. Meaning, however, is an abstract notion that reflects only what is determined by a knowledge of the language. The significance of an utterance goes beyond meaning because it depends on recovering referents and some minimal idea of the speaker's intentions. The truth conditions of the proposition expressed by a sentence therefore depend on the meaning of the sentence, its context of utterance (as represented in the current mental model), and the implicit inferences that it triggers from background knowledge." In this way, Johnson-Laird's mental models are representations of the context or background by which propositional reasoning is possible, i.e., his 'mental models' include the intuitive knowledge which escapes the representation by the explicit formulation in terms of the semantic nets of the AI community.

In this respect, Johnson-Laird continues a well established tradition. The need for a representation of the context for understanding language as well as for control of skilled movements has long been discussed in the philosophical literature. Polanyi (1967) has made thorough studies of the importance of "tacit" knowledge. Mackie (1975) found it necessary to introduce the notion of a "field" as the representation of the context in his efforts to define causality in common sense descriptions of event sequences. Recently, Searle (1983) has argued the importance of the "background" which in his terms is the "non-representational" something underlying mental representations, "intentional states". Mental representations form a network of intentional states, and the semantic content of a state depends on its location in this network. However, "anyone who tries seriously to follow out the threads in the network will eventually reach a bedrock of mental capacities that do not themselves consist in intentional states (representations), but nonetheless form the preconditions for the functioning of intentional states. His arguments for the existence of the "background" is very analogous to the present arguments for the internal world model: "The background is necessary to account for the fact that the literal meaning of a sentence is not a context-free notion, for understanding of metaphors, and to explain physical skills as for instance needed in expert skiing".

Other approaches to the mental model concept from the artificial intelligence point of view have been presented by Gentner and Stevens (1983). Typically, the contributions to this collection focus on the representation of reasoning procedures by means of computer programs and, consequently, the problem domains discussed are rather simple and derived from 'naive physics' or from the immediate experience of computer scientists with, for instance, calculators or word processors. In the present discussion, the tentative taxonomy of features of mental models discussed by Young (1983) is of interest. He mentions several classes of models, but focuses the discussion of models on surrogates (i.e., analogies) and cue-action mappings of students during the use of calculators. His conclusion is that surrogates are biased towards the "reasoning criteria", and suited for explanation and prediction while they are limited in the use of a device. Mappings are better suited to "provide an overall characterisation of the machine to orient the user's behaviour". These categories and their performance implications are closely related to declarative and procedural models underlying knowledge-based and rule-based performance discussed below.

A natural consequence of the computational approach is a focus on a well bounded aspect of mental representation in the form of a 'mental model' in order to be able to embed it in a computer program. This, in turn, means that only rather simple and well structured problems can be approached or the danger will be that the reasoning procedure will turn out rather artificial. A case in point is the efforts of Brown and De Kleer (see for instance 1983) to develop computational models of qualitative reasoning about the functioning of physical devices. In order to have a manageable model for simulation, they assume that explanation of the functioning is inferred bottom-up from a representation of the structure of the device in terms of the topology of component connections together with component properties. This approach can be useful to model 'naive physics' reasoning e.g., on simple kinematic problems such as predicting the movements of objects given the initial conditions. When considering, however, the functioning of rather complex goal oriented artefacts from a general question of "how they work", the resulting reasoning procedure becomes very artificial. We will return to this topic in a subsequent section discussing the use of means-end relations for functional reasoning.

The cognitive engineering approach

Approaching the question of mental representations from the point of view of actual work performance, a focus on selected, well-formed aspects of mental models cannot be maintained. From the analysis of verbal protocols from actual work (Rasmussen and Jensen, 1973) our attention was drawn towards the interaction of several different kinds of mental representations (Rasmussen, 1986). Furthermore, the analysis of human errors in process plant operation has shown that the interaction of performance under control of basically different kinds of mental representations has to be considered (Rasmussen, 1980). Other studies of human performance in actual industrial work situations also have shown the need for analysing the difference between the representations brought to work by persons with different professional backgrounds and levels of training (De Keyser, 1987; Herry, 1987).

A natural consequence of this approach will be that the mental representations under work situations cannot be formulated in one well structured simulation language. Several different research models of the various mental representations have to be accepted (see the 'catalogue of models' in Rasmussen, 1986), and validation of the models will basically be a test of their predictive ability for systems design, i.e., validation depends to a large degree on evaluation of system during actual work conditions. In order to have a framework for mapping the properties of different kinds of mental representations, a discussion of the cognitive control of skilled work performance will be useful.

Modes of cognitive control

The point of view of the following discussion, therefore, is taken from the analysis of performance in complex work situations and from the requirements met when designing computer based interfaces. For such purposes to be satisfied, it is necessary to study the interaction of a wide variety of mental strategies and models. In particular, study of the interaction and interference between different modes of cognitive control appear to be important for the understanding of erroneous performance.

When we distinguish categories of human behaviour according to basically different ways of representing the properties of a deterministic environment as a basis for control of actions, three typical levels of performance emerge: skill-, rule-, and knowledge-based performance. These levels and a simplified illustration of their interrelation are shown in figure 1.

Skill-based behaviour represents sensori-motor performance during acts or activities that, after a statement of an intention, take place without conscious control as smooth, automated, and highly integrated patterns of behaviour. In most skilled sensori-motor tasks, the body acts as a multivariable, continuous control system synchronising movements with the behaviour of the environment. This performance is based on feed-forward control and depends upon a very flexible and efficient dynamic world model. In some cases, performance is one continuous, integrated dynamic whole, such as bicycle riding or musical performance. In these cases the higher-level control may take the form of conscious anticipation of upcoming demands in general terms, resulting

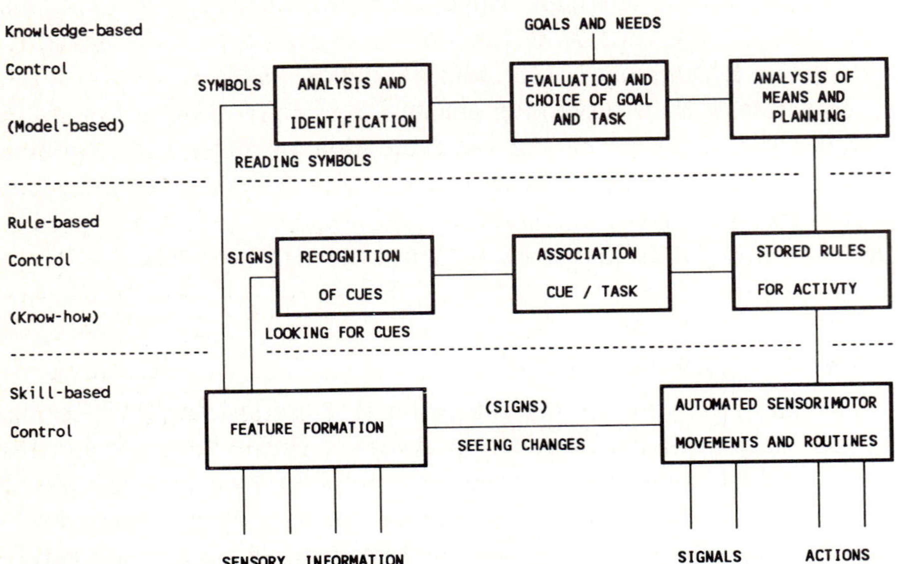

Figure 1. Schematic map illustrating different levels in cognitive control of human behaviour. The basic level represents the highly skilled sensorimotor performance controlled by automated patterns of movements. Sequences of such sub-routines will be controlled by stored rules, activated by signs. Problem solving in unfamiliar tasks will be based on conceptual models at the knowledge based level which serve to generate the necessary rules ad-hoc. The figure illustrates the flow of information, not the control of this flow. The figure is not meant to show humans as passive and subjects to information 'input'. On the contrary, they actively seek information, guided by their dynamic 'world model'.

in an updating of the state of the dynamic world model and thereby in the appropriate "modulation" of the skilled response. In general, human activities can be considered as a sequence of such skilled acts or activities composed for the actual occasion. The flexibility of skilled performance is due to the ability to compose from a large repertoire of automated subroutines the sets suited for specific purposes. The individual routines are activated and chained by perceived patterns that are acting as signs, the person is not consciously choosing among alternatives.

At the next level of rule-based behaviour, the composition of a sequence of subroutines in a familiar work situation is typically consciously controlled by a stored rule or procedure that may have been derived empirically during previous occasions, communicated from other persons' know-how as an instruction or a cookbook recipe, or it may be prepared on occasion by conscious problem solving and planning. The point is here that performance is goal-oriented, but structured by "feed-forward control" through a stored rule, in other words, the person is aware that alternative actions are possible and has to make a choice. The choice is based on 'signs' in the environment which have been found to be correlated to one of the alternative actions. Very often, the goal is not even explicitly formulated, but is found implicitly in the situation releasing the stored rules. The control is teleologic in the sense that the rule or control is selected from previous successful experiences. The control evolves by "survival of the fittest" rule.

In general, skill-based performance rolls along without conscious attention, and the actor will be unable to describe the information used to act. The higher-level rule-based co-ordination in general is based on explicit know-how, and the rules used can be reported by the person, although the cues releasing a rule may not be explicitly known.

During unfamiliar situations for which no know-how or rules for control are available from previous encounters, the control must move to a higher conceptual level, in which performance is goal-controlled, and knowledge-based (knowledge is here taken in a rather restricted sense as possession of a conceptual, structural model or, in AI terminology, of deep knowledge. The level, therefore, might also be called 'model-based'). In this situation, the goal is explicitly formulated, based on an analysis of the environment and the overall aims of the person. Then a useful plan is developed - by selection. Different plans are considered and their effect tested against the goal, physically by trial and error, or conceptually by means of 'thought experiments'. At this level of functional reasoning, the internal structure of the system is explicitly represented by a "mental model" that may take several different forms. A very important aspect of the cognitive control to be captured by models of human behaviour is the dynamic interaction between the activities at the three levels.

Skill, rules and knowledge in problem solving

Problem solving takes place when the reaction of the environment to possible human actions is not known from prior experience, but must be deduced by means of a mental representation of the 'relational structure' of the environment. This structure must be represented symbolically in a mental model. A major task in knowledge-based problem solving is to transfer those properties of the environment which are related to the perceived problem to a proper symbolic representation. The information observed in the environment is then perceived as 'symbols' with reference to this mental model.

Formation of a proper representation depends on knowledge about the basic laws governing the behaviour of the environment. This phase of problem solving is finished when a representation in a framework familiar to the person is obtained - which means a mental model for which a set of rules for information processing is available. The representation then ceases to be an informative, symbolic framework and turns into a prescriptive system of signs that control the application of stereotyped process rules.

If the representation then is externalised in the form of a physical or graphic model, it is evident that the same kind of rule- and skill-based operation can be developed, as it is found for operation on a physical environment. The efficiency of formal, mathematical models and technical graphs and diagrams, as e.g., control engineers' Bode plots and pole-zero graphs, depends on the existence of a large repertoire of stereotyped manipulation rules used for solutions and predictions - often to a degree where the engineer's fundamental understanding of the conceptual basis has completely decayed.

The conclusion of this discussion is that patterns in a symbolic model configuration, as is the case with perceptual patterns of the physical environment, can act as signs. This is most clearly seen if externalised representations of the mental model are actually available in the form of physical models, e.g., an abacus for calculation, or in the form of graphs or other symbolic representations on paper or on visual information displays, forming artificial objects for manipulation. For display formats this means that rule- or skill-based control - "direct manipulation" - at a higher abstract level can be obtained if a symbolic display can be designed where there is a one-to-one mapping between the immediate appearance of the display and properties of the process to be controlled. In this way, the same conceptual model may act as a symbolic representation when considered in relation to the elements of the environment and the laws controlling their relationships, and as a system of prescriptive signs when considered in relation to the rules for model transformation and data processing.

The distinction between signs and symbols in representations in the sense discussed above is equivalent to the distinction in semiotics and information science between prescriptive and informative texts (Morris, 1971; Eco, 1979). The important point in the present context is, however, related to the fact that the same text - or model - will be considered as either prescriptive or informative by the same person, depending upon the situation. An important question is therefore how the cognitive level needed is activated and what information in fact serves this activation.

The role of a functional representation as prescriptive signs has been studied from a semiotic point of view by Cuny and Boye (1981). They analysed the role of electrical circuit diagrams in terms of signs controlling activities during design, installation, and repair of electrical power supply systems in private houses, and investigated how different appearance of the same functional diagram was effective for support of the different activities.

Skills, rules, and knowledge as stages in learning a skill

It is clear from the discussion in the previous section that the three levels of control are intimately interacting. In order to evaluate the degree to which the underlying models are separate concepts or just different aspects of the same internal representation, it may be useful to discuss how they relate to learning.

Distinctions between different categories of human behaviour similar to the SRK-levels have previously been proposed in relation to learning a skill. Fitts and Posner (1962) distinguish between three phases: the early or cognitive phase, the intermediate or associative phase, and the final or autonomous phase. If we consider that in real life a person will meet situations with a varying degree of training when performing his task depending on variations and disturbances, the correspondence with the three levels in the present context is clear.

In the three-level model, the final stage in adaptation to a task environment is the skill-based level. During training the necessary sensori-motor patterns develop, while the activity is controlled by other means. It may happen directly at the skilled level by imitation and trial-and-error, as for instance, learning to play an instrument by ear or children learning to talk, walk, etc. In other cases, control at the rule-based behavioural level will be efficient during development of the automated skill. The rules may be obtained from an instructor or a text-book, as is typically the case when learning to drive a car, to operate tools and technical devices supplied with an instruction manual, or to manage social interactions from "rules of good manners". And, finally, persons with a basic knowledge of the structure and functioning will be able to generate themselves a set of rules to control activities related to various purposes during early phases of learning. This involves what Anderson (1983) calls 'compiling declarative knowledge.'

Human errors are closely related to this learning process. Fine-tuning of manual skills depends upon a continuous updating of the sensory-motor schemata to the time-space features of the task environment. If the optimisation criteria are speed and smoothness, the limits of acceptable adaptation can only be found by the once-in-a-while experience gained when crossing the precision tolerance limits, i.e. by the experience of errors or near-errors. Also at the more consciously controlled rule-following level, development of know-how and rules-of-thumb is depending upon a basic variability and opportunity for experiments to find shortcuts and identify convenient and reliable signs which make it possible to recognise recurrent conditions without analytical diagnosis. Involved in problem solving, test of hypothesis becomes an important need. It is typically expected that for instance process operators check their diagnostic hypothesis conceptually - by thought experiments - before operations on the plant. This, however, appears to be an unrealistic assumption, since it may be tempting to test a hypothesis on the system itself in order to avoid the strain from reasoning in a complex causal net.

An important point is that it is not the behavioural patterns of the higher levels that are becoming automated skills. Automated time-space behavioural patterns are developing while they are controlled and supervised by the higher level activities - which will eventually deteriorate - and their basis as knowledge and rules may deteriorate. In fact, the period when this is happening may lead to errors due to interference between a not fully developed sensori-motor skill and a gradually deteriorated rule system. This kind of interference is known also to highly skilled musicians when they occasionally start to analyse their performance during fast passages. It seems plausible also that this effect can play a role for pilots of about 100 hours flying experience, which is known to be an error-prone period among pilots.

Anderson (1983) also discusses the interaction between declarative knowledge and procedural knowledge. He describes the development of procedural knowledge during learning as a 'compilation'. Generally, compilation refers to a transformation of knowledge by means of a formal procedure. According to the SRK-framework, however, procedural knowledge derived by compilation of declarative mental models is a possible, but not an inevitable, first phase of rule-based behaviour. In later phases procedural knowledge is typically not derived from the basic, 'deep' knowledge, but has an empirical, heuristic basis, and compilation is not a suitable metaphor.

Following the lines of reasoning suggested above, the transfer of control to new mental representations is a very complex process involving change along several different orthogonal dimensions. First, when trained responses evolve, the structure of the underlying representation shifts from a set of separate component models toward a more holistic representation. This is discussed by Bartlett (1943) in relation to pilot fatigue, and Moray (1986) analyses how such model aggregation can lead process operators into trouble during plant disturbances, because the process is irreversible, i.e., the regeneration of a structured model needed for causal reasoning in unfamiliar situations is not possible from the aggregated model. The learning model implied in the SRK-framework indicates that skill acquisition involves not only an aggregation of mental models. Typically, control by a structural, declarative model will also be replaced by an empirical procedural representation concurrent with a shift from a symbolic to a stereotype sign interpretation of observations. This means that training involves at least three concurrent and structurally independent shifts, in terms of aggregation, of declarative- procedural knowledge, and of interpretation of information.

If this model of learning a skill is accepted and skill/rule-based performance is characteristic of professional activities in general, one would expect the basic causal or functional understanding to deteriorate. This is in fact what is the evidence found by Ackermann and Barbichon (1963) from their analysis of the organisation of knowledge and the explanation of phenomena as presented by electrical and chemical technicians in industry. Based on an analysis of interviews, their conclusions were that the professional knowledge of the technicians was fragmented, showed a lack of relationship among phenomena, had barriers between theory, practice, and extra-professional life, and lack of relationship among various representations - mathematical, graphic, concrete, and analogical - of a particular phenomenon. One explanation could be, as the authors suggest, that theoretical knowledge is not used and that their findings reveal rudimentary memories from basic education. But, seen in our context, it could also be that basic symbolic knowledge and representations are typically used to support stereotyped lines of functional reasoning in various typical situations, and causal reasoning therefore turns into rule- and skill-based manipulations of symbolic representations which will thereby lose their symbolic nature and theoretical relationship. Analysis of the functional explanations offered by the technicians interviewed by Ackermann and Barbichon was characteristic by resort to what the authors call verbal nominalisms, i.e., the use of technical terms without understanding their content or relationship, or verbal logicism, as for instance pseudo-analogies or replacement of logical sequences with chronologic sequences from the problem context. A general trend found is the replacement of functional arguments by reference to human interaction, a tendency that can be explained by the tight relationships between human acts and symbols which are degenerated into mere signs.

A taxonomy of mental representations

From this discussion, a taxonomy of mental representations can be proposed. It is proposed to restrict the term mental model to the representation of the 'relational structure' of the environment, to follow Craik's definition. This means, the mental model is a representation of the fundamental constraints determining the possible behaviour of the environment, i.e., it is useful to anticipate its response to acts or events when instantiated by state information. The study of errors have made it clear that a taxonomy of representations should not only consider the higher level cognitive functions related to inference and reasoning, the role of the body in the control of sensori-motor performance is an integrated part of the system. In the following section, the representations related to actual working performance according to the skill-, rule-, and knowledge distinction are discussed in more detail.

Representations at the skill-based level

Performance at the skill-based level depends on a dynamic world model which has a perceptual basis, like Johnson-Laird's mental model. The model is activated by patterns of sensory data acting as signs, and synchronised by spatio-temporal signals.

This dynamic world model can be seen as a structure of hierarchically defined representation of objects and their behaviour in a variety of familiar scenarios, i.e., their functional properties, what they can be used for, and their potential for interaction, or what can be done to them. These elements of a generic analogue simulation of the behaviour of the environment are updated and aligned according to the sensory information during interaction with an environment. The model is structured with reference to the space in which the person acts and is controlled by direct perception of the features of relevance to the person's immediate needs and goals.

This conception is similar to Minsky's (1975) "frames". The main - and fundamental - difference is that Minsky's frames depend on a sequential scene analysis; they are structured as networks of nodes and relations, and they are basically static. Minsky defines frames as a data structure for representing stereotyped situations which are organised as a network of nodes and relations. Gibson's (1966) concepts related to "direct perception" are far more convincing, viewed as a model of the high-capacity information-processing mechanisms underlying perception, sensori-motor performance in fast sequences, etc., than Minsky's symbolic information processing. The latter is more adequate for higher-level conscious information processing, i.e., the manifestations of the "dynamic world model" at the conscious level in terms of natural language representations.

The "dynamic world model" in the present context is very similar to the mechanisms needed for the "atunement of the whole retino-neuro-muscular system to invariant information" (Gibson, 1966, p. 262), which leads to the situation where "the centres of the nervous system, including the brain, resonate to information". This selective resonance relies on the existence of some kind of dynamic model of the environment. The control of skilled performance by an active analogue model raises some interesting modelling problems, in particular as seen from the point of view of digital computer based AI. Skilled behaviour cannot meaningfully be decomposed into parts without a shift in domain of description to neuro-physiology. Behaviour of an active model is not controlled by rules, but by the laws controlling the behaviour of the involved physical system or, as Searle has phrased it "there is no computational answer to that; it is just done by the hardware" (Searle, 1984). The role of the dynamic world model for representation of the context - 'background' - of higher level cognitive functions makes this a basic problem of simulating intelligent human behaviour by present AI technology, as mentioned already by Dreyfus (1972): the problem with computers is not that they lack a brain; but that they lack the human body. From this point of view it is worth noting the recent revival in terms of 'connectionism' (Feldman et al., 1986) or PDP, i.e., 'parallel distributed processing' (Rummelhart et al., 1986), of the interest in parallel processing and self-organising networks which was characteristic of the bio-technological research of the 60'es (see for instance Oestreicher et al. 1966).

To Gibson, perception is not based on processing of information contained in an array of sense data. Instead, the perceiver, being attuned to invariant information in space and time in his environment, samples this information directly through all senses. That is, arrays of sense data are not stored or remembered. Instead the nerve system "resonates". In my terms, the world model, activated by the needs and goals of the individual, is updated and aligned by generic patterns in the sensed information, but the idea of an organism "tuning in" on generic time space properties is basically similar and leads to the view of humans as selective and active seekers of information at a high level of invariance in the environmental context.

Like the perceptual function, motor control is not based on stored behaviour patterns from prior encounters, but on a constructive process that generates the proper patterns on demand (Bernstein, 1967). This is demonstrated by the fact that the success of rapid movements is independent of the initial positions of limbs and that movements can be transferred to other metric proportions and limbs. This function must depend on schemata for generating complex movements with reference to the internal dynamic world model. An important ingredient in motor control is the dynamic feed-forward generation of patterns within this internal dynamic map which is updated and aligned by the sensory information.

From the role in human behaviour, some of the functional features of the world model can be summarised:

- It is able to control bodily movements in a feed-forward mode of control during fast sequences, i.e., it is capable of real time, quantitative, and precise simulation of the time-space patterns of the environment, and it is an active model.
- It is a hierarchical representation; it enables recognition of objects and scenes at the level of physical appearance; it makes it possible to identify objects by their functional values rather than their appearance; and patterns of purposive behaviour can be activated by high level intentions.
- There is a very efficient mapping between features of the environment and the model; i.e. a very efficient updating of the model is possible in response to changes, as well as easy transfer to "similar" scenarios. This points to an analog model with elements representing objects and their functional properties and values, and consequently a one-to-one mapping of elements in the environment onto the model.

It is important to repeat that the three levels of control are not alternatives. The skill-based level is always active; the dynamic world model supplies the contextual basis for all performance (compare the role of Johnson-Laird's mental model), it directs attention, activates higher level performance, and based on higher level intentions expressed in terms of goals or activities it controls information gathering and transforms intentions to control of movements.

Representations at the rule-based level

At the rule-based level, system properties are only implicitly represented in the empirical mapping of cue-patterns representing states of the environment and actions or activities relevant in the specific context supplied by the underlying dynamic world model. According to the definition adopted here, this representation does not qualify as a mental model since it does not support anticipation of responses to acts or events not previously met, and it will not support explanation or understanding except in the form of reference to prior experience.

In order to prepare for rule-based control of activities, however, conceptual relations may be important. Descriptive relations are useful in assigning attributes to categories and, therefore, to label scenarios and contexts for identification of items to retrieve from memory. Descriptive labels are the basis for updating of the focus for intuitive judgements and for establishing the proper "background" of action and communication. As could be expected from research on memory (Bartlett, 1932; Tulving, 1983), episodic relations are important for structuring of memory. Episodic relations appear to be important for labelling prototypical situations to serve as tacit "frames" or context for intuitive judgements and skilled performance.

Representations at the knowledge-based level

In the present context, the representations at the knowledge-based level constitute the proper 'mental models' being representations of the relational structure of the causal environment and work content. Many different kinds of relationships are put to work during reasoning and inference at this level, depending on the circumstances, whether the task is to diagnose a new situation, to evaluate different aspect of possible goals, or to plan appropriate actions. Two kinds of relationships, i.e., part-whole and means-end relations appear to be particularly important for the specification of the content and direction of problem solving processes and will be considered in some detail. These two dimensions constitute the problem space. The part-whole dimension is well suited to delimit the section of the problem environment which is actually within the span of attention, whereas the means-end dimension specifies the level of generality at which the problem present will be considered, i.e., the language in terms of model concepts which is used. Figure 2 illustrates the trajectory of the changing focus of attention in this problem space of an engineer during fault-finding an a digital computer system.

In the functional means-end hierarchy, the functional properties of the environment are represented by concepts that belong to several levels of abstraction (see figure 3). In the present discussion, the focus will be on mental models of a physical system built to serve some human

PROBLEM SPACE IN COMPUTER TROUBLE SHOOTING.

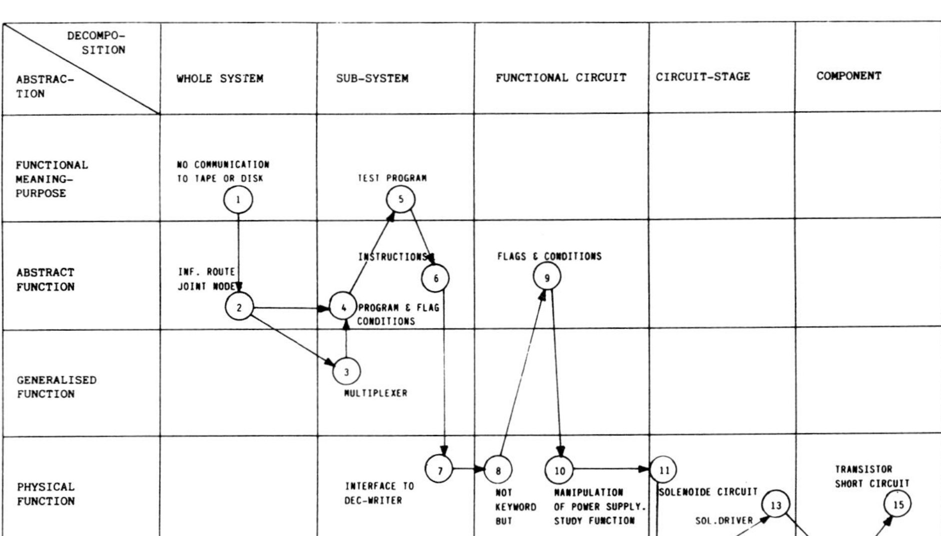

Figure 2. The problem space of computer trouble shooting can be illustrated by a map of two dimensions reflecting the levels of abstraction and decomposition considered in the individual statements of knowledge about the state of the system. Generally, in a resource-demand matching decision task, it will be expected that the decomposition is considered independently at each level of abstraction. In the present very selective task of locating a fault with reference to only one, normal, system state, a common decomposition at all levels with reference to the physical equipment was feasible for describing the trace found in verbal protocols. The figure illustrates the unstructured path of a specific case; each case will be different. Therefore, the process description is unsuited for a design basis model.

goal. The lowest level of abstraction represents only the physical configuration of objects and their locations, the material configuration of the system. The next higher level represents the physical processes or functions of the various components and systems in a language related to their specific electrical, chemical, or mechanical properties. Above this, the functional properties are represented in more general concepts without reference to the physical process or equipment by which the functions are implemented, and so forth.

When moving from one level of abstraction to the next higher level, the change in system properties represented is not merely removal of details of information on the physical or material properties. More fundamentally, information is added on higher-level principles governing the co-ordination of the various functions or elements at the lower level. In man-made systems these higher-level principles are naturally derived from the purpose of the system, i.e., from the reasons for the configurations at the level considered. A change of level of abstraction involves a shift in concepts and structure for representation as well as a change in the information suitable to characterise the state of the function or operation at the various levels of abstraction. Thus an observer asks different questions of the environment depending on the nature of the currently active internal representation.

In other words, models at low levels of abstraction are related to a specific physical world which can serve several purposes. Models at higher levels of abstraction are closely related to a specific purpose which can be met by several physical arrangements. Therefore shifts in the level of abstraction can be used to change the direction of paths, suitable for transfer of knowledge from previous cases and problems. At the two extreme levels of models, the directions of the paths available for transfer are in a way orthogonal, in that transfer at one level follows physical, material properties, while at the other it follows purpose.

At each level of abstraction reasoning depends on a particular type of model and rules for information processing. Therefore, shifting the level of modelling can be very effective in a problem situation because data processing at another level can be more convenient, the process rules can be simpler or better known, or results can be available from previous cases. A special instance of this strategy is the solution of a problem by analogy, which depends upon the condition that different physical systems have the same representation at higher levels of abstraction. Higher level models for one physical configuration may therefore be re-interpreted to solve problems related to a quite different, unfamiliar configuration.

Physical systems with known and invariant internal structure are responding to changes and to human acts according to basic laws of

MEANS-ENDS ABSTRACTION HIERARCHY

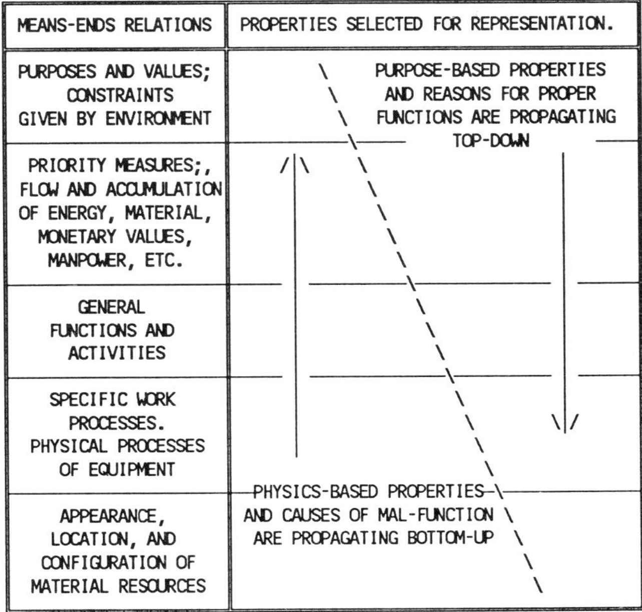

MEANS-ENDS RELATIONS
PROPERTIES SELECTED FOR REPRESENTATION.
PURPOSES AND VALUES; CONSTRAINTS GIVEN BY ENVIRONMENT
PURPOSE-BASED PROPERTIES AND REASONS FOR PROPER FUNCTIONS ARE PROPAGATING TOP-DOWN
PRIORITY MEASURES;, FLOW AND ACCUMULATION OF ENERGY, MATERIAL, MONETARY VALUES, MANPOWER, ETC.
GENERAL FUNCTIONS AND ACTIVITIES
SPECIFIC WORK PROCESSES. PHYSICAL PROCESSES OF EQUIPMENT
APPEARANCE, LOCATION, AND CONFIGURATION OF MATERIAL RESOURCES
PHYSICS-BASED PROPERTIES AND CAUSES OF MAL-FUNCTION ARE PROPAGATING BOTTOM-UP

Figure 3. The functional properties of a physical system designed to serve human purposes can be described at several levels of abstraction. The figure illustrates that properties related to the purpose of the design, intentional relationships are predominant at the higher levels, while properties derived from physical properties are predominant at lower levels.

nature which therefore can be used to predict their behaviour. They are causal systems, and their response to physical changes for which no experience is available to an observer can be explained or predicted by means of bottom-up reasoning in the abstraction hierarchy, i.e., by functional analysis.

This approach is not possible for all the environments in which humans have to make decisions. Systems with a high degree of autonomous internal functioning, with self-organising and highly adaptive features (as for instance when humans are part of the work environment), will change their internal functional organisation continuously in order to meet the requirements of the environment and to suit their internal goals or performance criteria. Even though such systems basically may be controlled by laws of nature, their complexity in general makes it impossible to explain or predict their performance by functional analysis during real-life decision making. The alternative is to consider such systems as intentional systems controlled by motives or intentions together with the constraints on performance posed by the environment - physically or in the form of conventions and legal requirements - and by the limiting capabilities of their internal mechanisms.

Decision making in control of intentional systems is based on knowledge of the value structures of the system, the actual input from the environment of the system, and its internal, limiting properties - i.e., it is based on reasoning top-down in the abstraction with little or no consideration of the internal causal structures or functions. This is probably the reason why top-level executive decision makers, according to Mintzberg's study (Mintzberg, 1973), do not behave according to analytical decision models, but prefer live action and constant consumer contacts instead of analysis of abstract reports, and current information even gossip and hearsay - for statistics and status reports. Meeting people and considering hearsay is probably the best sources of information on current trends in value structures.

Many technical systems such as control systems and information processing systems are very complex and have no simple relationship between their basic physical processes and their function in the information domain. Therefore, predictions regarding their behaviour are more readily made when considering the systems as intentional systems (Dennett, 1971). Even in case of relatively simple systems, operators can be seen in verbal protocols to develop an explanation of system behaviour from a top-down "re-design" of a reasonable functional structure from its supposed purpose, rather than to collect information on its actual, physical structure.

An illustrative example of the role of means-end relations can be found when comparing a decision task which has to be performed in a one-level formal description with the performance when the intentional context is also available. The difference may partly be due to the use of shifts in level of abstraction to find paths for transfer of solutions and strategies by analogy, but also due to support of memory and search for rules in terms of structures at other levels of abstraction. A good empirical piece of evidence is the reasoning experiment of Wason and Johnson-Laird (1972). Their experiment showed significantly better performance when a problem was embedded in the subjects' every-day experience, compared to the same problem in an abstract formulation. The difference in performance in the two cases probably can be explained by the role of means-end relations in the actual problem solving. In the abstract formulation, the problem solving is based on formal, logical arguments at only one level of abstraction, on syllogistic logic which requires manipulation of abstract symbols and storage of intermediate results in short-term memory. Embedded in a familiar setting, the context defines an intentional system, in which the effects of the different decisions can very easily be inferred at the higher levels. The reasons for proper states can be inferred top-down. The problem is solved by top-down model modification, by transferring to a model of "reasonable states of affairs".

The role of a multilevel abstraction hierarchy in problem solving is most explicitly seen in Duncker's (1943) research on practical problem solving related to physical, causal systems (radioactive tumour treatment and functioning of a temperature-compensated pendulum). Based on verbal protocols, Duncker describes how subjects go from the problem to a solution by a sequence of consideration where the items proposed can be characterised by a "functional value" feature pointing upwards to the problem, and a "by means of which" feature pointing downwards to the implementation of a solution. The relation to the means-end hierarchy is clear.

Yet another observation on the role of an abstraction hierarchy on understanding a mechanical device has been reported by Rubin (1920), who reports an analysis of his own efforts to understand the function of a mechanical shutter of a photographic camera. He finds that consideration of purpose or reason plays a major role in the course of arguments: he conceived all the elements of the shutter in the light of their function in the whole. He did not perceive the task to explain how the individual parts worked, but rather what their functions were in the whole. How they worked was immediately clear when their function was known. He mentions that he finds it an analytical task to identify the function of parts, the direction of thought being from overall purpose to the individual function (top-down considerations). The hypothesis necessary to control the direction is then readily available. This approach was found to have additional advantages: solutions of sub-problems have their place in the whole picture, and it is immediately possible to judge whether a solution is correct or not. In contrast, arguing from the parts to the "way they work" is much more difficult as a result of being a synthesis. Solutions of sub-problems must be remembered in isolation and their correctness is not immediately apparent.

An interesting, albeit indirect, demonstration of the importance of means-end relations for functional reasoning is the difficulties met by AI attempts to model the function of mechanical devices 'bottom-up' from the function of the components. De Kleer and Brown find that determining the function of a device like an electric buzzer solely from its structure and the behaviour of the parts require complex reasoning. The inference model proposed is based on an examination of the propagation of events through the structure. In an earlier presentation, a basic principle was the 'no-function-in-structure' assumption (Brown et al. 1981). In a later discussion, however, inference is guided by 'class-wide' assumptions and 'functional evidence' which in fact appear to be a representation of purpose in disguise. The resulting inference process appear to be very artificial, compared to the top-down inference process guided by functional considerations such as those described by Rubin. In the De Kleer-Brown model, it will be difficult to see the wood for trees, while Rubin's description appears to be guided by a birds-eye perspective.

A number of conceptual relations, in addition to part-whole and means-end relations discussed in the previous sections, will be useful for operation on a problem representation in the knowledge-based domain. When means for action has been chosen from perceived means-end relations in a particular work context, causal relations are used to judge the effect of actions. Value aspects are important for choice and for assignment of priority in decision situations when the constraints given by goal specifications and functional requirements leave freedom for optimising consideration, as for instance related to cost, reliability, effort required, emotional aspects, etc. Choice among possible strategies in a work situation will depend on performance criteria, i.e., value aspect assigned to the work process, as well as its product. Generic relations define a concept as a member of a set or category in a classical Aristotelian classification, and can be used to label part of the environment and assign it to a category for which functional properties are readily available. The generic relations are, in particular, useful for drawing formal logical inference (syllogistic reasoning).

Based on this discussion, a summary of mental representations is presented in figure 4.

SUMMARY OF THE BASIS FOR COGNITIVE CONTROL

BEHAVIOUR	REPRESENTATION OF PROBLEM SPACE	PROCESS-RULES
KNOWLEDGE-BASED	MENTAL MODEL; EXPLICIT REPRESENTATION OF RELATIONAL STRUCTURES; PART-WHOLE, MEANS-END, CAUSAL, GENERIC, EPISODIC, ETC. RELATION	HEURISTICS AND RULES FOR MODEL CREATION AND TRANSFORMATION; MAPPING BETWEEN ABSTRACTION LEVELS; HEURISTICS FOR THOUGHT EXPERIMENTS
RULE-BASED	IMPLICIT IN TERMS OF CUE-ACTION MAPPING; BLACK-BOX ACTION-RESPONSE MODELS;	SITUATION RELATED RULES FOR OPERATION ON THE TASK ENVIRONMENT, I.E., ON ITS PHYSICAL OR SYMBOLIC OBJECTS;
SKILL-BASED	INTERNAL, DYNAMIC WORLD MODEL REPRESENTING THE BEHAVIOUR OF THE ENVIRONMENT AND THE BODY IN REAL TIME	NOT RELEVANT - AN ACTIVE SIMULATION MODEL IS CONTROLLED BY LAWS OF NATURE, NOT BY RULES;

Figure 4. Schematic illustration of the representations of the regularities behind the behaviour of the environment which are used for control of behaviour at the different levels of cognitive control.

Conclusion

In conclusion, for planning human-computer interaction during actual work it is necessary to consider the interaction between several modes of cognitive control which are based on quite different kinds of mental representations. More research is needed for identification of the content and structure of such mental representations during complex tasks. In particular, the interaction between mental processes across cognitive levels and through time during actual work is important to be able to support decision making and work by modern information technology.

References

Ackermann, W. & Barbichon, G. (1963). Conduites intellectuelles et activite technique. *Bull. CERP* 12, (1), pp. 1-16.

Anderson, J.R. (1983). *The Architecture of Cognition.* Cambridge, MA: Harvard University Press.

Barnett, J.A. (1982). Some issues of control in expert systems. *Proceedings of the International Conference on Cybernetics and Society,* Seattle, WA, October 28-30, 1982, pp. 1-5.

Bartlett, F. (1932). *Remembering.* Cambridge: Cambridge University Press.

Bartlett, F. (1958). *Thinking, an Experimental and Social Study.* London: Unwin.

Bernstein, N. (1967). *The Coordination and Regulation of Movement.* New York: Pergamon Press.

Craik, K.J.W. (1943). *The Nature of Explanation.* Cambridge: Macmillan.

Cuny, X. (1971). *L'Approche Psycho-Semiologique: Etude d'un Code Gestuel de Travail.* Paris: Laboratoire de Psychologie du Travail de l'E.P.H.E. Report, November 1971.

Cuny, X. (1973). Les Commandements gestuels: Une experience avec ouvriers etrangers debutants. *Bull. Psychol.,* 307, (26), pp. 14-16.

Cuny, X. & Boye, M. (1981). Analyse semiologique et apprentissage des outils-signes: L'Apprentissage du schema d'electricite. *Communications,* 33, pp. 103-140.

De Keyser, V. (1987). Structuring of knowledge of operators in continuous processes: case study of a continuous casting plant start-up. In J. Rasmussen, K. Duncan & J. Leplat (Eds.), *New Technology and Human Error.* London: Wiley and Sons.

De Kleer, J. & Brown, J.S. (1983). Assumptions and ambiguities in mechanistic mental models. In D. Gentner & A.L. Stevens (Eds.), *Mental Models*. Hillsdale, N.J.: Lawrence Erlbaum.

Dennett, D.C. (1971). Intentional systems. *J. Philos.* 68, (4), February 25, 1971.

Dreyfus, H.L. (1972). *What Computers Can't Do*. New York: Harper and Row; New revised version, 1979.

Duncker, K. (1945). On problem solving. *Psychological Monographs,* Vol. 58, No. 5, Whole no. 270.

Eco, U. (1979). *A Theory of Semiotics*. Bloomington: Indiana University Press.

Feldman, J.A. & Ballard, D.H. (1986). Connectionist models and their properties. *Cognitive Science,* Vol.6, No.3.

Fitts, P.M., & Posner, M.I. (1962). *Human Performance*. Monterey, CA: Brooks/Cole Publishing Co.

Gentner, D. & Stevens, A.L. (1983). *Mental Models*. Hillsdale, N.J.: Lawrence Erlbaum.

Gibson, J.J. (1966). *The Senses Considered as Perceptual Systems*. Boston, MA: Houghton, Mifflin.

Herry, N. (1987). Errors in the execution of prescribed instructions. Design of process control work aids. In J. Rasmussen, K. Duncan & J. Leplat (Eds.), *New Technology and Human Error*. London: Wiley and Sons.

Johnson-Laird, P.N. (1980). Mental models in cognitive science. *Cognitive Science,* 4, pp. 71-115.

Johnson-Laird, P.N. (1983). *Mental Models*. Cambridge: Cambridge University Press.

Mackie, J. L. (1975). Causes and conditions. In E.Sosa (Ed.), *Causation and Conditionals*. Oxford: Oxford University Press.

Minsky, M. (1975). A framework for representing knowledge. In P. Winston (Ed.), *The Psychology of Computer Vision*. New York: McGraw-Hill.

Mintzberg, H. (1973). *The Nature of Managerial Work*. New York: Harper and Row.

Moray, N. (1987). *Intelligent Aids, Mental models, and the Theory of Machine.* Private communication. To be published.

Morris, C. (1971). *General Theory of Signs.* Paris: Mouton.

Oestreicher, H.L. & Moore, D.L. (1986). *Cybernetics Problems in Bionics.* New York: Gordon and Breach.

Polanyi, M. (1958). *Personal Knowledge.* London: Routledge & Kegan Paul.

Polanyi, M. (1967). *The Tacit Dimension.* New York: Doubleday & Co.

Rasmussen, J. (1979). *On the Structure of Knowledge - A Morphology of Mental Models in a Man-Machine Context.* Roskilde, Denmark: Riso National Laboratory, Report No. M-2192.

Rasmussen, J. (1980). What can be learned from human error reports. In K. Duncan, M. Gruneberg, & D. Wallis (Eds.), *Changes in Working Life.* London: John Wiley and Sons.

Rasmussen, J. (1986). *Information Processing and Human Machine Interaction: An Approach to Cognitive Engineering.* New York: Elsevier Science Publishers.

Rasmussen, J. (1983). Skills, rules, knowledge: signals, signs, and symbols, and other distinctions in human performance models. *IEEE Trans. Systems, Man, and Cybernetics,* SMC-13, (3), pp. 257-267.

Rasmussen, J. & Jensen, A. (1974). Mental procedures in real life tasks: a case study of electronic trouble shooting. *Ergonomics,* 17, (3), pp. 293-307.

Rubin, E. (1920). Vorteile der Zweckbetrachtung für die Erkenntnis. *Zeitschrift f. Psychologie,* 85, pp. 210-223. Also in *Experimenta Psychologica* (pp. 66-81). Copenhagen: Munksgaard.

Rumelhart, D. E., & Norman, D.A. (1981). Analogical processes in learning. In J. R. Anderson (Ed.), *Cognitive Skills and Their Acquisition.* Hillsdale, NJ: Lawrence Erlbaum Associates.

Rummelhart, D.E. & McClelland, J.L. (Eds.) (1986). *Parallel Distributed Processing: Explorations in the Microstructure of Cognition. Vol. 1 & 2.* Cambridge, MA: MIT Press.

Searle, J. R. (1981). Minds, brains, and programs. In J. Haugeland (Ed.), *Mind Design*. Montgomery, Vermont: Bradford Books.

Searle, J.R.(1984). *Minds, Brains and Science*. '84 Reith Lectures.

Tulving, E. (1983). *Elements of Episodic Memory*. Clarendon Press.

Wason, P.C. & Johnson-Laird, P.N. (1972). *Psychology of Reasoning*. Cambridge, Mass.: Harvard University Press.

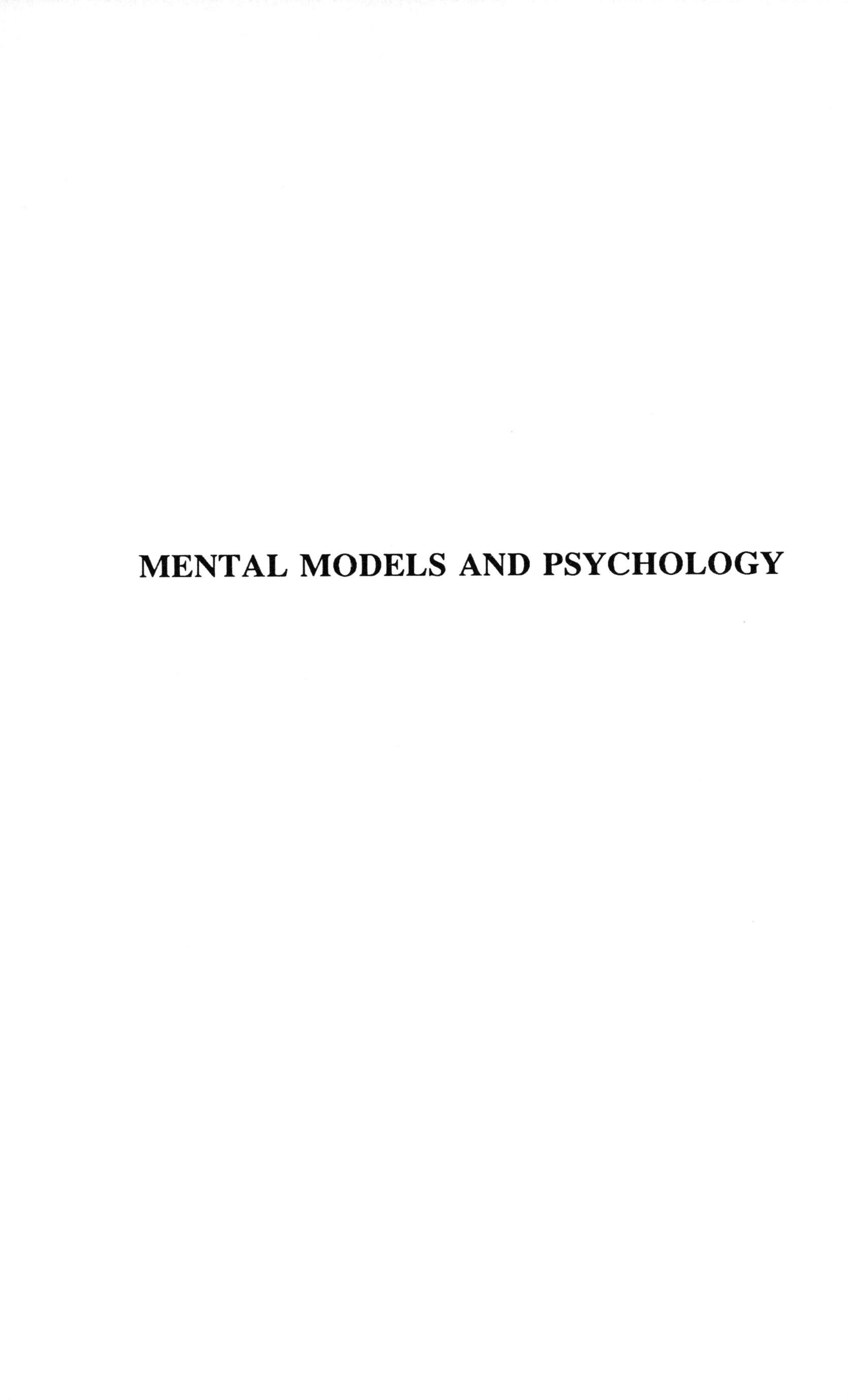

MENTAL MODELS AND PSYCHOLOGY

Mental Models and Human-Computer Interaction 1
D. Ackermann and M.J. Tauber (Editors)

ON THE DYNAMICS OF MENTAL MODELS

Yvonne Waern

Department of Psychology, University of Stockholm, Sweden

ABSTRACT

The present paper describes some theoretical concepts which are used to understand the dynamics of users' mental models and some data to illustrate these concepts.

The construction of a conceptual model will take place by a series of events, which can be iterated at any point:

- *Intention and attention.* Since human being's attention is restricted, the user will have to select some aspects of the current situation to start with.
- *Evocation of prior knowledge.* Prior knowledge is evoked on basis of the perceived (not the objective) characteristics of the situation.
- *Forming a plan.* The plan will contain a description of the goal, and a description of the method to reach the goal.
- *Action.* The action takes place in the outer world. A goal-directed, meaningful action is expected to change some aspects of the objects touched by the action.
- *Evaluation.* The result of the action is evaluated with respect to the task.
- *Memorization.* Some characteristics of the event can be stored for further use.
- *Interpretation.* The interpretation can take place at several levels, depending on the contents remembered in the events, and on the current conceptual model.

On basis of an example from a simple word-processing task it is claimed that novice users need help with each of these activities during learning. This help can only be provided if the developing model and its dynamics are understood.

Introduction

Within the field of human-computer interaction, it has for quite a while been recognized that a user's understanding of a computer system may not correspond to the working of that system. The terms "user's mental model" (Norman, 1983), or "user's conceptual model of the system" (Norman, 1986) have been suggested to stand for the knowledge about the computer system which the user constructs by interacting with the system.

This term is usually contrasted to the "Design model" of the system, i.e. the conceptualization of the system held by the designer. (Norman, 1986).

What do we need to know about these different models? That depends on the use to which we want to put the models. Here I shall discuss models from the standpoint of understanding a user's conceptual model so that we may instruct the user about the system during his learning of it. The instruction may take place outside of the system, as in manuals, by system education or by personal advisors. It may also take place inside of the system, as in computer aided instruction or adaptive help systems.

Different conceptualizations of model construction

In order to provide adequate instruction we cannot be content with regarding the user's conceptual model as static. We also have to cope with the fact that users change their conceptual model while constructing it. This means that the dynamics of the user's conceptual model also have to be considered.

Let's start by asking what ingredients that go into a mental model and how the construction process develops. Two in principal different approaches to constructing the model may be envisaged. One starts from the incoming bits and pieces of information and builds the model upwards towards a more consistent and complete model. The other starts from the already existing information (knowledge) that a user has available, and modifies, adds or restructures that according to the incoming information.

A learner who builds a conceptual model of the system solely on basis on the experiences of interactions with the system can be regarded to use a bottom-up learning approach. A proponent of that idea is Clayton Lewis, who also has attempted to model such a learning in a PROLOG program (Lewis, 1986). On the other hand, a learner who builds a conceptual model of the system on basis on his expectations of the system, derived from his prior knowledge of similar tasks or systems, can be regarded to use a top-down learning approach. Most modern psychological theories of learning build on the assumption that learning mainly uses the top-down approach (for an overview in the field of human-computer interaction see for instance Waern, 1986).

I will here develop the top-down idea, with particular consideration of its implications for the modelling of users' conceptual models.

Relationship between conceptual models

If we adopt the top-down idea of learning, an instruction about a system must take into consideration the current conceptual model which the user brings to the interactions with the system. This in turn means that the user's conceptual model must in some way be diagnosed, and that the instruction must be tuned to the model as diagnosed. Such a diagnosis is included in most ideas about adaptive user interfaces (cf. Totterdell & Cooper, 1986) as well as in intelligent computer aided instruction (cf. Sleeman & Brown 1982).

Different approaches can be used to perform the diagnosis. The most common approach is to take the "design model" as point of departure and diagnose the user's conceptual model as a subset of this. This diagnosis builds on the assumption that the user knows some, but not all aspects of the systems, and that all problems that the user encounters are due to lack of knowledge of particular aspects of the system to be used. Another approach starts with the user's knowledge as such, and assesses not only lack of knowledge, but also possible differences between the conceptual models. In that case it would be possible to diagnose problems occurring due to interference with knowledge of previous systems. Such interference can cause serious problems, as has been shown by Waern (1985).

In figure 1 I visualize the difference between these two approaches.

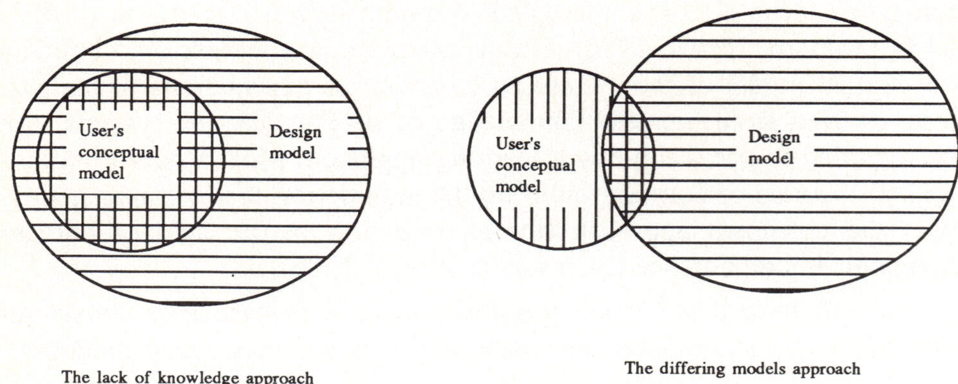

Figure 1. Different approaches to the relationship between design model and user's conceptual model

In the "lack of knowledge" approach, the user's conceptual model is included in the design model, in the "differing models" approach the models can be partially overlapping. The models can probably not be totally distinct, because in that case the user would not be able to understand at all.

Implications for instruction

If we regard the user's model as a subset of the designer's model, the implications for instruction are rather straightforward. We only need to provide less knowing users with the information about the system they lack. This is reflected in most systems which adapt their functioning according to users' prior knowledge. If, on the other hand, we regard the user's model as different, maybe even conflicting with the designer's model, we have to be able to handle misunderstandings as well as lack of knowledge. This will be a much greater problem, to which I will turn in the following.

I'll first describe how a user of a system uses his prior knowledge to understand his interactions with the system and how he constructs a conceptual model of the system on basis of both his prior knowledge and the feedback obtained from the system. I'll then try to find the implications of this analysis for the design of instructions about a system, either as conveyed by a human tutor or as embedded in the system.

The construction of a conceptual model

The construction of a conceptual model will take place by a series of events, which here are described in sequence. It should however be pointed out that one or several events in a sequence may be repeated during the construction process. The series here described applies to the construction which takes place during the performance of a single task. The events are to some extent similar to those suggested by Norman (1986), but my suggestion differs in terms of the stress laid on the user's prior knowledge.

Intention and attention

Let's start by assuming that people are given (or pose themselves) a particular task to perform in the system.

Since human attention is restricted, the user will have to select some aspects of the current situation to start with. The situation includes the task given, the system with which the user is confronted, and the instructions about the task which he is given.

The user can select aspects to be observed in two ways:

1) By *top-down selection:*
   The user will mainly rely on the prior knowledge evoked (see below) to select aspects to observe.
2) *Bottom-up selection:*
   The user will attend to characteristics of the situation which are not necessarily related to the evoked prior knowledge.

In both cases, attention gives rise to what will be called the "observed situation".

Evocation of prior knowledge

The observed situation will evoke some aspects of prior knowledge from long-term memory. With "evoke" is meant that some knowledge is actualized, which should be useful in the situation. The first evocation is instantaneous and is not governed by any conscious effort on part of the user. Some researchers describe the evocation as a simple "matching" of the characteristics of the situation to the characteristics of the knowledge residing in long-term memory. This is an oversimplified description, however, since knowledge is evoked on basis of the perceived (not the objective) characteristics of the situation, which in turn are due to the knowledge evoked. We thus have some knowledge evocation already at the selection (see above) and perceptual stage, and before we arrive at the conceptual stage, several aspects of knowledge might already have been evoked. Knowledge evocation is a complex process,. which is yet poorly understood. Let me therefore not dwell any longer here, but continue to the effects of the knowledge which has been evoked.

The perception of the situation can be regarded to be contained in a larger frame, the nature of which depends on the knowledge evoked. This larger frame has been denoted "frame" (Minsky, 1975), "script" (Schank & Abelson, 1977), or "schema" (Rumelhart & Ortony, 1976). By this frame, aspects of the situation which were not attended to can be inferred, and aspects missing from the situation can be added to the conception of the situation. The frame is thus responsible both for people's quick and adequate perception of familiar situations and for misunderstandings which can occur in nonfamiliar situations.

At the same time, the frame represents only a subset of all knowledge which could possibly be associated to the situation at hand. Thus if a frame is evoked, it will restrict the subsequent processing to its confines until the frame is found dysfunctional. This makes it possible for people to handle more information in an efficient way within the limitations of working memory than if they had to work with independent pieces of information.

We can now regard the evoked prior knowledge as the frame, within which the rest of the processing takes place, unless something happens which forces the user to radically change his conception of the task and the system. This means that the conceptual model will be built on the basis of the evoked knowledge.

Forming a plan

From the task and the current status of the conceptual model (be it solely evoked prior knowledge or prior knowledge enriched by the system experiences), the person may formulate a plan about what to do in order to perform the task. The plan can be formulated on several different levels. The lowest level concerns the actual actions to be performed. The user's conceptual model determines what levels of plans that are available, and if the plan can be realized directly in an action. The plan will contain a description of the goal, and a description of the method to reach the goal. This means that the user will expect to attain the goal by the chosen method. If the user does not see any direct way to attain the goal, he will try to divide the goal into subgoals, which may be attained one after the other.

Action

Actions can be determined in two different ways. Either the action is determined by a plan, as described above, or the action is exploratory, where the person just acts to see what happens. An exploratory action is not quite random, since it is based on either the presently evoked prior knowledge or the currently used mental model.

The action takes place in the outer world. A goal-directed, meaningful action is expected to change some aspects of the objects touched by the action.

Evaluation

The result of the action is evaluated with respect to the task. The feedback from reality here plays an important role. If the action was planned and no observable aspect of reality was changed due to the action, a noninformed user will have great difficulties in evaluating the action. Only a well-informed and experienced user would trust that the action had the intended effect. If the action was exploratory, the lack of feedback will give no information and lead to no change in the mental model.

A result which complies with the intent in the plan gives no impetus to change anything, neither in the action, the plan, or in the knowledge invoked to form the basis for the conceptual model. A nonexpected result may invoke an desire to change something, if the user is keen on having an adequate result.

Memorization

Some characteristics of the event can be stored for further use. The event includes the intended task, the conceptual model under construction, the observed situation, the plan, the action, the observed result of the action, as well as the evaluation of this result. The storage of all these entities takes some effort. It is probable that the user will forget at least some of them. The entities forgotten will most likely be those to which the user didn't particularly attend. We find, for instance, that users making typing errors will typically not remember these as possible causes for unexpected outcomes.

Interpretation of event

The action and its result are placed within the context of the model under construction. If they fall within the range of the permissible characterizations of objects and operations contained in the conceptual model, the event is easily assimilated into it. If they do not, the discrepancy may lead to a need to interpret the event, in order to explain the cause and find a better way of working for the future.

The interpretation can take place at several levels, depending on the contents remembered in the events, and on the current conceptual model. The actual actions performed can be blamed, which leads to the intention to change these the next time a similar situation occurs. The plan used can be blamed, whereby the user will try to change this. The conceptual model itself may be challenged, whereby the user will attempt to change it in some way. Further details about these possible changes will be discussed below.

Exploratory actions may also lead to a need to change something, through the interpretation of the results.

Continued construction

The events described above were related to a single task. For the continued construction of the conceptual model, different tasks, plans, actions and feedback will be involved. The user will forget some and remember some, will blame some aspects for failures and praise others for success. The history of all his encounters with the system in terms of the events and their outcomes as described above will determine the nature of his conceptual model.

To be able to continue my exposition of the dynamics on a higher level, I will now leave the specific details in the process and instead describe the concepts which I find useful for describing the conceptual model.

Concepts used in describing the conceptual model

In order to be able to talk about the conceptual model we must use some defined concepts. A user might talk about his mental model in a particular way, and a researcher in another way. As a researcher I should like to describe a computer user's conceptual model in terms of a "problem space". The problem space contains characterizations of objects (static entities) and operations (actions which change characteristics of objects or relations between objects), as these are related to the goal to be attained.

During learning to act in the system, the user constructs both a problem space (which corresponds to his understanding of the system) and strategies for searching the problem space. The strategies can be formulated as rules, containing actions to be performed, if the conditions specified by the rule are fulfilled by the attended situation. The conditions can concern characteristics of the objects, the results of the actions, or the goal. One particular set of condition-action rules was suggested by Card, Moran and Newell (1983), called GOMS-rules. GOMS stands for Goal, Operation, Methods, and Selection.

Changes in the mental model

What kind of changes can be imagined during a user's interaction with a computer system? The following is an account from the insights gained by modern researchers concerned with learning in problem solving contexts:

- The description of the objects considered can change by adding features to an object (discrimination) or by deleting features (generalization).
- The operations to be performed can be chunked together into greater units (composition).

These changes have been investigated at length by for instance John Anderson (Anderson, Kline & Beasley, 1978, Anderson, 1981, Anderson, Greeno, Kline & Neves, 1981) and also by Neches, Langley, and Klahr (1986). As we see, these changes imply changes in the problem space as well as in the strategic rules.

- The priorities put on the choice of one or several production rules among the ones which are applicable can be changed. As one example, take the difference between "correct" and "desirable" rules. Desirable rules are such which allow the person to attend to or to memorize only a limited amount of information, or rules which lead to short sequences of action (i.e. a more efficient procedure). I shall below analyse the situation of finding a rule, leading to a more efficient procedure.
- The conceptual model or parts of it may be discarded and substituted by a new one. This means that either new objects and operations are conceived, or that old objects are given new characteristics.

This last mentioned change has by the Gestalt psychologists been related to the "structure" of the situation. (see e.g. Wertheimer, 1945). Other kinds of changes which go beyond those mentioned above have been reported by modern information processing researchers. It has for instance been suggested that differences between novices and experts are due to their use of quite different methods. (Hunter, 1968, Simon & Simon, 1978, Larkin, 1981). Looking closely at the descriptions of the difference, it is found that sometimes different methods also require different understandings of the problem, or, in the term used here, different conceptual models. Since experts must have been novices at some point of time, they must have changed their conceptual model during experience. The structural rerepresentation of a problem is an important and interesting change which I will focus in the following.

Impetus to change

How can changes in conceptual models come about?

Let us first ask what conditions that may give an impetus to change. I suggest that a conceptual model does not change spontaneously. It only changes as a result from a discrepancy between the expectancies derived from the plan and the observed effect of the action. The first impetus to change thus lies in a detected discrepancy.

Next impetus for a user to change his conceptual model lies in the interpretation of the discrepancy. The conceptual model is but one of the links in the chain, consisting of observation, mental model, plan, action and evaluation. Some other links may be blamed as well. Only if the person has reason to believe that the conceptual model is the cause of the discrepancy observed, he will consider the possibility of changing it.

Another condition has to do with how concerned the person is by the discrepancy encountered. Only if the person finds the discrepancy serious enough (for instance leading to risks for big errors or repeated mistakes), the person will find it worthwhile to find the reason for the discrepancy.

A fourth condition has to do with how the person estimates his possibilities of succeeding in the attempts to change the conceptual model (once it is the one to be blamed). If the person can find no alternative prior knowledge to evoke, for instance, it will be difficult to find an alternative conceptual model. The person may then rather give up than trying in vain to come up with new suggestions. On the other hand, it may be equally difficult to find an adequate alternative conceptual model, if the range of possible models be considered is very large. Then the person will see himself entangled in a maze of alternative models, and rather give up than get lost.

Requirements for representational changes

I am here concerned with changes in the choice of objects and operations represented, and I will therefore not consider the changes due to discrimination, generalization, and combination.

Three different preconditions must be valid in order for a change to occur which concerns the choice of objects or operations to be represented.

The first requirement concerns attention. As long as the selection of observations is made top down, i.e. taking the current conceptual model as point of departure, the user has a chance to detect only such discrepancies which derive from the objects that he attends to. If the attended result differs from the expected result, the conceptual model (which is responsible for the expectation) may be blamed. Any other, potentially informative discrepancy cannot challenge the conceptual model, since it simply is not observed.

Thus, in order to be able to observe aspects not contained in the current conceptual model, the user must redistribute his attention. This can be done by a bottom-up procedure, where conspicuous events in the situation are observed, even though they are not selected by the current conceptual model.

The second requirement concerns interpretation of the discrepancy. The user has several options beside actively interpreting the discrepancy, once this has been noticed. The user can just go on, not worrying about the discrepancy at all. He can also choose to store the event as such in memory, in order to see if the discrepancy turns up repeatedly.

The third requirement concerns the knowledge evoked. The person may be caught in a circle of objects and operations which does not lead to any solution of the problem, either because he really does not know the crucial characteristics of the objects and operations which are required to achieve a solution, or because he is temporarily "fixated" to a certain way of looking at the world. People often report a feeling of "getting stuck", which can be explained in this way. In those cases, it is only by evoking new knowledge that there is a chance to reconceptualize the experiences in a more adequate conceptual model.

Some illuminating examples

In some studies of persons learning a word-processing system, I had the opportunity to observe some representational changes. Subjects were asked to perform a particular task, which is not commonly found in a word-processing situation (Waern & Rabenius, 1986, Waern, 1986). The task required the subject to realign a row with displaced numbers in a table of numbers. Table 1 gives an example of the task.

In this task, the numbers for year 3 have to be moved one step to the left. In the particular word-processing system used, the task can be performed in several ways.

One way consists in deleting and inserting each number in the row at a time, a rather tedious procedure. The "side" effect of this procedure is that the figures move to the left when something is deleted, and to

TABLE 1
An example of an aligning task

	Type 1	Type 2	Type 3
Year 1	32	45	28
Year 2	43	24	36
Year 3	33	27	55
Year 4	25	32	44

the right, when something is inserted.

The task can also be performed by a very simple procedure, i.e. by deleting a single blank somewhere before the number 33. Hereby the whole row moves to the left one step (or as many steps as the number of signs deleted). In other tasks, the numbers were displaced to the left, whereby the simplest method consists in inserting a blank.

Let us start by considering what conceptual model that would be needed in order to perform the task in the simple, efficient way, mentioned last.

In figure 2, the central objects, the operations on them and the results are shown in the form of a problem space. The figure is simplified by showing only the operations "move cursor" and "delete".

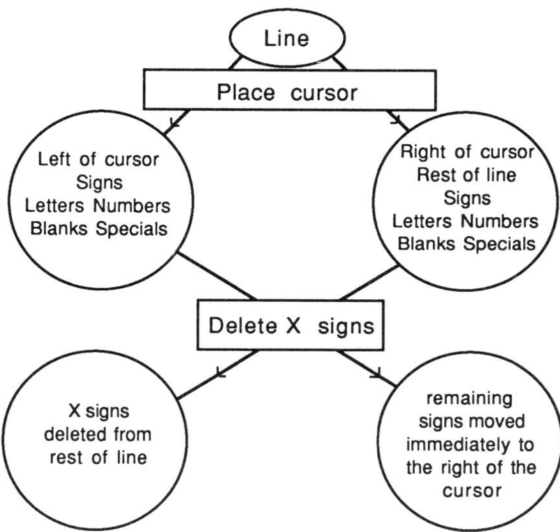

Figure 2. A simplified problem space for the aligning task

Observations of users attempting this task indicate that their conceptual models to start with were different from the one required for the efficient performance of the task. These observations and some interpretations of them have been described in Waern (1986) and Rabenius (1986). Different stages in the change of the conceptual model were detected. I want here to place the observations into the general framework described above.

First, it was found that many users to start with didn't observe the movements of what is here called "the rest of the line". They attended only to the number which should be changed. Since the rest of the line was not important to them, this might mean that they did not yet have the concept of "the rest of the line". This model is depicted in figure 3.

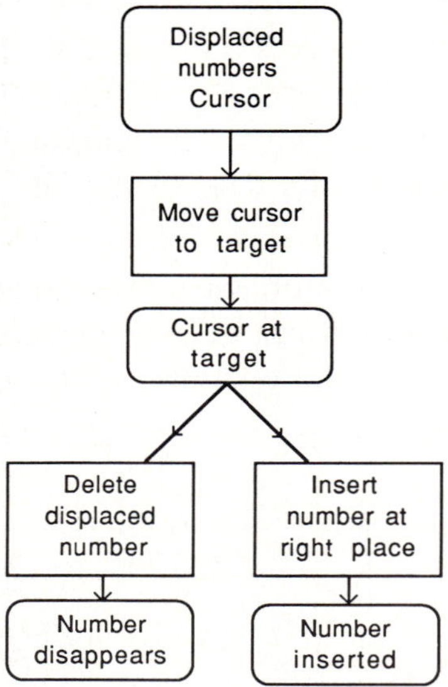

Figure 3. Suggested problem space at first stage of conceptual model. Only target numbers are attended to.

Next step consists in observing the other numbers. Some subjects started to observe the movement of these when they were instructed to find new ways of performing the task. It is as if the instruction forced them to distribute their attention to a wider field.

The observation of nonexpected movement could give the first impetus to change the mental model. However, the observation was not enough, as shown by comments as: "Why do the others move around?

Well, I'll not bother, but just go on." The movements of the other numbers were often regarded as annoying: "What shall I do to stop them moving around?". Such a comment indicates that the problem space now had changed to include the other numbers affected, not only those attended to. However, the plan derived from this model was still nonadequate for the task, since it contained the subgoal of NOT moving the other numbers.

When users detected that the rest of the line moved, some of them posed the goal to move this rest of the line (to the right or to the left according to the requirements of the task). However, they did not know how to do it. This finding indicates that the concept "rest of the line" was included in their conceptual model, but that their planned operation "move" could not find any correspondent in the design model.

Next, some subjects accidentally found that the rest of the line moved leftwards when they deleted a number. They then connected the intention of "moving" to the action of "delete". They were not yet clear about what to delete, however.

One subject thought that the "move" only affected the closest number, and not the others. Still another subject formulated the following rule: "If I want to move the line to the left, then I should delete a number".

The mental model at this stage can be represented as in figure 4.

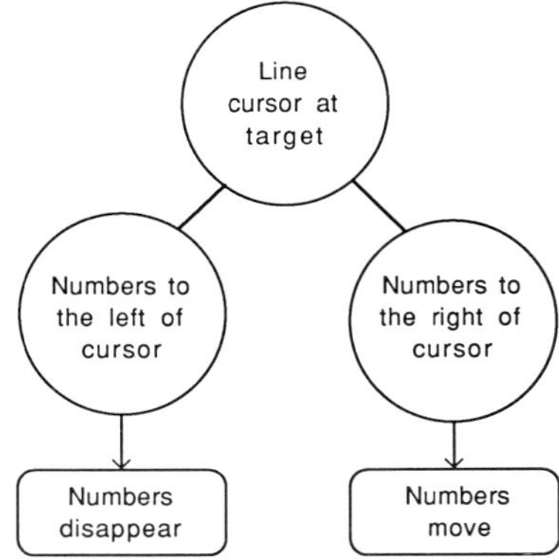

Figure 4. Another step in the construction of a conceptual model. Here both numbers to the left and to the right of the cursor are attended to. The actual action for the conceptual operation "move" has not yet been found.

It was possible for the subjects to perform the task efficiently, if they used the "movement" idea together with the idea that movements could come about by using the delete command somewhere. One subject expressed this as follows: "The delete command can be used either to take a number away or to move the row to the left". This rule is, as we see, not quite consistent with the design model, but can still be used to perform the task adequately and efficiently. This finding indicates that people do not have to have a conceptual model of the system which totally complies with the design model. For particular tasks, simple procedural rules can be sufficient.

The major problem in the design model consisted in the concept of "sign", which included blank signs, together with letters and numbers. Very few subjects found the solution of deleting blank signs or inserting them in order to move left and right respectively. A couple of subjects understood that deleting could be used on blank signs, but not that inserting could be used in a similar way.

To understand this difficulty, we have to understand how people, who are not accustomed to computers regard a screen composed of numbers. On paper, a number is placed on a background. The background is fix, but the number can be moved and removed. The spaces on the paper are just spaces. The concept of "blank sign" is quite nonsensical.

This is indicated by the comment by one of the subjects. She was shown the effect of deleting "blank signs". The experimenter explained the effect as "deleting empty signs". This subject expressed her difficulty in representing the screen as empty spaces in the following way: "You can't talk about 'empty signs'! Then people would think that you are empty in your head!"

The understanding of the meaning of the "blank sign" requires a major reorganization of the mental model. For most people, signs are something which are placed on a blank background. Signs are figures, blanks are just nothing. The subjects here thus had to reorganize their perception of numbers as figures on a background to a perception of numbers and blank signs with equal importance. They must see a new pattern on the screen, a pattern which might be as foreign to them as the relativity of time was before Einstein's insight. Figure 5 depicts the "natural" way of regarding signs on paper.

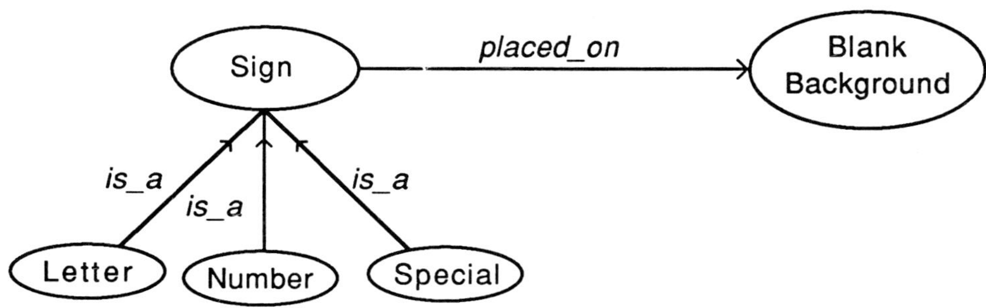

Figure 5. A suggested conceptual network for the concept "sign" for a user who does not know the present wordprocessing system.

In figure 6, the concept of "sign", as regarded by the system is depicted.

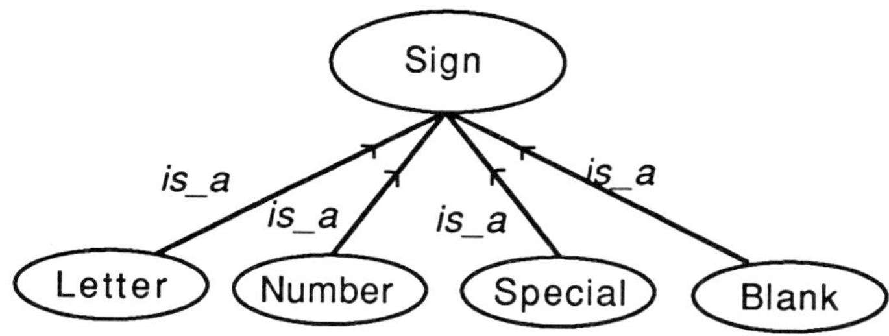

Figure 6. A conceptual network required for the concept "sign" in the wordprocessing system used.

Conclusion

From the analysis given above and the analysis of the empirical examples it can be concluded that it is not enough to consider a person's conceptual model as a static entity in order to inform the person about a system. Instead, the dynamics of the mental model must be taken into account.

Two aspects of the dynamics are important for the instruction to be successful. The first concerns the short-term dynamics of the model, the second concerns the possibilities to change the model in the long term.

For the short term it is essential to consider the selection processes which give rise to the first observed situation, and the processes which evoke the user's prior knowledge. People are usually unaware of these processes, and will therefore to a great extent be influenced by superficial details of the situation. In a computer situation, these superficial details concern the layout of the screen, the wording of the instructions, commands or menu options, and the way of describing the task. Interfaces which have been turned out to be easy to learn work with presentations of common objects and operations with which the user is already familiar. As long as the presentation and feedback of the system does not conflict with the user's prior expectations, no long term changes in the conceptual model have to be made.

In the long term, however, we all know that it will not be enough to use prior knowledge unchanged. Any use of a computer system which goes beyond tasks as conceived outside of the computer system will need some reconceptualization of objects and operations. We will therefore also have to consider how a conceptual model can be changed, when it no longer can cope with the concepts required to use a system successfully and efficiently. In current research on conceptual models of computer systems, this is a topic which yet has received very little attention.

From the observations and the analysis above, we see that a person's strategies for distribution of attention, willingness to spend effort on the task and perceived alternatives in prior knowledge play a great role in the potentialities for changing the mental model. This indicates that the instructions must take these dynamics of the mental model into account in order to help the user. In particular, the need for the user to make major reconstructions of the conceptual model should be considered. It is here that misunderstandings may occur. It is here that the user needs help in observing effects and interpreting them in a way that helps the reconstruction on its way.

How can this be done? The first step consists in accepting the idea that a user's model can concern concepts and operations outside of and different from the design model and not only a subset of those contained in it. Diagnoses of misunderstandings have to be worked out as well as diagnoses of lack of knowledge.

The next step consists in finding out what kind of instructions (outside or inside the system) that are needed to cope with misunderstandings. Here I have suggested that instructions which direct the attention to the "weak" spot would be helpful. A more tricky question concerns the explanations needed to get the user to reconstruct the model. Up till now, patience on part of the instructor and user seems to be the only solution. But further research may suggest more efficient tutoring methods also for that problem.

Acknowledgements

The preparation of this paper and the study reported has been supported by a grant from The Swedish Board for Research in the Humanities and Social Sciences.

I am indebted to Lars Oestreicher for drawing the figures.

References

Anderson, J.R. (1981). A theory of language acquisition based on general learning principles. In *Proceedings of the Seventh International Joint Conference on Artificial Intelligence* (pp. 163-170). Vancouver, B.C., Canada.

Anderson, J.R., Greeno, J.G., Kline, P.J. & Neves, D. (1981). Acquisition of problem-solving skill. In J.R. Anderson (Ed.), *Cognitive Skills and Their Acquisition.* Hillsdale, N.J.: Lawrence Erlbaum Ass.

Anderson, J.R., Kline, P.J., & Beasley, C.M. (1978). *A Theory of the Acquisition of Cognitive Skills.* Technical Report No. ONR 77-1. Department of Psychology, Yale University, New Haven, Ct.

Card, S.K., Moran, T.P. & Newell, A. (1983). *The Psychology of Human-Computer Interaction.* Hillsdale, NJ: Lawrence Erlbaum Associates.

Hunter, I.M.L. (1968). Mental calculation. In P.C. Wason & P.N. Johnson-Laird (Eds.), *Thinking and Reasoning.* Baltimore: Penguin Books.

Larkin, J.H. (1981). Enriching formal knowledge: a model for learning to solve textbook physics problems. In J.R. Anderson (Ed.), *Cognitive Skills and their Acquisition.* Hillsdale, N.J.Lawrence Erlbaum Associates.

Lewis, C. (1986). A model of mental model construction. In M. Mantei & P. Orbeton (Eds.), *Human Factors in Computing Systems* (pp. 306-313). CHI'86 Proceedings.

Minsky, M.A. (1975). A framework for representing knowledge. In P. Winston (Ed.), *The Psychology of Computer Vision.* New York: McGraw-Hill.

Murray, D. (1987). Embedded user models. In *Proceedings of the IFIP Interact'87.*

Neches, R., Langley, P., & Klahr, D. (1986). Learning, development, and production systems. In D. Klahr, P. Langley & R. Neches (Eds.), *Production System Models of Learning and Development.* Cambridge, Mass.: MIT Press.

Norman, D.A. (1983). Some observations on mental models. In D. Gentner & L.A. Stevens (Eds.). *Mental Models.* Hillsdale, NJ: Lawrence Erlbaum Associates.

Norman, D.A. (1986). Cognitive engineering. In D.A. Norman & S.W. Draper (Eds.), *User Centered System Design.* Hillsdale, New Jersey: Lawrence Erlbaum Associates.

Rabenius, L. (1986). *On Rerepresentation of Concepts in a Wordprocessing System.* Manuscript.

Rumelhart, D.E. & Ortony, A. (1976). The representation of knowledge in memory. In R.C. Anderson, R.J. Spiro, & W.E.Montague (Eds.), *Schooling and the Acquisition of Knowledge.* Hillsdale, N.J.: Lawrence Erlbaum Associates.

Schank, R.C. & Abelson, R.P. (1977). *Scripts, Plans, Goals, and Understanding. An Inquiry into Human Knowledge Structures.* Hillsdale, N.J.: Lawrence Erlbaum Associates.

Simon, D. P., & Simon, H.A. (1978). Individual differences in solving physics problems. In R. Siegler (Ed.), *Children's Thinking: What Develops ?* Hillsdale, N.J.: Lawrence Erlbaum Associates.

Sleeman, D. & Brown, J.S. (1982). *Intelligent Tutoring Systems.* New York: Academic Press.

Totterdell, P. & Cooper, P. (1986). Design and evaluation of the AID adaptive front end to Telecom Gold. *Proceedings of the Conference of the British Computer Society Human Interaction Specialist Group.* University of York, September 22-26, 1986.

Waern, Y. (1985). Learning computerized tasks as related to prior task knowledge. *International Journal Man-Machine Studies,* 22, pp. 441-455.

Waern, Y. (1986). *Learning Computerized Tasks.* HUFACIT reports, Department of Psychology, University of Stockholm, No.8, 1986.

Waern, Y. & Rabenius, L. (1985). *Metacognitive Aspects of Learning Difficult Texts.* Working Papers from the Cognitive Seminar, Department of Psychology, University of Stockholm, No. 18, 1985. Also in E. De Corte, H. Lodewijks, R. Parmentier & P. Span (Eds.), *Learning and Instruction,* 1. European Association For Research On Learning And Instruction, Leuven. (In press)

Waern, Y. & Rabenius, L. (1986). *On the role of models in the instruction of novice users of a word processing system.* Presentation at MACINTER workshop, Stuttgart, September, 1985. HUFACIT report, Department of Psychology, University of Stockholm, No. 6, 1986. Also in *Zeitschrift für Psychologie,* Suppl. 9.

Wertheimer, M. (1945). *Productive Thinking.* Chicago: The University of Chicago Press (First edition).

Young, R.M. (1983). Surrogates and mappings: two kinds of conceptual models for interactive devices. in D. Gentner & A.L. Stevens (Eds.), *Mental Models* (pp. 35-52). Hillsdale, NJ: Lawrence Erlbaum Associates.

Mental Models and Human-Computer Interaction 1
D. Ackermann and M.J. Tauber (Editors)

PROBLEM SOLVING RESEARCH AND HUMAN-COMPUTER INTERACTION

Uta Gumm and Herbert Hagendorf
Berlin Humboldt University, Berlin, GDR

ABSTRACT

The psychology of knowledge based problem solving processes can provide a framework for relatively high levels of the human computer interface. The critical elements are tasks and goals as concept-related units, which, as a result of cognitive processes, are subject to relevant formation laws. It is assumed that cognitive procedures are linked with these target concepts. This provides us with units to formulate planning networks on the basis of heuristic strategies of general nature. The cognitive effort, which is reflected in the remembering and processing effort required for structure recognition processes, is determinant of the chosen performance strategy. Experimental results on mapping of solution plans on sequences of actions for the computer are in accordance with these assumptions on the interaction between knowledge, representation and strategy use.

Introduction

In general, users interact on the basis of interaction languages. The tasks to be accomplished can be solved by using a variety of options. It is therefore apparent that human computer interaction could also be seen as a problem solving situation that involves routine mental processes. The user has to achieve goals represented as states in a problem space by means of operation sequences carried out by the computers. The problem space is characterized as the internal representation of the task and the corresponding knowledge states. Depending on the complexity of the task and the knowledge level of the user, planning processes have to be carried out. In order to understand some of the difficulties involved in using technological systems theoretically well founded knowledge of the users cognitive processes (Rasmussen 1983) is required. A number of authors have indicated that higher levels of user interface play a considerable role in matters of design (Tauber and Rohr 1984).

It is for this reason that this paper relies on our knowledge of the relations between knowledge, problem representation and solution strategy to provide a conceptual framework that helps to understand cognitive processes underlying user performance, and also helps to check our assumptions on the interaction between representation and process in the field of human computer interaction. Viewing the user as a processor of information provides a framework in which models of memory, problem solving and perception can be integrated.

Problem solving research

Studies of knowledge clean problems in the sixties and seventies illuminated the basic information processing capacities people employ when behaving intelligently in situations where they lack specialized knowledge. Recently, however, new results have been provided. It is shown that available knowledge units influence the induction of relevant implicit information (Kotovsky et al. 1985). Large differences in difficulty of various versions of the same problem rule out size of problem space as determinant of relative difficulty. Difficulty can be explained by considering memory load. Consistency of the structure within operator sets or rule sets with real world knowledge is one of the factors reducing memory load and therefore difficulty. Experience with problems of a certain type builds up knowledge which reduces the difficulty of problems, as well. Hesse (1986) came to the same conclusion in analyzing complex problems. Attempts to model solution processes showed that families of connected models for different stages of problem solving may be necessary (Sydow 1980). These outcomes emphasize the necessity to study the knowledge strategy for problem solving that regards progress as coming from expressing, recognizing and using diverse and particular forms of knowledge. Barnard et al (1986) recently stated that in cognitive tasks of even moderate complexity mental processes and knowledge are purposefully coordinated to control behaviour.

Rasmussen (1983) characterized the knowledge level as a sequence of activities which are not guided by preformed descriptions. Within the problem solving literature in more recent years knowledge rich tasks have been examined. Studies of high competence have attempted to describe differences between novices and experts in various domains such as radiology, programming, and physics (Glaser 1986). Much can be learned from this research. Here we mention only some results: extraordinary representational abilities of experts result in rapid access to an organized body of knowledge (proceduralized knowledge). Competence in one domain does not guarantee competence in other domains. Early learning seems to be dominated by task control whilst more experienced performance should be approximated by execution of methods more closely. Experts often can be characterized as opportunistic planners which means new features of problems result in changed representations. These results also provide us with characterizations of performance and of the changes that occur as learning progresses. They serve to constrain the model building process in problem solving research.

From our point of view the cognitive system is seen as a strategically adapting system which is goal oriented and uses knowledge. This cognitive system is able to view a problem or task in more than one way. Changing demands may lead therefore to altered strategies. One of the aims of our research should be the understanding of processes responsible for this flexibility of human performance, specifically in human computer interaction. This view emphasizing the representation of knowledge and its functional properties can be characterized as a user centered approach to human-computer interaction.

Human-computer interaction

We are going to confine ourselves to just one aspect of human-computer interaction: the user of a system is required to formulate expressions in a language that a computer can read, so that he can tell the system what operations to perform. We choose a seemingly simple variant from the realm of interactive graphics systems: the transformation of the intention of generating a geometrical object into the specification of an action sequence for making a drawing on the screen (Reisner 1981). With this task we wish to check our conceptual framework in this situation. In the upper part of figure 1 one of the patterns used in experiments with novices is shown.

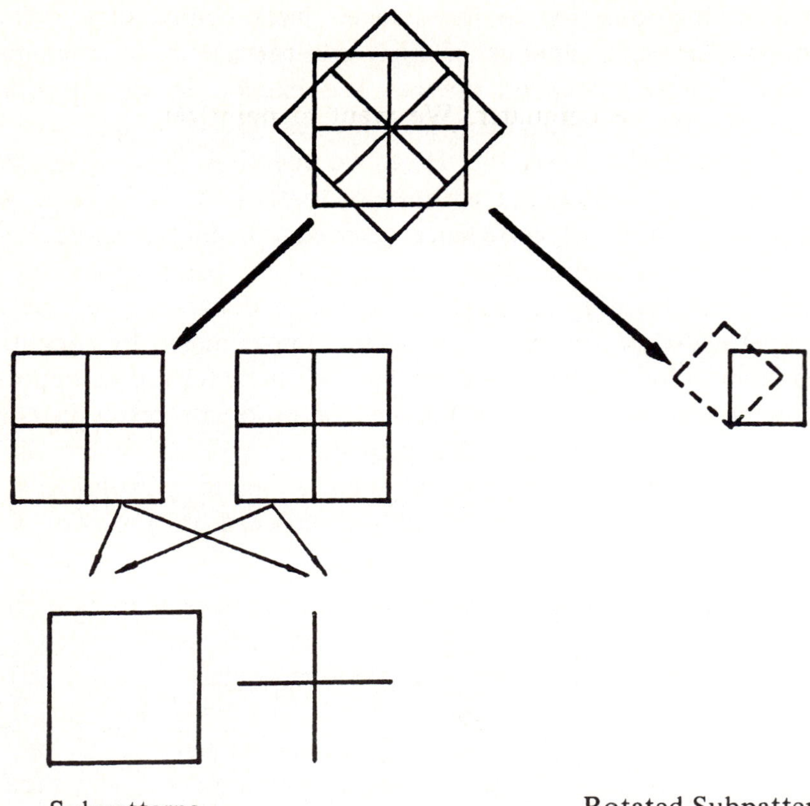

Figure 1. Decompositions of a pattern (upper part: original pattern, left part: subpatterns; right part: rotation of one subpattern)

For this reason we should like to say already at this stage what the characteristics of the simple LOGO-like language are that we made use of in our first investigations on specifying action sequences:

(1) The user can rely on an elementary set of commands to move a drawing pen on the screen. A distance that is to be covered can be given as a vector through the specification of direction and length. In accordance with its state which can be changed by a command, the pen either does or does not leave a visible trace on the screen. This allows generating all kinds of line drawings.

(2) The user can feed into the system a partial sequence (o_1, o_2, ..., o_m) of commands that is repeated n times, giving it an abbreviated form: (loop (n,&(o_1, o_2, ..., o_m))). This requires an appropriate

conceptualization of the task, i.e. the representation of the problem allowing the recognition of this loop-structure.

(3) A partial sequence (o_1, o_2, ..., o_m) that is required in the fulfilment of different tasks can be defined as a new linguistic element with a name of its own: (define ((name),& (o_1, o_2, ..., o_m))). This kind of procedure formation requires knowledge of the task space and is an adaptation of the ways in which language is able to express things. Definitions of such macros can be seen as expressions of semantic units in characterizing the internal problem space (Ackermann 1987, Eyferth et al 1986).

Choosing this kind of orientation, we only consider this stage of task delegation rather than the processing of the feedback from the system because we are mainly interested in planning processes as neglected components in human computer interaction (Hacker 1986).

Conceptual framework

We believe that user psychology can be properly understood on the basis of theoretical and empirical results from the psychology of knowledge. This allows substantiating approaches like those of cognitive grammar. In our considerations, which are still confined to qualitative aspects, we seek to estimate cognitive effort (Norman 1986) in psychological terms, thus making it accessible to influence.

The theoretical framework for our knowledge-based approach has been given by Klix (1985). Within this approach the existence of an initial knowledge base is assumed. In solving tasks users are faced with the problem of interrelating the preexisting repertoire in their long-term knowledge base and its operation with more transient information structures. Klix (1985) states that to explain mental performance we have to assume that knowledge consists of the following components (see figure 2):

(1) concepts and relations between concepts forming semantic networks;

(2) latent procedures to process concept-represented knowledge, e.g. a procedure to multiply numbers or to draw a geometrical pattern;

(3) heuristic strategies and checking procedures to set up planning networks because competence and performance are related by a logic of planning; and

(4) interaction between these types of knowledge and perceptually absorbed information in the operative compartment.

The generative nature of knowledge utilization which is typical of problem solving, can be explained through a goal-related combination of procedural modules as has been demonstrated in analogical reasoning.

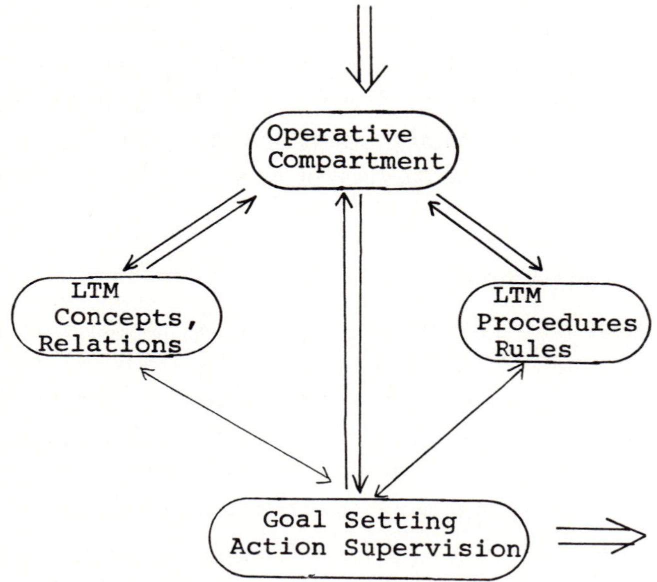

Figure 2. Functional components of problem solving competence

To bring about a heuristic separation between matter-related and interaction-related knowledge (Norman 1986, Streitz 1985, Hoppe 1985), we will have to assume that these components exist in either type of knowledge, since they become effective at different stages:

(1) relying on his matter-related knowledge, the user has to turn his intentions into a mental solution plan;

(2) applying his knowledge of interaction, the user has to turn the plan into a sequence of action specifications for the computer.

This is valid at least for the problem-oriented approach to learning.

To make the joint operation of these factors transparent in terms of human-computer interaction, we will have to relate the assumed units to both the problem sphere and the interaction sphere. For present purposes it is assumed that memory contains information which allows a person to manipulate mental descriptions of goals and actions:

(1) The tasks and targets in both the problem sphere and the interaction sphere are concepts and must be characterized as such by sets of features. The type and differentiation of the features are dependent on learning (see also Payne and Green 1986). Simple concepts of this kind are, for instance, angle, line, triangle and regular polygon. Psychologically, objects can be described in many different ways. This is also true for tasks and problems. One possible description of the pattern in figure 1 is given in figure 3.

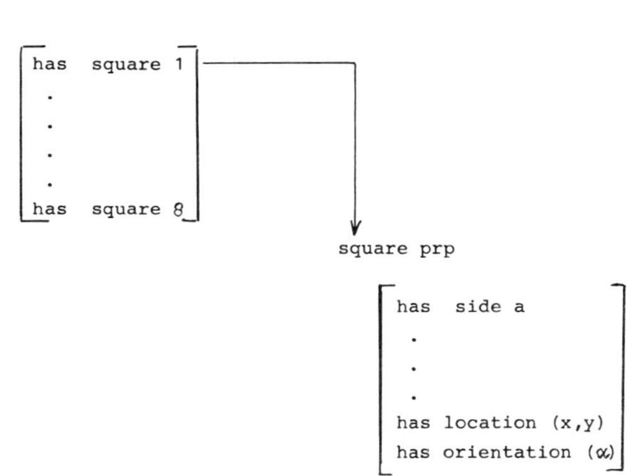

Figure 3. Feature description of a pattern (see figure 1)

(2) The assumed relational structures link concept-related representations of tasks and goals with concept-related representations of procedures. The concept-related representation of a procedure is an action concept, which forms the central unit of this kind of structure. In a simple case action concepts represent commands. According to Klix (1985), the link between action concept and goals is given through a relation of finality. Action concepts of this kind can stand for motor action sequences in manual sign production or for generalized plans in making action specifications for the computer. The information on preconditions for the use of procedures that is

required for linking procedures, and also the results from this can be mapped onto links of event representations. This provides us with all the elements that are assumed to be central to the deliberate control of the solution process. It is assumed that the knowledge base contains a set of such cohesive units. Beside this representation we have to assume an internal characteristic of each procedural unit characterizing the performance component. In figure 4 a possible description of such a unit is given for our task environment: different conceptual units representing accessible procedures are connected by means of finality relation to a concept LINE DRAWING. Each procedure has certain conditions (COND) and results (RESULT) represented by conceptual units as well. This knowledge structure is declarative. Therefore it can be used in multiple ways by interpretative procedures as stated by Greeno et al (1984). These units are the basis for working backward from the result of procedures by setting subgoals or for working forward by activating procedures. In analogy to the action programs (Mandler 1984), we assume that there is a two-fold representation for procedures.

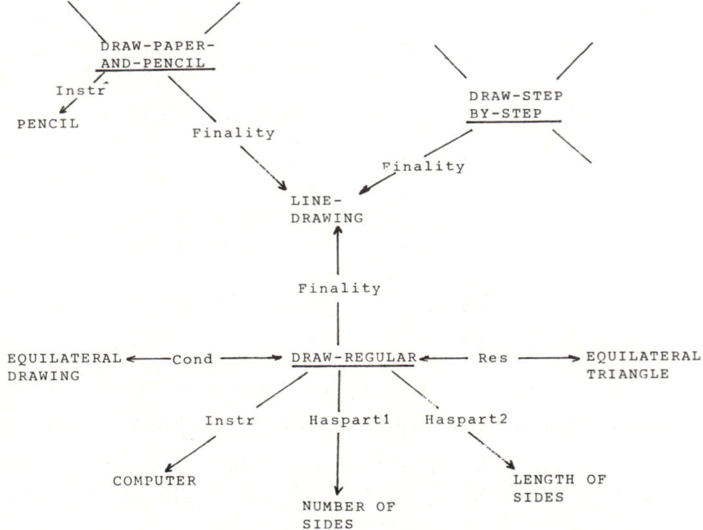

Figure 4. Conceptual knowledge structure containing different procedures for drawing a line pattern

(3) These operative units are dependent on learning. Subjects have to learn features that define a task concept, conceptual representations

of procedures that can be assessed quickly, and the performance component. The functional characteristics of the computer system can induce concept-related representations of goals that have features different from those of the targets in the content domain. The manual production of the drawing of a triangle requires interior angles to be given as features in the target representation. The language given above induces a representation of the triangle with the help of exterior angles. This is a simple example of re-conceptualization of the task space not to speak of restructuring of Gestaltpsychologie (Ohlsson 1984). Yet dependence on learning can also be manifest in the procedures: (a) According to the composition mechanism (Klix 1971, Anderson 1983), stable links between goal procedure units can be combined to form new conceptual units. (b) The language that we have given will allow the user to adapt the command language to his conceptualization of the task space. A reduction in the complexity of the task space is possible in either case (Eyferth et al 1986).

(4) Transient structure formations, which result from planning processes on the basis of the operative units available in knowledge, are made in the operative compartment. This is why these cohesive units in the knowledge base determine the depth of planning. Taking account of the limited resources of the operative compartment (remembering and processing capacity), we assume that when it comes to using the compartment, there is a "last effort principle" at work. A feature of a good strategy is that it will minimize the load on these limited resources. The all-important point is, however, that this mental load cannot be estimated on the basis of some knowledge-independent task analysis.

The usefulness of this conceptual framework will depend on the characterization of the temporary structure formations in the operative compartment and on the processes related to it. We wish to give a direct demonstration of this by referring to a number of results obtained in investigations by Gumm (1986).

Interpretation of experimental results

Figure 1 shows one of the patterns that allow making very different action specifications for the computer. We want to point out the characteristics of two rather extreme variations (see figure 5).

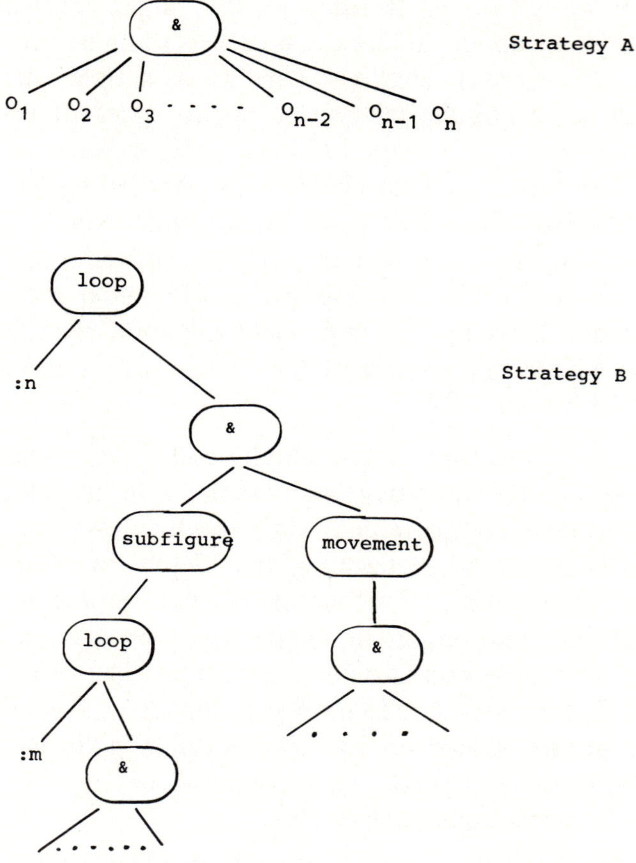

Figure 5. Main types of strategies

Step-by-step strategy A: The user conceptualizes the pattern as a sequence of line elements. This means that the target structures are given through the concept-related representations of the line segments, to which the concept-related representations of elementary commands for the specification of the length and angle of the line segment elements are directly attributed. As far as cognitive operations are concerned, there is need only for information seeking procedures that provide the actual parameters for the specification of the procedure for the command. Planning effort is extremely low since the required decomposition of the figures is affected by autonomous perception processes. This decomposition results in high effort for checking the intermediate results and in high effort in terms of motor reactions.

Planning strategy B: This high effort in terms of motor and checking operations can be reduced if the language's potentials are used. All the drawings in the experiments of Gumm (1986) can be produced through the bounding of variables in accordance with the following general procedure:

loop (n,&(subpattern, movement))
subpattern (triangle, square)
movement (translation, rotation)

To give an example, the pattern on figure 1 can be generated as a sequence of squares, with the following square resulting from the preceding one through a rotation by 45 degrees (see right part of figure 1): loop (8,(square(x),left(45))). Input effort is reduced to one seventh. Yet this requires a figure conceptualization that is entirely different from the one supplied by autonomous perception processes. The preferred breakdown of this pattern is shown in the left part of figure 1. What is required for the application of the procedure is a quasi-dynamic representation in the form of a repeated rotation of a subpattern (right part of figure 1) or a comparison of features of subpatterns whereby features refer to orientation and location of subpatterns. Regarding these patterns we have an assessment of the preferred interpretation in terms of both the preferred decomposition and the effort required to recognise subfigures (van Tuijl 1980). This allows characterizing the structure built up first in the compartment, which is to control the solution process.

Against this background, we should now like to interpret results. The list in figure 6 once again gives the factors that can be expected to effect strategy selection.

Strains placed on the operative compartment by additional remembering of processing effort as a result of realization conditions in task delegation should lead to use of strategy A. Strains of this kind result from an increase in the complexity of the figures or from a shift of perceptually aided information seeking processes to the mental level

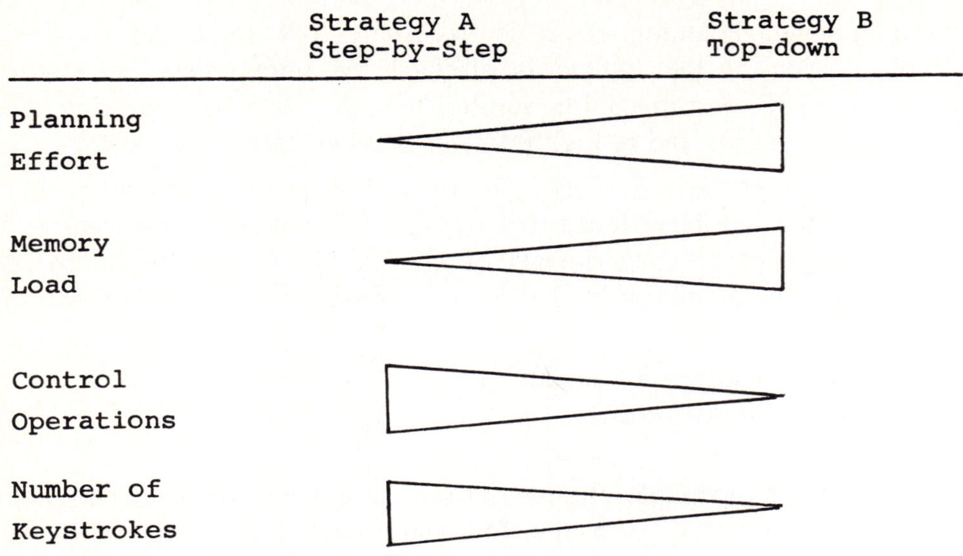

Figure 6. Main characteristics of strategy A and strategy B (see text)

of information seeking. We assume that tasks that impose higher processing loads do not allow planning to occur after short training sequences.

Inducing the construction of task-appropriate operative units trough the design of training examples should exert an influence on task decomposition and lead to more frequent use of strategy B, because the depth of the planning process is lower in the case of a strategy based on macros. This hypothesis is based on the assumptions of a problem-oriented approach to learning whereby the initial knowledge base is acquired through practicing sequences.

Gumm (1986) assessed the complexity of line drawings by means of coding times, the structural measure, and scaling procedures. Following a training stage, she had four patterns of different complexity implemented. The results, which are presented in figure 7, reveal a shift in favor of the utilization of the step-by-step strategy A in the case of patterns of fairly high complexity.

This expected outcome can be added on to by a secondary result: whatever the strategy used the structure in all programs is the breakdown that was expected on the basis of autonomous perception

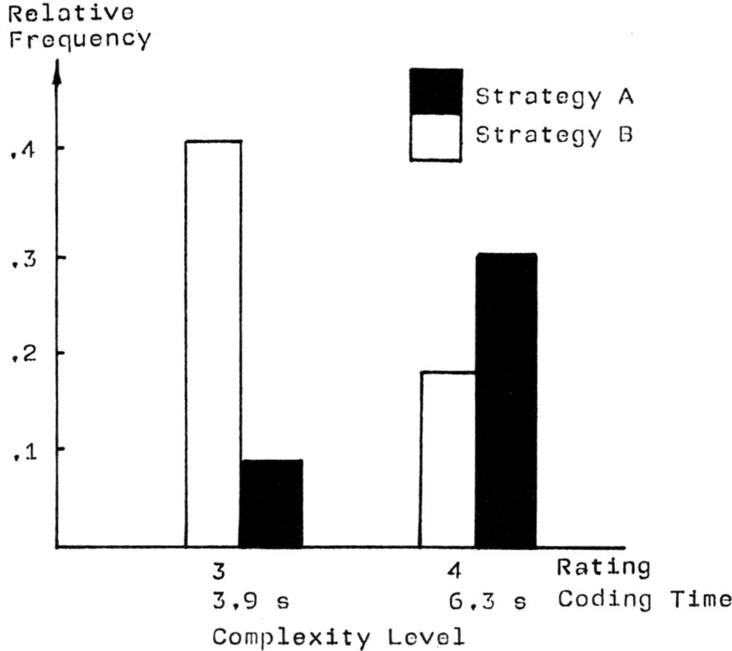

Figure 7. Proportion of strategy use as a function of the complexity of patterns

processes. This appears to indicate that difficulties mainly arise in the recognition and implementation of movements (rotation, translation) in accordance with strategy B. This is obviously the process requiring additional effort in the case of fairly complex patterns. There is a conceptualization, but it is not used. At this point it is worthwhile reminding ourselves of another result, which was obtained in an investigation by Wandke and Wetzenstein (in this volume). The investigation of utilizing procedure formations in the administration of a data base showed that subjects made use of procedure formation only when they were dealing with tasks with a prescribed breakdown into partial tasks. If subjects themselves had to develop this kind of structure after representation, they applied a step-by-step strategy there as well.

In another variation of the experiment, a comparison was made between two groups of subjects, one of which was allowed to rely on a preset pattern (visual group), while the other was asked to memorise the pattern and subsequently work relying on their imagination (imagery group). The increased strain due to the REGENERATE module after

Kosslyn et al. (1984) and the shift of parameter specification to the mental level led to a change in strategy selection (see figure 8), which confirmed our expectations.

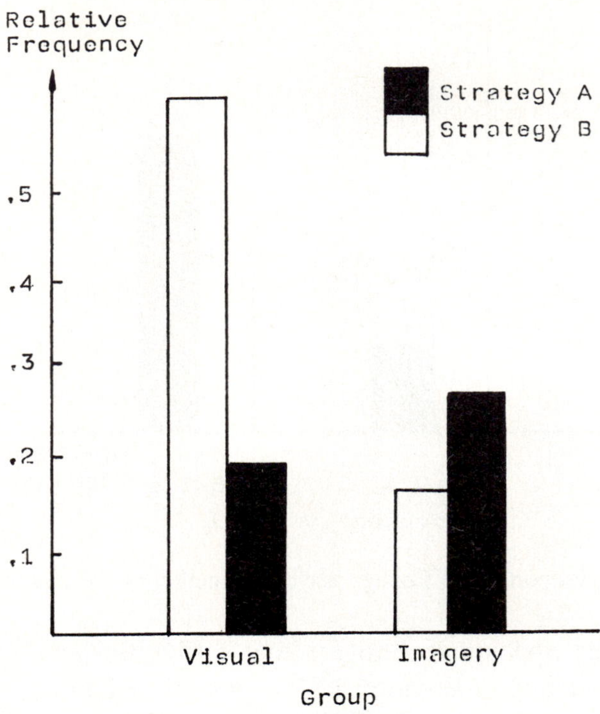

Figure 8. Relative frequency of strategy use depending on coding conditions

A critical assumption concerns the formation of operative units. In this context, the results of a training investigation are relevant. Two groups (S1 and S2) were given different training examples for inducing a concept-related representation of some general procedure: (loop (n,&(subpattern, movement))). We expected group S2 (extented sequence of training examples) to make more frequent use of the planning procedure because of proceduralized knowledge structures induced from the elaborated set of training examples. The results shown in figure 9 are conform with our expectations. This allows us to assume that these learning dependent units form the basis for the underlying processes. Evaluating the results, it should be remembered that we were using subjects who were inexperienced in terms of a requirement of

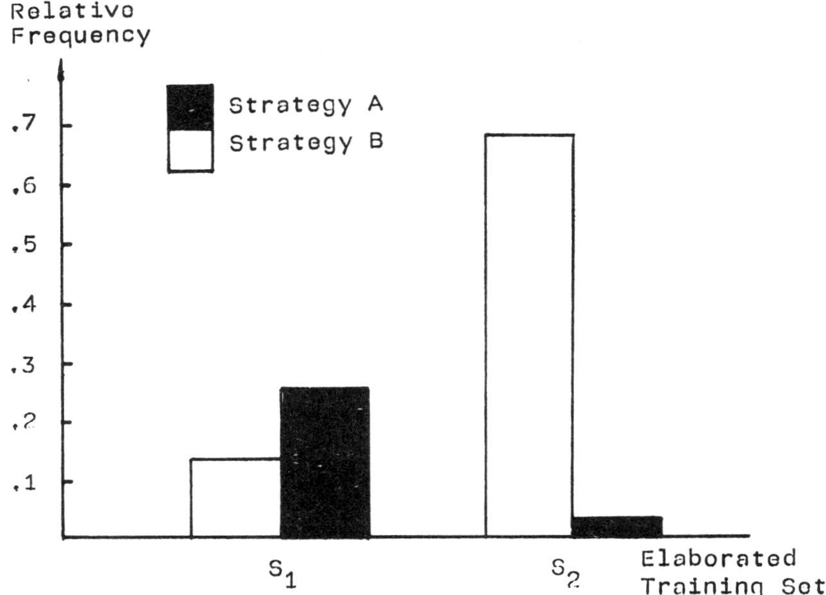

Figure 9. Relative frequency of strategy use depending on training conditions (S1: line combinations, triangle ; S2: rotations and translations of subpatterns, additionally)

that kind, and whose error profiles tell us about difficulties at fairly low levels still (Gumm 1986).

In summary, our results fit in well with the conceptual framework. It is the mutual relationship between knowledge, transient structure formations in the operative compartment and strategy that we have to study in more detail if we are going to justice to our claim at the beginning, which characterises our understanding of the mental model approach.

References

Ackermann, D. (1987). *Handlungsspielraum, Mentale Repräsentation und Handlungsregulation am Beispiel der Mensch-Computer-Interaktion.* Dissertation, Universität Bern.

Anderson, J.R. (1983). *The Architecture of Cognition.* Cambridge: Harvard University Press.

Barnard, P. (1988). Cognitive resources and the learning of human-computer dialogue. In J.B. Carroll (Ed.), *Interfacing Thought: Cognitive Aspects of Human-Computer Interaction.* Cambridge, Mass.: MIT Press.

Eyferth, K., Schömann, M. & Widowski, D. (1986). Der Umgang von Psychologen mit Komplexität. *Sprache und Kognition,* 1 (1986), pp. 11-26.

Glaser, R. (1986). On the nature of expertise. In F. Klix & H. Hagendorf (Eds.), *Human Memory and Cognitive Capabilities.* Amsterdam: North-Holland.

Greeno, J.G., Riley, M.S. & Gelman, R. (1984). Conceptual competence and childrens counting. *Cognitive Psychology,* 16 (1984), pp. 94-143.

Gumm, U. (1986). *Wissensabhängige Strategiebildung im interaktiven Problemlösen.* Diploma Thesis, Dept. of Psychology, Berlin Humboldt University.

Hacker, W. (1986). *Arbeitspychologie.* Berlin: Deutscher Verlag der Wissenschaften.

Hagendorf, H. (1978). On the acquisition of structures in problem solving processes. *Zeitschrift f. Psychologie,* 1 (1978), pp. 64-69.

Hesse, F.W. (1986). Wissenspsychologische Grundlagen der Wissensnutzung beim Problemlösen. In H. Mandl & P.M. Fischer (Eds.), *Lernen im Dialog mit dem Computer.* München: Urban & Schwarzenberg.

Hoppe, H.U. (1986). Anforderungen an Programmiersprachen für den Unterricht unter dem Gesichtspunkt des interaktiven Programmierens. In H. Mandl & P.M. Fischer (Eds.), *Lernen im Dialog mit dem Computer*. München: Urban & Schwarzenberg.

Kieras, D.E. & Polson, P. (1985). An approach to the formal analysis of user complexity. *Int. J. Man Machine Studies,* 22 (1985), pp. 365-394.

Klix, F. (1971). *Information und Verhalten.* Berlin: Deutscher Verlag der Wissenschaften.

Klix, F. (1985). Über die Nachbildung von Denkanforderungen, die Wahrnehmungseigenschaften, Gedächtnisstruktur und Entscheidungsoperationen einschließen. *Zeitschrift f. Psychologie,* 3 (1985), pp. 175-212.

Klix, F. (1986). Memory research and knowledge engineering. In F. Klix & H. Wandke (Eds.), *Macinter I.* Amsterdam: North-Holland.

Kosslyn, S.M., Braun, J., Cave, K.R. & Wallach, R.W. (1984). Individual differences in mental imagery abilities: A computational analysis. *Cognitive Psychology,* 6 (1984), pp. 195-243.

Kotovsky, K., Hayes, J.R. & Simon, H.A. (1985). Why are some problems hard? Evidence from tower of Hanoi. *Cognitive Psychology,* 17 (1985), pp. 248-294.

Mandler, G. (1985). *Cognitive Psychology. An Essay in Cognitive Science.* Hillsdale, New Jersey: Erlbaum.

Newell, A. & Card, S.K. (1985). The prospects for psychological science in human-computer interaction. *Human Computer Interaction,* 1 (1985), pp. 209-242.

Norman, D.A. (1986). Cognitive engineering. In D.A. Norman & S. Draper (Eds.), *User Centered System Design.* Hillsdale, New Jersey: Erlbaum.

Ohlsson, S. (1984). Restructuring revisited. *Scand. J. Psychology,* 24 (1984), pp. 65-78, 117-129.

Payne, S.J. & Green, T.G.R. (1986). Task-Action Grammars: A model of the mental representation of task languages. *Human Computer Interaction,* 1 (1986), pp. 93-133.

Rasmussen, J. (1983). Skills, rules, and knowledge: signals, signs, and symbols, and other distinctions in human performance models. *IEEE Trans. Systems, Mans, and Cybernetics,* 13 (1983), pp. 257-266.

Reisner, P. (1981). Formal grammar and human factor design of an interactive graphics system. *IEEE Trans. Software Engineering,* 2 (1981), pp. 229-240.

Streitz, N.A. (1986). Cognitive ergonomics: an approach for the design of user-centered systems. In F. Klix & H. Wandke (Eds.), *Macinter I.* Amsterdam: North-Holland.

Sydow, H. (1980). Mathematical modelling of representation and generation of structures in thought processes. In F. Klix & B. Krause (Eds.), *Psychological Research. Berlin Humboldt University 1960 - 1980.* Berlin: Deutscher Verlag der Wissenschaften.

Tauber, M.J. & Rohr, G. (1984). Representational frameworks and models for human-computer interfaces. In G.C. van der Veer, M.J. Tauber, T.R.G. Green & P. Gorny (Eds.), *Readings on Cognitive Ergonomics - Mind and Computers.* Heidelberg: Springer Verlag.

van Tuijl, H.J.F.M. (1980). Perceptual interpretation of complex line patterns. *J. Experimental Psychology: Human Perception and Performance,* 6 (1980), pp. 197-221.

Mental Models and Human-Computer Interaction 1
D. Ackermann and M.J. Tauber (Editors)

STYLES, SKILLS AND STRATEGIES: COGNITIVE VARIABILITY AND ITS IMPLICATIONS FOR THE ROLE OF MENTAL MODELS IN HCI

G Robert J Hockey

MRC/ESRC Social and Applied Psychology Unit, Sheffield

ABSTRACT

Designing an interface for effective human-computer dialogue is a task rightly associated with the need for a valid model of the normative cognitive processes of the user. The question addressed in this paper is whether anything further can be gained from a consideration of variability in cognitive functioning? Individual differences in how people use their cognitive systems are likely to be reflected in the kinds of mental models new users bring to the computer, and the kinds of models they develop in learning to use it. There has been increased interest in this issue in the recent HCI literature, in keeping with the desire to encourage the development of more usable or learnable systems. Cognitive style has been singled out in this context as being of particular importance for design and training (Robertson, 1985; van Muylwijk, van der Veer and Waern, 1987), yet the value of such an approach has been seriously questioned even within the applied psychometrics literature (Baron, 1982). Tests of general ability have also been used to assess individual differences in HCI, though, again, a clear rationale is lacking. The prime motivation in both cases seems to be the convenience of "off-the-shelf" tests. The present paper summarises the principal limitations of traditional measures of cognitive style and tests of general abilities. An alternative approach is proposed, based on a theoretically-derived analysis of individual differences in information processing skills. This leads to a framework in which individual differences in cognition are conceptualised in terms of skill in the management of competence.

Limitations of the psychometric approach: cognitive style and cognitive ability

The most traditional method for the assessment of individual differences involves mental testing. Cognitive ability is inferred from tests measuring achieved performance level - the effectiveness of behaviour, while cognitive style refers to the manner in which a test is completed. This distinction is an important one since it allows individual differences to be interpreted in terms of both quantitative and qualitative criteria, providing a functional link between intelligence and personality. There are, however, considerable problems with both style and ability tests.

Style tests

The best known dimension of style is field dependence- independence (FD-I), though many others have been used in particular contexts: e.g. reflectivity-impulsivity (R-I), convergence-divergence, risk-taking, cognitive complexity. The FD-I dimension, often treated as almost synonymous with the term cognitive style (eg, McKenna, 1984), was developed as a central construct in Witkin's theory of 'psychological differentiation' (Witkin et al, 1962), to reflect differences in the extent to which individuals made perceptual decisions independently of the context or background. Several studies have shown field-independent (FI) users to be more effective in learning to use computer systems. For example, Fowler, Macauley and Fowler (1985), using a filing task, found that field dependent (FD) users were more dependent on supportive, system-driven dialogue, and took longer to learn to use the system. There are, unfortunately, three major difficulties with style measures:

(1) They may not represent stable and fundamental features of behaviour. Stability estimates (test-retest reliabilities over several weeks) are moderate - about 0.6 for the embedded figures test (EFT) used to measure FD-I, while correlations across different types of FD-I test are often surprisingly low (eg, of the order of 0.3 between EFT and the rod and frame test, RFT). Similar results are found for other style tests. Thus, both stability (over time) and generality (over situations) are rather weak.

(2) There is little empirical evidence for the fundamental distinction between manner and level of performance. If style is truly independent of ability, it should be possible to find task situations in which the style identified as 'field dependent' (FD) should be more rather than less effective than that used by FI individuals (for example, perceptual judgements where the context or background provides relevant data for the identification process). In fact, there seems to

be no clear evidence of any such advantage for FD in the vast literature on FD-I (see, eg, Satterly, 1976; Laboratory of Comparative Human Cognition, 1978). The FI subjects in Fowler et al's experiment were simply more able to meet the demands of the task.

(3) The particular dimensions of style that have become popular may not be representative of cognitive operations across a broad range of activities. Although we have mentioned only some of the best known dimensions, Messick (1976) reported as many as 19 'styles' in common use, and more have emerged since. What has been notably absent from the style literature is any attempt to derive a coherent conceptual framework for specifying the (presumably) several fundamental dimensions of style that characterise human cognitive behaviour.

Cognitive ability tests

Cognitive ability is usually measured by broad-band tests of intelligence, or other general skills such as spatial or verbal ability. A distinction may be made (Horn, 1976) between tests of fluid ability (general cognitive capacity) and those of crystallised ability (dependent on specific knowledge or experience). It is assumed that tests of general ability draw on both these components, to a greater or lesser extent, but that some tests (sometimes referred to as 'culture fair') rely almost entirely on fluid ability (Raven's Progressive Matrices is a well-known example). Tests of ability have been rather disappointing in predicting success in learning, though this may be due to the use of routine tasks as learning criteria. When cognitively complex tasks are used predictive validity often increases substantially. For example, a study by Gomez, Egan and Bowers (1986) found correlations of about 0.5 between spatial memory and various indices of text editor learning. There is also good evidence of sex-linked differences in the patterning of verbal and spatial abilities, where women score relatively higher on verbal tests and men higher on spatial tests, making it important to take this factor into account.

The major limitation of ability tests, however, is that they rely heavily on domain-specific knowledge: they measure achievement, not potential for achieving. This would make such tests less useful for explaining the differential performance of novice computer users, for example, than for predicting success in new tasks for more experienced users. Exceptions to this are tests which measure fluid intelligence, since these are largely content-free. Again, though, there is no clear evidence that they can predict flexibility and adaptability to new demands.

The relationship between style and ability

Measures of cognitive style in fact correlate appreciably with scores on fluid intelligence, and tests of both spatial and verbal ability. Medians of correlations between various ability tests and EFT (based on the analysis of over 50 studies by McKenna, 1984) show an overall value of about r = 0.5; the relationship is stronger for spatial (or other non-verbal) tests, as might be expected given the primarily perceptual nature of EFT. This point is made most strongly, perhaps, in a factor analysis of various ability and task-derived style measures (Widiger, Knudson and Rorer, 1980). In this GEFT (the group version of EFT) was found to load 0.82 on the ability factor, but did not correlate at all with any of the task-based style measures.

Cognitive style is clearly not independent from ability. As a rough rule, individuals with high general ability are identified in standard style tests as (eg), field independent, convergent and reflective (this constellation is defined here as the 'focused' style). Low ability individuals tend to be field dependent, divergent and impulsive (the 'diffuse' style). There also seems to be an asymmetry in the pattern of use of stylistic strategies by individuals of differential ability. Widiger et al (1980) found that while high ability individuals showed a bias towards the analytic (focused) style, they could make effective use of both analytic and global strategies (equivalent to the focused and diffuse styles characterised here) when task demands required. Less able individuals, on the other hand, were restricted quite markedly to their preferred global (diffuse) style. The diffuse 'style' may, in fact, represent little more than the lack of ability to manage strategies effectively. I shall return to the implications of this interpretation shortly.

An information processing framework for variability

The psychometric approach has failed to provide a convincing account of individual differences in cognition. Measures of general ability seem rather remote from the behaviours we want to understand, while tests of style appear to reflect nothing more than a high-order ability dimension in disguise. In order to better understand cognitive variability, and, in our particular case, to predict individual differences in understanding and use of computer-based systems, it is essential to recognise both the complexity and the intrinsic flexibility of the human cognitive system.

A useful analogy for the regulation of human behaviour is a complex (albeit 'ill-defined') control system, providing a means of regulating system parameters in accordance with both preset values (internally-generated plans or task goals) and external disturbances, in order to maintain optimum system performance. Some control procedures operate automatically, while others require active (executive) intervention. In addition, control may be exercised at different levels, with higher levels having priority over lower levels. The overall behaviour of the system depends, above all else, on its efficiency at managing its competence, defined here as the sum of its basic capacities and IP resources. Cognitive performance is a complex function of the efficiency of control processes and the overall competence of the system. Table 1 summarises the essential components of the HIP system, with examples of functions.

TABLE 1
Components of the Human Information Processing System

COMPETENCE:

data processing skills :-
[encoding, access to stores, matching]

working storage :-
[holding, updating, computation]

permanent storage :-
[domain-specific knowledge]
[strategies, rules, heuristics]

CONTROL:

regulatory skill :-
[monitoring, strategy selection & implementation]

capacity:
[effort mobilization, regulatory power]

Competence

Competence is a property of the basic information processing facilities available to the system: data processing skills, working memory capacity and permanent memory contents. The management of competence requires a control system, which selects, implements and maintains the system in its use of resources.

Data processing skills are dependent on the use of various processors, specific low-level stores and associated communication channels, with characteristic ranges of speed and capacity (ie, the content-free system machinery). They are the essential elements of the keystroke level analysis of HCI (Card, Moran and Newell, 1983). Individual differences in the speed and efficiency of these fundamental processes have been shown to correlate with psychometric measures of verbal and spatial ability (Hunt, 1978; Cooper and Regan, 1982), and provide a 'hardware' basis for what Hunt calls "cognitive power". The size of this relationship is, however, quite small (about $r = 0.3$) within samples of normal adults, presumably indicating a narrow functional range of basic data processing capacities across the population. This makes such skills unlikely to be an important factor in accounting for variability in complex learning, and is one reason why the keystroke level of analysis may be quite inappropriate. When comparisons are made, however, across groups differing in verbal ability, including children and mentally handicapped adults, large differences are found in the efficiency of these processes (Hunt, 1978). It seems clear that data processing facilities may act as a limit on cognitive effectiveness only when they operate below a minimal functional level. Above this, other factors play a more prominent role.

The second component in table 1 is a general purpose working storage system. This is a limited capacity workspace, allowing high level storage, data manipulation and planning. The role of working memory (WM) in general thinking and problem-solving, in addition to its more obvious function in short-term memory, was identified convincingly by Baddeley and Hitch (1974). Individual differences in working memory capacity have been found to correlate highly with reading and comprehension, even within a group of high ability college students (Daneman and Carpenter, 1980), and are known to be a critical source of limitation in children's learning development (Belmont and Butterfield, 1977). Working memory ability, on this evidence is a major candidate for the determination of individual differences in cognition, notably in learning to operate computer systems.

The third component is a permanent store of acquired knowledge and skills, including information processing strategies. (We have separated strategies from other kinds of knowledge for the convenience of this discussion, though there is no reason to suppose that any fundamental distinction should be made). Differences in domain-specific knowledge are known to be the most significant difference between novices and experts in problem solving generally, and the influence of availability of IP strategies (Campione, Brown and Ferrara, 1982) can also be interpreted as a knowledge-based resource (Chi, 1981).

Control function

In contrast to these rather specific components of cognitive activity, control processes are general purpose skills for manipulating and managing specific resources. Of course, these are not structurally separate from the competence resources, since they are presumably stored in permanent memory (as high level strategies, for example), and operate through the use of the limited capacity working memory system (which is another reason for the pre-eminence of this HIP component). The separation is primarily one of function. A distinction may be made between control capacity and control skill. Control capacity refers to the degree of executive (WM) activity which the system is capable of, while control skill refers to the efficiency or appropriateness of control activity (with respect to task goals).

The central properties of control (or executive) function are its use in active tuning of the cognitive system, and the maintenance of particular configurations or states. More specific executive functions include goal setting, selection and implementation of strategies, and monitoring of the effectiveness of current actions (eg, Campione et al, 1982). It is now generally agreed in the educational testing field that the skilled use of executive control processes is central to the ability to behave effectively in practical problem-solving contexts, and is a central component of the teaching of thinking skills (Nickerson et al, 1985). In a recent summary Sternberg (1986) defines intelligence as 'mental self-government': in problem solving, executive activity is required to control the selection of either routinised skills (which are automatised, so may be run off-line) or flexible (real-time) management of system state.

The capacity of this latter kind of control appears to be limited, both in terms of the size of workspace available for planning and decision-making (Baddeley and Hitch, 1974) and in its resistance to fatigue with prolonged use or stress (Broadbent, 1971; Hockey and Hamilton, 1983). It is associated, both subjectively and physiologically, with the sustained use of effort, and is identified as a major factor in individual differences in susceptibility to stress and fatigue (Hockey, 1986).

The HIP analysis of ability and style

A large capacity for executive control is of limited value unless (a) a satisfactory level of competence is available for meeting task goals, and (b) appropriate strategies are available for control to be effective in tuning the system to the required configuration. All three factors are essential for the operation of an effective, adaptive cognitive system. In general, executive capacity may be thought to be typical of individuals characterised as 'high ability'. Individual differences in executive capacity have long been thought to contribute significantly to the variability observed in IQ scores. Although normally assumed to be a direct measure of ability the sustained nature of many of these tests almost certainly require persistence, or executive effort (Eysenck, 1967). Ability is, of course, directly comparable to what we have called competence, and effective levels of data processing power and high WM capacity are assumed. Fluid ability may be more dependent, however, on control skill, since it is a measure of content free information processing effectiveness, while crystallised abilities should be more closely determined by differences in domain-specific knowledge. While ability has a central place in the HIP analysis of individual differences, the mapping of cognitive style onto this framework is less direct. One approach is to consider what I will call Information Processing (IP) Styles. These may be defined in terms of characteristic use of particular kinds of control strategies, or processing mode, and may be discerned as strategic factors in skilled performance (Hockey and Hamilton, 1983). A detailed analysis of these, and the evidence in support of them cannot be undertaken here. A few examples may, however, suffice:

(1) *Internal / external bias.*

A distinction may be made in cognitive activity in terms of the source of the information being processed. Internally-based activity operates upon memory, while externally-based cognition operates upon sense data. This is approximately equivalent to the use of spatial or verbal IP modes. In practical terms, individuals may be identified in terms of whether their cognitive life is biased towards verbal/memory-based activities (eg, solving mental puzzles), or towards perceptual/sensory activities. This may be reflected in their preferred processing strategies across a range of tasks (eg, Hunt, 1978), and related to differences in verbal or spatial ability.

(2) *Attentional selectivity.*
Tasks which require the management of a number of separate activities, or the processing of information from several sources (including memory), are associated with strategies of attention deployment. In the extreme cases, individuals may exhibit a tendency to be overly-selective, focusing excessively on dominant task components, or too broad, failing to take account of inbuilt constraints and redundancies. An optimal strategy can usually be defined (eg, Moray, 1984), though particular individuals may consistently adopt a strategy which is biased towards one or the other of these extremes. Narrow or broad strategies may be associated with either internal or external focus of attention.

(3) *Degree of action control.*
In well-learned skills, actions are carried out without continuous use of feedback. With practice there is a shift from a highly controlled to largely automatic mode of regulation, though some active, feedback-directed control is still necessary. Individuals are likely to differ in the degree of regulation they indulge in; how much and how often they modify current plans with respect to available task information.

(4) *Speed-accuracy bias.*
Tasks requiring sustained speeded performance often exhibit a trade-off between speed and accuracy (consider the typing of a text by a computer user who is not a skilled typist). Some individuals may show a general bias towards either relatively greater accuracy or speed, whatever the general task constraints. At the extreme this results in performance which is ineffective, through either unnecessary delays or frequent errors, and may take the form of action slips that may need to be corrected.

What I have referred to previously as the 'focused' style may be seen as a composite of these IP styles, being characterised as highly selective, accuracy-biased and controlled (with an internal bias). There is little value in arguing that such variability in IP styles might underlie traditional style concepts such as reflectivity-impulsivity, convergence-divergence, field dependence and cognitive complexity. These are patterns of use of IP strategies, rather than fixed personality characteristics. They are, as such, more susceptible to situational demands, and may be assessed across a range of tasks. To the extent that such patterns are discernible, they are an indication only of might be called the individual's 'modal' cognitive state (Hockey and Hamilton, 1983), and not some inbuilt and inflexible limitation in what he or she can do. Furthermore, there is no reason to suppose that any one of these dimensions is primary. They are all variable settings of aspects of the cognitive state, and must be considered as a pattern.

A full assessment of IP styles, whether along the lines I have suggested, or based on some other HIP analysis, is badly needed. It could be carried out quite easily, probably involving peer assessment or diary analysis validation techniques. Such a test would provide a more fundamental style profile than that available from current cognitive style tests, and one which relates closely to underlying cognitive processes. While IP styles may be significant sources of variability in everyday cognitive life, however, they are only likely to play a major part in complex problem-solving when executive skill is rather low. Again drawing from our experience in the stress/performance field, any mismatch between modal state and that required by the task can normally be overcome by executive activity. The cost of such activity is determined by the degree of mismatch and by the individual's control skill. Individuals with good executive control are able to maximise their effectiveness by responding flexibly to task and environmental demands, both in terms of goal-directed use of appropriate IP strategies and in the patterning of primary processing activities. Such individuals are, in principle, capable of running any simulation of mental function that is stored in LTM, including variants of the diffuse mode, though the focused style is demanding and resource-consuming, in terms of both executive skills and control capacity: it can only be maintained over long periods at a cost. For low ability individuals a diffuse style will be much easier to maintain since moment to moment control is unnecessary, though effectiveness can only ever be moderate.

Implications for research on HCI and mental models

I wish to turn, now, to the problem of understanding individual differences in HCI, especially their implications for the use of mental models. It should be clear by now that standard measures of cognitive style such as FD-I are unlikely to be of any value in this respect. Ability measures, while providing a better overall prediction of the user's capabilities, give little insight into the basis for such skill or the individual's possibilities for flexibility or new learning. An ideal solution would require a set of tests developed specifically within the human-computer domain. These would provide measures of IP style profiles, as well as of functional competence in specific task areas. The emphasis of these tests should, however, be on high level cognitive skills such as planning and problem-solving, rather than on more fundamental processes which, as we have seen, have limited predictive value where a normal ability range is concerned (Cooper and Regan, 1982). Equally, such high levels skills are only likely to be evident in demanding tasks. We should look for their effect in window and database management, in complex problem solving (eg, debugging or system troubleshooting), and in planning and scheduling activities (as found in management of complex systems such as air traffic control). They are less likely to play a major role in text processing, data entry or accounts management.

With these points in mind, some illustrative comments may be made concerning the acquisition and development of mental models, and their deployment by experienced users. For this, I will focus on two broad aspects of variability in mental models: (a) What do they look like? and (b) How are they deployed?

Form and content

The form that models take may represent a genuine and quite stable source of individual differences. We tend to think of these in terms of spatial or imaginal properties, such as the 'mental pictures' of air-traffic controllers (Whitfield and Jackson, 1982). There are grounds, however, for thinking that some individuals typically use a verbal or rule-based form of representation (eg, Galotti, Baron and Sabini, 1986). It may be that there is an optimal or required form that should be taught, though this will doubtless vary with the task domain. The dependency on ability is quite complex. Hunt (1978) has shown that, where either IP strategy is suitable for a task, the tendency to employ verbal or spatial strategies is strongly determined by the existing bias towards one or the other area of competence (in terms of asymmetry of verbal and spatial abilities). On the other hand, he has also shown that individuals may be taught to use either strategy equally effectively, suggesting that such differences are based on habit or preference, rather than on their relative effectiveness. This has important implications for computer instruction, since it appears that we may safely ignore variability in natural preferences. The true test of this, however, requires a measure of the cost or effort in using less preferred modes of thinking. In terms of our IP framework, any available strategy may be implemented and maintained by executive control. It may only be practical however, if the cost is not too high: maintaining a cognitive state which is 'uncomfortable' for the individual may be risky, both to long-term health, and in terms of effective response to unforeseen operational problems.

Another implication of differences in the representational form of models is that these will affect their accessibility to observation and analysis. Protocol or interview-type methods, for example, are likely to be more successful with verbal models, and seriously distort those based on spatial or visual information. Mental models may very in terms of their degree of detail or articulation, ranging from an intuitive and unmodified analogy (such as the typewriter model of text processing) to a complete physical or chemical understanding. Within the domain of typical users of computer systems, such extremes are rare, though a large variability clearly exists. Models may also vary in terms of their generality, ranging from those which are highly domain-specific (eg, procedural heuristics used in printing a file from disk on a specific system) to those which are applicable to a wide range of tasks and systems. Both detail and generality are likely to be best accounted for by individual differences in competence, primarily in domain-specific knowledge. We may find evidence for the role of IP style factors, however, when we attempt to examine the use that individuals make of such models.

The management of models

The development of a mental model in acquisition of a new skill is widely regarded as necessarily involving the use of analogy or metaphor. It is likely that this process is influenced most strongly by competence factors, especially the prior knowledge the individual brings into the situation. Carroll and Mack (1985) argue against the imposition of standardised concrete metaphors in instruction; eg, those based on operational (Rumelhart and Norman, 1981) or structural (Gentner and Gentner, 1980) mappings. They advocate instead a central role for active learning, as a goal-directed process, in adapting existing knowledge by mismatch with current experience. Carroll and Mack's emphasis on learner-initiated model development, while it is certainly closer to the truth than a view of the user as a passive receiver of wisdom, may however be overstated. It assumes both the knowledge to generate useful base metaphors, and also the skill to manage the learning process in an effective way. Where interactive participatory learning is possible in a training environment, the ability to manage one's competence in order to develop a useful metaphorical base for the development of expertise may be more important than competence itself. We would thus expect those high in executive skill to benefit more from active learning, and to develop more appropriate models.

It is in the running of models to carry out cognitive tasks that the HIP framework may be most applicable. Whatever the form and content of models available to users (ie, in their permanent memory) it is likely that they access and use only parts of the model at any one time to guide action. Frese et al (1987) have used the term 'action styles' to refer to individual differences in planning, goalsetting and use of feedback.

The IP styles illustrated above may be regarded as underlying these action styles, and make predictions about how models will be used. Individuals with an internal focus of attention are more likely to be comfortable in the HCI situation, particularly if the interface places a heavy workload burden on the user. They should be able to gain access to different components of the mental model more easily, and exercise more effective control over its use. High selectivity individuals will tend to maintain in working memory only the currently most salient component (that relating to editing, say, but not to storing or printing), whereas low selectivity is associated with a lack of necessary bias towards currently relevant features of the model. Excessive selectivity is more likely to be a problem where the perceptual or decision-making load is high, or when individuals are under stress (Broadbent, 1971). Such effects have been recognised, for example, as a persistent problem in fault diagnosis in nuclear power plants (Sheridan, 1981).

Users who have an excessive degree of action control will monitor the adequacy of their dialogue activity more often and more completely than is necessary. They may load smaller chunks of model into WM on each occasion, planning only a small distance ahead, and changing the direction of planning frequently. Their use of the model may thus appear disjointed and their domain knowledge fragmentary. In contrast, a more open control mode, largely ignoring feedback, allows whatever model segments are accessed to control action for longer periods. This may also be sub-optimal, though the underlying model may appear more integrated. The task context is again important. In some tasks a more controlled mode may be essential (eg, the diagnosis of faults in process monitoring). In others, where prevailing goals are unchanging, active control may be inefficient (since it attracts costs in terms of management effort). Speed/accuracy bias has a more general role in the execution of all actions, but is likely to be a major factor in determining the adequacy of current goal-oriented activity. Independently of action control and selectivity, we might expect more unnecessary changes of control with a speed bias (premature evaluation). We might also anticipate problems of adjustment for users having an excessive speed bias when system response time is quite long.

Finally, I want to return to executive skill, which must be seen as the single most important factor in the management of mental models. Maintaining the appropriate amount and parts of the model in the planning foreground for the control of action is essential in complex human-computer systems for effective diagnosis and troubleshooting. It may be less obvious in the office environment, but the same principles apply.

References

Baddeley, A.D. & Hitch, G.J. (1974). Working memory. In G. Bower (Ed.), *The Psychology of Learning and Motivation,* Vol 8. New York: Academic Press.

Baron, J. (1982). Personality and intelligence. In R.J. Sternberg (Ed.), *Handbook of Human Intelligence.* Cambridge: Cambridge University Press.

Belmont, J.M. & Butterfield, E.C. (1977). The instructional approach to developmental cognitive research. In R.V. Krail, Jr & J.W. Hagen (Eds.), *Perspective on the Development of Memory and Cognition.* Hillsdale, NJ: Erlbaum.

Broadbent, D.E. (1971). *Decision and Stress.* London: Academic Press.

Broadbent, D.E. (1977). Levels, hierarchies and the locus of control. *Quarterly Journal of Experimental Psychology,* 29, pp. 181- 201.

Campione, J.C., Brown, A.L. & Ferrara, R.A. (1982). Mental retardation and intelligence. In R.J. Sternberg (Ed.), *Handbook of Human Intelligence.* Cambridge: Cambridge University Press.

Card, S.K., Moran, T.P. & Newell, A.L. (1983). *The Psychology of Human-Computer Interaction.* Hillsdale, NJ: Erlbaum.

Carroll, J.M. & Mack, R.L. (1985). Metaphor, computing systems and active learning. *International Journal of Man-Machine Studies,* 22, pp. 39-57.

Cooper, L.A. & Regan, D.T. (1982). Attention, perception and intelligence. In R.J. Sternberg (Ed.), *Handbook of Human Intelligence.* Cambridge: Cambridge University Press.

Daneman, M. & Carpenter, P.A. (1980). Individual differences in working memory and reading. *Journal of Verbal Learning and Verbal Behaviour,* 19, pp. 450-466.

Eysenck, H.J. (1967). Intelligence assessment: a theoretical and experimental approach. *British Journal of Educational Psychology,* 37, pp. 81-98.

Fowler, C.J.H., Macauley, L.A. & Fowler, J.F. (1985). The relationship between cognitive style and dialogue style: an exploratory study. In P. Johnson & S. Cook (Eds.), *People and Computers: Designing the Interface*. Cambridge: Cambridge University Press.

Frese, M., Stewart, J. & Hannover, B. (1987). Goal-orientation and planfulness: action styles as personality concepts. *Journal of Personality and Social Psychology,* 52.

Galotti, K.M., Baron, J. & Sabini, J.P. (1986). Individual differences in syllogistic reasoning: deduction rules or mental models? *Journal of Experimental Psychology: General,* 115, pp. 16-25.

Gentner, D. & Gentner, D.R. (1983). Flowing waters or teeming crowds? Mental models of electricity. In D. Gentner & A.L. Stevens (Eds.), *Mental Models*. Hillsdale, NJ: Erlbaum.

Gomez, L.M., Egan, D.E. & Bowers, C. (1986). Learning to use a text editor: some learner characteristics that predict success. *Human Computer Interaction,* 2, pp. 1-23.

Hockey, G.R.J. (1986). A state control theory of adaptation and individual differences in stress management. In G.R.J. Hockey, A.W.K. Gaillard & M.G.H. Coles (Eds.), *Energetics and Human Information Processing*. Dordrecht: Nijhoff.

Hockey, G.R.J. & Hamilton, P. (1983). The cognitive patterning of stress states. In G.R.J. Hockey (Ed.), *Stress and Fatigue in Human Performance*. Chichester: Wiley.

Horn, J.L. (1976). Human abilities. A review of research and theory in the early 1970's. *Annual Review of Psychology,* 27, pp. 437-485.

Hunt, E. (1978). Mechanics of verbal ability. *Psychological Review,* 85, pp. 109-130.

McKenna, F. (1984). Measures of field dependence: cognitive style or cognitive ability? *Journal of Personality and Social Psychology,* 47, pp. 593-603.

Moray, N. (1984). Attention to dynamic visual displays in man-machine systems. In R. Parasuraman & D.R. Davies (Eds.), *Varieties of Attention.* New York: Wiley.

Nickerson, R.S., Perkins, D.N. & Smith, E.E. (1985). *The Teaching of Thinking*. Hillsdale, NJ: Erlbaum.

Robertson, I.T. (1985). Human information processing strategies and style. *Behaviour and Information Technology,* 4, pp. 19-29.

Rumelhart, D.E & Norman, D.A. (1981). Analogical processes in learning. In J.R. Anderson (Ed.), *Cognitive Skills and their Acquisition.* Hillsdale, NJ: Erlbaum.

Sheridan, T. (1981). Understanding human error and aiding human diagnostic behaviour in nuclear power plants. In J. Rasmussen & W.B. Rouse (Eds.), *Human Detection and Diagnosis of System Failures.* New York: Plenum Press.

Sternberg, R.J. (1986). Intelligence is mental self-government. In R.J. Sternberg & D.K. Detterman (Eds.), *What is Intelligence?* Norwood, NJ: Ablex.

van Muylwijk, B., van der Veer, G.C. & Waern, Y. (1983). On the application of user variability in open systems. An overview of the little we know and the lot we have to find out. *Behaviour and Information Technology,* 3, pp. 313-326.

Whitfield, D. & Jackson, A. (1982). The air traffic controller's "picture" as an example of a mental model. In G. Johanssen & J.E. Rijnsdorp (Eds.), *Analysis, Design and Evaluation of Man-Machine Systems.* London: Pergamon.

Widiger, T.A., Knudson, R.M. & Rorer, L.G. (1980). Convergent and discriminant validity of measures of cognitive style and abilities. *Journal of Personality and Social Psychology,* 39, pp. 116-129.

Witkin, H.A., Dijk, R.B., Faterson, H.F., Goodenough, D.R. & Karp, S.A. (1962). *Psychological Differentiation: Studies of Development.* New York: Wiley.

EMPIRICAL INVESTIGATIONS

Mental Models and Human-Computer Interaction 1
D. Ackermann and M.J. Tauber (Editors)

EXPERIMENTAL RECONSTRUCTION AND SIMULATION OF MENTAL MODELS

David Ackermann and Thomas Greutmann

Work and Organizational Psychology Unit
Swiss Federal Institute of Technology, Zürich, Switzerland

ABSTRACT

Based on the assumption that individual differences in action regulation are influenced or caused by different mental models we tried to represent the knowledge of actors and used computer simulation as a method to identify individual differences. The results show different strategies in goal setting and use of memory. We hypothesize that this is implied by the dialogue structures. Cognitive modelling is a good tool to identify individual differences in the action regulation process and is also a useful tool in dialogue design.

Aims of research

Action regulation is based on mental models of the task. But what is a mental model and how does it work? Which are the components of the mental model and how are they organized? We have to understand these processes because we know that individual differences in action regulation exist. We suppose that they are caused by different styles of thinking. We know from work psychology that a given task will be redefined by the subject according to his own interpretation of the goals and degrees of freedom. Therefore we have to ask how a given task will be represented in memory and how this knowledge will influence action regulation.

Based on the hypothesis of semantic information transfer Krause (1982) confirmed the finding that learning processes will be improved by considering individual differences. He offered the subjects the possibility to arrange the material to be learned according to own preferences. The result confirms that the possibility to individualize the learning process will improve the efficiency. This agrees with the findings of Kaune (1985) and Cohors-Fresenborg (1987) that in teaching of mathematics different ways of the pupil's thinking have to be taken into account to optimize the learning process. They distinguish between sequential and conceptual strategies in the pupil's problem understanding and problem solving processes.

We have also evidence that individually developed dialogue structures are normally more efficient than prescribed dialogue structures (Ackermann, 1986). As stated by Ulich (1978) in his principles of differential and dynamic work design we have to consider these differences in the design of efficient worksystems. This will guarantee an optimal development of personality and competence.

The question: how is the dialogue projected into the mental representation?

What is the basis of individual differences in action regulation? We assume that they are influenced or caused by different mental models. This differences have to be shown and analyzed. Furthermore we have to ask how the degrees of freedom in choosing operations will be mentally represented and if there are influences on the type and kind of the actor's knowledge.

An answer to these associated (or interlinked) questions is only possible if we have (1) tools to represent the knowledge of the actor and (2) tools exist to simulate the thinking processes as adequate as possible. In other words: We need a medium to project the findings and to form a model of the process.

The topic: two dialogue forms of the same task

The task is simple: The player has to sort bottles into three rooms located in a maze. There is a robot which can be piloted in this maze. The bottles differ in their degree of filling (full, half, empty). In previous experiments, students of the electrotechnical department designed user friendly and efficient dialogue forms or command sets for potential users (Ackermann, 1984). We investigated the developed command sets further in long series of experiments. The main topics were structural qualities of the command sets, acceptance, efficiency and mental representation.

The game and the functionality of two command sets

Figure 1 shows the screen of the game. The maze with the three rooms is represented on the left. In the middle is a window for the memory (which is not used in this setting). Below is a window which shows the bottle the robot is carrying in his "hand". On the right there is the "screen" of the robot's video camera which shows the view into the maze and on the shelves with the bottles to be sorted. The task is represented in the lower half of the screen: all the bottles to be sorted are displayed with the indication of the goal room.

As mentioned before the player's task consists in sorting bottles into the three rooms according to the degree of filling. In previous experiments (Ackermann, 1986, 1987) students developed different command sets to solve the task. A subset of these dialogue structures is shown in figure 2.

Command set B-COMMANDS offers a lot of "little" - that is to say not so powerful and automatized commands - whereas command set E-COMMANDS offers few but powerful commands which automatize a lot of the piloting process. The functionality of B-COMMANDS consists of turn commands "left", "right", "turn" and commands such as "go until not free" (gstop) and two commands which pilot the robot along the shelves. E-COMMANDS has a much more powerful functionality, such as automatized search of empty or full racks or automatized exit of the rooms. E-COMMANDS offers all possible combinations of room-to-room commands. In this regard E-COMMANDS is comparable with B-COMMANDS.

The experimental design

To investigate the mental representation of the task and the influence on action regulation we used the cognitive modelling approach. For an experimental simulation by an expert system the user's knowledge was translated into production rules. There is criticism that the formulation of production rules is influenced by the experimenter and therefore not reliable (Schmalhofer & Wetter, 1987). To prevent this criticism we made use of an advantage of our general experimental design: we worked with students of the electrotechnical or computer science department. In the first part of all experiments, the students are their own test persons and later evaluate and discuss their

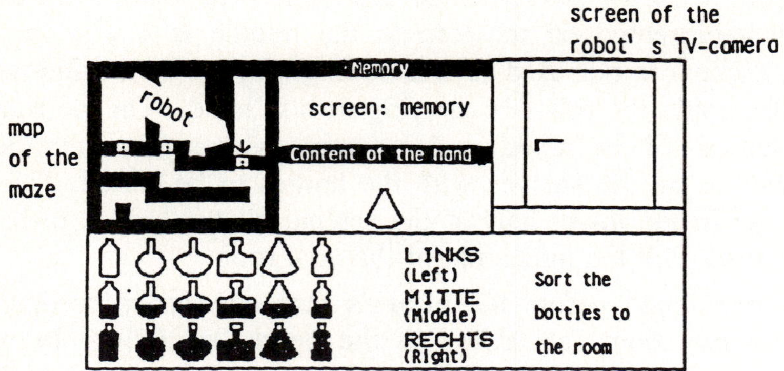

Display of the task

<u>Basic commands</u>

Go	The robot moves one field forwards
Turn	The robot turns 90 degrees to the left
Open	The robot opens the door
Take	The robot takes the bottle from the rack
Deposit	The robot deposits the content of his hand to the empty rack
Remember	The bottle of the rack in sight will be represented in the memory on the screen
Compare	The robot compares the bottle in the rack with that represented in memory

The commands can be combined with an editor. There are the following possibilities:

```
until    door, wall, rack, free, empty, equal
if       door, wall, rack, free, empty, equal
not
```

Example

```
Right = turn; turn; turn;
GT = Go until not free; Right; if door open;
```

Figure 1. Screen layout of the game

Command programs Type of Command	B-Befehle	ECMD2
left	LEFT	L
turn round	TURN ROUND	
right	RIGHT	R
go ahead	GSTOP	
(Combinations)	RUN	GL/GR/VL/VR
move left		XT
recognizing Corners	WLEFT	
checking for Walls		
move right		
recognizing Corners	WRIGHT	
checking for Walls		
search empty Rack		PUT +
search full Rack		NEXT
search Door		TOR
bottle in Memory		GET
(+ with deposit/take)		
(L left/R right)		
from Room(x) to Room(y)	x,y (x,y E A, B, C)	xGOy
to Room(y)		
from start to Room(y)	START (nur R)	BEGIN (only R)
from Room(y) to Start	GOSTART	GB (only R)
Bottle in Memory autom.		GETL/GETM/GETR

Figure 2. The functionality of two command sets

own behaviour together with the experimenter. This allows a good introduction of the students to psychological concepts based on their own experience.

In this experiments 12 students participated. They worked in groups of three students. They played the game with two selected command sets, documented their thinking and decision-making processes and translated their experiences into production rules afterwards. To facilitate the understanding of expert systems we offered one written in PASCAL (Bürge, 1986) the programming language most known of our students.

The students formulated the production rules as representations of their knowledge base of the action regulation. We consider these knowledge bases as the reconstruction of the "mental model". We tested these knowledge bases running them on the expert system and playing the game according to the inferences of the expert system. The simulation process and the results were discussed with the students.

The basic expert system and different forms of knowledge bases

The basic expert system consists of an *inference machine* which allows only forward chaining. The production rules are stored in a database. The basic operation cycle is shown in figure 3.

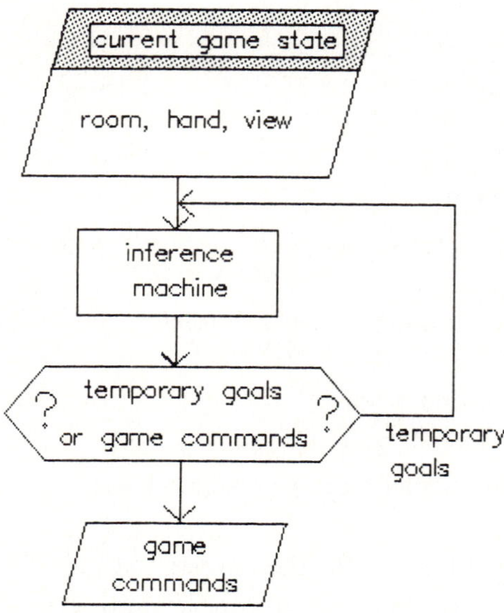

Figure 3. Basic operation cycle of the expert system

The input to the system is the state of the game (in which room the roboter is at the moment, the view and the contents of the hand). The inference machine of the expert system now searches for a rule matching the input conditions. This rule produces either commands for the computer game or goals. This goals can be defined for a certain stage of the game. In case of temporary goals, there are other rules that use these goals as input conditions which are now triggered. The system evaluates as long as there are no more rules that fit the conditions.

The production rules have the following format:

If (in the room on the left)
and (bottle in hand)
and (bottle intended for the room on the right)
*then give the command (LGOR) *)*

The responses of our subjects show that this form reflects best the decision making process when playing the game. Anderson (1983) claims that only further research can give evidence which form of cognitive modelling is best to represent thinking processes. We assume that production system representation is appropriate for this kind of task.

The developed knowledge bases for the expert system

The knowledge base for B-COMMANDS developed by the group of electro-engineer students is represented in figure 4. The first version contained 70 rules, but an analysis of these rules revealed some redundancy in the rules. The corrected rule base contained afterwards 55 rules.

Only 20 rules are in the knowledge base for E-COMMANDS constructed by the first group of students of the computer science department. The knowledge base for E-COMMANDS is shown in figure 5.

First impressions: where is the difference?

If we compare the two knowledge bases we observe that there are some interesting differences in the semantic structure. There are inferences in knowledge base "B-COMMANDS" (figure 4) which represent goals such as "I want to leave the room" (will raus) or "I want to deposit the bottle". We don't find this kind of inference in the knowledge base of E-COMMANDS (figure 5). The inferences are always commands of the dialogue.

In table 1 sample rules from figure 4 are presented which illustrate the structure and the use of temporary goals.

The knowledge base for E-COMMANDS (figure 5) contains no explicit goal settings. The goals are implicitly included in the command inferences. In contrary the knowledge base for B-COMMANDS

* Move from the left to the right room (Left GO Right)

```
----------        R E G E L N        ----------
location         sight   inference
  1 (p:in a)(s:vf)(flasche falsch)          | test if
  2 (p:in a)(s:hvf)(flasche falsch)         | bottle wrong
  3 (p:in b)(s:vf)(flasche falsch)          |
  4 (p:in b)(s:lf)(flasche falsch)          |
  5 (p:in c)(s:lf)(flasche falsch)          |
  6 (p:in c)(s:hvf)(flasche falsch)         |
  7 (s:wand)(keine tre)
  8 (s:hvf)(keine tre)
  9 (s:vf)(keine tre)
 10 (s:lf)(keine tre)
 11 (s:lr)(keine tre)
 12 (p:in a)(h:hvf)(will raus)          | inference of
 13 (p:in a)(h:vf)(will raus)           | subgoals
 14 (p:in b)(h:lf)(will raus)           |
 15 (p:in b)(h:vf)(will raus)           |
 16 (p:in c)(h:lf)(will raus)           |
 17 (p:in c)(h:hvf)(will raus)          | (a=in room a)
 18 (p:in a)(h:lf)(will depo a)         |
 19 (p:in b)(h:hvf)(will depo b)        |
 20 (p:in c)(h:vf)(will depo c)         |
 21 (anfang)(S)
 22 (flasche falsch)(h:leer)(N)
 23 (p:in a)(will raus)(keine tre)(LI,GS,WL)| look for door
 24 (p:in b)(will raus)(keine tre)(LI,GS)   |
 25 (p:in c)(will raus)(keine tre)(LI,GS)   |
 26 (p:in a)(h:vf)(s:tre)(O,AC,GS)           | piloting to
 27 (p:in a)(h:hvf)(s:tre)(O,AB,GS)          | goal room
 28 (p:in b)(h:vf)(s:tre)(O,BC,GS)           |
 29 (p:in b)(h:lf)(s:tre)(O,BA,GS,WR)        |
 30 (p:in c)(h:lf)(s:tre)(O,CA,GS,WR)        |
 31 (p:in c)(h:hvf)(s:tre)(O,CB,GS)
 32 (p:in a)(s:wand)(h:leer)(LI,GS)          | search of
 33 (p:in a)(s:wand)(h:lf)(LI,GS)            | bottles
 34 (p:in b)(s:wand)(h:leer)(KE,GS,LI,GS,RE) |
 35 (p:in b)(s:wand)(h:hvf)(KE,GS,LI,GS,RE)  |
 36 (p:in c)(s:wand)(h:leer)(RE,GS)          |
 37 (p:in c)(s:wand)(h:vf)(RE,GS)            |
 38 (p:in a)(s:lr)(h:leer)(WL)               |
 39 (p:in b)(s:lr)(h:leer)(WR)               |
 40 (p:in c)(s:lr)(h:leer)(WR)               |
 41 (p:in a)(s:lf)(WL)                       |
 42 (p:in b)(s:hvf)(WR)     decision: deposit |
 43 (p:in c)(s:vf)(WR)                       |
 44 (will depo a)(s:lr)(DE)]      | search of
 45 (will depo b)(s:lr)(DE)]      | empty racks
 46 (will depo c)(s:lr)(DE)       |
 47 (will depo a)(s:vf)(WL)       |
 48 (will depo a)(s:hvf)(WL)      |
 49 (will depo a)(s:lf)(WL)       |
 50 (will depo b)(s:vf)(WR)       |
 51 (will depo b)(s:hvf)(WR)      |
 52 (will depo b)(s:lf)(WR)       |
 53 (will depo c)(s:vf)(WR)       |
 54 (will depo c)(s:hvf)(WR)      |
 55 (will depo c)(s:lf)(WR)       |
```

Figure 4. Knowledge base for command set B-COMMANDS

```
Logfile
Regelsatz ECMDMAIN.RGL:


----------      R E G E L N      ----------

 1 if (Start) then (BEGIN)
 2 if (voll) and (R) then (NEXT)
 3 if (halbvoll) and (R) then (NIMM)
 4 if (leer) and (R) then (NIMM)
 5 if (halbvoll) and (R) and (hand) then (RGOM)
 6 if (leer) and (R) and (hand) then (RGOL)
 7 if (voll) and (M) then (NIMM)
 8 if (halbvoll) and (M) then (NEXT)
 9 if (leer) and (M) then (NIMM)
10 if (voll) and (M) and (hand) then (MGOR)
11 if (leer) and (M) and (hand) then (MGOL)
12 if (voll) and (L) then (NIMM)
13 if (halbvoll) and (L) then (NIMM)
14 if (leer) and (L) then (NEXT)
15 if (voll) and (L) and (hand) then (LGOR)
16 if (halbvoll) and (L) and (hand) then (LGOM)
17 if (R ok) then (RGOM)
18 if (M ok) then (MGOL)
19 if (L ok) then (LGOM)
20 if (regal leer) then (NEXT)


(Start)
 ->              BEGIN abgeleitet <-
 -> ---- Ableitung  fertig ---- <-
(leer)(R)
 ->              NIMM abgeleitet <-
 -> ---- Ableitung  fertig ---- <-
(leer)(R)(hand)
 ->              NIMM abgeleitet <-
 ->              RGOL abgeleitet <-
 -> ---- Ableitung  fertig ---- <-
(halbvoll)(L)
 ->              NIMM abgeleitet <-
```

examples of inferences

Logfile of inferences

Figure 5. Knowledge base for command set E-COMMANDS (main commands only)

(figure 4 and table 1) shows explicit goal inferences. The treatment of these temporary goals induces whole sequences of single commands. For instance, the goal "will raus" and the condition "keine tre" (table 1) induces the command sequence "LI, GS, WL".

TABLE 1
Sample rules for the expert system

a) Rules that generate temporary goals

if (p:in a) (h:vf) then (will raus)
if (p:in a) (h:hvf) then (will raus)

if the robot is in room a and has a full (vf) or half-full (hvf) bottle in his hand, then the temporary goal "will raus" (I want to leave the room) is derivated (the bottle has to be carried to another room).

b) Rules that use temporary goals

if (p:in a) (will raus) (keine tre) then (LI,GS,WL)

if the robot is in room a and wants to leave (will raus) and no door is visible (keine tre) then the commands LI, GS and WL are issued.

RoSi (Robbi Otter Simulation) **)

The simulation program RoSi was developed by a group of students one of them claimed that he could not translate his process of thinking for the game to the expert system described above. Especially, he needed a memory for keeping the contents of shelves and the state of rooms (completed or full) because he recognized that he memorized such facts towards the end of the game. A flowchart of the basic operation cycle is given in figure 6.

The current state of the game is the input to the inference machine. The state of the game has to be described in detail: the exact position of the robot (x- and y-coordinates), the orientation (north, west, south and east), the contents of the hand (empty, half-full or full bottle, nothing) and the view (same as for hand).

The memory serves as input for the inference machine as well. In the memory, knowledge about rooms and shelves is represented. A room may be known as "done" (that is to say it contains only bottles that belong there) or as "full" (no shelf in the room is empty). Shelves

**) The nickname RoSi was chosen by our students

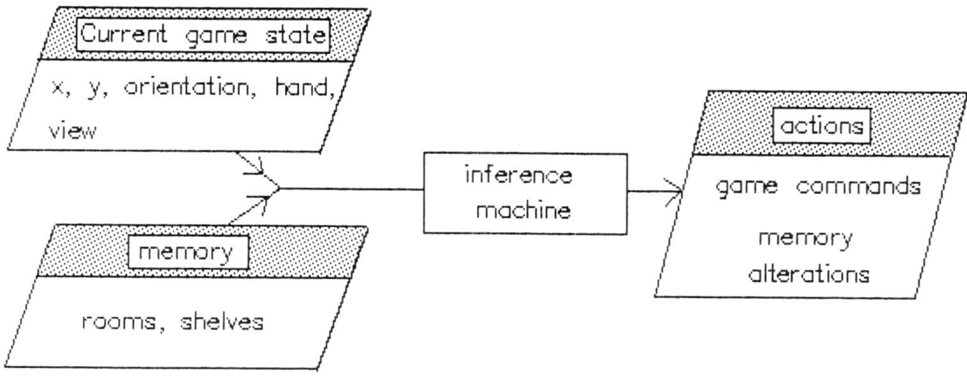

Figure 6. Basic operation cycle of RoSi

can be remembered as being empty or containing an empty, a half-full or a full bottle. This additional knowledge is not represented as production rules. The size of the memory is adjustable from 1 to 10 items by the RoSi operator. This allows studies about the influence of memory capacity on the actions with the computer game.

If the input conditions lead to a valid rule, the operations of the rule are executed. They consist of an output of the derivated command or sequence of commands for the game and an optional memory operation, eg. remembering or "forgetting" (deleting) the state of a room or a shelf.

The rules of RoSi can have three different structures as shown in table 2. The first structure (a) represents rules that do not use the memory. Rules of the second structure (b) take into account the remembered state of the rooms. The third structure (c) is for rules that depend on the state of memorized shelves. The system scans the rules of the third structure first. If no rule is found matching the state of the game, the rules of structure (b) are taken. Finally, if there is no matching rule, the rules of structure (a) are taken.

The rule knowledge is stored in three tables which resemble Turing tables. The rule knowledge is represented very atomistic: there may be some hundred rules for a command set, all very elementary. The structure of RoSi is tailored to the computer game: RoSi cannot be easily transferred to other system simulations.

TABLE 2
The three rule structures of RoSi

a) Simple rules					
x	y	orient	hand	view	operations
2	8	W	N	N	WR

if robot is at position (2,8) looking west, having no bottle in his hand and seeing no bottle, then perform command WR.

b) Rules for remembered state of rooms							
x	y	full	done LMR	orient	hand	view	operations
3	5	L	001	S	L	*	AB

if robot is at position (3,5) looking south, having an empty bottle in his hand, view = don't care and if the left room is full and the right is done, then execute command AB.

c) Rules for remembered shelves							
x	y	shelf	cont	orient	hand	view	operations
3	7	1	V	N	N	*	LINKS,GEHE,NIMM,&01

if robot is at position (3,7) looking north, having no bottle in his hand, view = don't care and if shelf 1 is remembered to contain a full (V) bottle, then issue the commands LINKS (left), GEHE (go) and NIMM (take) and remember the now empty shelf 1.

Aspects and results of the knowledge base development

The influence of memory on strategy

On a specific problem with B-COMMANDS we will demonstrate the influence of the memory facility on strategy. The robot has entered the left room and stands at position (3,7). He is carrying an empty bottle and has to dispose it on a shelf. The knowledge base of table 3 was constructed without memory facility. The player does not know where an empty shelf might be located, therefore he has to scan the walls for such a shelf. The first two rules cover position (3,7) just behind the door. If the robot looks north, he turns to the left (west), if he looks west he moves to the wall to position (2,7). For positions (2,7) thru (2,10) along the left wall of the left room, always the same set of rules is used: if the visible shelf is empty, the bottle is disposed, otherwise, the robot skips up one field to his right (north).

TABLE 3
Knowledge base without memory facility

x	y	orient	hand	view	operations
3	7	N	*	*	LINKS
3	7	W	*	*	GEHE
2	7	W	L	*	WR
2	7	W	L	N	DEPONIERE
2	8	W	L	*	WR
2	8	W	L	N	DEPONIERE
2	9	W	L	*	WR
2	9	W	L	N	DEPONIERE
2	10	W	L	*	WR
2	10	W	L	N	DEPONIERE

LINKS = turn left
GEHE = move on step
WR = shift on field to the right
DEPONIERE = deposit bottle

Table 4 shows part of the corresponding knowledge base with memory facility. It is memorized that shelf number 3 is currently empty. Therefore, there is no need for scanning the walls. Instead, the robot can be guided directly to the shelf. As one can see, there is only one rule needed which generates the appropriate command sequence in one inference step.

TABLE 4
Knowledge base with memory facility

x	y	shelf	cont	orient	hand	view	operations
3	7	3	N	N	L	*	GEHE,GEHE,LINKS, GEHE,DEPONIERE;!03

Such combinations of commands can be compared with the findings of psychological action theory which states that operations are combined into actions depending on the goal (Hacker, 1978). Therefore the command sequence of table 4 can be interpreted as an action unit belonging to the goal "deposit bottle in the empty shelf number 3".

The influence of memory on efficiency

In table 5 we present efficiency parameters for games with each of the simulation systems (the expert system and RoSi). The parameter "commands per bottle" can also be compared with the mean over a group of human players.

TABLE 5
An overview of the knowledge bases and simulation results

Player	Parameter	E-COMM.	B-COMM.
Expert System	Production rules	20	55
	Commands per bottle	2.05	15.05
	Basic robot steps per bottle	76.44	54.89
RoSi	Production rules	138	943
	Commands per bottle	2.1	11.2
	Basic robot steps per bottle	76.5	45.8
Human	Commands per bottle	2.3	15.25

The knowledge base for Rosi needs by far more production rules than the one for the expert system. The production rules of the expert system are much more general than the very atomistic rules of RoSi. A single rule of the expert system often covers several rules of the RoSi knowledge base.

As has been mentioned in chapter 4, the command set E-COMMANDS has more powerful commands than command set B-COMMANDS. This is the reason why the number of commands per bottle is much lower for E-COMMANDS. But these powerful commands are not optimized in regard to the basic robot steps. For instance, the robot makes unnecessary detours and turnings when leaving the room whereas the player of B-COMMANDS is invited to use the shortest path. So the number of basic robot steps is higher for command set E-COMMANDS.

We will now consider command set E-COMMANDS. The ratios "commands per bottle" for the simulated games are comparable with those of human players. The ratio is slightly higher for human players. We suppose that this is due to errors. In contrast to humans, the computer simulation is infallible. For the simulated games we find that the memory facility does not influence efficiency. The ratios "commands per bottle" and "basic robot steps per bottle" are almost equal for the expert system with or without memory facility.

If we look at the same efficiency parameters for command set B-COMMANDS we find that the average results of human players and simulated games without memory are comparable ("commands per bottle"). For the simulated game with memory facility there is a gain in efficiency: the ratios "commands per bottle" and "basic robot steps per bottle" are clearly lower. This is due to the possibility of piloting the robot directly to an empty shelf without having to scan the walls as discussed in chapter 8.1.

As mentioned in chapter 7 the memory facility was implemented according to the needs of a student who otherwise would not have been able to translate his own strategy into the knowledge base. His ratios "commands per bottle" and "basic robot steps per bottle" are only slightly higher (12.2 and 49.3 respectively) than those of the simulation. Still they are far below the ratios of average players. In previous experiments we observed two other players with comparable ratios (Ackermann 1986). We assume that they also used a strategy of memorizing bottles and empty shelves.

Discussion

As mentioned in chapter 7, the knowledge base on the expert system for B-COMMANDS contains explicit goals whereas the one for E-COMMANDS does not. The explicit goals of B-COMMANDS imply command sequences. The same command sequences can be found in the knowledge base for B-COMMANDS for RoSi. So the results are independent of the architecture of the simulation system. Moreover, the knowledge bases on RoSi and the expert system were independently developed by different students. This shows that the differences in goal settings are implied by the dialogue structures (command sets).

One group conceived a strategy requiring the use of the memory. The other group did not even think of such a possibility. This fact demonstrates the individual differences in action regulation. We have hints from previous experiments that such differences can also be found (Ackermann, 1987). This is not independent of the dialogue structure. The knowledge bases and the experimental results show that whether the possibility of memorizing shelves exist or not, all players use the same strategy with command set E-COMMANDS. The efficiency parameters are all nearly equal. On the contrary B-COMMANDS invites the player to develop own strategies and to use his abilities (e.g. memory).

Control experiment with human players in Berlin (Eyferth et al., 1986) have shown that users of B-COMMANDS know by far more about the game than users of E-COMMANDS. In the light of our findings we assume that these differences are caused by the differences in goal settings. Only cognitive modelling of the process of thinking is suited to reveal which factors and influences are responsible for such differences in task-related competence.

Based on the fact that the goal settings of B-COMMANDS imply fix command sequences we developed a modified version of B-COMMANDS which combines these fix sequences to single commands. This improves the efficiency of the command set as the amount of command input is strongly reduced. The degrees of freedom remain the same. The user can still make use of his own strategies and abilities. This is a good example how dialogue design can benefit from cognitive modelling.

When doing cognitive modelling, one is confronted with three problems (Schmalhofer & Wetter, 1987):

(1) *The problem of architecture.* What are the basic structures of cognitive processes? Are the structures invariant? For our computer game task, the production system approach was sufficient as long as no memory was involved. For RoSi, the mechanism of the inference machine had to be modified. Three knowledge bases are hierarchically arranged: The rules of the lower-level knowledge bases are only invoked if the higher-level knowledge base fails. Both systems include a working memory which is rather organized in a declarative form rather than as a production rule system.

(2) *The problem of representation.* What is the format of the stored knowledge? Although both system are based on the mechanism of a production system, the grain of the production rules is very different. RoSi uses very atomistic rules with a lot of redundancy whereas the expert system has very general and compact rules without redundancy.

(3) *The problem of the involved processes.* Is there a finite set of processes operating on the mental structure of represented information? What are the basic mental processes? How are the processes controlled? This problem was not faced in our experiments. We do not know if the production system mechanism is the only possible one. Yet we found that it reflects the thinking processes when playing the game. When asked, students formulated their thinking processes as production rules: "If I am in a room and I see a wrong bottle, I take it and leave the room".

Despite of the above criticism our experiments show interesting interactions between dialogue structure and possible mental representations. It is important to investigate individual differences in human-computer interaction to get evidence about the action regulation processes. Moreover, cognitive modelling will serve as an useful explorative tool in dialogue design.

Acknowledgements

We gratefully appreciate the collaboration of the following students in this experiment: D. Gruntz, R. Kannappel, B. Zürcher, A. Meister, G. di Pietro, M. Kohler, and Ch. Widmer.

References

Ackermann, D. (1986). A pilot study on the effects of individualization in man-computer interaction. In G. Mancini, G. Johannsen & L. Martenson (Eds.), *Analysis, Design and Evaluation of Man-Machine-Systems.* Proceedings of the 2nd IFAC/IFIP/IFORS/IEA Conference, Varese, Italy, 10. - 12. September 1985 (pp. 293- 297). Oxford - New York: Pergamon Press.

Ackermann, D. (1987). *Handlungsspielraum, mentale Repräsentation und Handlungsregulation am Beispiel der Mensch Computer Interaktion.* Doctoral thesis, University of Bern.

Anderson, J.R. (1981). *Cognitive Skills and their Acquisition.* Hillsdale, New Jersey: Lawrence Erlbaum Associates.

Bürge, U. (1985). Entwurf und Programmierung eines minimalen Expertensystems. *Micro- und Kleincomputer,* 1985, 6, pp. 95-99.

Cohors-Fresenborg, E. (1987). The benefits of microworlds in learning computer programming. In E. Brueger (Ed.), *Computation Theory and Logic.* Berlin - Heidelberg - New York: Springer Verlag.

Eyferth, K., Kafai, Y., Ottenroth, M., Strümpfel, U. & Widowski, D. (1986). *Lernen in der Steuerung einer computersimulierten Aufgabe.* Arbeitspapier zur Präsentation an der Tagung experimentell arbeitender Psychologen, Saarbrücken, 1986. TU Berlin.

Hacker, W. (1978). *Allgemeine Arbeits- und Ingenieurpsychologie.* Bern: Huber.

Kaune, Ch. (1985). Schüler denken am Computer. Eine Untersuchung über den Einfluβ von Repräsentationsformen und kognitiven Strategien beim Konstruieren und Analysieren von Algorithmen. *Schriftenreihe des Forschungsinstituts für Mathematik* Nr. 5, 1985. Universität Osnabrück.

Krause, B. (1982). Semantic information processing in cognitive processes. *Zeitschrift für Psychologie,* 1982, pp. 37-45.

Oschanin, D. A. (1976). Dynamisches Operatives Abbild und konzeptionelles Modell. *Probleme und Ergebnisse der Psychologie,* 1976, 59, pp. 37-48.

Schmalhofer, F. & Wetter, Th. (1987). Kognitive Modellierung: Menschliche Wissensrepräsentation und Verarbeitungsstrategien. In E. Richter & Th. Christaller (Eds.), *Künstliche Intelligenz: Frühjahresschule Dassel 1986.* Informatik Fachberichte. Berlin - Heidelberg - New York: Springer-Verlag.

Ulich, E. (1978). Über das Prinzip der differentiellen Arbeitsgestaltung. *Industrielle Organisation,* 1978, 47, pp. 566-568.

Mental Models and Human-Computer Interaction 1
D. Ackermann and M.J. Tauber (Editors)

MENTAL MODELS AND STRATEGIES IN THE CONTROL OF A COMPLEX SYSTEM

Olaf J. Ringelband, Carlo Misiak and Rainer H. Kluwe

Institute for Cognitive Research
University of Federal Armed Forces, Hamburg, FRG

ABSTRACT

The research reported here is based on single case studies in the domain of complex system control. Subjects operate an artificial complex system, sim006, implemented on a computer. The analysis of behavioural data obtained during system control led to the assumption that some subjects elaborate a rather simple mental model when running the system. This model is far from being a mathematically correct description of the system and its behaviour. A program 'simstrat' based on few declarative and procedural knowledge has been constructed. The results of Simstrat when operating sim006 are compared to the subject's performance. Similarities and differences of the results are discussed.

Introduction

The research reported here is concerned with mental models and strategies that can be involved in the control of a complex system.

In the context of a comprehensive research project on learning by doing several experiments with a complex system named sim006 were designed. They were concerned with the question of how subjects learn to operate such a system (Kluwe et al. 1985a, Kluwe et al. 1985b, Kluwe et al. 1986).

The analysis of the mathematical structure of the complex system sim006 used in our studies leads to the assumption that simple strategies might be sufficient for controlling the system; that is, a set of rules based on little knowledge about the system and its behavior. Most of all, the system's structure, i.e. the relation between system variables, should not be heeded. Our empirical data so far provide evidence for this assumption. Some subjects occasionally operate the system with such strategies during the experiment.

Having this in mind we wrote a program named SimStrat which incorporates such strategies. SimStrat controls sim006 without any knowledge about the system's structure. Thus we wanted to get additional evidence for our assumption derived from theoretical and empirical analyses. The performance of the program can be compared with the subjects' behavior.

In the following, the structure of the system sim006 is described first. Then the role of mental models when operating a complex system is discussed. After that the program SimStrat and its performance is examined. The final section includes a discussion of the results.

System sim006

The basic approach of our studies so far can be described as follows:

(1) Subjects are run in single case studies; since we are interested in the analysis of long learning processes, 10 sessions per 20 trials are performed. There is one session each day over a period of 10 days (90 to 120 minutes); a trial is a set of control operations.

(2) The task of the subject is to operate a specific complex system named sim006 implemented on a computer. The instruction informs the subject to operate the system in order to approximate its state to a set of reference values (there is one reference value for each system-variable). The subjects may subtract or add values in order to influence the states of the system variables. They may also decide not to intervene. There are 15 system variables with artificial labels in one condition, and with meaningful labels in a second condition. Before each trial a subject has to decide which of the 15 variables will be displayed. Only a maximum number of 8 (out of 15 variables) can be seen. However, always all 15 variables can be manipulated in a trial. After having chosen up to 8 out of 15 variables, the variables' states are displayed both as numeric values and as barcharts on the monitor. Furthermore the variables' reference

values are shown as a line in, resp. above, the variables' barchart. Figure 1 shows the screen as it is presented to the subject during the session.

(3) Contrary to systems that are used in other psychological studies the formal characteristics of the system sim006 can be described. In addition, we now use systems which attributes are known a priori. That is, we construct systems with predefined attributes in order to study their effects on the learning process of subjects that have the task to control the system (Kluwe et al. 1986).

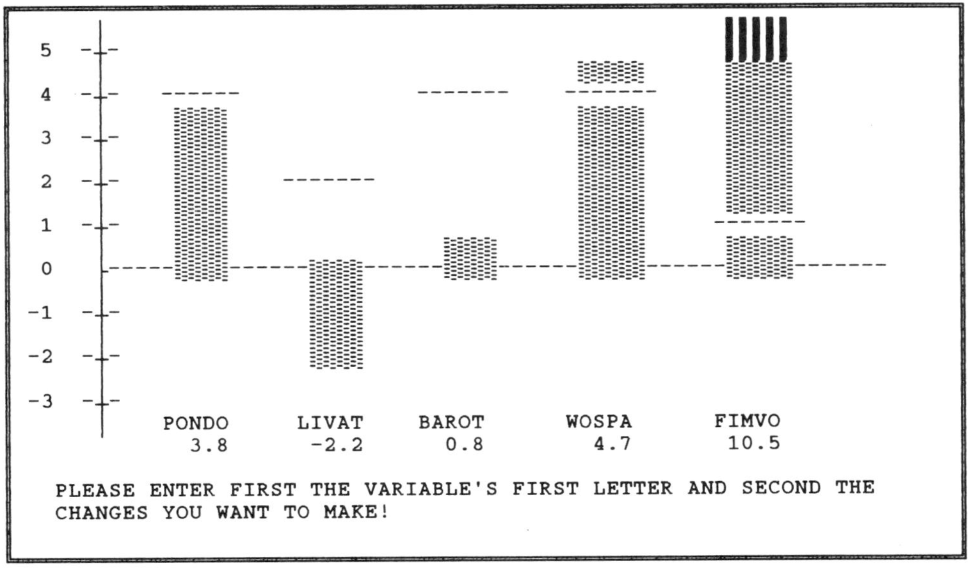

Figure 1. Screen dump of system sim006

The system sim006 can briefly be described as a time-invariant, linear, discrete-time system. The formal description is given by

$$V(t+1) = M * (V(t) + E(t)) \tag{1}$$

where V is the state-vector of the system's 15 variables, E is the vector of the input at time t, and M is the 15x15 transition matrix. M is the system's distribution matrix as well.

The characteristics of the system's behaviour are determined by the characteristics of the matrix M (e.g. eigenvalues of the matrix).

If the inverse of the transition matrix M exists, one can easily show that the system in question is observable and state-space controllable. To reach an arbitrary state vector of reference values V(s) at time t+1 one just has to compute

$$E(t) = M^{-1} * V(s) - V(t) \tag{2}$$

whereby M^{-1} is the inverse of M. This means that there is an optimal input vector E(t).

With regard to the controllability of the system the following considerations have to be added: the optimal control inputs would be the difference between the observed value and the reference value if the system- and distribution matrix would be the identity matrix I:

$$V(t+1) = I * (V(t) + E(t)) \tag{3}$$

$$E(t) = V(s) - V(t) \tag{4}$$

With regard to our system, however, this is not valid. The constant part $M^{-1} * V(s)$ does not represent the vector of reference values s. This means that there is a vector of differences

$$d = V(s) - M^{-1} * V(s) \tag{5}$$

Therefore, it is not possible just to change the system state according to the reference values. It is necessary to take into account the combined effects of dynamics and distribution that constitute the difference. This means

$$E(t) = V(s) - d - V(t) \tag{6}$$

We assume that the control is difficult for those system variables where the component of the vector of differences is large. It is easier where these components approximate zero. Given a large component of the vector of differences it is necessary first to identify the right "dosage" of control. Since in our system the values of "d" (see eq. 5) are not very large we assumed that it is possible to control the system by taking the difference between observed value and reference value of a variable as input.

A much better control performance is achieved, however, if a subject tries to find out the adequate quantities in "d". Such a strategy would treat each variable as a single problem. The task would be, to find out the right "d" for each variable. The mental model underlying such a strategy needs not necessarily correspond to the mathematical model of the system as described above.

The relevance of mental models when dealing with complex systems

When confronted with the task of controlling a complex system like sim006 a subject is trying to build an internal representation of the system's structure and behaviour. This representation is termed 'mental model'. According to Kluwe (Kluwe, in press) a mental model is an individual's mental make-up of a specific problem domain. It includes knowledge of structures and processes as well as inferential rules. It may be brought towards a problem situation, but also it may be developed in the course of gathering experience in the domain in question. The function of these models is to direct the process of coping with a complex problem environment.

Mental models are difficult to identify, because different techniques of modelling are involved in their exploration. Considering a problem situation with structure S, we postulate two classes of models:

(1) Scientific models S(S) which are developed by scientists and other experts;

(2) Mental models M(S) which are constructed by various individuals.

On a meta-level psychological research aims at the elaboration of models of mental models P(M(S)). Mental models may vary significantly with respect to their completeness and correctness because there is a strong interrelationship between the way of acting in a task environment and the mental model of its structure. Goal directed search in a problem space attached to a structure results in the modification of the related mental model. That, in turn, alters the way the situation is approached. A commonly held opinion is that the success of acting in a complex environment with structure S depends on the completeness and correctness of the associated mental model M(S). In other words, the chance of failure is proportional to the distance between M(S) and an appropriate S(S). Tauber (Tauber, 1985) states: "... the most important psychological factor is the mental model serving as a representation of the virtual machine ... mental models represent cognitive processes like understanding and predicting system processes as well as explanations of system behavior" (1985, p.776; translated by the authors). Likewise, Funke (Funke, 1985) assumes an interdependence of (a) the correlation between the subjects' mental models and reality, (b) his system's mathematical structure and (c) the efficiency of subjects' control operations. In his studies, Funke (Funke, 1985) asks subjects to fill in forms in order to obtain data on the subjects' knowledge of the interrelation between system variables. He then defines the appropriateness of subjects' mental models as the degree of correspondence with the formal architecture of the system he used as a tool of research.

Another piece of evidence is given by Jagacinsky & Miller (Jagacinsky & Miller, 1978). There, the subject's task was to control an oscillating movement of a spot on a CRT-screen. Jagacinsky & Miller assume that successful control depends on the construction of a mental image that maps the movement's underlying cause as a time-invariant second order system: "The representational form of the internal model is not obvious. For purposes of this analysis, it is assumed that a second-order, time-invariant system is satisfactory. That is it is assumed that the switch locus is adequately described by an equation (..)" (Jagacinsky & Miller, 1978, p. 429).

Dörner et al. (Dörner et al., 1983, p. 39) point out that it is necessary to obtain knowledge of the interdependence of a complex system's variables in order to master implicit difficulties. This knowledge is termed 'structural knowledge'. Furthermore, Dörner et al. (Dörner et al., 1983) emphasize that besides searching for interrelations of variables it is necessary to implement an adequate mental image of a system in order to operate it properly. They claim that a mental model is adequate if it is 'well-structured' and 'each of its variables is connected with many other variables' (1983, p.250).

The results of our research, however, do not indicate the correctness of the assumptions described above. Subjects who controlled a system successfully did not particularize the system's structure (see Kluwe et al., 1986). This seems to be in accordance with results of Broadbent et al. (Broadbent & Aston, 1977; Berry & Broadbent, 1984; Broadbent et al., 1986) who in several experiments unsuccessfully tried to solicit structural knowledge from subjects being able to control small but complex systems efficiently. The question arises whether it is suitable to ask for knowledge that is implied by the architecture of a scientific model

S(S). It seems reasonable to assume that a subject's mental model M(S) consists of different and probably less knowledge than a model S(s), but still is sufficient to control a system S appropriately. In the following it will be shown that simple mental models produce strategies which are commensurate to control a complex system.

Description of implemented control strategies

A program called SimStrat, which is able to operate the system, sim006 has been written. SimStrat embodies four different strategies which are selectable before the program is run. All strategies are considered to be simple because the underlying knowledge that constitutes the corresponding mental models does not include much information.

The strategies are described in terms of the essential declarative knowledge specific to the task given, which basically is the same for each strategy, and the procedural knowledge, which is not much in strategy 1 but considerably more in strategy 4. It is important to note that we consider the rules that are part of the strategies as procedural knowledge because rules are the written instantiation of the dynamic processes that occur in an inference engine at run time. Knowledge of very basic skills like counting or adding is not part of the models discussed here. The declarative knowledge common to all strategies can be listed as follows:

- there are 15 variables each of which has an associated state,
- one can select up to 8 variables to obtain information about the variables' states,
- it is useful to gather as much information as possible, i.e. to select the maximum of eight variables always,
- the task is to approximate the variables' states to the variables' reference values which can be achieved by adding or subtracting values to or from all 15 states,
- it is useful to work on those variables the state of which is visible.

In strategy 1 there is no additional declarative knowledge. The procedural knowledge consists of two rules, one rule governing the choice of variables, the other one the control operations. The rules can be easily written as:

- if the goal is choice, choose eight variables at random
- if the goal is controlling the system, compute the difference if state and reference value for each variable displayed on the screen and subtract it from the state.

Strategy 2 differs only slightly. The common knowledge base is augmented by the following rules:

- it is useful to group variables.

Its choice rule part is represented by three rules:

- if the goal is choice, choose the variables or the group of variables you did not see in the last cycle
- if you did not choose eight variables yet, use the choice rule of strategy 1 for the rest of the variables
- if it is the first time you choose, consider the variables as a group.

With these rules, the strategy in the first cycle chooses variables at random, then chooses seven variables it did not see before plus one variable at random, then the group of variables it saw first and so on. Both of the strategies considered so far do not use any information about the characteristics of the system's dynamics.

The following strategies are a little more sophisticated. The main difference between strategy 3 and 4 is the set of choice rules. They are more elaborate in the fourth version, while strategy 3 still includes the choice rule part of the second model described above. In order to avoid redundance we only discuss strategy 4 here.

The knowledge base of strategy 4 is augmented as follows:

- in addition to the state, there is a ?characteristic value associated to each variable, which is of importance in order to control the system successfully
- it is useful to ?prefer to choose the variables that tend to show a ?substantial deviation from their reference value, a fact that is indicated by the ?'characteristic value' (note that this assertion is not included in the knowledge base of strategy 3).

Strategy 4 is the most sophisticated strategy and we summarize its rule system below. The rules are:

1. The choice rules
- if the goal is choice, choose the variables that tend to deviate ?substantially
- if you did not choose eight variables yet, choose the variables you did not see in the last cycle
- if you did not choose eight variables yet, use the choice rule of strategy one for the rest of the variables not yet chosen
- if you have chosen eight variables remember them and the values of their attributes.

2. The control rules
- if the goal is controlling the system, compute the deviation of each variable, one at a time
- if the deviation of a variable is substantial, ?recompute its ?characteristic value and adjust the variable according to the ?combination of deviation and ?characteristic value.

It is important to realize that the question mark denotes declarative (?substantial, ?characteristic value) or procedural (?prefer, ?recompute, ?combination) parameters that determine the success of the strategy substantially.

Results

Table 1 shows the control performance of two subjects RB and AE operating sim006 as well as the performance of all four strategies.

TABLE 1
IDAB (Deviation from optimal input) - average per session

Session	1	2	3	4	5	6	7	8	9	10
S AE	11.8	13.9	5.1	2.6	3.1	3.1	2.6	1.9	1.7	2.1
S RB	25.8	15.0	6.6	6.8	10.5	25.9	8.2	5.6	4.7	4.7
Strat I	4.0	4.4	5.9	4.5	4.6	3.8	5.1	4.7	4.8	3.5
Strat II	3.3	3.4	3.2	3.3	3.6	3.4	3.6	3.5	3.4	2.9
Strat III	3.0	2.8	2.8	2.9	2.9	3.0	3.2	3.4	3.3	3.2
Strat IV	3.7	2.7	3.0	3.0	3.3	3.3	3.7	3.5	3.7	3.3

The level of efficiency of control performance is determined in terms of the difference IDAB between actual input and ideal input (which is computed as shown in eq. 2) averaged over all variables and per session. An optimal system control would show an IDAB of zero. On the other hand, letting the system run without any input would lead to an average IDAB of 64. Compared with this all of the subjects show remarkable success in controlling the system.

First, the result of SimStrat working with strategy 1 is considered. This strategy chooses 8 variables by chance and subtracts or adds the difference between observed value and reference value from or to the reference value. SimStrat on the average achieves an IDAB between 3 and 6; that is better than most subjects' performance in the first sessions but still below the best subject's (AE) performance in the last sessions. Strategy 2, which is working in the same manner as strategy 1 but chooses the variables alternatively, achieves a similar result. It is also better than most subjects but weaker than the best one.

The peaks in the plot of strategy 1 can be explained by its choice rules: it chooses the 8 variables at random. If, in the course of 20 trials, the more difficult variables are not selected for some trials, which also implies that they are not manipulated, those variables increase rapidly. The performance of strategy 2 shows a smaller range of average values IDAB because it is monitoring the whole system by its alternating choice.

It is important to note that both strategies 1 and 2 include no learning process. The results are similar to the subjects' results after 4 or 5 sessions, i.e. there is no explorative stage at the beginning which produces weak control performance during sessions 1-3.

Strategy 3, however, includes a process of learning; the program tries to find the right characteristic value for each variable. Strategy 3 is again better than subject RB and also slightly better than strategy 2. It approximates the performance of subject AE. However, SimStrat produces weaker results in the last sessions. This can be explained by looking at the variables' characteristic values (see table below).

SimStrat does not compute a non-zero characteristic value for the variables of subsystem 2 as well as for the 3 non-oscillating variables of subsystem 3.

TABLE 2
The ?characteristic values of variables that are added to the deviation from the reference value as input after 200 trials (SimStrat strategy 3).

Sub-system 1:	-8.80	6.80	-9.80	-3.00	0.00
Sub-system 2:	0.00	0.00	0.00	0.00	0.00
Sub-system 3:	0.00	2.40	0.00	1.60	0.00

The both oscillating variables show a characteristic value of 2.4 and 1.6. During the 200 trials those values were in the range of -8.0 to +8.0. That means, SimStrat tries to find the right "dosage" for those variables without success. Briefly said, SimStrat does not "recognize" the character of the oscillating variables.

Four variables of sub-system 1 show high characteristic values; three have negative values and one has a positive value. It does not seem reasonable to add a much larger value to one variable and subtract a large value from another if both are connected with each other. However, it leads to a satisfying but suboptimal result. It is more efficient, though, to add a smaller characteristic value to all 5 variables of sub-system 1. SimStrat does not "recognize" that the variables are connected with each other. Strategy 4 chooses and influences the variables with a high characteristic value more often. The performance of strategy 4 is close to that of strategy 3. The rules of strategy 4 make up two competing processes. (a) Difficult variables are chosen more often. This leads to a better control. (b) SimStrat makes useless efforts to control the two oscillating variables by recomputing the characteristic value. This is the main reason for the decrease of performance compared to strategy 3.

Discussion

The performance of SimStrat and our earlier theoretical and empirical results show the following:

(1) Simple internal models with respect to a computer simulation allow a control of a complex system. The control performance is much better then the result of letting the system run without any input. Compared with subjects the control performance is in the range of the subjects' performance.

(2) The strategies implemented in SimStrat are not a complete and perfect model of the system. They do not take into account the mathematical structure of the system. Consequently it can be concluded that it is not necessary to have a complex and complete mental model of an environment in order to act successfully.

(3) All subjects exhibit an initial explorative phase during the experiment. This is not the case for the strategies as described above. There is no interaction between SimStrat's "mental model" and the system, i.e. the mental model does not change during the run.

This can easily be achieved by combining the four strategies: in this case an additional procedure would have to take care of the stepwise transition from strategy 1 to strategy 4. In such a model strategy 1 is taken as the first phase of the learning process; the program then proceeds to the more advanced strategies until strategy 4 is reached in the final phase.

SimStrat sometimes obtains non-optimal results in controlling sim006. It fails at the end when using strategy 4. This can be explained by its efforts to compute the adequate characteristic value for each variable. It leads to the undesired effect that SimStrat adds a large amount to one variable and subtracts a large amount from another while both variables are highly connected. A better strategy is to add a smaller amount to highly connected variables. Subjects who can shift to an explorative stage probably are less troubled with those variables. The two oscillating variables in sim006 "confuse" SimStrat. The program adds and then again subtracts large values without success. This is not an adequate strategy for operating oscillating variables. Avoiding control operations would lead to a better performance in this case.

We assume that, contrary to a wide spread opinion, it is possible to show that it is not necessary to develop a complete mental model of the formal mathematical structure of a system in order to operate a complex system. We are convinced that in reality a considerable part of everyday acting can be explained on this basis.

Acknowledgements

Supported by Deutsche Forschungsgemeinschaft (DFG), Bonn-Bad Godesberg; Az Kl. 488/3-1

References

Berry, D. & Broadbent, D.E. (1984). On the relationship between task performance and associated verbalizable knowledge. *The Quarterly Journal of Experimental Psychology,* 36 A, 1984, pp. 209-231.

Broadbent, D.E & Aston, B. (1978). Human control of a simulated economic system. *Ergonomics,* 21, 12, 1978, pp. 1035-1043.

Broadbent, D.E., Fitzgerald, P. & Broadbent, M. (1986). Implicit and explicit knowledge in the control of complex systems. *British Journal of Psychology,* 77, 1986, pp. 33-50.

Dörner, D., Kreuzig, H.W., Reither, F. & Stäudel, Th. (1983). *Lohausen: Vom Umgang mit Unbestimmtheit und Komplexität.* Bern: Huber.

Funke, J. (1985). Problemlösen in komplexen, computersimulierten Realitätsbereichen. *Sprache & Kognition,* 4, 1985, pp. 113-129.

Jagacinski, R.J. & Miller, R.A. (1978). Describing the human operator's internal model of a dynamic system. *Human Factors* 1978, 20(4), pp. 425-433.

Kluwe, R.H. (in press). Gedächtnis und Wissen (in press). In H. Spada (Ed.), *Allgemeine Psychologie.* Bern: Huber.

Kluwe, R.H., Misiak, C. & Ringelband, O. (1985a). Learning to control a complex system. Invited paper for the *1st European conference on learning and instruction, June 10-13, 1985.* University of Leuven, Belgium.

Kluwe, R.H., Misiak, C. Ringelband, O. & Haider, H. (1986). Learning by doing in the control of a complex system: the benefits from experience and the effects of system characteristics on the learning process. Extended version of a paper presented at the *35. Congress of the German Psychological Association.* University of Heidelberg, Sept. 1986.

Kluwe, R.H., Misiak, C. & Schmidle, R. (1985b). Wissenserwerb beim Umgang mit einem umfangreichen System: Lernen als Ausbildung subjektiver Ordnungsstrukturen. In D. Albert (Ed.), *Bericht über den 34. Kongress der Deutschen Gesellschaft für Psychologie* (pp. 255-257). Göttingen: Hogrefe.

Tauber, M.J. (1985). Entwicklung mentaler Modelle und kognitive Stile in der Mensch-Rechner-Interaktion. In D. Albert (Ed.), *Bericht über den 34. Kongress der Deutschen Gesellschaft für Psychologie (Band 2)* (pp. 775-777). Göttingen: Hogrefe.

Mental Models and Human-Computer Interaction 1
D. Ackermann and M.J. Tauber (Editors)

AN EXPERIMENTAL STUDY ON MENTAL MODELS IN DATABASE SEARCH

Lena Linde and Monica Bergström

Department of Psychology, University of Stockholm, and
Department of Human Studies, National Defense Research Institute.

ABSTRACT

An experimental study was performed to investigate whether pretraining on textual information, pertaining to database content, has any effect on the ability to learn search principles in a database system. Twentyfour subjects, distributed over three different experimental conditions, were studied. The 1st condition comprised pretraining on textual information that was partially identical with the informational content in the database. The 2nd condition comprised pretraining on textual information that was partially analogous to but not identical with the informational content in the database. The 3rd condition comprised an irrelevant "placebo" task. Differences between the three conditions were analysed with respect to the time it took to complete a search task, errors, and assistance given by the experimenter. Pretraining on textual information that was identical with the content in the database was found to facilitate the learning of search principles. Also, the subjects were categorized, by a blind procedure, as " Visualizers" and "Non-visualizers", respectively. Visualizers tended to have a better search performance. A closer analysis of the data indicated that this could be attributed to the fact there were more "Visualizers" in the 1st condition than in the 2nd. Specific properties of the text that was identical with the content in the database were assumed to account for the larger proportion of "Visualizers", which in turn gave a better search performance. A possible relationship between these results and the mental model framework suggested by Johnson-Laird (1983) is pointed out.

Introduction

The purpose of the present study is to investigate the effect of prior knowledge of informational content in a database on the ability to learn its search principles. We are also interested in the mental representation of information given about the content.

In a recent study prior knowledge of informational content was found to affect the ability to learn the search principles in a database (Linde and Bergström, 1987). The subjects' task in that study was to retrieve information from a relational database in order to answer a set of questions. The aim was to investigate how search performance is influenced by procedural knowledge of table search (that is, the searching in tabular information on paper) and declarative knowledge of informational content (that is, knowledge from textually given facts about the content). The distinction between procedural and declarative knowledge was based on Anderson (Anderson, 1977). The facts were about the content and abstracted essentials, i.e. macrostructural information in the database (cf Kintsch and Van Dijk, 1978). The pretraining on the facts about content was found to facilitate the learning of the search principles. Prior training with tables presented on paper seemed to increase the frequency of inadequate search schemes, while also possibly helping the subjects to construct a mental representation of the database organisation. Subjects given table training learned more quickly than subjects given no pretraining. A significant interaction between table search and content training appeared.

The present study was designed as a further investigation of the effect of macrostructural information about content found by Linde and Bergström (1987). In that experiment the prior given information about content entailed

(1) that the database concerned groups of persons (their names were given) engaged in certain activities at certain places and times,

(2) that all persons occurring in the database and engaged in a particular activity had the same profession (the profession of every person was given), and

(3) that every person occurring in the database was seen at more than one time and place.

In the present experiment we test the hypothesis that pretraining on a content that is not identical with the content in the database in its specific details but is analogous with respect to conceptual structure, will have the same impact on the learning of the search principles as the effect found by Linde and Bergström (1987). We therefore use alternative versions of the facts about content: one identical with the facts given by Linde and Bergström and another in which all activities, professions, names and places have been replaced and never occur in the database. The two different versions comprise different scenarios. We hypothesize that both versions have a significant effect on the learning of the search principles. If so, the crucial factor affecting this learning ought to be the possession of knowledge of the type of entities in the database and examples of "possible" entities. We also wish to get some direct information about the mental representations which are created by the facts about content in either version. We hypothesize that a relationship exists between the form of mental representation of the content and the ability to learn the search principles. In addition, we are looking for information about whether the experimental conditions differed with respect to how much difficulty and mental strain the subjects perceived during the searches.

Why should knowledge about the semantic content in a database facilitate the learning of the logical search principles? One explanation may be that knowledge of the content affects the subjects' information analysis during the subsequent stages of learning the search task, such as when reading the queries, studying the instructions and performing actual searches in the database. Bransford and Johnson (1972) found that prior information about contextual relationships in a text, presented from a picture, increased comprehension and recall. Linde and Bergström (1987) gave prior information textually about semantic relationships and links between informational bits in the database. From these facts, given prior to database search, it could also be inferred, that some facts were contextually related (i.e. that there was a relationship between events distributed into different records and tables). Moreover, an inference task related to the facts about content was also given by Linde and Bergström (1987). This task may have rendered the subjects prone to make a "deep level" processing of the information about content (cf Craik and Lockhart, 1972). That is, they encoded the meaning of the information about content rather than its verbatim details. Therefore, we hypothesize that the subjects may construct some kind of mental model from the information about content. It might be that a mental representation (or a mental model, cf Johnson-Laird, 1983) of contextual and semantic relationships in textual information, induced directly from a picture or indirectly from textual information, facilitates encoding and analysis of task-relevant information (Linde, 1986).

Methods

Design of the experiments

Three preexperimental conditions were created. One was prior training with facts whose content was identical with the content in the database. Another was prior training with facts, whose structure was conceptually analogous with the content in the database. One was a placebo condition. The subjects were randomly distributed to the experimental conditions.

Subjects

Twenty-four undergraduate students of psychology took part in the experiment. There were eight subjects for each experimental condition. The subjects participated on a semivoluntary basis - serving as subjects was part of their course requirements but they were free to choose among current projects; they were not paid. The subjects were supposed to have no prior experience of computers and they all stated that they had none.

Database information, database system and dialogue

The database, stored in a databank called Report, contained fictitious information, about events occurring at different times at different places in the south of Sweden. An event featured the name of one person, his activity, the time and the place of occurrence. The subjects were encouraged to imagine that the information had been gathered by private detectives, each following a particular object of investigation and writing reports about that person. A relational database system, MIMER, was used for the experiment and this system's query language was used to create a data organization comprising three tables: Events, Persons, and Groups, with five, two and three columns respectively. A search dialogue, partly menu-based and partly organized as a question-answering dialogue, had been constructed, using procedures in the query language of MIMER. The dialogue was constructed for use without special training. The organization of the dialogue is shown in figure 1.

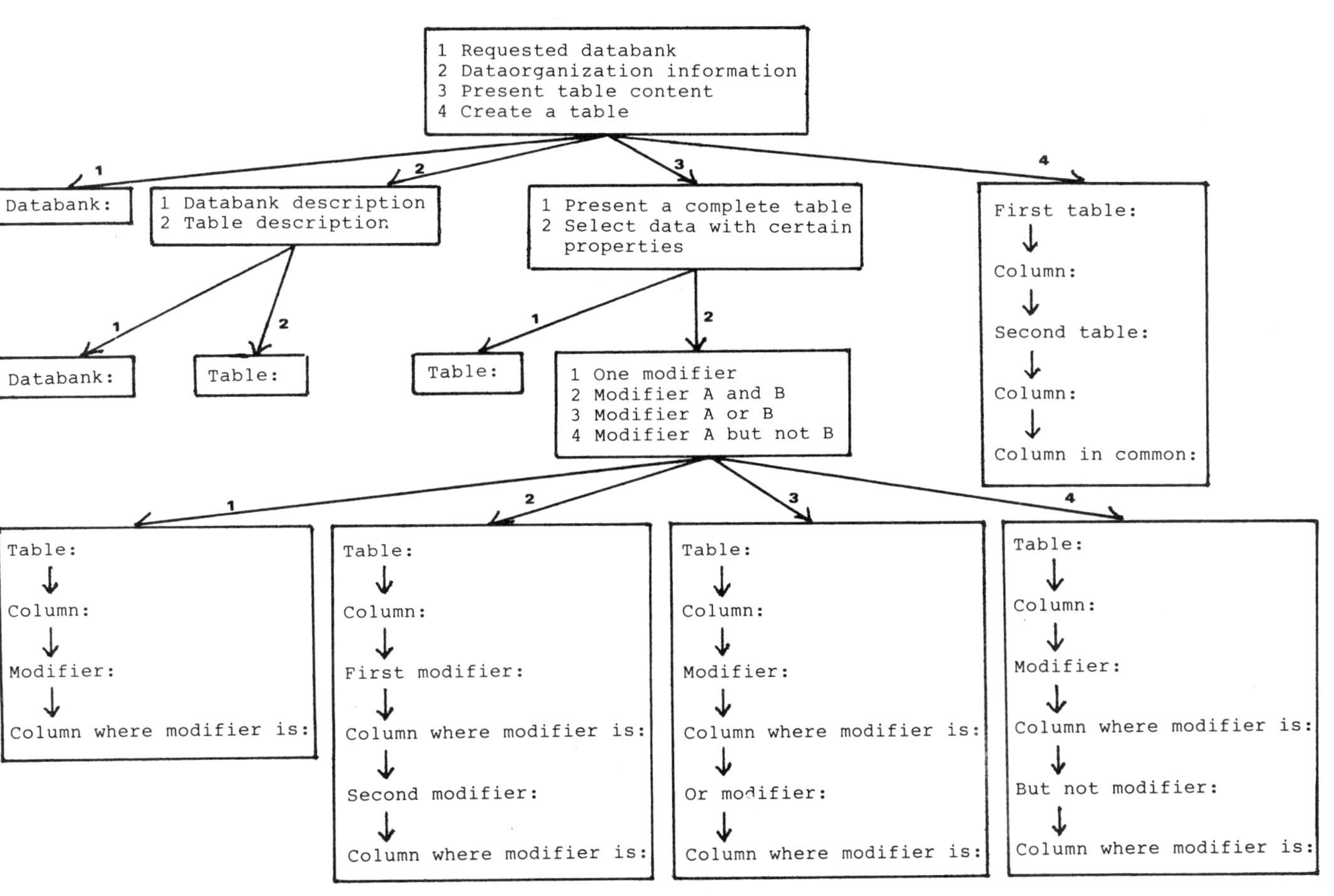

Figure 1. Graphic overview of the dialogue as presented to the subjects

Queries and search tasks

Five different queries or "search tasks" were given to each subject. The first two queries had one modifier. The third query had two modifiers, to be combined with a Boolean AND operator. The fourth query had two modifiers to be combined with a Boolean OR operator. The fifth query involved the creating a "new" two-column table from different tables linked by a common column with common values. All subjects were given the queries in the order mentioned above.

Prior training on facts about content

The facts about the content had the following form:

Example of type 1: A group consisting of August, Hjalmar, Anton, Vincent, Paulus, Torgny and Torbjörn performed in a street show in Eslöv at 3 30 pm.

Example of type 2: August, Hjalmar, Anton, Vincent, Paulus, Torbjörn and Torgny are all actors.

Example of type 3: August was observed at five different places and times.

There were five sentences each of types 1 and 2 and 10 sentences of type 3. To ensure that the subjects encoded the facts, they were given 15 propositions and asked to infer whether they were true or false, given the facts. In one version all activities, names, professions and places were identical with some of the entities in the database. The other version was analogous with the first except that all activities, names, professions and places were replaced by ones that never occurred in the database. The two versions were intended to depict different scenarios.

Procedure

First, all subjects were given the facts about the content or the irrelevant placebo task, which comprised choosing between charter trip alternatives. Afterwards every subject who had received the facts about content, was asked about his/her representation of the facts. This question ran: please tell me how you imagine the information that has just been presented to you. Then the subjects were given a written instruction about the information in the database and the search principles and a figure comprising an overview of the database organisation. When the subjects had read this instruction they were given a set of questions pertaining to it. Then the experimenter gave an oral instruction about the menu and the subjects received a set of questions about the menu. After that the experimenter demonstrated the database search task for the subject, using a block of queries that were analogous but not identical to queries that the subjects subsequently were given. Finally, the subjects performed the search tasks individually and at their own pace at a VDU. Information to the system was given at an alphanumeric keyboard. The subjects were asked to make as many search attempts as they needed to retrieve the correct information for each query to the screen. If they got "stuck", the experimenter could provide assistance. The subjects were asked to think aloud during the whole experimental search session. After some search attempts the subjects were prompted by the experimenter to explain their reasons for giving information to the system in the particular way. When the correct information for a query had been retrieved, the subjects were also asked to assign on scales, from 0 to 10, how "difficult" and "strenuous", respectively, each search task had been. Scale values were assigned interactively. The subjects' answers to the question about how they imagined the content were tape-recorded and so was the verbal interaction during the search sessions. Log-files over the search sessions were also provided.

Data analysis

Two dependent variables, measuring search performance, were assessed. One was the elapsed time from the moment the subject had read the search question (aloud) to the moment he/she had retrieved the correct information. This was assessed from the tape recordings. The other dependent variable had three components: a) number of assistances provided by the experimenter (assessed from the verbal protocols), b) dialogue errors such as incorrect menu choices or incorrect information given to the system (assessed from logfiles and verbal protocols), and c) self-detection of errors (assessed from logfiles and verbal protocols).

Each protocol of the subjects' imagining of the information about the content was scored blindly by one author. "Blindly" implies that the scorer had no knowledge of the search performance of the subject in question. The subjects were categorized as "Visualizers", and "Non-visualizers", respectively. The criterion for scoring a subject as

Visualizer was that the subject should affirm that some part of the information about content had given him/her a visual image and that s/he described some features of that image.

Results

Table 1 shows the average search time and standard deviations over subjects for each query and experimental condition. The average search times over all queries are also given. Two-tailed probabilities of T-testing between pairs of conditions for each query and overall means are given in Table 2. It can be mentioned that when using F-values as statistics, significant effects were obtained for mean search time between condition 1 (pretraining on identical content) and condition 3 (the placebo task), and between condition 2 (pretraining on analogous content) and condition 3. The probabilities were 0.05 and 0.04, respectively.

TABLE 1
Means and standard deviations of search times for each query and experimental condition (Condition 1=identical information, Condition 2=analogous information, Condition 3=placebo task).

	Condition 1		Condition 2		Condition 3	
	M	S	M	S	M	S
Query 1	377	178	840	347	907	748
Query 2	193	93	316	192	425	270
Query 3	314	160	356	182	331	200
Query 4	150	77	165	96	183	69
Query 5	608	286	440	139	645	485
M total	329	92	424	91	498	210

Table 3 shows the number of errors made, the number of assistances given and the number of self-detected errors. Menu-errors and menu-assistances refer to events in connection with the menu-dialogue. Question/answer errors and question/answer assistances refer to events in connection with filling in information prompted by the system. As can be seen from table 3, subjects given pretraining on information identical with the database content made least errors, while subjects given pretraining on information that was analogous with the content in the database made most errors. It is also worth noting that, while

TABLE 2
Two-tailed probabilities with T-testing of pairs of experimental conditions (C1= identical information, C2=analogous information, C3=placebo task).

	C1,C2	C1,C3	C2,C3
Query 1	0.01*	0.07	0.82
Query 2	0.13	0.04*	0.39
Query 3	0.64	0.86	0.67
Query 4	0.75	0.39	0.27
Query 5	0.16	0.86	0.37
M total	0.06	0.06	0.37

subjects in the placebo condition made fewer errors and got less assistance than subjects given pretraining on analogous information, the former still had a larger number of self-detected errors.

TABLE 3
Number of errors, self-detected errors and assistances, respectively, for each experimental condition. Concerning type of errors and assistances, see text. (C1=identical information, C2=analogous information, C3= placebo task).

	C1	C2	C3
Menu errors	27	76	53
Question/answer errors	75	123	103
Menu assistance	3	28	11
Question/answer assistance	11	15	10
Self-detected errors	33	40	50

Table 4 shows the average rated difficulty and mental strain for each query and experimental condition. It can be seen that condition 2 tended to be rated as somewhat more difficult and mentally strenuous than conditions 1 and 3 but that the differences between groups are small.

Table 5 shows the average search time over all queries for individuals categorized as "Visualizers" and "Non-visualizers", respectively. As can be seen the Visualizers have a shorter average search time than Non-visualizers. Visualizers are most frequent in Condition 1 (identical information), and Nonvisualizers in condition 2 (analogous information). The ratios have been computed as the mean of Visualizers in Condition 1 divided by the total mean for Condition 1, the mean of

Visualizers in Condition 2 divided by the total mean in Condition 2, etc.. From these means one can see that Visualizers deviate only slightly from the rest of the subjects in the same experimental condition.

TABLE 4
Average rated difficulty and mental strain (Condition C1=identical information, C2=analogous information, C3=placebo task).

	Difficulty			Mental strain		
	C1	C2	C3	C1	C2	C3
Query 1	4.3	7.8	6.2	6.3	8.0	5.8
Query 2	3.9	6.8	5.3	5.0	6.1	5.9
Query 3	5.4	6.6	3.9	6.3	6.4	4.1
Query 4	4.4	5.5	5.3	5.1	4.8	4.2
Query 5	6.4	4.9	6.0	6.1	4.8	7.1
M total	4.9	6.3	5.2	5.8	6.0	5.2

TABLE 5
Mean search time for Visualizers and Non-visualizers, number of Visualizers and Non-visualizers from condition 1 (identical information) and condition 2 (analogous information) and Ratios (see text).

	Visualizers	Non-visualizers
Mean search time	348	423
No of Ss from C1	7	1
No of Ss from C2	3	5
Ratio, C1	0.99	1.02
Ratio, C2	0.93	1.04

Discussion

The present results indicate that the pretraining given in Condition 1 facilitated the learning of the search principles of the database. The same effect was obtained by Linde and Bergström (1987). However, taking search time, errors and assistances into account indicates that pretraining on analogous information did not facilitate the learning of the search principles, which had been hypothesized. Why was the identical information more efficient than the analogous information? First, it should be pointed out that the specific names and entities mentioned in the queries were not the same as any mentioned in the facts about content (identical information). Therefore we can rule out the possibility that the subjects simply retrieved the answers from memory. The theoretical framework we suggest is the mental model proposed by Johnson-Laird (1983). That is, when trying to understand the search principles the subjects may have needed a mental model of the information in the database to figure out the conceptual organisation and the relationships between different pieces of content in the database. Such an understanding of the conceptual organisation and contextual relationships may have been of assistance in the understanding of the instructions about the database and dialogue with it. Evidently, the pretraining on the identical content was most efficient. However, we suggest that this effect was not due to the fact that the content was identical, as such, but rather that these textual facts gave a more vivid and realistic scenario relating to the information in the database that was the most easy to memorize. One might also suggest that the subjects were more familiar, that is, had more knowledge about the "identical" scenario. It is noteworthy that there were more "Visualisers" in condition 1 (identical information) than in condition 2 (analogous information).

Furthermore, we want to comment on table 4. It may not be totally clear what "difficulty and "mental strain", respectively, meant to the subjects. We suggest that difficulty refers to "the extent to which the subjects encountered problems" when trying to perform each search task, and that mental strain refers to the "effort" that the subjects put into each task.

Finally, we want to point out some practical implications of the present study. For one thing, Artificial Intelligence techniques for abstracting essential information in databases might be useful for the information seekers. Second, and as we believe most important, when designing database systems and teaching search principles one should use well-known and realistic models of the information.

References

Anderson, J.C. (1976). *Language, Memory and Thought.* Hillsdale, New Jersey: Lawrence Erlbaum Associates.

Bransford, D.J. & Johnson, M.K. (1972). Contextual prerequisites for understanding: some investigations of comprehension and recall. *Journal of Verbal Learning and Verbal Behavior,* 11, pp. 717-726.

Craik, F.I.M. & Lockhart, R.S. (1972). Levels of processing: a framework for understanding memory. *Journal of Verbal Learning and Verbal Behavior,* 11, pp. 671-684.

Johnson-Laird, P.N. (1983). *Mental Models.* Cambridge: Cambridge University Press.

Kintsch, W. & Van Dijk, T.A. (1978). Toward a model of text comprehension. *Psychological Review,* 85, pp. 363-394.

Linde, L. (1986). The information-seeker's mental model of the content in a database. *Proceedings of the Third European Conference on Cognitive Ergonomics,* Paris, September 1986.

Linde, L. & Bergström, M. (1987). The impact of prior knowledge of informational content and organization on the ability to learn search principles in a database. *Contemporary Educational Psychology,* in press.

Mental Models and Human-Computer Interaction 1
D. Ackermann and M.J. Tauber (Editors)
Elsevier Science Publishers B.V. (North-Holland), 1990

EMPIRICAL STUDY OF THE REFERENCE INTERVIEW IN BIBLIOGRAPHIC ONLINE RETRIEVAL

Manfred Wettler and Angelika Glöckner-Rist

Fachgruppe Informationswissenschaft
Universität Konstanz, FRG

ABSTRACT

We report on a research project aimed at finding empirically grounded rules for the design and implementation of an interface to facilitate the access to online bibliographic information systems. Interviews between professional searchers and end-users are analyzed in order to uncover how the colloquial problem descriptions of end-users are translated into query-language expressions. The feasibility and usefulness of this approach is demonstrated and discussed.

Introduction

Information retrieval can be considered as a problem solving task in which the search problem of a user, formulated in colloquial or technical language, has to be specified and translated into a query (Soergel, 1985; Jahoda & Braunagel, 1981). This translation is dictated by the query language and the thesaurus of the database. It involves several decisions, for instance the choice of words and expressions of the problem description to be included in the query, the assignment of field indicators to the terms of the query, the connection of the terms with boolean and other junctors, the truncation, masking and explosion of the query terms. Figure 1 gives an example of the kind of bibliographic search which constitutes the object of our study.

The upper part of figure 1 shows the problem description of an end user of the PSYNDEX database, which comprises psychological literature from the german speaking countries. Its lower part gives the corresponding query used in the online search. The query was formulated by a professional searcher at the Psychological-Information Center *problem-description*

Current research literature about memory training with old people

query-formulation (Grips/Dirs 3)

36	471	FIND CT=MEMORY
37	3452	FIND CT=EDUCATION$
38	568	FIND CT=(AGE$;GERONT$)
39	5074	FIND 37 OR TRAINING/TI
40	5	FIND 36 AND 38 AND 39
41	438	FIND GEDAECHTNIS/PQ
42	15	FIND 40 OR (41 AND 38)

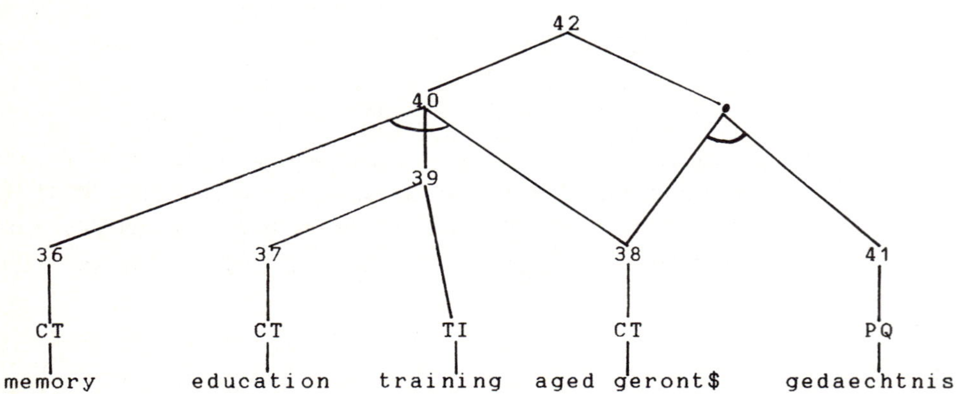

Figure 1. Example of a problem-description with its corresponding query-formulation

of the University of Trier, which maintains the PSYNDEX database.

Previous investigations about the formulation of queries used in information retrieval have been mainly concerned with the syntactical aspects of this process, such as variations in style between different groups of searchers or structural patterns of the queries. In contrast, we are primarily concerned with lexical aspects of this process, i.e. with the translation of the different words of the problem description into terms of the query. A point of departure for the investigation of this process is to describe the query as a function of the problem description and of the features of the information system. An example of an analysis using this approach is shown in table 1.

TABLE 1
Tranformation of problem-terms into query-terms

		query-terms			
		thesaurus terms	free-text terms	dropped	
problem-terms	thesaurus terms	10	9	4	23
	uncontrolled terms		4	9	13
		10	13	13	36

The data in table 1 derive from 11 searches. An example of them was displayed in figure 1. The problem descriptions of the end users, which had no face-to-face contact with the searchers, contained a total of 36 nouns and adjectives. 23 of these words correspond directly to terms included in the "Thesaurus of Psychological Index Terms" (American Psychological Association, 1985) used to index the PSYNDEX documents. Four out of these thesaurus terms were not used at all in the queries, ten were searched as descriptors and nine as free-text words. Of the remaining 13 uncontrolled terms used in the problem descriptions only four became part of the queries.

In the eleven searches from which these data are derived, thesaurus terms thus play a dominant role: they constitute the majority of the content words in the problem descriptions as well as in the queries, even in free-text searches. The Thesaurus of Psychological Index Terms thus conforms well to the vocabulary of the inexperienced end users and also of the searchers.

This kind of analysis, however, leaves many questions open. It cannot tell us, for instance, which words of the problem description of the end user will be included in the queries and which ones will be left out, nor does it show which words will be searched in descriptor fields and which ones in free-text fields.

In order to approach these questions one needs additional observations which allow further insight into the cognitive processes of the searcher during the translation of the problem description into the query. Such data may be gained through analyses of reference interviews, conducted by professional searcher and end user in order to prepare and perform bibliographic online searches. In the direct user search or in the absence of direct contact between searcher and end user the process of translating problem descriptions in query formulations is covered. The only observable behaviour is the result of the translation process, i.e. the input of the user/searcher. In contrast to this, the formulation of the query for an intermediary search is the result of an observable process, namely of the dialogue between the end user and the searcher/intermediary. The analysis of such dialogues can thus provide insight into how this translation process comes about.

Previous work on search strategies and reference interviews

Although the investigation of reference interviews became the subject of scientific interest early on, there has been little empirical work in this area to date.

Lynch (1978) and Auster & Lawton (1984) investigated which questions are posed in reference interviews in libraries and how the grammatical form in which questions are posed influences the quality of the search result and the user's satisfaction.

Hitchingham (1979) analyzed interviews between intermediaries and recipients of MEDLINE-Information with the aid of interaction categories employed in clinical psychological interview research. It became apparent that significantly differing interaction models are employed in presearch- and in online interviews, and by the client and by the searcher.

Fidel (1984, 1985) observed differing search strategies among experienced searchers: in an operational search, the searcher employs mainly the properties of the system in constructing the query. For example, he/she replaces descriptors by free-text words. In the conceptual search, he/she employs mainly descriptors, i.e. few free-text words, and tries to enhance the quality of the search by selecting suitable descriptors.

Oldroyd & Citroen (1977) describe two further search strategies: in the first, the searcher initially selects few descriptors. The later optimisation of the query is achieved by adding further descriptors with AND-connectors. In the second search strategy, a greater number of descriptors is initially selected, of which a part is later deleted. Neither

Fidel nor Oldroyd & Citroen, however, provide statistical data on the frequency or the characteristics of the strategies they describe.

Canter, Rivers & Storrs (1985) developed a formalism to describe online searches from which standards can be derived to characterize various search strategies. To design an intelligent assistant to help end users or searchers not only in conducting online searches but also in the identification and specification of the search problem and in the formulation of search queries Belkin, Brooks and coworkers (e.g. Belkin & Windel, 1984; Belkin, Seeger & Wersig, 1983; Brooks, Daniels & Belkin, 1986; Brooks & Belkin, 1983) subjected reference interviews to a number of different conversation analyses. On the basis of these analyses a mental model describing the formulation of the search problem and the query and an user modelling function has been derived. Until now, however, only six presearch interviews have been analyzed, with the help of only a limited number of observational categories which in addition were tailored primarily to an analysis of the behaviour of the searcher. Moreover, to date apparently no statistical analyses have been carried out that could provide reliable data about the logical and temporal sequences and relations between those searcher and/or client behaviours or interactions which have been found to be effective in the process of information mediation.

The interpretation and evaluation of the cited research results is restricted by the fact that the impact of a) the search problem and b) the specialist and system-specific knowledge of searchers and clients have been taken into account only insufficiently or not at all. Thus, the quality of the search results could only be estimated via subjective judgments of the user. These are influenced, however, by attitudes, which are only partially dependent on the quality of the search results.

Furthermore, on the basis of present observations, it can be only inadequately assessed how the communication between searchers and clients is influenced by differing and varying specialist and system-specific knowledge. These questions can only be adequately answered on the basis of transcribed reference interviews and searches and when the search problem and the system-specific knowledge of searchers and clients are experimentally controlled.

An approach to describing and investigating online retrieval

General characteristics of information retrieval

(1) The online-information search is a problem solving task. Its aim is the identification of documents which are useful in satisfying the information need of an end user.

(2) The usual intermediary search in online bibliographic databases is guided by two kinds of dialogues: the dialogue between the user/client and the professional searcher, the reference interview, and the dialogue between the searcher and the information system, the search proper. While the reference interview is thus a person-to-person dialogue, the search proper is a person-machine dialogue.

(3) The reference interview can be divided into the presearch interview that takes place before the search, and the online interview that takes place during the search. In these conversations, the client's search problem is specified and translated into a query by providing and commenting on information about the search problem and the information system. The contributions to these conversations can be classified a) according to the kind of speech acts initiated and executed by each conversation partner, b) according to their topics, c) according to the form of the statements, and d) according to the way various themes are linked up.

(4) Reference interviews are asymmetrical. Searcher and client have different kinds of knowledge relevant to constructing the query. The searcher knows the thesaurus and the query language, the client knows the specialist concepts that have to be delimited by a sentence in the query language. The terms of the thesaurus and the vocabulary of the client's specialist language are intersecting sets. At the beginning of a search the client often does not yet know which terms of her/his specialist language are also terms of the thesaurus, and the searcher does not know which terms of the thesaurus are relevant for delimiting the client's search problem.

(5) A query can be described syntactically as a structure of descriptors, free-text words and junctors, and semantically by the set of information or documents they delimit. 'Precision' and 'recall' and the

quality of the query calculable from them are thus part of their semantic description.

(6) Searches can be divided into consecutive steps. Each step begins with an output of the system and ends with a query by the searcher. System outputs contain descriptions of the number of delimited documents. The aim of individual search steps is to produce an improved search question, or to acquire information relevant for this purpose. In single steps, further interactions can be embedded, e.g. interrogations of the thesaurus. The individual steps can be described syntactically by the kind and the position of junctors added and deleted, and semantically by changes in the sets of delimited references. In this way, exact criteria can be defined to describe changes in the query.

Experimental design

The reference interview and the search are thus defined by the following six kinds of knowledge:

- the user's knowledge regarding the information sought after, the so-called information need
- the client's knowledge of the information system
- the client's knowledge of the subject area from which the search problem comes
- the searcher's knowledge of the information system
- the searcher's knowledge of the subject area from which the search problem comes
- the semantic breadth of the previous queries

To investigate how this knowledge affects the structure and the course of reference interviews and searches, we conduct an experiment in which the client's search problem is controlled, the quality of the query is assessed, and the influence of specialist and system knowledge of both searcher and end user on the result of the search can be estimated.

In various university libraries, professional searchers look for a total of 12 specialist articles either directly (direct-user-search) or as intermediaries for inexperienced users (mediated-search). Each of the 12 articles is relevant for three different disciplines (medicine, biology and psychology) and treats a topic pertinent for each discipline (e.g. colour vision, aphasia, neurotransmitters). The searchers have each studied one of these disciplines. They are experienced searchers carrying out online searches regularly. The end users each study one of the three disciplines in an advanced semester. They have no previous experience with online searches.

The articles are presented to the experimental subjects without author, title, abstract and list of references, together with the instruction to find out via an online search whether this article or a comparable article has already been published. In the direct-user search, the article is handed to the searcher to read before looking for related articles. In the mediated search, the articles are handed to the end users to read before turning to one of the searchers who have not read the article in question. Under this condition the elaboration of the query is the result of the conversation between the searcher and the client. Under no condition the searcher or the client are allowed to refer back to the text during the search or - in the case of a mediated search - during the presearch or online interviews. The databases to be searched and the maximal search times are determined by the experimenter. All 12 articles are contained in databases offered by the same host (DIMDI) and thus can be searched for in a common query language.

This experiment allows to test the following assumptions central to the understanding of reference interviews:

- A common specialist language of searcher and client affects how often the information system or the search problem are spoken about, how knowledge is ascertained, communicated and commented on in the interview, and who guides the choice of topic.
- In discussing a search problem a complex problem description is built up. Modifications in the query can be represented as the translation of individual elements of this problem description into the query language. In doing so, the problem descriptions are on the one hand abridged by omitting translated elements and on the other hand extended by the addition of further determinants. Linguistic characteristics of the problem-description determine subsequent changes.
- The semantic changes in the query are independent, the syntactic changes are dependent on the interviews: whether the number of

delimited documents increases or decreases with a modification of the query is mainly a function of the number of documents delimited in the previous query. The kind of modification caused by this extension or restriction is a function of the preceding interview.

- The style of interaction in the reference interview affects subsequent modifications of the query. We assume that conceptual modifications tend to arise from client dominated conversations, and operational modifications from searcher dominated conversations. In addition, we expect that the query's quality increases when the reference interview treats both the information system and the search problem, when the conversation is guided by both partners, and when specific questions are posed.
- Reference interviews can be described as interlocking context spaces (Reichman, 1986) derivable from characteristics of the linguistic surface. Each search step is guided by a context space with one of the topics: 'enhancement of recall' or 'enhancement of precision'. Within these further context spaces are embedded, dealing with the information system or the search problem.

Preliminary results

Up till now we have evaluated some reference interviews from a pilot study. These results show that the methods of analysis described above are feasible and useful. In addition, they allow the general hypotheses to be specified. The data analyzed were gathered from the interviews and search protocols of eight literature searches. All the searches were conducted by professional searchers at the Online-Information-Retrieval Center of the University Library in Konstanz.

Six users participated in the searches, four undergraduate students and two faculty members of the psychology department of the university. All users were searching for literature pertinent to psychological topics, the students with respect to their master's thesis in psychology, the faculty members with respect to research publications. Six searches were conducted in the DIMDI Psyndex and PsycInfo database, one search in the DIMDI Medlars database. In three searches, the DIALOG SSCI and PsycAlert database were used in addition.

All verbal interactions between the user and the searcher were recorded on tape from the moment when the user approached the searcher with her/his search request, until the end of the search, i.e. when the searcher logged off the system. The transcriptions of these conversations and the search logs form the material for the following evaluations. All statements of the clients and intermediaries were alloted to one of the following 4 classes:

(1) Description of content or form of the search-problem or the query

(2) Description of the information system

(3) Comments on the search results

(4) Description of information sources

In these first evaluations it became apparent, as has already been observed in other kinds of conversations, that there is a very clear thematic structure: in all the transcripts the conversation starts with a description of the search problem by the client. In some cases this consists of one nominal phrase "The question is - about bruxism - nocturnal teeth-grinding" and in other cases of several sentences "Eeh - the question is, I'm looking for something dealing with homicide (Totschlag) - with the problem of homicide - and - eeh more specifically, if there is anything at all, eeh, the perception - that is the perception of the person commiting homicide (Totschläger) - at the moment of the act"

Following this problem description the searcher tries to clarify the boundary conditions of the search. For first-users explanations concerning the information system follow, i.e. about the thesaurus and the query language. Then normally the translation of concepts and their interrelations into a query is started. This phase of the conversation is thus dominated by the goal to match as exactly as possible expressions from the query language with the problem description of the client. The dominant goal of the subsequent online interviews is the enhancement of recall and precision of the search results.

Figure 2 shows the thematic structure of a segment of an online interview. It was compiled according to the discourse grammar proposed by Reichman (1986). O stands for output of the system; I for input commands of the searcher ; C for utterances of the client and S for utterances of the searcher.

```
O: 19 NUMBER OF HITS IS  34
C: Should we enter "biochemistry" and "genetics" in addition? (1)
S: No. Because you don`t look specifically for that          (2)
C: Mhm,                                                       (3)
     but too                                                  (4)
S: It'll come anyhow,                                         (5)
     but, if you name it, only this will come                 (6)
C: Right,                                                     (7)
     but, I need that certainly                               (8)
I: 19 AND BIOCHEMISTRY AND GENETICS
```

```
context space 1
     topic = enhancement precision

     context space 2
          topic = AND-ing
                    descriptor1 = biochemistry
                    descriptor2 = genetics
          initiator = client
          speech act = (1) class = propose
                           speaker = client
                           form = question

          context space 3
               topic = search problem
               initiator = searcher
               speech acts = (2) class = direct challenge
                                 speaker = searcher
                                 form = "no"
                             (3) class = support
                                 speaker = client
                                 form = "mh"
                             (4) class = indirect challenge
                                 speaker = client
                                 form = "but"

               context space 4
                    topic = information system
                    initiator = searcher
                    speech acts = (5) class = agreement
                                      speaker = searcher
                                      form = "anyhow"
                                  (6) class = indirect chall.
                                      speaker = searcher
                                      form = "but"
                                  (7) class = agreement
                                      speaker = client
                                      form = "right"
                    terminator = client

                             (8) class = indirect challenge
                                 speaker = client
                                 form = "but"
               terminator = searcher
```

Figure 2. Thematic structure of a segment of an online interview

The segment begins with a system output. After that, the client suggests delimiting the query with the descriptors 'biochemistry' and 'genetics'. These have not yet occurred in this conversation, but in the presearch interview. The client changes the topic abruptly from the search for the first name of an author. The client's suggestion is questioned by the searcher who refers to the client's search problem (2). The client's reply cannot be put into question by the searcher, because in his previous objection he referred to the client's search problem, i.e. to an area in which the client is competent. In his next objection (6), the searcher mentions the information system, an area of knowledge in which he is competent. But even this is not accepted by the client. This conflict may be a result of the fact that the client uses the expression "and" in the vernacular sense, whereas the searcher interprets it as a Boolean operator, i.e. in the sense of the query language. A second ambiguity arises through the fact that in the further course of the conversation, the new descriptors are pronominalised, so that the referent of "it" remains unclear.

The four determinants alloted to the context spaces (topic, initiator, speech act and terminator) and the three determinants alloted to the speech acts (class, speaker and form) have to be supplemented by further parameters that describe the relations between the various context spaces and between context spaces and speech acts.

TABLE 2
Initiation and transformation of query-terms by client and searcher (absolute frequencies, combined across searches)

		transformation		
		client	searcher	
initiation	client	12	54	66
	searcher	1	40	41
		13	94	107

Loglinear Analysis (Brecht et al., 1985)

	chi square	df	p <
Initiation:	6.88	1	.01
Transformation:	23.93	1	.001
Initiation X Transformation:	5.87	1	.02

Table 2 shows who of the two interlocutors mentions the terms of the queries first, and who transforms them into the form which is used in the query. 66 of the 107 terms appearing in the queries of the eight searches were introduced by the client, but out of these 66 terms, 54 were transformed by the searcher into their final form. These transformations included replacements of the client terms by synonymous thesaurus terms and explosions, translations from German to English, the language of the database, truncations, etc. The 41 terms introduced by the searcher are mainly specifications of the publication year and the type and language of documents.

The user and the searcher thus make specific contributions to the formulation of the query: the user introduces the terms which outline the search problem, the searcher introduces the terms which delimit the search results on the basis of formal characteristics of the documents. In addition, the searcher transforms the terms introduced by the client into the form which is used in the query using his knowledge about the information system as well as his knowledge about the domain of the search problem.

During their interactive problem solving, the user and the searcher apply a common strategy that can be designated as the serial working up of the search problem. It consists in discussing the individual terms of the problem description one after the other. Each term is elaborated for as long as it takes for it to be transformed into a term of the query language satisfactory to both partners. A continual change between conceptual and formal moves takes place in this process (Fidel, 1984). Figure 3 shows an example of this strategy.

Conclusions

The results of this preliminary analyses of the reference interview can be summarized as follows:

1. A lexical analysis of the reference interview is feasible and a useful tool for understanding the transformation of a problem description into a query.
2. The structure of the reference interview reflects the underlying problem solving activity adhered to in solving the information retrieval task. It is started by a global description and analysis of the search problem and it is continued by a sequentially organized translation of problem terms into query terms.

"Eeh - the question is, I'm looking for something dealing with homicide (Totschlag) - with the problem of homicide - and - eeh more specifically, if there is anything at all, eeh, the perception (Wahrnehmung) - that is the perception of the person commiting homicide (Totschläger) - at the moment of the act (Augenblick der Tat)"

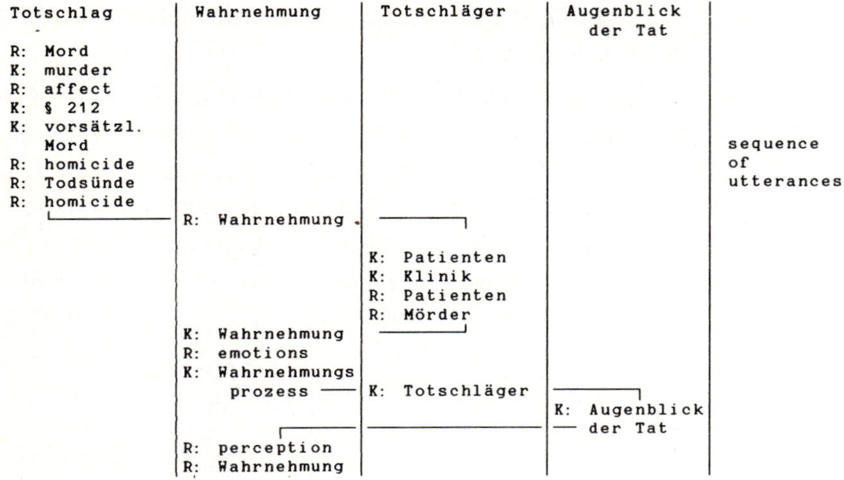

Figure 3. Example of the sequential processing of problem terms

3. The functions of the searcher in the information retrieval process are not limited to applications of his knowledge about the information system. The searcher also participates in the analysis of the search problem, and he contributes to the specification and selection of the query terms defining the search topic.

References

Auster, E. & Lawton, S.B. (1984). Search interview techniques and information gain as antecedents of user satisfaction with online bibliographic retrieval. *Journal of the American Science for Information Science,* 1984, 35, pp. 90-103.

American Psychological Association (1985). *Thesaurus of Psychological Index Terms*. Washington, D.C.

Belkin, N.J. & Windel, G. (1984). Using monstrat for the analysis of information interaction. In H.J. Dietschmann (Ed.), *Representation and Exchange of Knowledge as a Basis of Information Processes.* Amsterdam - New York: North-Holland, Elsevier Science.

Belkin, N.J., Seeger, T. & Wersig, G. (1983). Distributed expert problem treatment as a model for information system analysis and design. *Journal of Information Science,* 1983, 5, pp. 153-167.

Brecht, M-L., Bonett, D.G. & Woodward, J.A. (1985). *GENLOG II* (Microcomputer program and documentation).

Brooks, H.M. & Belkin, N.J. (1983). Using discourse analysis for the design of information retrieval mechanisms. Research and development in information systems. *Sixth Annual International ACM SIGIR Conference, ACM,* Washinton D. C., 1983, pp. 31-47.

Brooks, H. M., Daniels, P. J. & Belkin, N. J. (1986). Research on information interaction and intelligent information provision mechanisms. *Journal of Information Science,* 1986, 12, pp. 37-44.

Canter, D., Rivers, R. & Storrs, G. (1984). Characterizing user navigation through complex data structures. *Behaviour and Information Technology,* 1985, 4, pp. 93-102.

Fidel, R. (1984). Online searching styles: a case-study-based model of searching behavior. *Journal of the American Society for Information Science,* 1984, 35, pp. 211-221.

Fidel, R. (1985). Moves in online searching. *Online Review,* 1985, 9, pp. 61-74.

Hitchingham, E.E. (1979). Online interviews: charting user and searcher interaction patterns. *Proceedings of the American Society for Information Science,* 1979, 16, pp. 66-74.

Jahoda, G. & Braunagel, J.S. (1980). *The Librarian and Reference Queries. A Systematic Approach.* New York: Academic Press.

Lynch, M. J. (1978). Reference interviews in public libraries. *The Library Quarterly,* 1978, 2, pp. 119-142.

Oldroyd, K.K. & Schroder, J.J. (1982). Study of strategies used in online searching: 2. positional logic - An example of the importance of selecting the right boolean operator. *Online Review,* 1982, 6, pp. 127-133.

Reichman, R. (1986). *Getting Computers To Talk Like You and Me. Discourse Context, Focus, and Semantics. An ATN Model.* Cambridge, Mass.: MIT Press.

Soergel, D. (1985). *Organizing Information. Principles of Data Base and Retrieval Systems.* Orlando: Academic Press.

LEARNING

Mental Models and Human-Computer Interaction 1
D. Ackermann and M.J. Tauber (Editors)

THE ROLE OF THE USER MODEL IN LEARNING AS AN INTERNALLY AND EXTERNALLY DIRECTED ACTIVITY

Pamela Briggs

MRC/ESRC Social and Applied Psychology Unit,
University of Sheffield

ABSTRACT

A fundamental distinction in this paper is made between learning as an internally versus externally driven process. The role of the user's a priori understanding - discussed here in terms of the user's "mental model" - differs with respect to these different learning processes. When learning is seen as an externally directed process, i.e. when users are taught, or follow an explicit program of instruction, then the user's model plays a role in the process of communication between teacher and student, or computer-based tutor and user. Clearly novice users have prior expectations which can be seen as providing both aids and obstacles to the communication of task- or machine-relevant information. These are discussed below, in the context of a case study of forty women attending a Women's Technology Training Workshop.

When learning is an internally directed process - as is often the case with 'casual' computer users - then the role of the model becomes more pro-active, directing the learning experience so that the end result, in terms of the user's knowledge and understanding of the new system, is in some way dependent upon the initial model. This process is described in the second half of the paper, with respect to a study in which users' questions about a new computer system are used to illustrate the way in which a user's model can drive learning behaviour.

Learning as an externally directed process

We typically associate the learning process with something resembling the classroom setting. Someone, or more recently something (in the case of Computer Assisted Instruction), directs the learning process in a number of ways: by providing a structure for the information to be learned; by describing new concepts in terms of already existing ones (through some process of metaphorical reference); by establishing explicit and realistic goals which can act as 'mileposts' in the learning process; and by providing some means of assessment. An important feature of this process, as opposed to some process of self-directed learning, is that control lies in the hands of the 'expert'. All too often this means that the learning process is structured in a way which is appropriate for the subject area rather than the student. It is possible, however, to bridge the learning gulf between teacher and student, expert and novice, by presenting information in a way which is meaningful to the student. For students of computing, or for novice users, this means (a) evaluating their naive understanding of computers; and (b) presenting new information in a manner which is both compatible with this prior understanding, in order that it can be readily assimilated; and which is also compatible with the subject area, so that the new knowledge provides an appropriate base upon which to build.

A case-study of a women's computing class

As an illustration of the role of prior experience and analogy in an externally directed learning situation, a case study is presented which describes the learning experiences of a group of forty women, attending a one-year, part-time course in computing, at the Sheffield Women's Technology Training Workshop. These women are unusual students, in that they have no formal educational qualifications, having left school at fifteen; and are all unemployed, with most having spent years in the home without any experience of computers, nor any understanding of new technology. The course, too, can only be seen as an unusual choice for such women, in that it involves maths, practical and theoretical electronics, and computing hardware and software instruction, in addition to the more obvious practical skills in the use of computers.

The women described above present a particularly interesting sample, in that they are all engaged in the process of learning something entirely new, and would seem to have very little relevant experience to draw upon. They invite the following questions: 1. What kinds of understanding do these women have of the various spheres of computing, before starting the course, and 2. To what extent can their prior experience be used as a resource in the construction of suitable models i.e. is it possible to construct analogies which are both consistent with the women's prior experience, but are also useful as tools for understanding?

With these questions in mind, a series of structured individual interviews and subsequent group interviews were conducted. Within the individual interviews the women were asked about their educational background; experiences at school, work and home; and about their attitudes both past and present to maths and science and the growth of new technology. In addition they were asked detailed questions concerning their progress on the course, and their reaction to the different course components. All of the women were asked to note 'critical learning incidents' - either positive, when they felt they had mastered some difficult concept; or negative, when an issue proved particularly intangible.

In terms of their experience and understanding prior to the course, these women showed a very weak understanding of computers in general, and also virtually no knowledge of electronics and programming. They began with no functional models appropriate to these areas, and were able to draw upon only gross analogies; as when comparing a computer to "a giant brain". This particular example illustrates that an analogy can not only be useless as a learning tool, but can also be harmful to the learning process, in that it engendered in many the inappropriate belief that the computer was "clever". From an analysis of the interview transcripts, five categories of response to the question "what is a computer", were felt to represent the women's naive understanding of computers. These categories are as follows:

1. *An emotive response.*
   The naive views espoused by the women typically contained some affective component, usually negative. Thus the computer was seen as threatening in some way. Computers were described as "frightening", or as "monsters", and these views were usually associated with the belief that any attempt to use the computer would swiftly meet with disaster.

2. *An attributive response.*
   Responses in this category were indicative of a belief that the computer possessed some particular human attribute - usually intelligence. Computers were discussed in these anthropomorphic terms as being possessed of a brain, and therefore clever. Several women had been shocked to learn that they themselves would have to learn to create algorithms for problem-solving, having previously simply believed that the computer could solve any problem.

3. *A functional response.*
   Related to this, the students possessed vague and ill-formed notions of the computers capabilities and functions. While they occasionally had some notion of it being "like a calculator" they more typically drew woolly pictures of functions they had witnessed in former workplaces - related vaguely to the notion of automation, and reduction of paperwork.
4. *A featural response.*
   Here the women used the most obvious features of the computer in their models of just what a computer was. Thus computers were typically described as being rather like typewriters or televisions, and while these were reasonably accurate visual descriptions, they carried with them associations and expectations which were unfounded.
5. *A structural response.*
   This was obviously the smallest of the response categories, very few of the women had any notion of the structure of a computer. Indeed the only responses in this category were vague references to components, or one specific reference to a "silicon chip". However, these allusions were not supported by any evidence of deeper understanding, either of the function of these components, or of the essential ingredients in any computer system.

These responses, when taken together, reflect a view of the computer which could hardly be described as a 'model' in any functional sense. The problem for these women was that they lacked the specific building blocks by which appropriate models are constructed, and were therefore unable to break down a problem area into meaningful units. Unfortunately, this led to many of the women rejecting topics outright as being far too difficult for them. An example was provided by one woman, who, prior to the course, had been able to view electronics only in terms of the meaningless spaghetti of the "back of the television set". Perhaps the best illustration that these women lacked even the simplest functional models of the devices around them, was given by one student who, never having seen a floppy disc, inferred that it might be "rather like a pancake". Clearly the challenge for course trainers was to draw upon concepts familiar to the women which could also be used to build up functional models appropriate to the technology environment. At the stage of writing this report they had done this with a moderate degree of success, but there were some distinct problems. The success was reflected in the women's attitude to the course: none of the women felt that the course was beyond them, and each of the individuals interviewed expressed some amazement at the ease with which they had taken to previously 'impossible' subjects.

However, a number of problems resulted from the use of analogies which were familiar to the women, but inappropriate as learning aids, in that they could not act as functional models for that particular knowledge domain. The best illustration of this occurred within the maths classes, where the women experienced tremendous difficulties with negative numbers, largely as a result of being told to view the numbers in terms of a bank balance. The quotation below, taken from a problem diary, illustrates this point:

> "I have been thinking about a personal bank account, e.g. I have an overdraft of -7 and I have 7 (+7). I am taking the seven I have away from the -7 I am overdrawn, which seemed as though I was just clearing off the debt. But if I think I am the bank manager, I have an account here with 7 in and one that is overdrawn by 7, which is 14 altogether, now that makes sense!"

Clearly one of the problems with this analogy is that knowledge of mathematical laws takes second place to intuitive understanding of what it is to have and have not. The latter places quite severe bounds upon reasoning: almost precluding any possibility of understanding the still more complex operations of multiply and divide. It is possible to relate the real learning experiences of this type to some of the theories current within cognitive psychology. In particular the analogies generated by students and teachers can be seen in terms of Gentner and Gentner's (1983) distinction between the use of analogy to convey relations among objects, and its use to convey simple characteristics of objects. While the women more readily take to the latter, the former would seem to be more fruitful. However, analogies which can truly model the system or process being taught, and which can be readily assimilated by the students are clearly rare.

Learning as an internally directed process

While some people will undergo short training courses on the use of a new computer, many will simply be content to learn by a process of trial and error, relying upon a manual, or local expert for advice. Under these circumstances the entire learning process is driven, not by some external "expert", but by the user's own mental model of what the system is likely to offer. This point has already been made by John Carroll and his colleagues, in a series of studies of self-directed (active) learning (e.g. Carroll and Mack, 1984; Carroll and Mack, 1985; Carroll, Mack, Lewis, Grischkowsky, and Robertson, 1985). They have stressed that, in the absence of formal training, the process of acquiring new knowledge about a system is driven by the user, and is therefore contingent upon the user's model of the system and of the task at hand. Most notably, users will very rarely make systematic use of a manual, which presumably represents the "system image" (Norman, 1986) being promoted by the designer. Instead, they will create and test hypotheses about the system, and will often construct their own goals within the learning process, rather than adhere rigidly to those set by the manual.

Clearly the extent to which the user possesses a generalisable model of a computer system will affect this learning process, so that an expert will have available a metastructure to facilitate the acquisition of new information, and the subsequent development of a model particular to the new system. This metastructure is unavailable to the novice, who must simply build upon the little knowledge he or she already possesses. Here lies the fundamental difference between this learning process, and that described in the first section: novices cannot introspect into the nature of their own ignorance, and are unaware of just how to structure the learning process. The problems inherent in this type of learning procedure are anticipated by Miyake and Norman (1979), who point out that "in order to ask a question, one must first know enough to know what is not known". If one doesn't know what is not known, then one must rely upon metaphors which are often inappropriate, or upon the few cues which are available from the system itself, or which are obvious from the task. A demonstration that computer users will structure their own learning behaviour in this way is given below.

Experimental studies of novice computer users

The focus of interest in these studies was upon the kind of information users of differing experience would seek of a new system. It was felt that this was best reflected in terms of questions a user would ask about the system, given an explicit task. This situation was believed to capture something of what happens in the real-world, when people will often avoid using a computer until they have to complete an important task for which the use of the computer is essential (c.f. Carrol and Rosson's "production bias"). The task reported here was that of editing, saving and printing a letter.

In an initial study, six participants were recruited: all were students attending a one year part-time womens' course in basic computing. These women were given a letter in its complete form and asked to create a duplicate, using the personal computer system in front of them. The women were told that they could ask as many questions as they wished in order to successfully complete the task, but that they should ask these questions before they switched the machine on. Although they were discouraged from asking questions after the machine was switched on, it was recognised that this group of users would be unlikely to request sufficient a priori information to actually complete the task, therefore they were told that they could ask for information during the task, but this only if they were unable to continue. They were advised to take time and to think carefully about their preliminary questioning, and to signal clearly when they felt that they had learned enough to complete the task. They were also encouraged to take notes. The entire session was audio-taped, and extensive notes were made of the behaviour of each participant.

Transcriptions were made from the audio-tapes, and the participants' questions both before and during the task were identified. During the initial question period four categories of question emerged quite clearly: the largest category of questions were those prompted by surface features of the task. In other words, the women used the features visible in the letter before them to generate specific questions of the type: "How do I underline?"; "How do I centre text?" etc. They also asked questions prompted by the visible or 'surface' features of the system itself: concerning the 'on' switch, and various of the labelled keys. However, it was notable that while these users were systematic in their task-based questions, going through each feature of the letter in turn, they were fairly erratic in their inquiry about features of the machine. This discrepancy was also reflected in their questions about the 'hidden' features of task and machine, i.e. features not present as visible cues. Few questions addressed these hidden features, and these few were almost entirely based upon the women's limited experience with other systems, and also reflected their use of a typewriter analogy.

In general participants were ludicrously overconfident at this stage, asking on average only seven questions before asserting that they had sufficient information to complete the task. In addition, the questions generated from their own previous experience - questions which addressed the 'hidden' (and, in many cases more difficult) aspects of the task, were poorly worded from the viewpoint of extracting information. For example, the question "Do you use commands?" was met with the reply "Yes, you can ask me about the commands", but the participant didn't follow up this prompt to ask about the form of commands in general, nor about the nature of the menu system and how to access menus from the edit screen. Instead she asked for specific commands related to the surface features of the task. Also the question "Is it like a typewriter?" was in many ways too open ended to be of use. In general, participants were only successful when asking for specific procedures - but they did this almost solely for the explicit formatting demands of the letter before them. None, for example, asked "What do I do after I switch the machine on?", although this would clearly have generated a good deal of useful, procedural information. Clearly these naive users were very bad at asking a priori questions.

Holes in the participants' questioning strategies became obvious when they were forced to seek additional information during the task. Here the questions were of a slightly different nature. Participants had obviously been systematic in generating questions around the surface features of the task, since they needed to ask very few questions in this category once they had started. However, questions related to the surface features of the machine (i.e. questions inspired by features visible to the user) increased markedly. This was unsurprising given that the actual information immediately visible to the user suddenly increased as a consequence of switching on the computer. It is, however, interesting that these users felt the need to ask about on-screen information. This was obviously not self-explanatory, and seemed to lead to considerable anxiety. In particular users queried the meaning of a "status-line" which offered information as to the current mode of operation (e.g. 'insert' vs. 'typeover'; current cursor position, etc.). This information was offered in a fairly terse manner, and clearly reflected a design philosophy which assumed a certain understanding on the part of the user.

Perhaps more interesting were the questions concerning the hidden aspects of the task. The information in this category was essential to the successful completion of the task, but had been largely neglected in the question period before the task began. Users were simply better at identifying crucial information necessary to task completion if it had some obvious visual correlate, rather than simply being an essential, but implicit component of the task. The perfect example of this concerned the insertion and deletion functions. The need to delete a word is contingent upon user behaviour, and is not a visible component of the word-processing task. In an ideal situation the deletion function could be entirely redundant. However, any experience in using a word-processor, particularly in the case of a novice, should create a perceived need to know how to delete. It would seem that the users in this study were not drawing very well upon their previous experience to direct their questioning. This was also true of the save and print functions, - even when users were explicitly instructed to save and print the document, in half of the cases they forgot to ask for this relevant information until they had completed typing the document.

Since this poor performance could easily be attributed to the lack of experience of this particular user group, a further study was conducted, in which three groups of users, of differing experience, completed a task identical to that described above. The first user group were secretarial students, each with six months word-processor experience. Group two were also students, but of business studies, which meant that they had had only two weeks word-processor training, but had been given training with other software packages, so that their experience included updating spreadsheets and database inquiry. The third user group were studying to become word-processor trainers, and as such had had a number of years experience, not only of a variety of word-processing packages, but also of a variety of systems. It was anticipated that the level of the users experience would influence their questioning strategies prior to the commencement of the task i.e. the more experience, the better the metaknowledge available to guide their learning experience. This was indeed the case, but once again their relative inability to request suitable information was apparent. This was most obvious with the secretarial students who asked an average of only five questions, which fell almost entirely into category 1: visible features of the task (see figure 1). In other words, these students were no better at requesting information than those described in the first study, despite their six months word-processing experience!

SURFACE FEATURES OF THE TASK	*HIDDEN FEATURES OF THE TASK*
HOW TO UNDERLINE? HOW TO RIGHT-ALIGN? HOW TO CENTRE? HOW TO INDENT EACH PARAGRAPH? HOW TO SET THE MARGINS? HOW TO SET THE TAB STOPS?	HOW TO ACCESS THE WORD-PROCESSING PACKAGE? HOW TO CREATE A DOCUMENT? HOW TO NAME A DOCUMENT? HOW TO SAVE A DOCUMENT? HOW TO PRINT A DOCUMENT? HOW TO INSERT? HOW TO DELETE?
SURFACE FEATURES OF THE MACHINE	*HIDDEN FEATURES OF THE MACHINE*
HOW TO SWITCH ON THE MACHINE? THE FUNCTION OF THE 'PRINT' KEY? THE FUNCTION OF THE MICROSCREEN?	IS IT A WYSIWYG SYSTEM? DOES IT HAVE MENUS? DO THE MENUS STAY ON-SCREEN? DOES IT HAVE AUTOMATIC WORD WRAP? DOES THE UNDERLINING APPEAR ON-SCREEN? WILL IT APPEAR AS A BLANK SCREEN IN EDIT MODE?

Figure 1. Examples from the four question categories

Perhaps most revealing, was the contrast between the three user groups tested in the current study. This is best illustrated in figure 2. The extent to which the users were able to capitalise upon their experience, in order to acquire information about the new system, was indicated by the quality of their questioning strategies, before task commencement. It is clear from figure 2 that the secretarial students differ from either the business studies students or the experienced secretaries in that they ask significantly less questions about the hidden features of the task ($p < .05$); and it is also clear that in turn, they, and the business studies students, differ from the experienced secretaries in that the latter ask more questions about the hidden features of the machine, i.e. about the interface design ($p<.05$). Thus we find a step-like function which is explicitly related to the diversity, but not the extent, of the

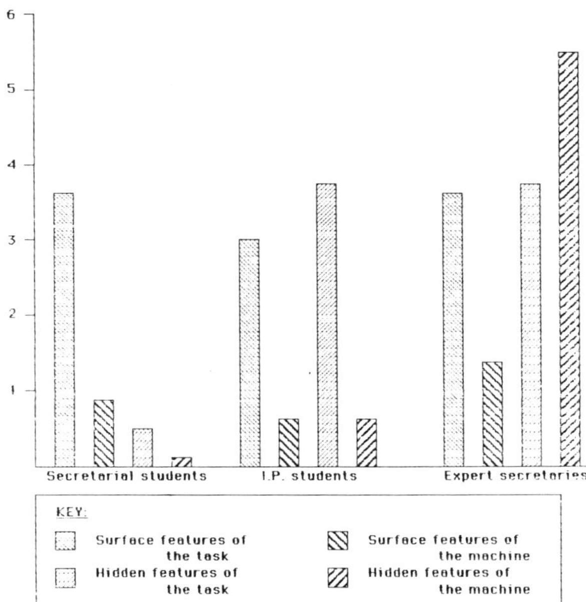

Figure 2. Number and type of questions as a function of the experience of the user group

users experience: business studies students, having had experience of more than one type of task (spreadsheet and database enquiry), seem able to understand the parameters of a word-processing task better than secretaries with solely word-processing experience. Similarly, experienced office staff, who have used different systems, in addition to different software packages, seem able to understand the ways in which one interface can differ from another. We might argue that while the secretarial students have a procedural knowledge of word-processing, gained from six months training; they lack the metaknowledge by which they can understand just what it is that they do know, and what information is lacking. As stated, this metaknowledge would seem dependent upon diversity of experience: users become aware of task and system components when they are able to compare one task/system with another, and discover those components which are invariant.

This study provides a demonstration of the way in which knowledge of a new system is acquired in the absence of any formal training. There are a number of characteristics of this learning process which are relevant to the design of an interface, manual or training package. A particularly salient feature is the absence of a good conceptual model of the system, which can act as a framework or metastructure for learning. Without this, users are forced to rely on available cues to guide the learning process, the most obvious of which are surface features of the task and the machine. Users with limited experience of systems, may also call upon experience, or analogy to aid the learning process - but there are clear disadvantages to this. Whereas users elicit information concerning surface features of the task in a fairly systematic and coherent manner to obtain straightforward descriptions of procedures they can readily adopt; they tend to call upon previous experience in a fairly ad hoc manner, and, rather than consciously generate hypotheses which they can then test, they simply make generalised and untested assumptions about the way the new system will work.

As users experience becomes more diverse, they can draw more systematically upon this experience to build up a suitable metastructure which can guide the learning process, but it is presumably only a very experienced user who is able to totally free herself from any direct reliance upon previous experience, or analogy, and use a sophisticated model, which is generalisable across systems, to influence her questioning and learning strategies. Under these circumstances the internally directed learning process might follow a pattern similar to that which would be externally imposed, although there would naturally be no problem of assimilation - given that student and teacher are one.

Discussion

In conclusion we return to the role played by the user model in an externally versus internally directed learning process. Naturally, learning will be a difficult process if the naive model possessed by the user is inappropriate; but the actual implications for the learning process are different for the different types of learning discussed above.

For externally directed learning, the information which is communicated to the user is appropriate, in so far as it is presumably (a) correct, and (b) information that the user needs to know. However, it may be inappropriate in that it is presented in a manner which doesn't allow the user to assimilate the new information. This relates to what Norman (1982) describes as the accretion of information into an already existing structure. If the user lacks an appropriate model (Norman's "existing structure"), then learning will fail. Traditionally this scenario is interpreted in terms of the user (or student) being ignorant or stupid; and yet a user who believes a floppy disc to be rather like a pancake is clearly no more stupid than someone who believes that Bombay Duck is fowl, given that both are errors which could naturally result from over-reliance upon linguistic cues. Such value judgements are useless to the learning process, and are better replaced by a viewpoint in which the communication process has simply failed. The solution involves the instructor firstly evaluating the user's naive model, and then either providing information which can be readily assimilated into this existing structure, or spending time correcting existing misconceptions.

With internally directed learning, the consequences of inappropriate or impoverished models of the computer are more severe. The casual user who structures his or her own learning process is given complete freedom. What this usually means is that users will learn what they believe they need to know, and very little else. Unfortunately, as demonstrated in the studies reported here, users will respond only to fairly obvious cues when deciding just what it is they need to know. Where users do have some model, either of the computer, or the task, then this model can be helpful in that it acts as a metastructure for the learning process; but it can also be harmful in encouraging the user to generate inappropriate hypotheses and maintain these in the face of contradictory evidence (as research scientists we are all familiar with this process). In this sense a model can act rather like a jigsaw puzzle: under those circumstances where the sketch (model) is correct, the puzzle will be assembled quickly and completely, because the user knows what to look for; but under those circumstances where the sketch is misleading, the user may waste hours searching for the wrong pieces, and may try to fit them together using force rather than perception. The task for those constructing computer manuals and help systems, is to provide a good 'sketch' for both novice and expert, at the appropriate level of complexity.

References

Carroll, J.M. & Mack, R.L. (1984). Learning to use a word-processor: by doing, by thinking and by knowing. In J.C. Thomas & M. Schneider (Eds.), *Human Factors in Computer Systems*. Norwood: Ablex.

Carroll, J.M. & Mack, R.L. (1985). Metaphor, computing systems, and active learning. *International Journal of Man-Machine Studies,* 22, pp. 39-95.

Carroll, J.M., Mack, R.L., Lewis, C.H., Grischkowsky, N.L. & Robertson, S.R. (1985). Exploring exploring a word-processor. *Human-Computer Interaction,* 1, pp. 283-307.

Carroll, J.M. & Rosson, M.B. (1987). Paradox of the active user. In J.M. Carroll (Ed.), *Interfacing Thought: Cognitive Aspects of Human-Computer Interaction.* Bradford Books: MIT Press.

Gentner, D. & Gentner, D.R. (1983). Flowing waters or teeming crowds: mental models of electricity. In D. Gentner and A.L. Stevens (Eds.), *Mental Models.* Hillsdale, N.J.: Lawrence Erlbaum.

Miyake, N. & Norman, D.A. (1979). To ask a question, one must know enough to know what is not known. *Journal of Verbal Learning and Verbal Behaviour,* 18, pp. 364.

Norman, D.A. (1982). *Learning and Memory.* San Francisco: Freeman and Co.

Norman, D.A. (1986). Cognitive engineering. In D.A. Norman & S.W. Draper (Eds.), *User-Centred System Design: New Perspectives on Human-Computer Interaction.* Hillsdale N.J.: Lawrence Erlbaum.

Mental Models and Human-Computer Interaction 1
D. Ackermann and M.J. Tauber (Editors)

ON THE RELATIONSHIP BETWEEN A USER'S SELF-TEACHING AND HIS KNOWLEDGE

Raimund Schindler and Alwin Schuster

Humboldt University, Department of Psychology, Berlin, GDR

ABSTRACT

We propose an iterative design procedure that can be regarded as a rapid-prototyping approach to user assistance. Relying on a special text-editing system some of the first steps to be taken in such an iterative developing procedure are described. In the first part of the article psychological experiments are described revealing the information using and searching behavior of self-directed learning subjects working with the text editor. In the second part, two different learning procedures - learning by examples and learning by rules - are described. Conclusions are drawn regarding the application of the experimental results obtained.

Introduction

The community of computer users is growing, yet is also becoming increasingly heterogeneous. In general, people wish to use application systems as tools to facilitate their own work. They are therefore only willing to acquire the body of knowledge that is required to achieve this goal. Conditions of this kind make certain demands on training procedure:

1. In order to meet the ever-increasing training needs the training of users should be decentralized, i.e. it should be provided at the place of work.
2. The greater the functionality of an application system and the greater the differences between the future users with regard to their individual dispositions, the greater is the need for individualizing the training procedure.
3. It must be ensured that training procedure will never require more than a very small number of instructors. Thus, computer assisted

learning is also of growing importance in user training. The application system itself can be extended by tutorial components that may assist the user in acquiring und using the knowledge required for interactive task/problem solving.

At present, the extension of application systems by tutorial or help components is not only expensive but also raises a large number of unresolved questions (Sleeman & Brown, 1982; Spada & Opwis, 1985). At this point, we should like to stress no more than two basic problems:

1. The design of a tutorial has to start with the specification of the knowledge to be taught. At present, this requires experimental or empirical investigations to be made because the system is not generally described in a way that allows deriving the body of knowledge that the future user has to acquire if she/he wishes to use the system properly. There are very interesting approaches to modelling the user's knowledge, but most of them have certain limitations (see Green, Schiele & Payne, 1988); above all, they are not at present used by system designers to give a user related description of the system.
2. It is also very difficult to formulate a control or tutorial strategy. How can learners in view of their specific dispositions (e.g. personality factors, cognitive styles, preferred personal strategies, and personal knowledge) be given efficient assistance or guidance? The system has to provide methods and means of guiding the trainee in educational terms. This means that it must specify when to interrupt a user's task solving, what to say, and how best to say it in order to provide the learner with instructionally effective advice. These decisions should not be based on the intuition of the tutorial's designer but on experimental and/or empirical findings on the user's learning in this domain.

In order to tackle these problems, we propose an iterative strategy that can be regarded as a rapid-prototyping approach to user assistance. The starting point is a self-guided learning procedure that is gradually being extended by external interventions. In the first step, future users are asked to complete tasks by using the device. The user can gather the required information from an external source (at the very beginning by asking a human expert for instance). The task relevant entities of the system can be derived from analysing the information searching behavior of future users; and learning problems can be specified in this way. On the basis of the results obtained, external interventions can be designed that aimed at assisting users in meeting the demands. The effect that every intervention has on the efficiency of user learning is analysed in experimental and/or empirical investigations. This procedure can be stopped if external interventions do not provide efficient assistance to the user, or if there are hardware limitations to the application system.

Relying on this iterative procedure of developing tutorials, we can meet training needs at a very early point (efficiency is not, of course, very high when the procedure begins). We should like to stress that we hope that we shall get results that not only deepen our understanding of user learning in a particular domain, but will also allow deriving of generalizable approaches to assisting or guiding users in acquiring and using knowledge in further application programs.

In this paper we are going to describe this procedure in some detail. Our work is based on a text-editing system (TEXT 20), which is menu driven and has no capacity for direct manipulation. What we wish to do is to assist future users in operating the system.

Method

To find useful approaches to assisting future users in operating the text-editing system, we used the method of question asking. The method can be regarded as a prototype of self-guided individual learning in communication with other persons, written materials, or the computer system itself.

According to the general framework developed by Flammer (1981), question asking is considered as resulting from cognitive processes; it is an indicator of both productivity and goal formation in task/problem solving. It begins by establishing a shortage of information and ends with the decision to ask a question. Question asking can therefore give us information on the regulation of knowledge based task/problem solving behaviour (Krause & Hagendorf, 1986).

In our investigations, subjects were asked to use the device to accomplish four different text-editing tasks. The tasks were selected in a way that allowed them to cover the whole scope of the functionality of the system. Each text-editing task consisted of several subtasks (e.g.

specify subprogram, load text file, name text file, delete a character, insert a word, etc.). The subtasks were either different, or identical, or similar. The order of the four learning tasks was decided by the experimenter; it was the same for all of the subjects. Subjects were instructed to accomplish the four text-editing tasks without making errors. To analyse the information that subjects called up in building their knowledge of the interactive environment they were allowed to ask the experimenter for all the information that they thought relevant to understanding the way in which the task was to be completed with the help of the device. To emphasize this part of the instructions, the experimenter asked subjects to explain to an uninitiated person how to operate the system, after they had finished the self-teaching learning procedure. Each editing task had to be repeated till each subject met a predefined learning criteria: 80 per cent of the subtasks that the learning tasks consisted of had to be completed correctly and without any help by the experimenter. To control the information searching and using processes the experimenter did not allow subjects to operate the system directly. They had to verbalize everything that they intended to do. The experimenter provided feedback about the correctness of the subject's activity. It is clear that this experimental procedure does not simulate learning by exploration. The dialogue between subjects and experimenter was recorded on tape.

Experiment 1: aim and test subjects

In the experimental situation described above the user had to organize his/her learning activities him-/herself. Self-teaching is generally difficult for a lot of pupils and does not lead to high levels of attainment. So, the question can be asked: how can this self-teaching be given assistance?

One of the critical points of self-teaching through question asking is that the learner can select and process those items of information from the environment that are relevant to meeting the learning goal: task completion with the help of the device. The general barrier in this learning process is that the learner can only ask questions with regard to the knowledge currently existing in his/her memory. We therefore assume that a user can be effectively assisted if a specific knowledge base is established before she/he starts the self-guided learning procedure.

It could be argued that human learning does not only depend on the knowledge that a learner already has but also on other personal dispositions (Jenkins, 1979; van Muylwijk et al., 1983; van der Veer et al., 1984; Frese et al., 1987). This is to say, personal knowledge can be regarded as only one of the personal characteristics that the efficiency of learning depends on. The efficiency of learning may therefore depend to a greater extent on, e.g., personality factors, cognitive styles and preferred personal strategies than it does on the actual knowledge of the learner. Both the verification and the rejection of this hypothesis are of importance to the design of tutorials.

Our first experiments put the hypothesis to a very crude test. We used two groups of subjects whose relevant knowledge differed. In the first group (*OW*), there were six undergraduate students of psychology who had no specific knowledge of the hard- and software of interactive computer systems in general and of the text editor in particular. The second group of subjects (*IN*) consisted of six undergraduate students of informatics who did have a knowledge of the hard- and software of dialog systems and of how to operate interactive systems, but had no specific knowledge of how to operate the text editor.

If the efficiency of self-guided learning really depends to a considerable extent on a person's knowledge of the learning domain, there should be a difference between these two groups regarding learning efficiency.

Experiment 1: results

Difficulty of learning

In order to assess the learning difficulty in each of the subtasks that the four editing tasks consisted of, we counted the instances of incorrect activity (faulty reproduction, production or hypothesis) that the subjects realized until the subtask was correctly completed. In this way we calculated the average for each text-editing task (learning task). Figure 1 presents the results, which are quite unambiguous: learning demands could be fulfilled more easily by the students of informatics (IN) than by the subjects who were complete computer novices (OW). With the exception of trail 3.1, this statement is true from the first

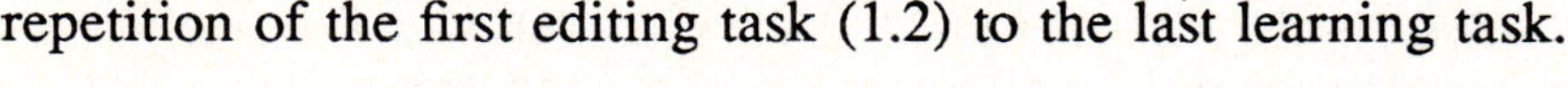
repetition of the first editing task (1.2) to the last learning task.

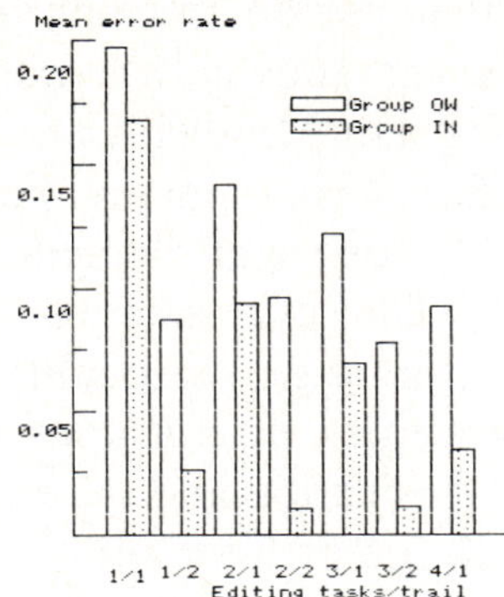

Figure 1. Difficulty of self-teaching and prior knowledge

We can hence confirm our hypothesis: personal knowledge influences self-guided learning to a considerable extent. Regarding practical novice user assistance, this result is worthless because user training will never use instruction techniques to realize the knowledge that students of informatics have acquired. But on the basis of this result we can now ask a more precise question: what kind of knowledge base can be used for effectively assisting the self-guided learning of novice users?

To obtain knowledge bases of this kind, let us analyze the information searching and using behaviour of the two groups in greater detail.

Problems of the acquisition and use of knowledge

Elements of human-computer interaction

To establish the reasons for the advantage that the IN group enjoyed in learning how to operate the device, we analyzed the items of information that the subjects of the two groups called up to build their knowledge structures.

The subjects of either group used (i.e. asked for, produced, or reproduced) exactly the same classes of information. The most important ones were:

a) Verbal phrases to label the actual transformation (*W*). Phrases of such kind consisted of a verb representing the transformation (e.g. delete, load, insert, etc.) and a noun representing the objects that the transformation acted on (e.g. a character, or a subprogram).

b) Combinations of alphanumeric features displayed on the screen, or word markers to label them (*X*). They were used by subjects to represent both the initial and the anticipated perceptible states of the system.

c) Units of action (*HE*), which represent the physical actions that the user has to perform in order to accomplish an anticipated object transformation. In our experiments the units of action consisted of specific keystroke sequences on the keyboard.

d) System processes (*SV*), which represent task relevant processes of the system that are not made visible. They were used by subjects for understanding why a particular unit of action or a specific state of the system had to be realized in the completion of the text-editing tasks.

These four classes of information represent the task relevant entities of the device that the subjects of the two groups called up to understand task completion with the help of the text editor. According to Tauber (1987) they can be regarded as the system's components that the user's virtual machine consists of. We are going to call them *elements of interaction.*

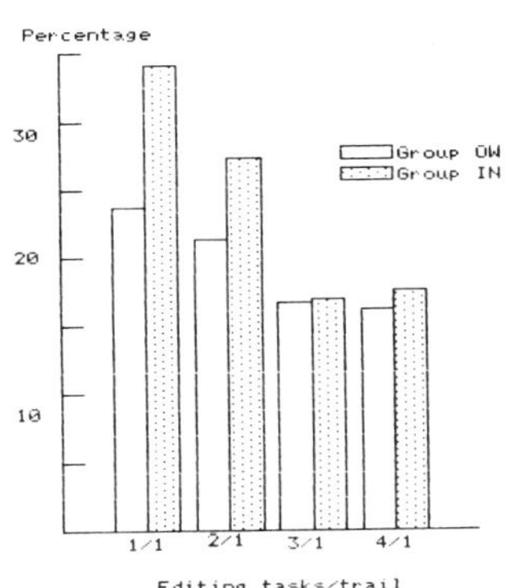

Figure 2. Percentage information used

Figure 2 shows that there were differences between the two groups concerning the extent to which the elements of interaction were made use of in the course of learning. In order to complete the first two learning tasks, the students of informatics (IN) used the elements of interaction to a larger extent than the OW group did. The differences were not, however, significant because there were considerable great inter-individual differences between the subjects of the OW group.

Units of human-computer interaction

It is generally accepted (e.g. Klix, 1976, 1985, 1986; Hoffmann, 1986) that human beings acquire and structure knowledge in terms of the mental operations and physical activities that they have to perform to meet the demands made in a given domain. Text-editing tasks are tasks of object manipulation. Real objects (e.g. text units, i.e. characters, words, sentences, etc.) have to be built on virtual objects and transformed by being delegated to the system until there are no differences between the features of the objects and the anticipated state. The top level goal (text editing) is subdivided into a hierarchical sequence of subgoals (transformations, dialogue steps) that have to be complete with the help of the device.

Our experiment showed that the subjects of the two groups used the elements of interaction with regard to the subgoals that they had to achieve in reaching the top level goal. As a result, they acquired situational or event related knowledge (Klix, 1985, 1986). It consisted of concepts that were linked by semantic relations representing the role (functional meaning) of the concepts. As regards HCI, we are going to call such conceptual entities *units of interaction.*

Units of interaction represent the informational base that the subject's completion of object transformation relied on. In terms of the elements of interaction that they consisted of, different types could be distinguished. Figure 3 presents a few examples. Type 1 represents the simplest unit of interaction: nothing but a unit of action (HE, i.e. a single keystroke or a sequence of keystrokes on the keyboard) is used to carry out a transformation. The empty circle symbolizes the fact that the unit of action can be conditionally related to either the actual system state (X), or to the last transformation (W), unit of action (HE) or system process (SV). The labelled arcs represent the role that the elements of interaction can play in task completion. We can see from figure 3 that either the transformation (W), the visible state of the system (X) or the non visible system process (SV) can play the role of the user's actual goal (represented by FIN1, FIN2, FIN3). Type 8 represents the most complex of the unit of interaction: all the four elements of interaction were used for completing the transformation. It is clear from figure 4 that this type was used very rarely in either experimental group.

The kind of role played by the elements of interaction depended on the conditional relation that triggered the unit of interaction. To illustrate (see type 3 in figure 3), if the unit of action was conditionally related to one of the four conceptual entities, the system state played the role of the user's actual goal (represented by FIN2).

But if the unit of interaction was triggered by a conditional link between the system state and one of the elements of interaction (symbolized by dotted arcs) the unit of action played the role of an instrument (represented by INS 3). Generally speaking, a unit of interaction could be triggered by all conceptual entities it consisted of.

All in all, the examples given make clear that subjects made very flexible use of the four elements of interactions to complete a transformation.

Figure 4 presents the percentage of the different types of interaction for the first two editing tasks. At this point we should merely like to focus our attention on the result showing that, in the first two trails (SA1 and SA2), the group OW used only the unit of action for task completion more often than the students of informatics did.

Integration and composition of knowledge

Because subjects had to verbalize everything that they intended to do in accomplishing the given learning tasks, we were able to analyse two questions: first, to what extent were the subjects of the two groups able to reproduce or produce the information required; and secondly, what kind of compositions did they realize in the course of learning.

Let us first look at the first question. The results are presented in figure 5. The upper part of figure 5 shows the percentage of those of the subjects' activities that make clear that they had no problems in reproducing and/or producing the task relevant entities of the system.

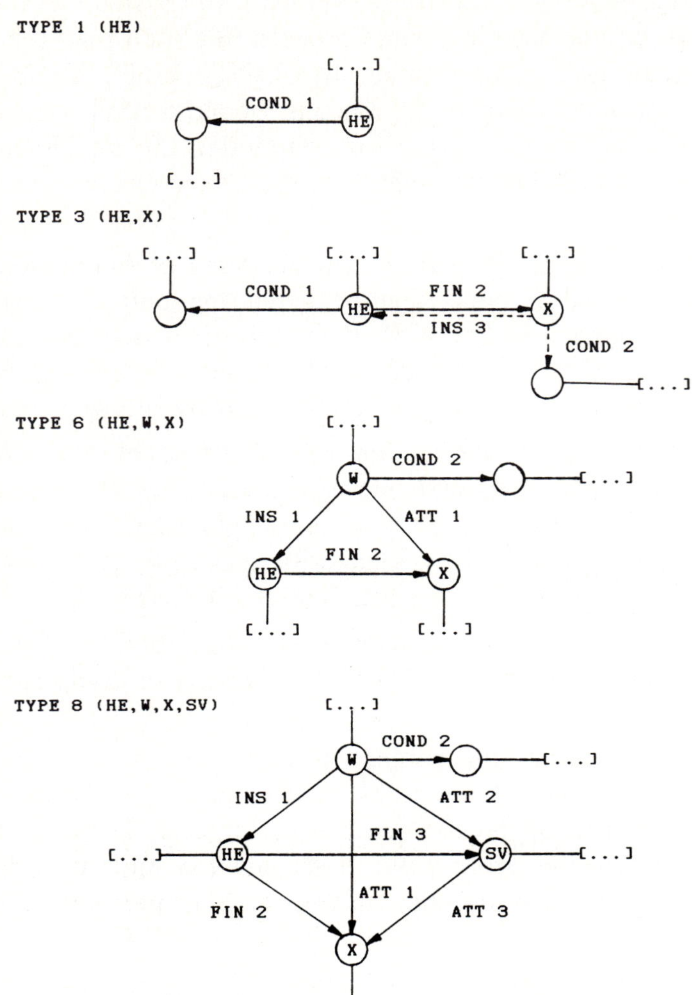

Figure 3. Types of units of interaction (selected examples). Symbols enclosed in circles represent the elements of interaction (HE: unit of action, X: system state, W: transformation, SV: system process). Brackets represent the properties of the elements of interaction. The empty circles can be filled by all of the four elements of interaction. The labelled arcs represent the role that the elements of interaction can play (COND: condition, FIN: finality, ATT: attribute, INS: instrument). Further explanations are given in text.

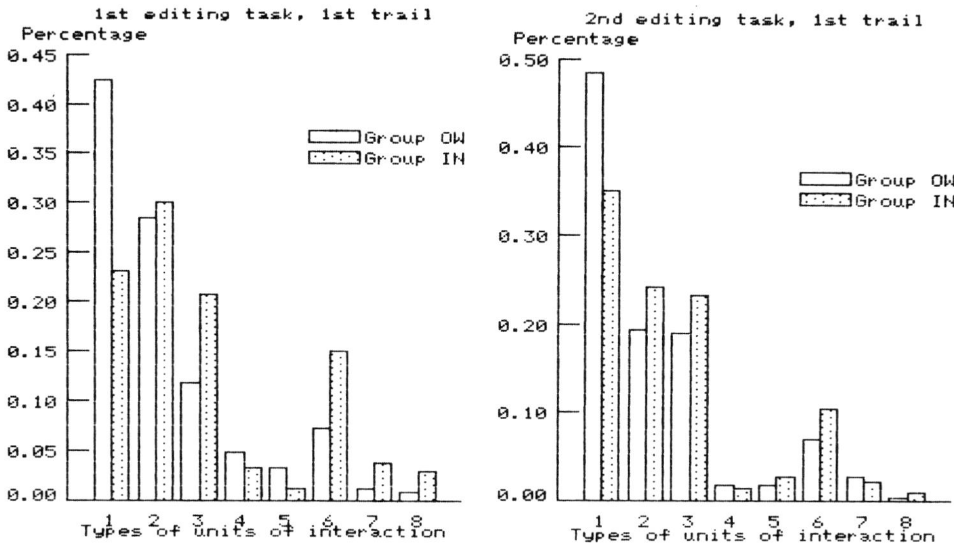

Figure 4. Used types of units of interaction. 1: HE; 2: HE, W; 3: HE, X; 4: HE, SV; 5: HE, W, SV; 6: HE, W, X; 7: HE, SV, X; 8: HE, W, SV, X. : Group OW; : Group IN; upper part: first editing task, first trail; lower part: second editing task, first trail.

The lower part presents the percentage of the activities that makes clear that subjects had such problems.

All in all, we can be gather from figure 5 that the students of informatics (IN) were better capable of reproducing items of information that they had asked the experimenter for, and they were also better able to produce task relevant conceptual entities of the system on the basis of the knowledge actually stored in their memory than group OW was.

Now let us turn to the second question. In the course of learning, the units of interaction are changed as a result of two processes. The

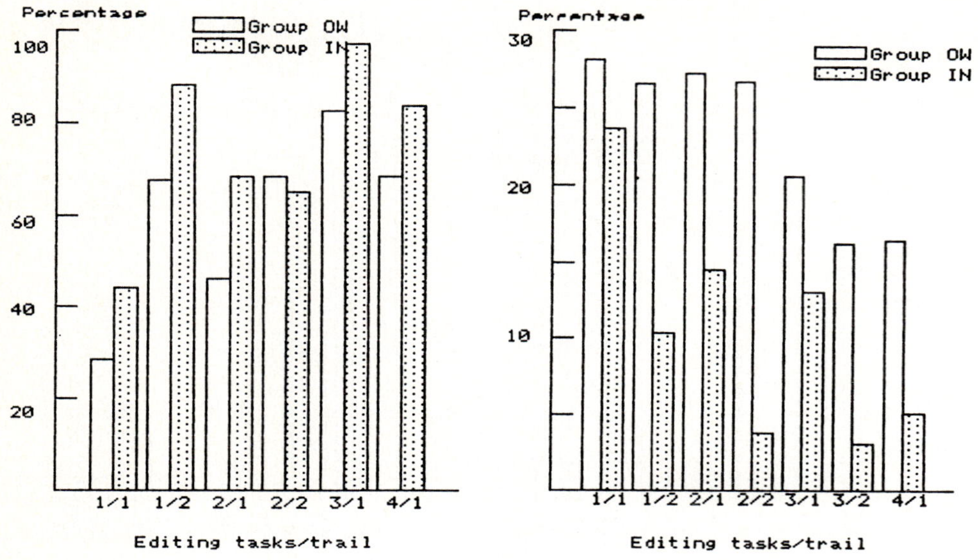

Figure 5. Integration of information; left part: no integration problems; right part: integration problems.

first process, generalization, is based on recognized similarities between different units of interaction and creates a new unit, which captures what the individual units of interaction have in common (Anderson, 1982). Our experiments produced a great deal of evidence showing that both groups of subjects realized generalization processes of this kind; yet we had to use another methodical approach in order to analyze processes of this kind in detail.

As a result of the second process, composition, the number of units of interaction can be reduced by building "macrounits" (Anderson, 1982). The creation of such macrounits is based on recognized regularities in sequences of transformations. For instance, in order to accomplish an editing task with the help of the system, the user has to load the application program. This requires two steps to be taken: first, to input in the command "call" (by means of the unit of action call, FERT), and second input in the argument "text" (by means of the unit of action of text, FERT). At the beginning of their learning, subjects used two units of interaction to accomplish the goal, but later it was a macrounit that embodied this sequence of transformation.

We used data reproduction to analyze composition processes of this kind in both of the experimental groups. Figure 6 shows that the students of informatics created appropriate macrounits to a larger extent than the novice learners did.

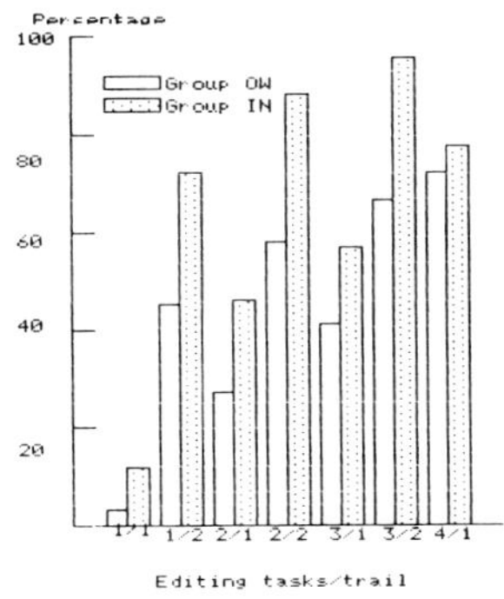

Figure 6. Knowledge composition.

To sum up the results: the difficulty of a user's self-teaching depends to a considerable extent on his personal knowledge.

There were significant differences between the two experimental groups with regard to the items of information they used to meet the learning demands. At the beginning of their learning, the students of informatics used the information available (elements of interaction) to a larger extent than the novice learners did. Furthermore, in the course of learning there were also differences with regard to the informational base (units of interaction) that subjects called up to complete the transformation required. At the beginning of their learning, the novice learners used only the units of action for task completion more often than the students of informatics did.

There was also evidence showing that the students of informatics could organize information to be learnt, in a more appropriate manner than the novice learners could. This can first be gathered from the result that the IN group was better able to produce and/or reproduce the task relevant components of the system than the OW group was and, second, from the result that the students of informatics created more appropriate "macrounits" than the novice learners did.

Experiment 2: aim and independent variables

The results obtained allow drawing the following conclusions. In order to assist the user in his self-teaching the following three requirements have to be taken into account:

First, future users must be able to recognize the task relevant components of the system; second, they must understand what role (functional meaning) these components play in task completion; and third, they must be able to classify in an appropriate manner, the conceptual entities to be learnt. The data obtained suggest that all of the three requirements depend to a considerable extent on the learner's prior knowledge.

Since we shall never be able to use instruction techniques to realize the knowledge that students of informatics have acquired, we shall have to look for another knowledge base that can assist novice users in meeting this requirements. Waern (1986) investigated the role of metaphors in instructing novice users on how to learn a word processing system. She showed that a metaphoric description of the system is only useful at the initial step of learning. So, we focused our attention on more detailed knowledge bases.

In order to support the above mentioned requirements of self-teaching, we realized two different learning procedures:

- learning by examples, and
- learning by rules.

The first procedure was realized as follows: Subjects who were complete computer novices were gradually being instructed on how to complete the first editing task. This is to say they were taught some of the task relevant components of the system on the basis of an example. Afterwards, they had to complete the other three editing tasks. Any shortages of information could be supplied by question asking (see section on method). Three different groups of subjects were used in the second set of experiments. Each group consisted of six undergraduate students.

The three groups were instructed on the completion of the first editing task with the help of different types of units of interaction. Type 3 (HE,X) was used in one group (*B1*), Type 6 (HE,X,W) in a second group (*B2*) , and Type 8 (HE, X,W,SV) was used in a third group (*B3*). This variation was aimed at a more accurate analysis of the role of the different elements of interaction in the self-guided learning procedure. It is generally assumed that learning by examples is the main influence on the information searching behaviour of the learners.

Our last group (RE) was taught metarule knowledge before the self-teaching procedure started. This means that before the subjects of this group had to learn the completion of the four editing tasks, they were taught eight generalized units of interaction. Conceptual entities of this kind represent possible classifications of the set of concrete units of interaction regarding existing regularities of task oriented HCI.

Generally speaking, metarules of this kind represent event types (Klix, 1985, 1986). Klix uses this term instead of schema, because the latter is used in different contexts and with different meanings. Event types represent the classification and explanation of an external domain by human beings. In metarules of this kind the semantic relations can be regarded as functions that map one particular set of conceptual entities on another. Both of them are characterized by a well defined set of properties.

The metarules were given verbally by means of IF/THEN statements. For instance:

IF (X: A word is displayed on the screen, and there are six (or less than six) marked positions behind it, and the cursor is located at the first of the marked positions)

AND (W: Your goal is to put in a string so as to fill all the positions)

THEN (HE: You will have to strike particular numerical keys and, afterwards the FERT key).

The actual state of the system was taught not only verbally, but also by presenting schematic screen layouts. In order to test their understanding of the eight metarules, subjects were presented concrete screen layouts and subtasks, and had to write down the properties of the correct unit of action.

Experiment 2: results

In order to assess the influence that the knowledge bases provided had on the efficiency of the user's self-teaching we evaluated the difficulty of learning (see above). The results from all of the four groups are presented in figure 7. To allow easy comparison the results of the two groups of the experiment 1 (OW and IN) were added. At first, let us focus our attention on the three "example" groups (B1, B2, B3). It can be seen that the learning difficulty does not depend in a negative monotonous relationship to the complexity of the instructed units of interaction taught.

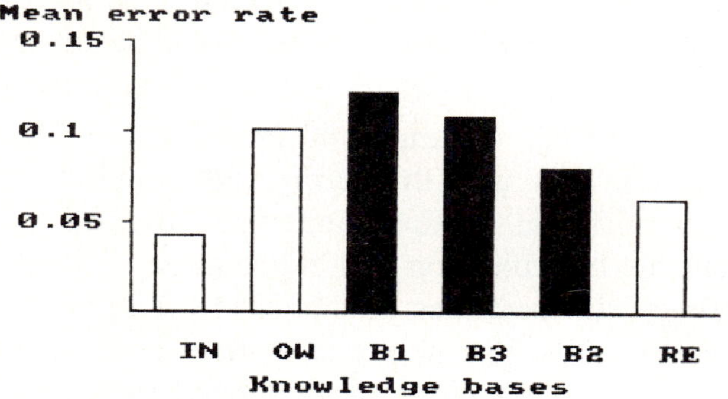

Figure 7. Difficulty of self-teaching and prior knowledge (IN : students of informatics; OW: novice learners;
"example" groups:
B1: HE, X (type 3 of units of interaction)
B2: HE, W, X (type 6 of units of interaction)
B3: HE, W, SV, X (type 8 of units of interaction)
"rule" group: RE)

The best group (i.e. the one with the least learning difficulty) was the group B2, which was instructed to carry out the first editing task with the help of Type 6 (HE,X,W) of unit of interaction. The additionally teaching of the system processes (Type 8 of unit of interaction ; see Group B3) did not reduce the learning difficulty.

Furthermore, it can be seen from figure 7 that the RE group, which was given metarules before the self-teaching procedure started, tended to have less difficulty in meeting the learning demands than the three "example" groups had. Not all of the differences were significant, though, group B2 had the same learning difficulty as group RE had.

Discussion

To sum up, the following conclusions can be drawn from the results. System processes are not generally task relevant components of the system. In this paper we cannot explain in greater detail why they were mainly used by the subjects when there were either inconsistencies in the human-computer interface, or the perceptible system state did not make clear which particular transformation had to be performed.

Now let us turn to the result that rule based learning did not generally exceed learning by examples, as might have been assumed. One problem is related to the construction of metarules of such kind. Since we did not know any method by which the task relevant regularities of an existing human-computer interface can be derived (as far as we know, the existing approaches do not take into account the features of the system states; see Green, Schiele & Payne, 1988), the metarules taught would probably not cover the whole range of regularities.

A second problem is that the interface of the system that our investigations were based on were not completely consistent. We anticipate that this will be true of most of the existing human-computer interfaces. Hence, there are regularities regarding the task relevant components of a system, but there are exceptions to the rules, too. It can be assumed that the effectiveness of rule based learning depends on the consistency of the human-computer interface: the greater the consistency, the greater can be the efficiency of rule based learning. In order to test this hypothesis, a method is needed that allows realizing a quantitative assessment of the consistency of human-computer interfaces.

Conclusion

Since there are a large number of unsolved theoretical and practical problems in designing efficient tutorials or assistances, we outlined an iterative designing procedure that can be regarded as a rapid-prototyping approach to user assistance. The main idea is that the design process should start with careful investigations into the user's self-teaching processes. On the basis of results that can be obtained, conclusions may be drawn as to the external interventions that will allow future users to be efficiently assisted in acquiring and using the task relevant knowledge regarding the system.

Relying on a special text-editing system we described some of the first few steps to be taken in an iterative developing procedure of this kind.

Although there were no significant differences between groups B2 and RE, we propose that the self-teaching of future users of the text-editing system should be taught the metarule knowledge used in our experiments. The units of interaction used by the subjects to build their own knowledge about the system are very useful in implementing the knowledge base of a passive help system. Our future research will be aimed at adding active components to this system.

References

Anderson, J.R. (1982). Acquisition of cognitive skills. *Psychological Review,* 89, pp. 369-406.

Flammer, A. (1981). Toward a theory of question asking. *Psychol. Res.,* 43, pp. 407-420.

Jenkins, J.J. (1979). Four points to remember: a tetrahedal model and memory experiments. In L.S. Cermak & F.I.N. Craik (Eds.), *Levels of Processing in Human Memory* (pp. 429 - 446). Hillsdale, N.Y.: Erlbaum.

Frese, M., Albrecht, K., Altmann, A., Lang, J., Papstein, P., Peyerl, R., Pämper, J., Schulte-Göcking, H., Wankmüller, I. & Wendel, R. (1987). *The effects of an active development of the mental model in the training process: Experimental results on a word processing system.* Department of Psychology, Ludwig- Maximilians-Unversität. München.

Green, T.R.G., Schiele, F. & Payne, S.R. (1988). Formalisable models of user knowledge in human-computer interaction. In G.C. van der Veer, T.R.G. Green, J. Hoc & D. Murray (Eds.), *Working with Computers: Theory versus Outcome.* London: Academic Press.

Hoffmann, J. (1986). *Die Welt der Begriffe.* Berlin: VEB Deutscher Verlag der Wissenschaften.

Klix, F. (1976). Über Grundstrukturen und Funktionsprinzipien kognitiver Prozesse (Aspekte eines Zugangs zur Analyse und Synthese geistiger Leistungen). In F. Klix (Ed.), *Psychologische Beiträge zur Analyse kognitiver Prozesse* (pp. 9-56). Berlin: VEB Deutscher Verlag der Wissenschaften.

Klix, F. (1985). Über die Nachbildung von Denkanforderungen, die Wahrnehmungseigenschaften, Gedächtnisstruktur und Entscheidungsoperationen einschließen. *Z. Psychol.,* 193, 3, pp. 175-211.

Klix, F. (1986). Memory research and knowledge engineering. In F. Klix & H. Wandke (Eds.), *Macinter I.* Amsterdam: North-Holland.

Krause, B. & Hagendorf, H. (1986). Exploratory investigations in acquiring and using information in problem solving. In F. Klix & H. Wandke (Eds.), *Macinter I.* Amsterdam: North-Holland.

Park, O.C., Perez, R.S. & Seidel, R.J. (1986). Intelligent CAI: old wine in new bottles or a new virtage? In G.P. Kearsley (Ed.), *Artificial Intelligence and Instruction: Applications and Methods.* Reading, MA: Addison-Wesley.

Schindler, R. & Fischer, F. (1986). Effectiveness of training as a function of the knowledge structure taught. In F. Klix & H. Wandke (Eds.), *Macinter I.* Amsterdam: North-Holland.

Schindler, R. & Fischer, F. (in press). Vermittlung von Handlungswissen - Ein Ausbildungskonzept zur Bedienung mikroelektronischer Textverarbeitungssysteme. *Psychologie für die Praxis.*

Schindler, R. (1987). Hilfen für Benutzer: Möglichkeiten und Probleme aus psychologischer Sicht. In W. Schönpflug & M. Wittstock (Eds.), *Software-Ergonomie '87*. Stuttgart: Teubner.

Schindler, R. & Schuster, A. (1987). Rechnergestützte Benutzerschulungen: Gestaltungsprobleme und -möglichkeiten aus psychologischer Sicht. *Wiss. Z. der Humboldt-Universität zu Berlin, Math.-Nat. R.,* 36, 5, pp. 448 - 455.

Sleeman, D. & Brown, J. S. (1982). *Intelligent Tutoring Systems*. London - New York: Academic Press.

Spada, H. & Opwis, K. (1985). Intelligente tutorielle Systeme aus psychologischer Sicht. In M. Mandl & P.M.Fischer (Eds.), *Lernen im Dialog mit dem Rechner*. München - Baltimore: Urban & Schwarzenberg.

Tauber, M.J. (1986). Top-down design of human-computer interfaces. In S.K. Chang, T. Ichikawa & R.P.A. Ligomenides (Eds.), *Visual Languages*. New York: Plenum Press.

van Muylwijk, B., van der Veer, G.C. & Waern, Y. (1984). On the implications of user variability in open systems - An overview of the little we know and of the lot we have to find out. *Behaviour and Information Technology,* 2, pp. 313- 326.

van der Veer, G.C., van Muylwijk, B. & van de Wolde, J. (1984). Introducing statistical computing of the cognitive system of the naive user. In G.C. van der Veer, M.J. Tauber, T.R.G. Green & P. Gorny (Eds.), *Readings on Cognitive Ergonomics - Mind and Computers* (pp. 62-73). Lecture Notes in Computer Science, Vol.178, Berlin, Heidelberg, New York: Springer Verlag.

Waern, Y. (1986). *On the role of mental models in instruction of novice users of a word processing system.* HUFACIT report, Department of Psychology, University of Stockholm, No 6.

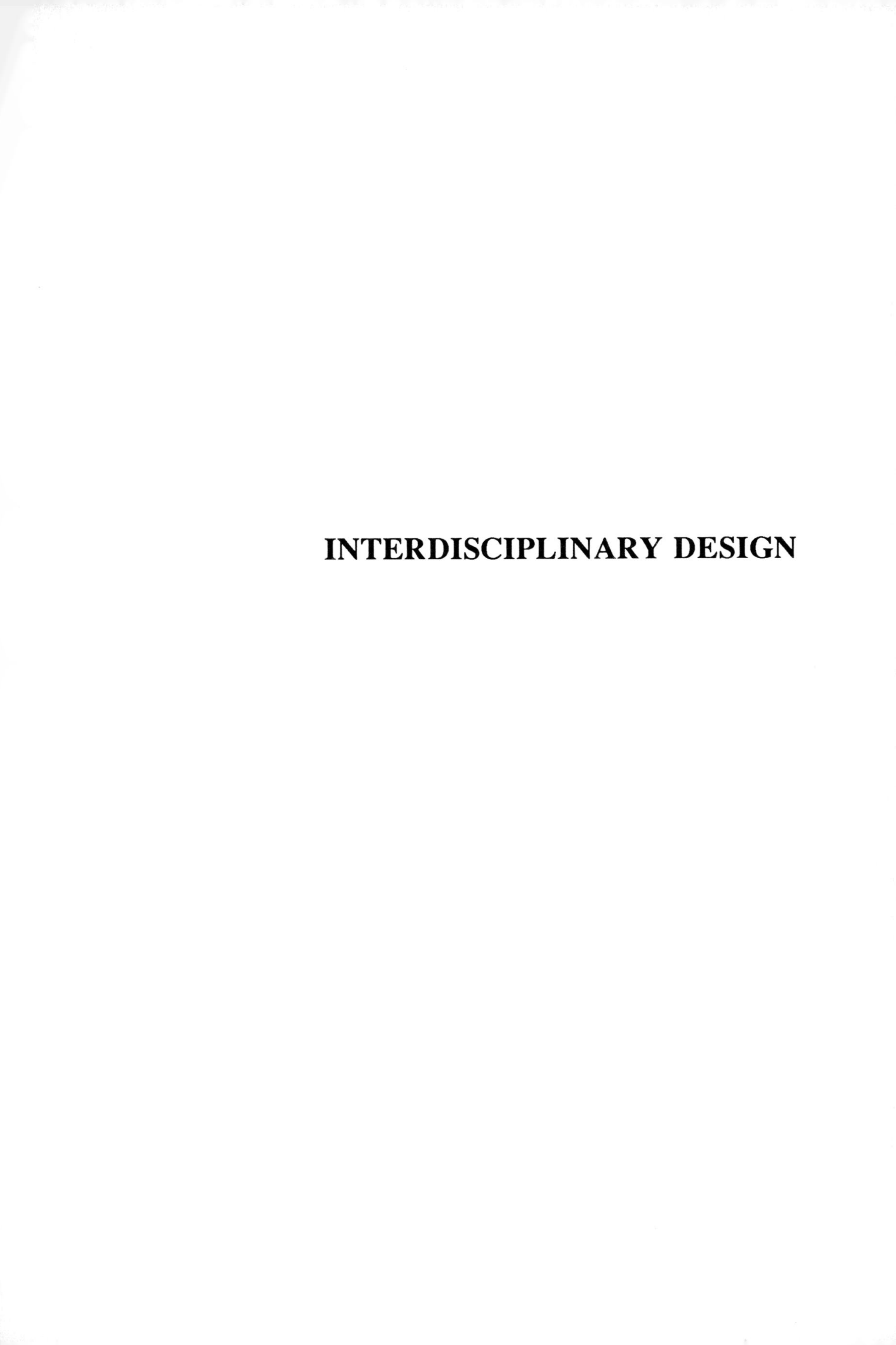

INTERDISCIPLINARY DESIGN

Mental Models and Human-Computer Interaction 1
D. Ackermann and M.J. Tauber (Editors)
Elsevier Science Publishers B.V. (North-Holland), 1990

TOWARD ADAPTIVE HUMAN-COMPUTER INTERFACES

Elke Wetzenstein-Ollenschläger and Hartmut Wandke
Humboldt University, Berlin, GDR

ABSTRACT

In the applied research of engineering psychology, particularly in the field of HCI, we are faced with a problem for which there is no generally applicable approach. A well founded theoretical frame does not exist. That is why a singular specific interface is designed either on an experimental basis or just following the subjective opinion or intuition of the designer. From our point of view, the following course should be followed to obtain general design solutions for practical application. This requires a multi-step approach. Based on the scientific knowledge of cognitive psychology it is possible - as it is shown for the example - to design interface components through the analysis of knowledge and task dimensions. As a further step, methods for analysing the user's knowledge and tasks should be worked out. The implementation of such methods and rules in User Interface Management Systems could lead to an interface design adaptive or flexible with regard to changing classes of tasks and user characteristics.

Present-day problems of interface design

In the course of increasing the efficiency of personal computers and their extensive application for very different groups of users and due to the variety of tasks, it becomes more and more necessary to lay out user interfaces variably. In addition, users while handling the system, change their qualifications by practising and learning thus putting varied demands on the interface even during one session. So the concept of "one best way" design becomes doubtful at least from two points of view. It becomes necessary to adapt the system design to inter- and intraindividual differences of the users. Thus differential work design demanded by many authors, especially to guarantee promotion of personality in the working process (Hacker, 1980; Ulich et al., 1983), must also to be aim and demand in laying out human-computer interfaces (HCI).

Roads to differential design

Three fundamental ways are shown in table 1. They differ in: how system layout should meet inter- and intraindividual differences and which problems arise. These are:

- *the flexible expert solution,*
- *the flexible user solution, and*
- *the adaptive solution.*

The flexible expert solution

The layouts are fixed by the dialogue author as an expert solution. He especially adjusts the interface to a population of users or a class of problems. However, this is only possible if software is split into user program and interface, as it is the case with User Interface Management Systems (UIMS). The author is "prompted" by the system in specifying interface characteristics to consider psychological design rules or to formulate help texts for the user. This can be done in the form of metarules or be based on if-then decisions, which the author will be offered by the system. This would, at least, solve one problem: the psychological training of authors. But, on the other hand, this is no answer to the problem of the analysis of tasks and knowledge, which, actually, is the "independent" variable for current design decisions. The analysis of tasks and knowledge has to be performed by the dialogue author.

The flexible user solution

One possibility to evade this difficulty is, to shift the task of designing the interface from the author to the user. But this shift cannot be complete. The designer has to provide the interface versions from which the user can select. Before or during a session, the user has to decide, what the individual interface components should be like. This requires additional efforts and knowledge because he does not know, which advantages and disadvantages could result from the different possibilities. But in this case of interface design, too, several questions remain open which, in part, are discussed in the literature in a controversial manner.

These are such questions as:

Which users make use of the alternatives offered?
Which extent of flexibility is allowed and what should be flexible?
Is it possible for users to decide on the optimum variant?

Wetzenstein et al. (Wetzenstein et al., 1984), for example, could show that demands on inexperienced users due to necessary decisions in the framework of flexible design are higher than in the case of consistent solutions. In contrast, Spinas et al. (Spinas et al., 1982) demand the flexible layout as a condition sine qua non for user friendly dialogues. From the psychological point of view it seems to be necessary to carry out some basic experimental research.

The adaptive solution

Another access is adaptive specification of interface components by the system itself. Thus the system adopts a specific function of the designer, on the base of behavioural data of the user and well defined task characteristics which can be assigned to the configurable interface components. A precondition, however, is the feasibility to collect behavioural data and task characteristics, to assign them to configurable interface characteristics and to implement rules defining the relationships between currently logged data and interface characteristics. One could imagine this to be a kind of expert system for user interface design. Now, we have to answer the question how the system "recognizes" which interface is optimal for the user at a given time. Furthermore it has to be proved, that this way of interface design leads to higher efficiency in interaction.

The intention is to show, by means of an example, how such an approach could practically look like. A user is solving a task using a special interaction techniques (for example menu or graphic parameter input). The "adaptive" interface analyses this solution and checks whether the solution was optimal (with regard to number of steps, helps, errors). For this purpose, corresponding knowledge on optimum task-interface relations has to be stored, of course. In the non optimal case, the user, when solving the next task, gets the proposal to continue with another interaction techniques. The user may but need not accept this proposal.

TABLE 1
Ways to flexible and adaptive human-computer interfaces

WAY	ADVANTAGE	DISADVANTAGE	EXAMPLE
Flexible Expert Solution	dialogue author can set the interface corresponding to current conditions tools are at disposal (meta-rules, if-then-decisions)	analysis of task and knowledge has to be carried out by the dialogue author changes in user's degree of experience can hardly be taken into account during one session	UIMS (RIG, COUSIN, INTUIT)
Flexible User Solution	user selects versions from the interface or defines them by himself individual solutions are possible	high programming effort user does not know what versions do include user has to set interface before solving the task	RIG (WPU Rostock) INTAK (AdW-IIR) alternative information presentation (RAUM 1986)
Adaptive Interface Layout	current user characteristics (learning state, knowledge) and classification of tasks can be considered inter- and intraindividual differences are considered	no experience how to implement practically user characteristics cannot be assigned yet to interface characteristics	not any first approaches in CADHELP

Theoretical foundation of differential interface layout

From the facts mentioned above it becomes evident that the decision on one of the discussed variants will not solve the fundamental problems of differential work design from the psychological point of view. We can put this as follows:

Interface components are to be designed in such a way that they meet the cognitive mechanisms as well as the semantic aspects (concerning the contents) of human information processing. According to theoretical considerations of Moran (Moran, 1981) and Tauber (Tauber, 1985; Tauber, 1986) the semantic components of the user interface can decisively contribute to higher efficiency of HCI. And that, above all, because it is the semantic aspect of the interface which activates knowledge in the process of HCI. The layout of all other components, such as the syntactic or lexical ones is determined by these semantic properties. That means, to carry out interface design in the sense of cognitive ergonomics, at first the analysis and, if necessary, the mediation of knowledge is required and, secondly, an interface layout that allows the optimum use of available knowledge.

Differential interface design must be based on valid theories or models of human information processing. Which models are now available and how can they be operationalized to serve as tools for design? We agree to Schiele (Schiele, 1987) and Ackermann (Ackermann, 1987) that the current models of HCI can particularly be used for the exact description of input and output processes. They can hardly be used for real design. Different components of interface can at most be compared with the help of HCI models. This is especially true of the syntactic and interaction level, if we stick to the level description of interface by Moran (Moran, 1981). Those types of approach summarized under the term "performance models" (e.g. Keystroke-level-Model and GOMS-Model by Card et al., 1983; Production Systems by Kieras & Polson, 1985) can be helpful in estimating interaction times. Their limitations are evident. The models presuppose error free interaction. On the other hand, "competence models" include several assumptions concerning knowledge. Evaluation of learning effort becomes possible (cf. Action Grammar by Reisner 1984; Task Action Grammar by Payne 1985 or Green et al. 1986). Assumptions as the modifications of knowledge structures during interaction or interindividual differences in storing, existence and availability of knowledge, which would have to be the starting point of differential design of work, are taken into account only with limitations.

At this point we can resume: a relatively reliable knowledge about more peripheral information processes (perception, motorics) essentially allows well founded statements how to lay out hardware components of the interface (screen, keyboard) also including standardization. Cognitive psychology often sees no need of individualization in these interface components. Of course, this does not mean an approach aimed at changing monotonous work or preventing saturation effects through variable interface layout. We hold that in this case the contents of work tasks should be changed and the tasks should not be solved through more flexible system upgrade of the computer.

Peripheral information processes are usually the level where model like descriptions are derived, enabling the evaluation of interface components by means of times and formal performance parameters. However, semantic aspects of information processes based on activation and storage of knowledge in the HCI process resist to thorough modeling. Hitherto, there is no general theory in cognitive psychology to model these processes comprehensively.

Possibilities to involve psychological results in interface design

The question arises how, from the psychological point of view, well founded design solutions can be reached. Let us start with some remarks on the fundamental approach to including psychological results in interface design. Table 2 characterizes four ways recently followed more or less successfully.

1) A series of rules concerning the design of interfaces and dialogues (Wandke et al., 1985; TGL 44690/05; DIN 66234/8; Murchner et al., 1987) have been worked out. Their application, however, requires certain basic knowledge of psychology. Due to their large interpretation range, the application of rules and recommendations sometimes results in contradictory solutions.
2) At present, the way of experimental analysis is mainly directed to specific design solutions. Due to the lack of theoretical foundation, generalization is limited. Testing versions by experiments also presuppose fundamental knowledge of the methodology of experimental psychology.
3) There are preconditions for teaching methods concerning the analysis of tasks and knowledge to designers of dialogue systems that are difficult to realize. There is neither an easy-to-handle inventory of methods for the diagnosis of knowledge nor a complete classification of tasks. At present, this way would come to a short course in methodology of experimental psychology or to lessons in psychology for students of informatics.
4) The system designer's attention, quasi automatically, would be directed to psychological problems of interface design in implementing rules, methods etc. in User Interface Management Systems

(UIMS). Additionally, he would be given support by rules and decision aids in laying out interface features. It is disadvantageous that only the lower levels of the interface are taken into account. Considering the interface as direct and hierarchically constructed (Moran, 1981), UIMS would handle all aspects starting from the lexical level. Semantics and syntax of the interface are handled by the application program, and not by the UIMS.

We assume, that a combination of the ways 2 and 4 could lead to an approach practicable for the design of user interfaces. Our goal is to develop methods for the analysis of tasks and user knowledge during current interaction. The application of these methods should result in characteristics of users and tasks which can be assigned to specific interface features. Thus, it would become possible to implement methods, rules and performance criteria as a frame program in UIMS. All the interfaces developed by means of this future UIMS could incorporate the accumulated knowledge in the UIMS. We consider this way as the most efficient option for psychological results to take effect on interface design. Hereby, we are in agreement with Fähnrich et al. (Fähnrich et al., 1987) who discuss the same way for the project HUFIT.

Summing up the above arguments from a psychological point of view, the following way of carrying on interface design will be suitable for us. Based on positive knowledge of cognitive psychology, interface solutions have to be worked out for each interface component and, if possible, to be implemented in a UIMS as a mode which enters into each concretely defined user interface. At present, we do not see a way to a model approach for the interface as a whole (see table 2).

Experimental approach

General procedure

Which experimental approach is possible or necessary for a differential interface layout based on cognitive psychology?

1) *Step one:*
   On the basis of the knowledge of cognitive psychology we have to develop a "cognitive model" of the cognitive mechanisms, underlying the mental information processing. This "cognitive model" is

TABLE 2
Possibilities of including psychological knowledge into interface design

Meta-Rules and Recommendations to System Designers		
ADVANTAGE	DISADVANTAGE	EXAMPLE
comprehensive treatment of all interface problems is possible	rules and hints are mostly not precise basic knowledge of psychol. is required for application large interpretation range	DIN 66234/8 TGL 44690/05 rules for interface design (WANDKE, 1985, SPINAS 1982, MURCHNER 1987)

Experimental Analysis		
ADVANTAGE	DISADVANTAGE	EXAMPLE
precise statements for the special case of design	very narrow validity range generalizability limited experimental analysis of many special cases required	various findings in literature

Instructions for System Designers in Methods of Task and Knowledge Analysis		
ADVANTAGE	DISADVANTAGE	EXAMPLE
meta-rules can be applied more successfully and without substantial knowledge of psychology designer can develop solutions for new problems by himself	general task classification is required, does not exist yet methods for knowledge analysis lacking too	seminars on cognitive psychology for software engineers rapid prototyping

Implementation of Rules and Methods in User Interface Management Systems		
ADVANTAGE	DISADVANTAGE	EXAMPLE
software designer is supported by UIMS in solving psychol. problems tools for layout are available multiplication effects of good solutions can occur	UIMS consider only low design levels level of tasks and semantics are not involved multiplication effects for bad UIMS solutions too	RIG (Berndt et. al. 1986) COUSIN (Hayes et. al. 1985)

needed for the interface components to be investigated or to be designed. It must be possible to derive from this model hypotheses about the relations between task characteristics, knowledge and corresponding interface characteristics. If the design of flexible or adaptive systems is intended, it must be possible to derive assumptions on inter- and intraindividual differences in cognitive mechanisms. From the psychological point of view there is no foundation for a flexible or adaptive layout of interface components without such assumptions and thus the design becomes doubtful.

2) *Step two:*
There must be evident relations between task characteristics and interface characteristics. The consideration of these relations leads to an increase in the efficiency of HCI. Compatible solutions are only possible in this case.

3) *Step three:*
It must be proved that the user (flexible solution) and the programmer (expert solution) are able to choose interfaces which are compatible with classes of tasks. In this context, it must also be investigated how efficient flexible solutions really are, in comparison with consistent ones, if there is a great variety of tasks, which possibly would render necessary a permanent change or adaptation of the user interface to ensure information processing adequate to the task. Furthermore, it must be shown whether and to which extent users do work with flexible solutions. This examination also includes the clarification of the relations between behavioural data (operations, time, errors, demands for help) and interface characteristics.

4) *Step four:*
The relationships found in the preceding steps must be formalized. Doing this means designing an interface module. Using this module the system will analyze the user inputs (their contents, time patterns, sequence, correctness etc.) and derive hints and recommendations as to how the interface could be changed by the user. The system can offer this change as an active help function. The user may or may not accept these recommendations.

This approach includes experimental methodology in all its stages (1 - 4). As an example of this step-by-step technique investigations concerning flexible layout of command languages will be presented. The same approach was and is realized for other interface components, for example for the coding of information on the screen (Wetzenstein et al., 1984) and the layout of input techniques (Metzler, 1987).

Experimental example: formation and use of macros

Theoretical knowledge in cognitive psychology (step one of the general methodology)

Many task solving processes are transformation processes. On the basis of a given situation, a goal is achieved through a sequence of transformation operations and intermediate states. In HCI, the user delegates some of the transformations to the computer. Thus, they become system operations. The specification of these system operations is made through commands and parameters.

It is well known from natural task solving processes, that sequences of transformations occurring frequently will be condensed and shortened by human abstraction. Abstraction processes result in a reduction of memory load and mental load. In other words, frequent solving of problems results in a changed structure of knowledge. With Klix (Klix, 1973; Klix, 1983) we start from the assumption, that such abstraction processes generally characterize human problem solving. The design process should take this into account. How could this be taken into consideration in constructing command languages for HCI? We should proceed from the general requirement, that basic system operations and the corresponding elementary commands should be compatible with cognitive transformations in the task solving process. Since we have to assume abstraction processes occurring after a longer time of interaction with the system, the original sequences of cognitive transformations will be shortened. Constant system operations and commands then should demand from the user more and more incompatible cognitive operations. In this case, flexible or adaptive designs are of advantage because they take into account such intraindividual changes. As to the construction of command languages this means, that the user at any moment should have the option of constructing macro operations by himself. Those macro operations should correspond to his level of knowledge in the learning process. Subsequently, these operations shall be called procedures.

Assumptions on the relation between task characteristics and procedure construction (step two of the general methodology)

At least, two conditions must be met when procedure construction and use should occur:

- The construction of procedures presupposes frequent occurring of the same sequence of elementary commands (basic commands). That means in the tasks to be accomplished, a set of basic commands must by partly or completely repeated.
- The construction of procedures is reasonable and effective only on condition that sufficient knowledge has been obtained and regularities in the spectrum of tasks have been recognized.

Our assumption on the use and construction of procedures and on intra- and interindividual variations in this field is based on an interaction effect between both factors. The following hypotheses were formulated for the experimental investigations:

a) If variety of tasks is low, procedures will be constructed more frequently, because regularities of task sequences can be recognized earlier than in the case of high variety.

b) The use of procedures becomes more efficient if the complexity of tasks increases. Complexity is the number of basic commands necessary to solve the task. Solving complex tasks requires longer sequences of commands.

c) Users who have acquired comprehensive and adequate knowledge about system properties and task classes will construct procedures more frequently.

Experimental approach

To verify the hypotheses we used a fictive information system for warehouse processes (Engel, 1984; Rohls, 1986) as an experimental paradigm. The subjects (Ss) could issue queries about different materials stocked and about orders and solve simple optimization problems. Solving the tasks requires only linear command sequences without control structures and decision criteria. Twenty Ss without any experience in computer handling took part in the experiment. They had to solve eighteen query tasks during two sessions.

In the first session they had to learn and use a simple command language using German words. In another session, they could solve the tasks by constructing and using procedures. The procedures were constructed by entering the command PRODEF followed by a name and the sequence of the basic commands to be substituted by the procedure. Therefore, two independent variables were introduced into the experiment:

- task variety:	high:	6 types of tasks with 3 tasks per type
	low:	3 types of tasks with 6 tasks per type
- task complexity:	variation of the number of basis commands, necessary to solve the task (5,6,7,8,10)	

Before and after solving the problems and at the moment of procedure construction different methods were applied for knowledge diagnosis. Times, mistakes, number of helps and number of procedures defined and used were registered as additional dependent variables. The construction of the methods for knowledge diagnosis (questionnaire and card-sorting test; Schult, 1985) was based on assumptions by Klix et al. (Klix et al., 1984) on the storage principles for knowledge in the long-time memory. They allowed the prediction of specific types of errors and other performance data during the procedure construction, dependent on knowledge components required.

Results and conclusions for a differential approach

It had to be proved that, corresponding to our theoretical assumption, there is a relation between task characteristics, interface components and knowledge, which could be used for a flexible or adaptive design of interface components.

In figures 1 to 3 the main results of the experiment are summed up. They can be interpreted as follows:

- The task variety (figure 1) influences the definition and use of procedures. Low task variety results in a more frequent use of procedures. If the task variety is high there will be, however, a greater number of different and short procedures.

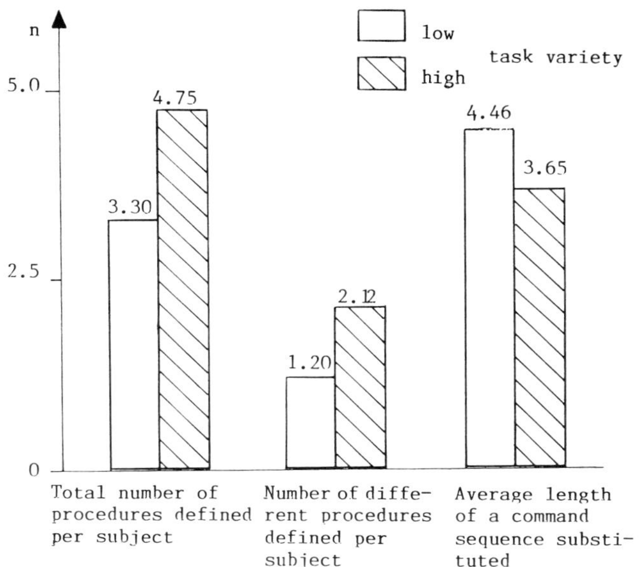

Figure 1. Number and types of procedures and task variety

- The efficiency of using procedures depends on the task complexity (figure 2). We determined the task complexity only as the length of command sequences. Therefore the conclusion in view of complexity only applies to classes of tasks with the same kind of complexity. This distinguishes our investigations from those made by Gumm and Hagendorf (Gumm & Hagendorf, 1987) or Ackermann (Ackermann, 1987). A higher degree of task complexity makes the use of procedures more effective in terms of solution time. If the solution of a task requires a sequence of only 5 elementary commands, the use or non use of procedures makes no significant difference as to the solution time. If the sequence, however, is longer than 10 elementary commands, differences are significant.

- But the two variables variety and complexity of tasks can only explain 50 - 60 percent of the variance. From figure 3 it is evident, that individual knowledge is decisive for the explanation of interindividual differences in performance. Ss with a better starting knowledge request a lower number of helps, commit fewer errors and define less ineffective procedures. The feature oriented,

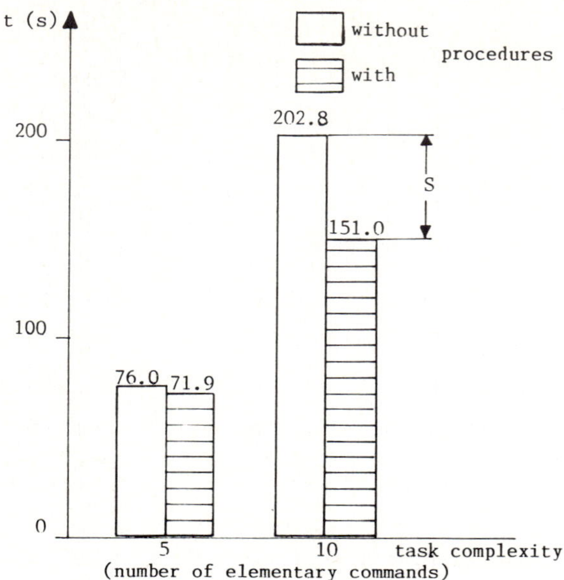

Figure 2. Use of procedures, task complexity and solution time

procedural knowledge seems to be the main factor determining the starting moment for the definition of procedures.

Which conclusions can be drawn with regard to a differential layout of command language:

- The versions for flexible or adaptive interfaces have to take into account variety and complexity of tasks. With low variety, few, powerful procedures can be recommended at an early stage of use. On the other hand, for high task variety several shorter procedures are more appropriate. Specially for solving tasks of high complexity, procedures are efficient and should be suggested to the user.
- Helps and errors are important external criteria for evaluating the store of knowledge of Ss. Individual knowledge, in turn, is decisive for the beginning of the work with procedures. The number of helps and errors can be a criterion for the system to suggest to the user to use procedures.

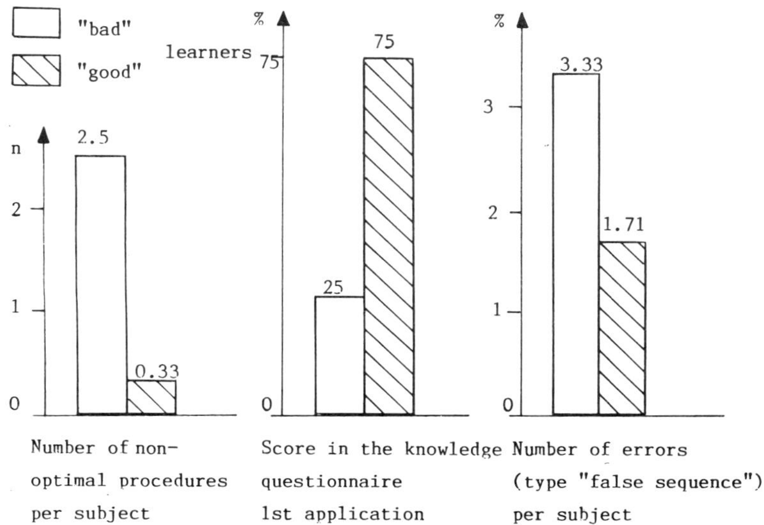

Figure 3. The influence of knowledge on the using of optimal procedures and the numbers of errors

Efficiency test for flexible or adaptive solutions (steps 3 and 4 of the general methodology)

Now, the findings in view of the relation between task, knowledge and command language must be brought into an experimental approach for differential layout. For this purpose we selected the flexible and the adaptive approach. Since the experiments are still running, we shall only present a few tentative results.

As a paradigm we used again the fictive information retrieval system, described above: three versions of the dialogue were implemented. They were different in the amount of learning and keying effort required. The types of tasks were the same as in part two in this investigation. Table 3 characterizes the three versions. Both dialogue version 1 and 2 do not permit the construction of procedures, therefore the keying effort is decisively higher than in version 3, where Ss can use procedures. The learning effort is defined trough the number of commands and increases from version 1 to 3. The complexity and variety of tasks were kept constant.

TABLE 3
Characteristics of dialogue versions

DIALOGUE VERSION	LEARNING EFFORT	INPUT EFFORT
1	*2 commands:* ANZEIGEN, LOESCHEN	average *101 commands* per task
2	*4 commands:* SUCHEN, LOESCHEN, EINSCHRAENKEN, AUFLOESEN	average *5 commands* per task
3	*5 commands:* SUCHEN, ANZEIGEN, EINSCHRAENKEN, AUFLOESEN, *2 procedures:* *Prodef, Prozeig*	average *1 command* per task if procedures are applied

Now let us consider some results referring to one of the questions discussed above. Among other things we wanted to clarify: to which extent do users make use of alternatives in a flexible or an adaptive interface?

- *Results with the flexible interface.*
  Ss could decide on one of the three dialogue versions before interaction. Furthermore, they could change from one version to another during interaction. Ten unexperienced (students of psychology) and ten experienced (students of informatics) users took part in the experiment.

  From figure 4 it is evident, that some users prefer versions connected with a higher learning and a lower keying effort even if their level of practice is still low. About one third of the users work with procedures right from the beginning, if task variety is very low. This result confirms our first hypothesis. Of course, both test groups do not significantly differ from each other. Figure 5 shows that users only exceptionally change versions during interaction. Only one of the Ss changed the dialogue version.

- *Results in view of the adaptive interface.*
  Making use of the adaptive interface all Ss started with the easiest dialogue version - the first one. During their solving the task, errors and helps were registered and a "knowledge criterion" was defined. On arriving at it the user got the recommendation to work with the next dialogue version. The "knowledge criterion" was fixed as follows: within 5 commands, not more than 3 mistakes or 2 helps or,

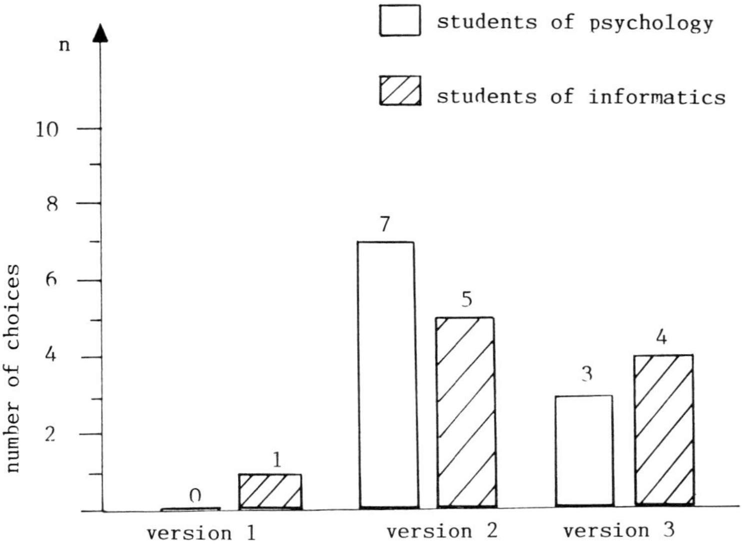

Figure 4. Frequency of using dialogue versions with a flexible interface

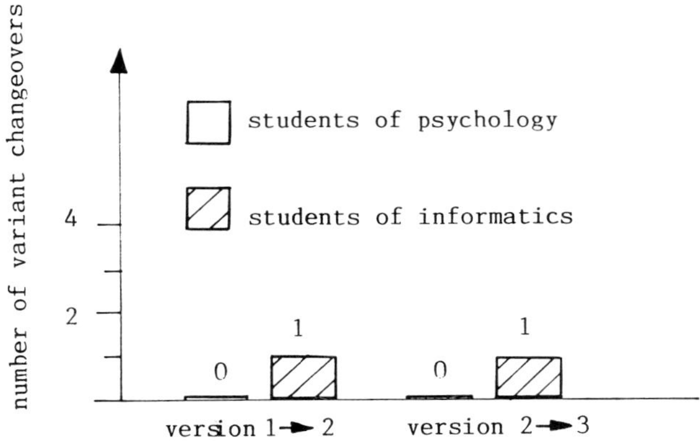

Figure 5. Number of variant changeovers during interactive task solving with a flexible interface

altogether, more then 4 mistakes and helps should occur. The Ss may or may not accept the dialogue version, recommended under this condition.

Figure 6 shows the result. All Ss follow the first or second recommendation of the system. That means all Ss solve their tasks using procedures at the end. Thus, they are able to solve more tasks and the solution time will decrease.

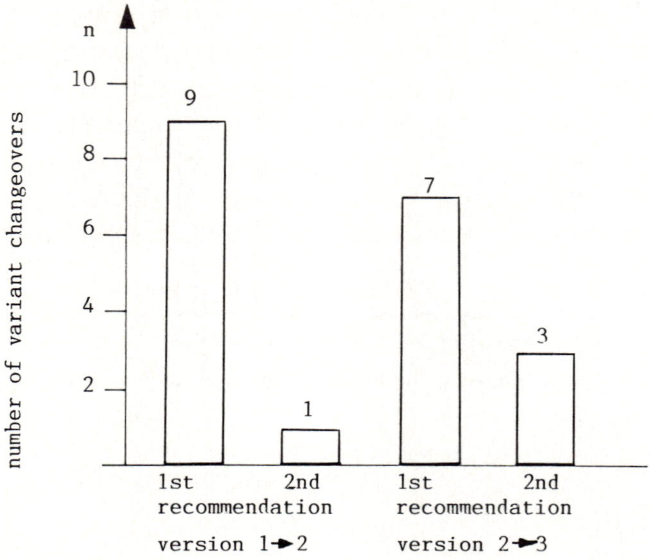

Figure 6. Number of variant changeovers according to the recommendation of the system in the case of adaptive interface

Conclusions

Comparing flexible and adaptive interfaces, one can conclude, that flexible offers are accepted by users only to a limited extent. There is a trend towards a "mean" difficulty. Only in exceptional cases dialogue versions are changed depending on training state or knowledge during a dialogue.

On the other hand, support and positive affirmation in the case of the adaptive variant result in a broad use of the variable system facilities, which is corresponding to the user‘s performance level. The adaptive solution offers the better way to come up to inter- and intraindividual differences and to completely use the facilities implemented in the system.

In this paper, however, it is not possible to draw general conclusions for all three of the described versions of differential interface design: flexible version (selection by the user), flexible expert version or adaptive version. For this our experimental approach must be extended and more data will have to be collected in order to use the results for the evaluation of design versions. But now, it is already evident - and this is confirmed by results of earlier investigations concerning flexible information layout (Wetzenstein et al., 1984) and flexible interaction techniques (Metzler, 1987) - that inexperienced users are not fully able to select system's options, appropriate to the task characteristics and their current knowledge. Adaptive interfaces support the inexperienced user in taking his choice and therefore yield higher efficiency.

References

Ackermann, D. (1987). *Handlungsspielraum, mentale Repräsentation und Handlungsregulation am Beispiel der Mensch-Computer-Interaktion.* Dissertation, Universität Bern.

Berndt, E., Karstens, B., Pätz, Th. & Vatterrott, H.R. (1986). Anwendung des Nutzerinterface-Verwaltungssystems RIG. *Rostocker Informatik Berichte,* (4) 1986.

Card, S.K., Moran, T.P. & Newell, A. (1983). *The Psychology of Human-Computer Interaction.* Hillsdale, NJ: Erlbaum.

Cullingford, R.E., Krueger, M.W., Selfridge, M. & Bienkowsky, M.A. (1982). Automated explanations as a component of a computer-aided design system. *IEEE Transactions on Systems, Man and Cybernetics,* 12 (1982), pp. 161-181.

DIN-66234, Teil 8, *Bildschirmarbeitsplätze - Grundsätze der Dialoggestaltung,* Draft December 1984.

Engel, U. (1984). *Empirische Untersuchungen zur Verwendung von Prozeduren innerhalb einer Kommandosprache.* Diplomarbeit, Humboldt-Universität, Sektion Psychologie, Berlin.

Fähnrich, K.P. & Ziegler, J. (1987). HUFIT - Human factors in information technology. In: W. Schönpflug & M. Wittstock (Eds.), *Software-Ergonomie '87* (pp. 219-227). Stuttgart: Teubner.

Green, T.R.G., Payne, S.J. & Schiele, F. (1988). Formalisable models of user knowledge in HCI. In G.C. van der Veer, T.R.G. Green, J. Hoc & D. Murray (Eds.), *Working with Computers: Theory versus Outcome.* London: Academic Press.

Gumm, U. & Hagendorf, H. (1987). Aspekte rechnergestützter Problemlöseprozesse aus psychologischer Sicht. *Rostocker Informatikberichte,* 5 (1987), pp. 28-30.

Hacker, W. (1986). *Psychologische Bewertung von Arbeitsgestaltungsmaßnahmen.* Berlin: Verlag der Wissenschaften.

Hayes, P.J., Szekely, P.A. & Lerner, R.A. (1985). Design alternatives for user interface management systems based on experience with Cousin. In L. Borman & B. Curtis (Eds.), *Human Factors in Computing Systems - II,* (pp. 169-175). Amsterdam - New York: North-Holland.

Hoppe, H.U. & Schmalhofer, F. (1987). Software-Ergonomie und "Cognitive Science": Die Bedeutung von Experimenten und Modellen. In W. Schönpflug & M. Wittstock (Eds.), *Software-Ergonomie '87.* Stuttgart: Teubner.

Kieras, D.E. & Polson, P. (1985). An approach to the formal analysis of user complexity. *Int. J. Man-Machine Studies,* 22, pp. 365-394.

Klix, F. (1973). *Information und Verhalten.* Berlin: Deutscher Verlag der Wissenschaften.

Klix, F. (1983). Begabungsforschung - ein neuer Weg in der kognitiven Intelligenzdiagnostik? *Zeitschrift f. Psychologie,* 191 (1983), pp. 360-384.

Klix, F. (1984). Über Wissensrepräsentation im menschlichen Gedächtnis. In: F. Klix (Ed.), *Gedächtnis, Wissen, Wissensnutzung.* Berlin: Deutscher Verlag der Wissenschaften.

Klix, F. & van der Meer, E. (1984). Über Begriffsbeziehungen: Untersuchungen an Organisationsformen der menschlichen Gedächtnistätigkeit. *Wiss. Z. der Humboldt-Universität-Berlin, Math.-Nat. Reihe,* III (1984), Heft 6, pp. 556.

Klix, F. & Wandke, H. (1986). *Macinter I.* Amsterdam - New York: North Holland.

Metzler, W. (1984). *Bildschirmarbeitsplätze.* Amt für industrielle Formgestaltung, Dresden.

Moran, T.P. (1981). The command language grammar: a representation for the user interface of interactive computer systems. *Int. J. Man-Machine Studies,* 15, pp. 3-50.

Murchner, R., Oppermann, R., Paetau, M., Pieper, M., Simm, H. & Stellmacher, J. (1987). EVADIS - Ein Leitfaden softwareergonomischer Evaluation von Dialogschnittstellen. In W. Schönpflug & M. Wittstock (Eds.), *Software-Ergonomie '87* (pp. 307-316). Stuttgart: Teubner.

Payne, S.J. (1985). *Task Action Grammars.* University of Sheffield, Dept of Psychology. Memo 639.

Raum, H. (1986). Alternative information presentation as a contribution to user related dialogue design. In F. Klix, F. & H. Wandke (Eds.), *Macinter I* (pp. 339-348). Amsterdam - New York: North Holland.

Reisner, Ph. (1984). Formal grammar as a tool for analyzing ease of use - some fundamental concepts. In J.C. Thomas & M.L. Schneider (Eds.), *Human Factors in Computer Systems* (pp. 53-78). Norwood, NJ: Ablex Publishing Corp.

Rohls, J. (1986). *Prozedurbildung und -verwendung bei komplexen Aufgaben.* Diplomarbeit, Humboldt-Universität Berlin, Sektion Psychologie.

Schiele, F. (1987). Formale Modelle des Benutzerwissens als Mittel der Spezifikation und Bewertung von Benutzerschnittstellen: Stand und Perspektiven. In W. Schönpflug & M. Wittstock (Eds.), *Software-Ergonomie'87* (pp. 504-506). Stuttgart: Teubner.

Schult, S. (1985). *Die Erfassung interindividueller Unterschiede beim Mensch-Rechner-Dialog.* Diplomarbeit, Humboldt-Universität Berlin, Sektion Psychologie.

Spinas, P.H., Troy, N. & Ulich, E. (1982). *Leitfaden zur Einführung und Gestaltung von Arbeit mit Bildschirmsystemen.* Duttweiler-Institut, Rüschlikon.

Tauber, M.J. (1985). Top down design of human computer systems from the demands of human cognition to the virtual machine - an interdisciplinary approach to model interfaces in human-computer interaction. In *Proceedings of the IEEE Workshop on Languages for Automation - Cognitive Aspects in Information Processing.* Palma de Malloraca, June 1985.

Tauber, M.J. (1986a). Top down design of human-computer interfaces. In S.K. Chang, T. Ichikawa & P. Ligomenides (Eds.), *Visual Languages.* New York - London: Plenum Press.

Tauber, M.J. (1986b). An approach to metacommunication in human-computer interaction. In F. Klix & H. Wandke (Eds.), *Macinter I.* Amsterdam - New York: North Holland.

Ulich, E. (1983). Differentielle Arbeitsgestaltung - ein Diskussionsbeitrag. *Z. f. Arbeitswissenschaften,* 37 (9).

Wandke, H., Wetzenstein-Ollenschläger, E., Schulz, J. & Kossakowski, M. (1985). *Richtlinien zur Gestaltung von Mensch-Rechner-Interfaces.* Informationsmaterial der Sektion Psychologie, Humboldt-Universität Berlin.

Wetzenstein-Ollenschläger, E. Scheiderreither, U. & Geißler, H.G. (1984). Psychologische Beiträge zur anforderungsgerechten Informationsgestaltung bei Bildschirmarbeitsplätzen. *Psychol. für die Praxis,* 4 (1984), pp. 283-296.

Mental Models and Human-Computer Interaction 1
D. Ackermann and M.J. Tauber (Editors)

DESIGNING FOR THE MENTAL MODEL

AN INTERDISCIPLINARY APPROACH TO THE DEFINITION OF A USER INTERFACE FOR ELECTRONIC MAIL SYSTEMS

Gerrit C. van der Veer, Steve Guest, Pim Haselager, Peter Innocent, Eddy McDaid, Lars Oestreicher, Michael J. Tauber, Ulfert Vos, Yvonne Waern*

*Department of Psychology, Cognitive Psychology Division, Free University, Amsterdam

ABSTRACT

This paper describes the work in progress on a multidisciplinary international project in human factors and telematic systems sponsored by the CEC. The goal of the project is to contribute to the standardisation of definition languages for user interfaces in open system networks. Representational problems and languages are considered with respect to an idealised open system, an electronic mail system, and a users mental model of this application. Detailed specifications are developed and a prototyping tool is described which translates a system representation into a working prototype for human factors experiments. In this first phase of the project, it is concluded that it has been possible to use the proposed representations to describe an existing application so that it can support prototyping specification and execution as well as be understood by all members of the project team. Future work will consider the problem of formally representing a system from a users point of view in carrying out a specific task so that it can be evaluated with respect to the acceptability from a cognitive psychology perspective.

Introduction

This contribution describes the progress of the working group "Human factors in telematic systems", a project within the COST-11-ter Human Factors action, sponsored by the Commission of the European Communities, DG X1II, information technologist and telecommunications task force. The project coordinates research on the feasibility of human factors (cognitive psychological) requirements and guidelines for the definition and design of human-computer interfaces in OSI (Open Systems Interconnections). An important role in this effort is played by the distinction between categories of users and between categories of tasks or task elements. The goal of the project is to contribute to the standardisation of definition languages for user interfaces in OSI environments, enabling the application of human factor guidelines by the designer.

History of the project

The working group has thus far completed work on the inventory of theoretical and empirical knowledge on human factors in OSI (Van Muylwijk, Van der Veer and Waern, 1983; Wheeler and Innocent, 1983), and on the feasibility of design criteria (Hannemyr, 1983). A representational framework and design strategies have been developed (Hannemyr and Innocent, 1985), and a feedback model for metacommunication inside the virtual machine (Van der Veer, Tauber, Waern and Van Muylwijk, 1985).

Prior work on the language for defining user interfaces (Hannemyr and Innocent, 1985) had a broad goal of describing a strategy whereby alternative user interfaces could be available within the context of a user of an application in an open system. Some of the general guidelines for human factors in designing open systems provided by Wheeler and Innocent (1983) were taken into consideration. The paper integrated a computer and user perspective and proposed broad mechanisms for implementing the suggested strategy. Use was made of a standard notation in computer science (Backus-Nauer Form, BNF) for representing user transactions with an open system application. This was a first stage on making some formal representation available in the context of an open system standard.

Within the same area, work by Tauber (1985) considers fundamental issues and the representation of cognitive aspects of user interactions with a system. Van der Veer, Tauber, Waern and Van Muylwijk (1985) suggest suitable areas for investigation in order to capture the characteristics of user interactions within an open system application. It should be possible to formally describe such characteristics within the notation of Tauber (op cit) within a formally well defined system.

Current status of the project

The project "human factors in telematic systems" has as its main goal to investigate the feasibility of an interdisciplinary approach to the problem of human-computer interaction. We try to solve the problem users face when confronted with a system they do not know in all its details (and which they may never be able to know completely). We are currently trying to answer the following four questions:

a. Is it possible to actually *describe* the user interface part of the conceptual model of an existing real life computer application.

b. Is it possible to actually *define* the conceptual model for the user interface component of a real life computer application that is acceptable from cognitive psychological and cognitive ergonomic viewpoint, taking care of interactions at the user interface, individual differences, and learning processes.

c. Is it possible to *construct* a user interface according to the conceptual model as we have defined it.

d. Is it possible to *demonstrate* that the new user interface leads to "better" man-machine interaction than does the already existing interface.

To answer these questions we have chosen an example of an application that makes sense in an OSI environment, e.g. UNIX mail, further called UMAIL. We have defined a new mailsystem called IMAIL, for the same task domain (or a subdomain), according to the psychological knowledge of mental models of different groups of users. We will construct a user interface of IMAIL on UMAIL with the help of a user interface management system (SYNICS, see Guest, 1982). We will compare interfaces from the user's point of view: teaching novices, construction of metacommunication (both implicit and explicit), and development metaphors in order to induce valid mental models.

Representation of interactive systems

Users of a computer application need clear and consistently structured knowledge of the system they interact with. This knowledge only concerns that part of the machine that is directly relevant to the task delegation by the user to the system: the *user's virtual machine*. The cognitive ergonomic approach that will be illustrated combines methods for the representation of the user virtual machine, with the mental model concept. Our basic ideas are:

a. The mental model is an important cognitive aspect of the human-computer interaction (Norman, 1983).
b. Specifying the user virtual machine means to define explicitly the conceptual model for the user interface in a knowledge based way.
c. The conceptual model can be described with the help of a multi level approach derived from Moran (1981), which should also apply to the user's mental model.
d. This conceptual model should be presented to the user, taking into account relevant characteristics of human learning and user variables.

The question of how to represent systems, interfaces, and models of systems will be analysed from two different aspects, the "human factors" approach and the "informatics" approach. Figure 1 presents a schematic representation of the different concepts and their relations in these two domains.

The domain of human factors (psychology)

Norman (1983) makes a clear distinction between a system, the conceptual model of the system, and the mental model of the system:

a. *target system*
   The actual thing, e.g. a computer system.
b. *conceptual model*
   A correct description of the target system, as far as the human-machine interface is concerned; an accurate and consistent representation, that is invented or developed by a teacher and/or designer. This includes both relevant aspects of hardware of screen and keyboard (meaningful for the user, e.g. audible signals on hitting keys that do not have a meaning in the current mode, blinking cursors), and application software, as far as the user interacts with these. Aim of teaching a novice is to transmit this model.
c. *mental model*
   This concept denotes the knowledge structure the user applies in his interaction with the computer. The user predicts reactions of the

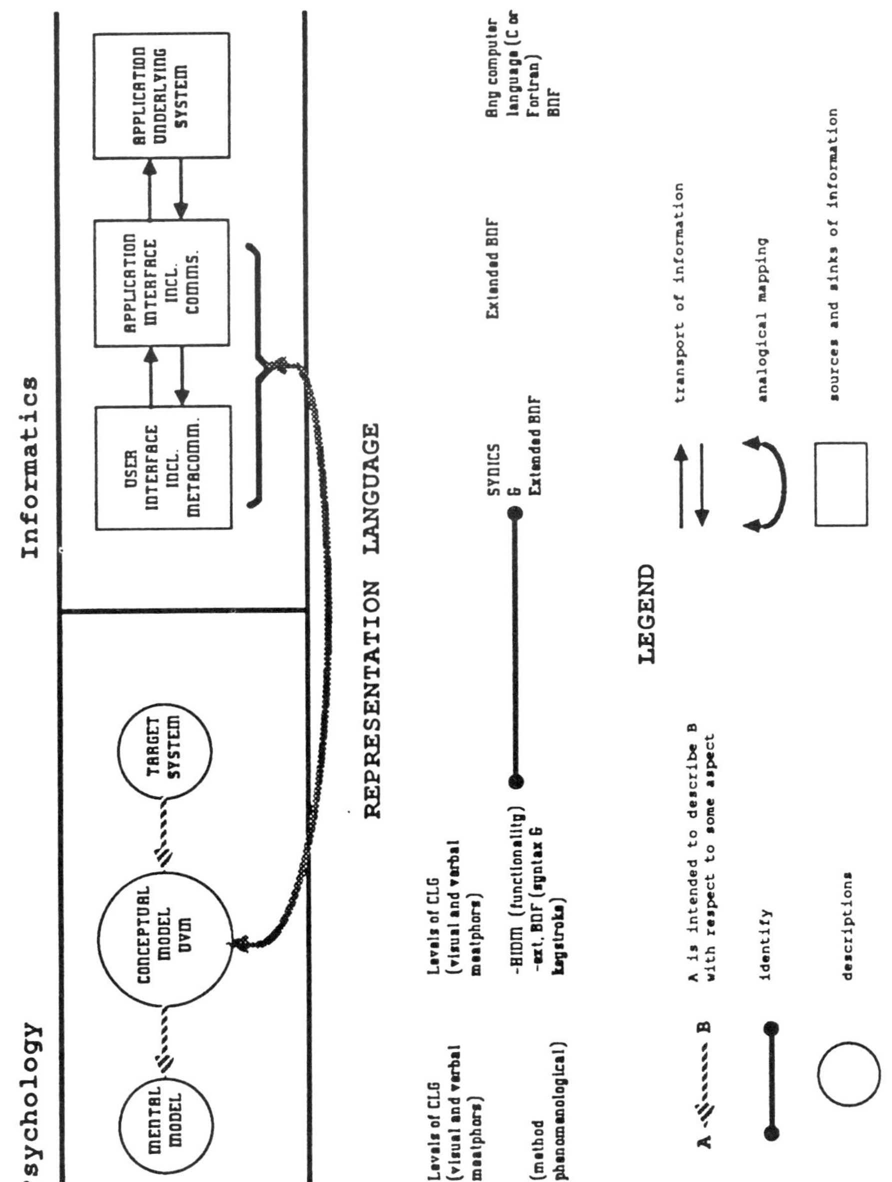

Figure 1. Relations between representations

system to his own behaviour. Decisions and planning are based on the mental model, as is explanation of unexpected system behaviour. This model evolves during interaction with the target system, especially in the initial learning phase. A user "understands" a system if predictions based on his mental model are consistent with the behaviour of the user interface of the target system. Or, in other words, if his mental model maps completely to the relevant part of the conceptual model, e.g. the user virtual machine. Unexpected effects and errors point to inconsistency between the mental model and the conceptual model.

The relation between the target system and the conceptual model may be defined as follows: the conceptual model is intended to describe the target system with respect to some aspects. The same definition is valid for the relation between the conceptual model and the mental model. The conceptual model and the *user's virtual machine (UVM)* overlap. The UVM is a subset of the conceptual model, defined only for a special user group and a specified task domain.

The representations we will use for these different concepts will differ, related to the nature of the models (or the system). The four levels of Moran's CLG (1981) will provide a framework for description of both the mental model and the conceptual model (see a later chapter). In the case of the mental model a phenomenological method of analysis may be useful (Van der Veer and Felt, 1988). For the functionality (task level and semantic level) of the conceptual model the Heidelberg Interface Description Method (Tauber, 1987) will be used, and for both the syntax and keystroke level we will use the "extended BNF notation" (see a later chapter). For our purposes it is irrelevant to give an exact description of the target system, although some user oriented aspects are considered in BNF.

The development of the conceptual model may start from two different sources: either an existing system is described with respect to its relevance to the user (point a. of the introduction) or a conceptual model is defined from the analysis of the functionality of some intended human-computer interaction (point b. of the introduction).

The development of mental models (cognitive representations of computing systems) is a process in which structures in semantic memory are built or changed. The process of acquisition or change of mental representations is generally considered to be strongly based on analogies: Known concepts and structures are related to the new situation. This process can be activated if the metacommunication in the user interface (see a later chapter) refers to existing semantic knowledge and schemes. Metaphors may be used to activate knowledge and act as analogies. The choice of appropriate metaphors is crucial for the development of adequate mental models (Carroll and Thomas, 1982; Carroll, 1983; Clanton, 1983; Houston, 1983). Several distinct metaphors might be referred to for the same conceptual model, each illustrating a few aspects of the new system to be learned (Van der Veer and Felt, in press; Rumelhart and Norman, 1983).

The domain of systems' design (informatics)

In this domain the components are linked by lines of information flow. Therefore a protocol must be adopted to ensure the integration of this communication. The components may exist as independent processes, or groups of processes. In other cases the components may be combined in a single process. We apply a distinction between system, application, several interfaces, and different types of communication.

a. *user interface*
The user communicates only directly with the user interface. The user interface includes both explicit metacommunication, and implicit metacommunication aspects of mnemonics and tokens.

b. *application and application interface*
The application interface includes all communication between the user and the application regarding task delegation. All communication between the user and the application interface goes through the user interface, where tokens and mnemonics may be transformed on behalf of implicit metacommunication.

c. *the system*
The user interface and application(s) are supported by a computer based system. Functions like data storage and retrieval are processed by the host system. Such functions may introduce time delays at the application interface, and hence at the user interface.

d. *communication*
Information is communicated between the user, the user interface, application and system relating to data objects and control. In an

open system network, delays in communication may arise. Information may come from different system layers following strict protocols, finally arriving at the application layer. Some information may relate to the state of the system/application/user interface. For example, if the network breaks down, higher levels are informed, including the user. Communication between the system and the user is normally through the user interface.

e. *metacommunication*
This refers to the communication of information between a user and the system about how to communicate. Within the process of interaction, users may be given help about entities in the system space. For example, help requests and error messages often *explicitly* regard syntax and semantics of commands. The mnemonic or icon chosen to represent a token (command or prompt) in the user interface may *implicitly* refer to semantic aspects of the object or command that is denoted. One of our aims is to work with metacommunication as a way to adapt the user interface to the user's needs.

For every component of an informatics system, there are different languages for description. We have used SYNICS (see a later chapter) for the user interface (including metacommunication), "Extended BNF" for the application interface (including communication about the task delegation by the user to the application), and several portable languages (C, LISP, FORTRAN) for the system. It should be noted that SYNICS has Extended BNF as a subset of its pattern match. Therefore it can provide the ability to implement the application interface in an environment that facilitates rapid prototyping.

The relation between the two domains of representation

There is a complete, analogical mapping of the conceptual model (including the user's virtual machine) of the "human factors domain" to the user interface and the application interface of the "informatics domain" and vice versa. In fact they represent exactly the same, but are merely seen from two different points of view. Depending on the case (either a. or b. of the introduction) this mapping may start from the systems designer *describing* a system on behalf of the users, of from a human factors specialist *defining* an intended conceptual model to the designer. Extended BNF notation may bridge the gap between the two disciplines, enabling them to communicate in a uniform and unambiguous way.

Since the mental model is intended to describe the conceptual model with respect to some aspects, it can be said to be aiming to describe the user- and application interface. The target system is a concept that can be used in the "psychological domain" to refer to everything in the "systems designer domain", including the physical aspects of the computer system.

4 levels of user-computer interaction

Moran (1981) distinguishes between 4 levels in describing interaction between users and systems. The first two levels refer to the functionality of the system. The lowest CLG level is the interaction level. In our work we need to represent physical aspects of interaction as far as they are meaningful to the user and thus we replace this level by a keystroke level.

a. *task level*
At the task level it should be noted that a user always regards a computer system as a tool to perform a task. Applying a system, at this level, may be described as delegation of subtasks to the machine. The conceptual model consists of a complete review of the possibilities in this respect. Knowledge of the target system (the mental model) is understanding which subtasks may be delegated, and which cannot. This means that a user not only needs a list of subtasks that the system can perform, but also requires an explicit account of how these subtasks can be delegated as part of an envisaged task. The particular task may be an old familiar one or one which has been added due to the new possibilities offered by the system. Whatever is the case, the user needs to relate the system to the task in question. It may be difficult to incorporate sensible metacommunication at task level in the user interface (Van der Veer, Tauber, Waern and Van Muylwijk, 1985). Teaching and documentation will have to supply this, outside the system.

b. *semantic level*
The task level maps down into the conceptual operations and conceptual entities within the user's virtual machine. As users learn about a system their mental models are revised. If a system

recognises that a user cannot achieve a task successfully then some remedial interaction (metacommunication) should be taken. In a simple view, this could take the form of a change in the error messages and related information. This metacommunication can also be adaptive (Fischer, Lemke and Schwab, 1984) and they are aimed at improving the ease of learning of an application system. Hence there is a strong and complex interaction between the application system and the metacommunication (Rich, 1983).

c. *syntax level*
This level gives the commands available for accomplishing the conceptual operations defined in the semantic level. There are many guidelines (Shneiderman, 1980) provided at this level on, for example, uniformity and consistency in command language syntax. The syntax level includes naming conventions and the use of mnemonics in commands and these are particularly important to users. Unless the link between the syntax level and the semantic level is through transparent intermediaries (e.g. visual metaphors and icons), users can have considerable difficulty. These can be overcome by metacommunication.

d. *keystroke level*
The dialogue interactions through physical devices is defined at this level and maps directly into the syntax level. Dialogue modes (e.g. natural language, menu, command, graphical), are partially equivalent at a syntax level and it is possible to separate this level out for implementation.

Adaptation and individual differences

Research on the possibilities to adapt interfaces and modes of interaction to individual users has shown a variety of results, with seemingly casual cases of success and failure. At least part of these phenomena seem to be due to the fact that some personality characteristics are easy to adapt to, whilst others require educators to invest a lot of time and effort in producing minor effects. Van der Veer and Van Muylwijk (1984) introduced a model of changeability of cognitive functions.

Personality factors such as intelligence, introversion/extroversion and negative fear of failure are generally considered to be stable features. It seems very difficult, to change them in a reasonable amount of time. In as far as such stable personality traits influence the learning process, it is obvious, that adaptation of the learning environment is necessary.

On the hand, knowledge and skills, production rules, schemes and semantic nets are the result of influences of the environment and education (external conditions) in combination with more stable personality characteristics (internal conditions).

In the middle of the dimension of changeability is the domain of cognitive styles and strategies. Strategies are conceived as domain-specific and adjustable, cognitive styles as rather stable products of talent, education and experience.

Adaptation in human-computer interaction is directed at adjustment to individual differences. Optimal interaction is only to be expected if the user interface (including the metacommunication) closely matches the characteristics of the user. There are situations in which matching is impossible, since the abilities needed to perform a certain task are beyond an individual's potentialities. Selection of users (possibly self-selection) is the only way to solve this problem. Matching means tuning the system and the user to each other. This process may take two different directions:

a. Adaptation may take the form of an educational activity, taking care of individual differences between users, their special wishes, abilities and problems, aiming at changing the human partner and at improving the individual's possibilities. The educational activity can take place either within or outside the computer system. Within the system, it can take the form of a tutorial, separated from the main activity, or help- and error-messages, related to the user's main activity. Our main effort will be directed towards designing adaptive help- and error messages. Hereby the application as such and its communication to the user can remain fixed. This is a requirement for an open system situation, where the application itself cannot be changed.

b. The interface may react to the individual user in a flexible way. In this case the designer will have to accept the fact that the mode and quality of interaction will not be of a uniform nature for different users. To accomplish an adaptation, the system must be constructed with a built-in model of the user. The required data about the user can be obtained by asking the user himself (before the session is started, or on request during the session) or by diagnosing the user during the session. The adaptation of the interface can then take place either by the user himself (customisation), or automatically by the system. Customisation should be preferred in order not to confuse users. Here the user is offered different options, for instance for help, undo, documentation and renaming. The system may even offer users a choice of interaction formats. Automatic adaptation may be recommended for cases where the system detects simple, recurring errors in the user's interaction behaviour. A user who consistently writes "flie" instead of "file", for instance, could be helped by a system which understands what he means and does not ask every time the misspelling occurs.

Often the optimal situation combines elements of both directions. The most successful way of adaptation is determined by the possibilities and desirability of changing the user's characteristics and by properties of the task domain.

Analysis of an application

Analysis of an application presupposes that both the human requirements and the application have to be considered. It was decided to formulate the human requirements as a "wish list" for features in an imagined "ideal" for the application chosen, i.e. mail. It was further decided to analyse one particular existing mail system in detail, in order to see what concepts and operations were involved. This parallel development of a "wish list" and a description of an existing system makes it possible in the future to suggest changes of features of the existing system, where these are found not to correspond to the "ideal" situation. The formal descriptions of the "ideal" and existing system make it possible to compare the ideal and existing system on the same level.

It may show up that the wish list derived is to some extent unrealistic. Also, it does certainly not restrict the ideal system to one particular implementation. Rather, the analysis of an ideal should be regarded as a range, within which future implementations should lie.

UNIX mail from a user's viewpoint

The present section tries to categorise users' observations and provides some (modest) guidelines for the construction of an electronic mail system. At first glance criticism seems to dominate, but the goal is to summarise experiences, not to derogate a powerful and useful tool. The specific system which was studied was the seventh edition of the system, update 2.1 (/bin/mail).

Strong Points

The UNIX† mail system gives (especially in combination with "write") tremendous opportunities for inter-user communication. The strong points in this respect are:

a. power
   - It is relatively easy to send mail to other institutes (when UUCP is installed).
   - It is possible to send secret mail (using xsend).
   - Sophisticated and fast mail handling are provided (e.g. looking through your mail in reversed order).

b. speed
   - To send a short letter to another user can be done within 15 seconds.

c. complete integration with the UNIX operating system. For instance:
   - Sending of files from your directory to other users (using pipes or re-directs).
   - The possibility of giving commands to the shell while looking through your mail.

Weak Points

The strong points described above all refer to the functionality of the system. Some of the weak points below refer to the semantic aspects of the system, most of the weak points described here refer to the lower levels of the interaction, i.e. the syntax and keystroke levels.

---

† UNIX is a trademark of Bell Laboratories.

a. inconveniences
The word "inconveniences" is used for aspects which are not vital shortcomings but do cause loss of time, increased error rate etc. This refers to the semantics of the system. The aspects mentioned below are of course an arbitrary choice but probably most "heavy users" will recognise them as unhandy.

- When sending a message fails the message is saved in the file "dead.letter". When another mailing fails this file is overwritten without informing the user.
- When a letter prepared with "mail" has been sent successfully there is no possibility to save a copy of this letter (except when you send it to yourself).
- A user is informed if he has any mail just after a successful login. But there is no (fast) way of finding out who has sent the mail or how many letters there are.
- When entering the UMS there is no way of knowing how to invoke the help-menu before you have seen it.
- While working with your mail "x" and "q" turn out to be not the only ways to go back to the shell. "Control-d" gets you back. And if you are viewing your last message so do "+", "d", "n", "s", "m" and "return".

b. inconsistencies
With "inconsistencies" are meant events, feedback and commands which are not logical or consistent with the rest of the system. This refers to syntax aspects of the interface. Some examples:

- When using the mail system, the command "ddddghtyt&&543*" will delete a message. Obviously the shell does more error checking. Strangely ,"sfgrthg" is not equal to "s" but "nfhytnvc" is to "n".
- If a message is sent from the shell to two users who are not listed (Ziggy and Elton) the following error message appears:

```
mail: can't send to Ziggy.
mail: can't send to Elton.
Mail saved in dead.letter.
```

If you do the same from the mail system (using "m") you get:

mail: can't send to Ziggy.
Mail saved in dead.letter.
mail: can't send to Elton.
Mail saved in dead.letter.

Although not entirely cryptic, it is more confusing.

- When the user wants to see the previous message in the mail system and there is no one, then the same message is shown again. If he requests the next and there is no next one he is send back to the shell automatically.
- "mail xxxxx" (from the shell) and "m xxxxx" (from the mail system) are essentially the same commands. So why not give them the same name? (typing "mail xxxxx" in the mail system causes an error)

c. lack of feedback
The UNIX operating system and all its utilities give no feedback if a process is started correctly. The only evidence of a successful completion of the process is the re-appearing prompt. This approach is called "silent mode". Especially novice users would like to have more feedback when they use mail. ("But how do I know my message is sent?") Before we criticise this unfriendly behaviour it is good to know that UNIX, when it was developed in the early seventies (!), was intended as programmer's workshop. Its users therefore, would be well-trained professionals who do not need and want "useless" feedback messages. But today the system is used by people with very little experience and the lack of feedback is often a problem.

Conclusion

The UNIX mail system is still a powerful and useful utility but these characteristics are not sufficient. Today, many non-experts are using UNIX mail and sortlike programs. Their demands are of cognitive ergonomic nature: userfriendliness, learnability etc. If software is developed without considering the human factors, it will take longer to learn and will result in more errors by users. The great advantage of UNIX and its components is adaptability. Until now this advantage has only been used to improve the system technically. Since the system is becoming popular very fast in the world of office-automation maybe this is the right time for improvements concerning the area of human factors.

An example of various problems encountered in UNIX mail

An exploratory study was performed, where one subject who did not know anything about computers was asked to perform some simple tasks in UNIX mail. The subject was given a short introduction to UNIX mail. The subject was not given the manual (the reason is that in an open system you might not have all manuals available). The subject was told that he could get help by pressing the "?" key. At the operating system level, help was given orally (according to some simple rules). At the mail level, only the in-built help was used.

The following difficulties were encountered:

a. The subject did not understand how to send a letter (once he had written it). From the subject's comments and the registrations of the interactions, the following reasons for this difficulty were found:
   - There is no way to check that a letter really has been sent. The subject tried hard to find a way, and ultimately gave up. He never found out that his intention to check was in vain.
   - The subject could not understand the description of commands in the help menu. In particular, he tried to use commands in "send" mode which were only applicable in "read" mode. (For instance he tried to "remail message", when he had finished his writing.)
   - The subject did not know "where he was" (i.e. in the operating system, in "send" mode or in "read" mode). The cursor changes slightly in the different modes, but the subject did not notice this slight change.
   - The subject was uncertain about the difference between received mail and written mail. This uncertainty showed up when he tried to check that the letter was sent by checking his own letters.
   - The subject did not know how a written letter is treated by the system, i.e. he did not know that finishing the mail session by "ctrl-d" also sends the letter.

b. The subject did not understand when the help-text could be derived. This difficulty is related to the layout of the screen. In fact, the help-text is only available in "read"-mode. However, in this particular case, the subject had first read a letter, and then asked for help. Thereby the help-text was available all the time he tried to send his own letter. It was this help-text that the subject used to find out how to send the written letter.

The system does not make the most important distinction sufficiently clear: the distinction between "send" and "read" mode. The very faint hint lies in the prompt, which consists in a "?" in read mode and nothing in send mode. Combined with the cluttered screen, which showed the "read" commands also while the user was writing, it is easy to understand that the user did not notice the important distinction. Not noticing it, it was of course impossible for the user to understand which actions lead to which results, and thus to make a coherent plan for writing letters.

Conclusions for an "ideal" mail system

It is often hold that an "ideal" system should conform to users' expectations. However, users of new computer systems do not usually hold any particular expectations on the system. The new system offers new facilities, and it is not necessary that these comply with the facilities which already are familiar to users.

Instead, it is necessary that the system as a whole complies with the users' cognitive requirements:

a. *attention*

Human beings' attention is restricted. It is therefore essential that attention is directed to the right place. Users' prior knowledge will make them attend to particular things (and neglect others). If a system includes an important distinction (such as between "read" and "write" mode as here illustrated) users should also be made to attend to that distinction.

The "ideal" system would start with "refreshing" the screen when changing "mode". This would avoid the confusion the user encounters when nonrelevant help messages are still visible on the screen. It would also be advisable to invoke some active help to make the users attentive to the distinctions which the system performs (i.e. between read and write-mode). The actual method to draw attention to the relevant facts has still to be determined.

b. *evaluation*

The user will evaluate the result achieved with reference to his goal. It is thus essential that the system gives some information about the result. One of the main difficulties in the UNIX mail system is that it normally operates in "silent mode". It does not give any indication at all about the outcome of a certain command once it has been given by the user. This absence of feedback was responsible for most of the problems encountered by our example user.

An "ideal" system should strive for as much feedback as possible to novice users (and maybe less to experienced users). We here encounter the problem of trade-off: A great amount of feedback will compete with the user's attention when other aspects are concerned. The user's planning of the next action may for instance be hampered if he has to wait for the feedback to appear and has to process it before he can continue. Frequent users of the same system may not need much feedback at all.

c. *memory*

When new and unfamiliar procedures are presented, people will have difficulties memorising them. Users will differ in terms of what procedures that are unfamiliar to them, and will thus need different reminders.

The "ideal" system should thus have the possibility to tailor the information about the system (metacommunication) to the needs of the particular user. The knowledge the user brings to the particular situation can be assessed in advance by some simple questions. This assessment should cover not only information about whether or not the user knows this particular system, but also information about what other systems the user is familiar with. It has been found that both negative and positive transfer results between different systems (Waern, 1986).

There are some different ways of helping memory: giving concrete, procedural reminders and trying to fit the procedures into an overall structural model. We do not know what way is best, but suppose that different kinds of users may need different kinds of memory helps.

d. *interpretation*

Users have to make sense of what they themselves and the system are doing, both in order to ease the working memory load and in order to plan future actions. We here encounter the big problem of what mental model of the system a particular user creates, and how this mental model may differ from the system's actual virtual machine (i.e. the conceptual model of the system).

In this particular project we have found that it is no trivial task to define the conceptual model of the UNIX mail system, even less to define the different mental models which users might create from the metacommunications and interactions with the system. An "ideal mail" must in a similar way specify the conceptual model of the system envisaged.

e. *generalisation*

Whereas interpretation refers to particular procedures to be performed to achieve a particular goal, generalisation implies that some rules can be found which can generate different procedures for different circumstances.

In the UNIX mail study we found that one particular difficulty was related to the inconsistency of the commands used to invoke the "read" and the "send" mode respectively. Whereas the command "mail" would be expected to refer to an invocation of the mail system as such (as in DEC-type systems), in this particular version of UNIX-mail here used (and other types of mail systems as well) this command leads the user directly to the "read" mode. To write, the user has to give the command "mail", followed by a user-identity. This command structure is not very consistent and contributes to keeping the user to the procedural type of knowledge, where the difference between "read" and "write" modes is not clearly understood.

An ideal system is built on consistent rules to help the user with his generalisation attempts. A careful consideration of the functions which the system should perform can help system designers to create a consistent "grammar" (Payne, 1985). Starting at the functional level, further developments of the systems can then be made by specifying the corresponding command structures and the interaction rules (Moran, 1981).

Definition of IMAIL

In this section we will present a definition of the functionality of a mail system, that might be expected to be consistent with the "natural" mental model a novice user may develop from an electronic mail system. The conceptual model that will be described in this way will be called "IMAIL". We have no pretension that this will be the "ideal" mail system, but it will at least be more close to a description of the task analysis and related semantics of an electronic mail service as might be understandable for a naive user. Our analysis derives both from a collection of descriptions of existing mail systems and related applications, from intuitive reasoning, and from experience in psychological field studies on introductory courses in computer applications. We describe the mail facilities according to task level and semantic level. In this way a virtual machine is defined on these levels, for which the syntax may be derived from two sources:

a. consistency
The different layers of the virtual machine should be consistent to each other from the user's point of view, so the semantic level will put constraints on the design of the syntax.

b. knowledge of human factors
Psychological knowledge of human perception, attention, learning and memory will provide a potential source of guidelines. Thus far both at task level and at semantic level of the virtual machine the functionality of a mail system has been defined, which we call IMAIL, although we are aware of the fact that this cannot be a real "ideal" mail system, since too much of the preparation has been based on guesswork.

The Task Level

We restrict the task level to a small number of main mail tasks, and some tasks of metacommunication. Editing of messages is deliberatedly left out of the task domain. The primary subtasks, related to a message in a computerised world are:

Preparing
Sending
Receiving
Administration
Learning

If the world is the UNIX world the message should be manipulated as a "file". For all of these subtasks, the user will need the possibility to delegate parts to the system, in an interactive fashion.

In providing possibilities for delegation, the level of expertise will ask for adaptation of the interface. Novices will need other possibilities for decomposition of task to be partly delegated to the system, than do UNIX programmers.

Semantic Level

objects:	
-message	original message (opened/unopened) copy of message
-marks	
-highlighted object	(marked by the sender, or first line)
-system object	(folder, dir, file)
-receiver	(list, group)

attributes:	
-sender	
-date	of receiving
-date(s)	of sending
-1st line/ highlighted object	

actions:		
-create	>	original message
-send	>	copy of message
-receive (system action)	>	unopened message
-read	>	message
-browse	>	list of messages
-mark	>	message
-locate and read	>	message
-notify (system action)	>	unopened message
-destroy	>	original message
-copy	>	message to system object
-move	>	message to system object
-terminate session		

metacommunication action:	
-help_status	where to go to what is possible here where from
-help_semantic	tree structure menu
-help_syntax(action)	specification/prescription
-error	(system action)
-feed back	(system action)

A prototype system

In this section a method will be presented to defined a prototype user interface with built in tools for adaptation and metacommunication. We choose SYNICS to describe the interface.

Dialogue description in SYNICS

The design philosophy of SYNICS is that the end-user dialogue can be seen as a state transition network. This design is simple to follow and it has been found that most non-computing personal can easily deal with this description of the interface. Each nodal point in a state diagram equates to a "dialogue event" in the SYNICS system. At each event there may be some output, there may be some input, and there will be a decision made on which is the next event. To decide which is the next event there are several options. Normally the designer would indicate that input should come from either the end-user or the application, then depending on how this input was recognised the system would proceed to the next event in the dialogue.

The method of recognising the input, and therefore deducing the next event in the dialogue, is performed by a pattern matching operation. This is done by a simple BNF style description. The SYNICS system works through the various descriptions until it finds one that matches. On locating a match it allows for a translation of the input, or some form of output string to be constructed, that can be used later. Then a directive that was associated with this pattern match is used to invoke the next event. There is a fail safe explicit directive option which can be used should none of the templates find a match with the input.

This pattern matching system can be used to accept invalid strings and search for expected embedded keywords. There is some contextual searching facility also. These features are not very common with pattern matchers, but our experience has shown that they are very often needed when attempting to recognise end-user input strings.

Dialogue language format

There are a principal set of commands with which a dialogue can be constructed. The designer needs only to know how to name a event, output to the screen, read from either the end-user or background task, and then make a decision as to which event to progress to next.

Each event is described with an introduction statement giving the number by which it is to be defined, any output required to be printed on the terminal when entering this event, and the strings (with their relevant actions) to be followed on leaving this event.

There are seven different types of action which can be engaged at an event, each of which causes the dialogue to progress (EXIT, GO TO nn, TO nn IF, CALL nn, TO mm IF rr, RETURN, RESTART). The next event to be accessed is, in most cases, named explicitly. There is also the final termination command.

Representation of conceptual model and of interfaces

Early work by members of the COST working group (Hannemyr and Innocent, 1985) introduced the idea of representing a user session within an Open Systems Application environment using a language model. That is, transactions between users and the system could only take place within a formally described grammar. The syntax of these transactions was defined formally within a grammar notation based on the Backus-Nauer Form (BNF). The semantics were also described in Hannemyr and Innocent (op cit).

This section describes formally the interface between the user interface and the background system for a user in a testbed environment. It is intended to be a fixed component of the test bed for experiments with the user interface being a variable component. The work is presented in a general form which relates to the context of developing standards in open systems interconnection (OSI). The test bed application is based on a subset of UNIX mail and does not include the specification of the user interface.

Brief overview of Extended BNF

It is assumed that the reader is familiar with reading standard BNF rules. The extension to the use of the notation is made by applying the language to represent interactive grammars between 2 or more parties. The following extensions are used:

a. label nonterminals with a party identifier

b. assignment of values to nonterminals and the use of square brackets to output the value

c. a nonterminal which matches any string if no other parse succeeds (represented by '*').

Example (modified from Shneiderman, 1982):

```
<dialog>       ::=   <1:greet> <2:respond> | <1:*> <2:what>
<1:greet>      ::=   good morning my name is <1:name>
<2:respond>    ::=   hello [<1:name>]
<1:name>       ::=   <1:identifier>
<2:what>       ::=   what?   { this is a comment }
<identifier>   ::=   ATOM
```

This is a two party dialogue with person 1 and person 2. (They may be given other symbols for names). The non-terminal <identifier> is an atom in this description, i.e. not expanded further. It stands for any string of characters. The [] enclose carried over parameters from another rule within the scope of the current parse. The * indicates that other words than <greet> signifies by person 1. Person 2 then responds with "what?". When no party identifier is provided, the default the party last involved in a non- or terminal transaction. e.g. "hello" in the above example dialogue is generated by party 2 since the generator, <2:respond> is the last labelled non-terminal involved in the parse.

A null response can be explicitly represented by the atom NULL in the notation and will be found in the following specification. In practice, NULL refers not to a lack of acknowledgement (NAK) but the none return of a token for further parsing.

{} enclose comments and are additionally used to signify ATOMS that are not further defined in any of the sections of this report. If there is a cross reference to other sections, it is included in the comment. ATOMs which are not enclosed in {} are further defined below.

Note that person 2 (or 1) could be machines if desired and are used in this way in this work. The user interface is one party and the application system is the other.

A further extension is made to accommodate mandatory or optional parameters and the number of repetitions of an argument. E.g. suppose a command (I) can have up to 5 arguments (all alpha) and must have 1 at least. This is represented as follows:

$$\langle command \rangle \quad ::= \quad I\ (\langle arg \rangle)_1^5$$

$$\langle arg \rangle \quad ::= \quad \langle alpha \rangle\ \{ATOM\}$$

Note that in the absence of delimiters on () the default is that it occurs once. {ATOM} is shorthand for stating the rule that <alpha>::= ATOM. Additionally, syntax conventions are that <sp> represents a space on input, <enter> represents typing an enter (or carriage return) key and NULL represents the absence of either an input or output or transaction nonterminal.

The BNF is presented in blocks corresponding to the expansion of the tree in left to right order. In the normal way, the binding precedence is that <AND> takes precedence over <OR> in interpreting the tree. i.e. the foregoing 2 party BNF top level is interpreted as either person 1 makes a greeting and person 2 answers, or person 1 makes a greeting and person 2 says "what?".

Within the context of this work two levels are defined for the formal description of a simple application in an imaginary open system:

a. top level - service provision

b. lowest level - application

Level a. is described in two sections; the first is an imaginary OSI environment but not simulated for this project. The second is a UNIX environment which is used in the project for portability. This is described as a substitute system. Level b. is simulated for the mail service requirements of the project and is described in full.

Service provision

At present, little account is taken of the other work on standardisation that is continuing in the open systems area. The following work is, however, not critically dependent on the standards that are being developed and serves to illustrate the idea of approaching human factors incorporation in a systematic framework. The open systems syntax and semantics are first described; these are not simulated in this project. The syntax and semantics of a UNIX environment are then partially described; these are simulated in this project. Finally, the syntax and semantics of part of the UNIX mail application service is described; these are also simulated in this project. The purpose is to describe the top levels of the BNF only. Hence, there are a lot of undefined "ATOM"s in the BNF which follows. Future work will be to fully revise this section to reflect actual standards and systems rather than the simulations used at present.

OSI syntax (not implemented)

This is a grammar where a single party is concerned at present but would develop into finer detail with more parties if expanded. This should be possible when other working groups have progressed on the standards levels of the application layer.

```
<OSIsession>              ::=  <open-OSI> <session-unit> <close-OSI>
<open-OSI>                ::=  <log-on-sequence>   {ATOM}
<close-OSI>               ::=  <log-off-sequence>  {ATOM}
<session-unit>            ::=  <service-activity> |
                               <session-unit> <service-activity>
<service-activity>        ::=  <initialise> <structured-sentence> <cleardown>
<initialise>              ::=  <set-parameters>     {ATOM}
<cleardown>               ::=  <restore-parameters>   {ATOM}
<structured-sentence>     ::=  <transaction> |
                               <structured-sentence> <transaction> |
                               <session-unit>
<transaction>             ::=  ATOM {further defined in the application syntax}
```

"log-on-" and "log-off-" sequences are not further defined but would involve multi parties (user and OSI system). "set-" and "restore-" parameters are also not defined further but would involve the user interface, user and OSI as parties in the developed grammar. When OSI standards have been set in these areas, it will be possible to define this grammar further.

Transactions are atoms in this grammar which are generated (or parsed) in an OSI session and represent the main interest in development within the context of this report.

OSI semantics (not implemented)

For a detailed description of the related semantics refer to Hannemyr and Innocent (1985). The following is a brief summary.

The model is built on the basis of the 7 layer ISO reference model for Open Systems Interconnection. This implies that the top layer (application) has within it a "user interface management system" (UIMS) which is a sub-system of the network management system and can be partially distributed in the network. There are three agents of interest to be represented: the user, the application and the session. The following three entities are defined to facilitate communication between them.

a. form: defines interaction semantics, controlled by the application.

b. frame: defines interaction instances, controlled by the user.

c. state: defines interaction context, controlled by both user and application.

In opening a session (open-OSI) a frame is created by the user which contains terminal (eg VDU setup) details, etc. An initial form (called an executive form) exists which contains the legal operations of adding and deleting a transaction. On entering a session (service-activity) legal transactions for that service are added to the form by the application. During user - system interaction by transactions, frames are created and accessed which determine the interaction level details (eg. mouse or light pen). The local system translates from transaction objects into interaction level components depending on the state. States are controlled by user or application but are initialised and restored by the initialise and cleardown tokens.

On leaving an OSI session (close-OSI) the UIM clears the frames and forms and sets the state to an initial state for the terminal. The transaction atom is currently of direct interest to this project.

Simulation syntax (implemented)

For the purposes of this project a UNIX system was partially simulated for the user. The only part of the system simulated was the logon and logoff procedures and invocation of the mail application program. Optional switches on the mail command (-r,-p,-q,-file), are not represented in this syntax. Default values are assumed such that all switches are off. The syntax of a session is described as follows:

```
<UNIX-session>          ::=   <logon> <session unit> <logoff> |
                              <U:*> <password> <UNIX-session>

<logon>                 :=    <U:logon-tokens> <U:name>
                              <S:response> <password>
<U:logon-tokens>        ::=   login <sp>
<U:name>                ::=   <valid-user-name> <enter>
<valid-user-name>       ::=   ATOM {defined by system and user }
<S:response>            ::=   NULL| <invalid user> | <mail-message>
<S:mail-message>        ::=   you have mail
<U:enter-passwd>        ::=   <text-string> <enter>
<invalid-user>          ::=   <user not known message> {ATOM}

<session unit>          ::=   <service-activity> |
                              <session-unit> <service-activity>
<service-activity>      ::=   <mail-service> | NULL

<mail-service>          ::=   <S:prompt> <U:response>
<S:prompt>              ::=   $
<U:response>            ::=   <mail-invoke> <mail-commands> |
                               <mail-to-users> | * <mail-service>
<mail-invoke>           ::=   mail <enter>
<mail-commands>         ::=   ATOM {defined in next block of syntax rules }
<mail-to-users>         ::=   <mail-invoke> <recipients> <compose>
<recipients>            ::=   <recipient> | <recipient> <recipients>
<recipient>             ::=   <valid-user-name>
<compose>               ::=   <text-string> <terminator>
<text-string>           ::=   ATOM
<terminator>            ::=   ?z <enter> | <enter> . <enter>

<logoff>                ::=   <U:logoff-tokens>
<U:logoff-tokens>       ::=   logoff <enter>

<password>              ::=   <S:password-tokens> <U:enter-passwd>
                              <S:prompt>
<S:password-tokens>     ::=   password
```

The mail commands and mail messages are described in a later section. Text preparation is not included in the mailbox simulation formally.

Simulation semantics (implemented)

As far as possible, a simple interactive session between an accredited user and a UNIX system has been simulated. This includes only logging in and out and the use of a single service-activity, viz use of a mail program. The full UNIX machine is not simulated. i.e there are no files/structures/pipes etc. A particular quirk of the UNIX simulation is that a successful logon does not include the password input. An unsuccessful logon (i.e. username not in the list of allowed users) requests a password! There are no UNIX objects visible to the user (remember the 'user' in the above syntax (U) is not a human user, but an interface program).

On invocation of the mail service, UNIX checks to see if there is any mail in the users mailbox and if so returns a message indicating so. The mail service is then initialised for providing services to read mail. If there is no mail, only compose and send services are initialised. Mail can be sent only to legally registered UNIX users on the system. Attempts to send mail to unknown or illegal persons results in an interruption. If there is mail, then the user can enter a wider range of mail services in the application.

Application

The project calls for two versions of a simple mail application based on UNIX mail. The versions are called UMAIL and IMAIL. Neither version includes such facilities as system calls, or editing messages for preparation to send. UMAIL is a minimal subset of UNIX mail as currently defined for Version 3 of UNIX. IMAIL is based on a desired mail facility comparable to UMAIL but including extra functions.

The syntax and semantics of each application is considered independently and uses cross reference atoms from the syntax descriptions of the implemented simulation of the service provision level. In this contribution, we will work out UMAIL only.

UMAIL Syntax (implemented)

```
<U:mail-commands>    ::=   <help> | <compose> | <quit> | <stop> |
                           <position> | <send> | <copy> | <delete> |
                           <* error><U:mail-commands>

<* error>            ::=   <S:help-menu>
```

```
<help>                ::=   <help-token> <S:help-menu>
<help-token>          ::=   ? <enter>
<S:help-menu>         ::=   ATOM

<compose>             ::=   ATOM

<quit>                ::=   <U:quit-token> <S:restore>
<U:quit-token>        ::=   q <enter> | <ctrl-D>
<S:restore>           ::=   ATOM  <S:UNIX-session>
                            {breaks the parse and takes to UNIX level}

<stop>                ::=   <U:stop-token> <S:stop-message>
<U:stop-token>        ::=   x <enter>
<S:stop-message>      ::=   ATOM <S:UNIX-session>

<go-back>             ::=   - <enter>
<go-on>               ::=   (p|NULL) <enter>
<S:show-message>      ::=   ATOM

<send>                ::=   <send-token> <recipients> <enter>
<send-token>          ::=   m
<recipients>          ::=   <recipient> | <recipient> <recipients>
<recipient>           ::=   <sp> <valid-mail-user>
<valid-mail-user>     ::=   ATOM

<copy>                ::=   <U:copy-cmd> <S:copy-response>
<copy-cmd>            ::=   <copy-token> <filename> <enter>
<copy-token>          ::=   s <sp>
<filename>            ::=   <UNIX-filename> | ATOM
                            <default-file>
<default-file>        ::=   mbox  {UNIX filename }
<S:copy-response>     ::=   <copied-message> {ATOM} |
                            <not-copied-message> {ATOM}

<delete>              ::=   <delete-token> <S:go-on-next>
<delete-token>        ::=   d <enter>
<S:go-on-next>        ::=   ATOM
```

UMAIL semantics (implemented)

The simulated mail machine has a sequential stack of messages which can be read in last-in first-out order by stepping through with the go-on commands. The user can go backwards as well with the go-back commands. If the user reads past the bottom of the list using go-on then he is returned to the top of the stack. If the user goes off the top of the stack with a go-back command then an implicit <quit> command is invoked.

Messages are marked for deletion during a session and the mailbox is only updated if a <quit> command is invoked implicitly or explicitly. Exit from the mail service by using the <stop> command does not change the contents of a mailbox. Saved messages are copied with a header which identifies the sender, subject and date.

IMAIL syntax (to be simulated)

```
<U:mail-commands>        ::=  <help> | <compose> | <send> |
                              <quit> | <restore> | <browse> |
                              <mark> | <read> | <look-at> |
                              <copy> | <destroy> |
                              <* error> <U:mail-commands>

<* error>                ::=  <S:help-general>
<S:help-general>         ::=  ATOM

<help>                   ::=  <help-status> | <help-semantic> |
                              <help-syntax> | <help-quit>
<help-status>            ::=  <status-token> <S:status-dialogue> <help-quit>
<help-semantic>          ::=  <semantic-token> <S:semantic-dialogue>
                              <help-quit>
<help-syntax>            ::=  <syntax-token> <S:syntax-dialogue> <help-quit>
<status-token>           ::=  ATOM <enter>
<semantic-token>         ::=  ATOM <enter>
<syntax-token>           ::=  ATOM <enter>
<help-quit>              ::=  ATOM <enter>
<S:status-dialogue>      ::=  <where-from> | <where-to> | <whats-possible>
<where-from>             ::=  ATOM { special dialogue not expanded }
<where-to>               ::=  ATOM { special dialogue not expanded }
<whats-possible>         ::=  ATOM { special dialogue not expanded }
<S:semantic-dialogue>    ::=  <help-menu>
<help-menu>              ::=  {ATOM}
<S:syntax-dialogue>      ::=  <command-syntax-help>
<command-syntax-help>    ::=  {ATOM}

<compose>                ::=  create <sp> <filename> <enter>
<filename>               ::=  <text-string>

<send>                   ::=  <send-token> <recipients> <enter>
<recipients>             ::=  <recipient> | <recipient> <recipients>
<recipient>              ::=  <sp> <valid-mail-user>
<valid-mail-user>        ::=  {ATOM}
<send-token>             ::=  m
```

```
<quit>                   ::=  <U:quit-token> <S:exit>
<S:exit>                 ::=  ATOM <S:UNIX-session> {leaves this parser}
<U:quit-token>           ::=  ATOM <S:UNIX-session> {leaves this parser }

<U:restore>              ::=  <restore-token> <S:restore>
<restore-token>          ::=  ATOM <enter>
<S:restore>              ::=  ATOM <S:UNIX-session> {leaves this parser }

<browse>                 ::=  <browse-token>
                              (<sp> <opened-list> | <sp> <unopened-list> |
                               <sp> <all>) <enter>
<opened-list>            ::=  <browse-dialogue-open> {ATOM}
<unopened-list>          ::=  <browse-dialogue-unopened> {ATOM}
<all>                    ::=  <browse-dialogue-all> {ATOM}
<mark>                   ::=  <mark-token> <position-mark>
                              <marker-identifier>
<position-mark>          ::=  ATOM
<mark-token>             ::=  ATOM
<marker-identifier>      ::=  ATOM
<browse-token>           ::=  ATOM
<read>                   ::=  <position> <S:show-message>
<position>               ::=  <find> <S:show-message>|
<find>                   ::=  <go-to-marker> | <locate-text>
<locate-text>            ::=  <find-token> <arguments>
<arguments>              ::=  <text-string> |
                              <text-string> <connective> <arguments>
<connective>             ::=  <conjunction> | <disjunction> | <negation>
<go-to-marker>           ::=  <goto-token> <marker-identifier>
<goto-token>             ::=  ATOM
<conjunction>            ::=  <sp> and <sp>
<disjunction>            ::=  <sp> or <sp>
<negation>               ::=  <sp> not <sp>
<S:show-message>         ::=  ATOM
<text-string>            ::=  ATOM
<marker-identifier>      ::=  ATOM
<look-at>                ::=  <look-at-token>
                              (<opened-message> | <unopened-message>)
<look-at-token>          ::=  ATOM
<locate-dialogue>        ::=  ATOM
<opened-message>         ::=  ATOM
<unopened-message>       ::=  ATOM

<copy>                   ::=  <U:copy-cmd> <S:copy-response>
<copy-cmd>               ::=  <copy-token> <filename>
<filename>               ::=  <textstring> | mbox
<textstring>             ::=  ATOM
<copy-token>             ::=  ATOM
<S:copy-response>        ::=  <copied-message> {ATOM} |
                              <not-copied-message> {ATOM}
```

<destroy>	::=	<destroy-token> <S:destroy-response>
<destroy-token>	::=	ATOM
<S:destroy-response>	::=	ATOM
<find-token>	::=	ATOM
<argument>	::=	(<sp> <arg>)$_0^N$
<arg>	::=	ATOM

IMAIL semantics (to be simulated)

The IMAIL system is designed to be built on top of UMAIL with a number of extra features. The most important of these is the distinction between two different classes of object held in the message; objects can be highlighted or not. In this context, highlighting means that an object has been marked by a user as being semantically significant.

A second difference is that messages can be opened but unread by a user. This is analogous to receiving a letter but not reading its contents. (Users know by various cues that the probable contents are about certain topics with a certain priority.) The first line of a message is by default a highlighted object which is given to the user when the message is received. Users can then leave the message unopened or open and read it. Inside a message, the user can scan the highlighted objects.

Users can browse through mail (which can be unopened or opened) by using a facility which allows selection via combinations of highlighted objects. Marking a message renders an object in it as highlighted.

Letters have the normal attributes of post date and sender. These constitute special highlighted objects which must always be present. Letters enter the users mailbox in time order. Access is normally via system presented scan used in browsing which defaults to the most recent letter being at the "top" of the pile, (i.e. the same as UMAIL). Major changes in help are provided in IMAIL. Help can be provided at semantic, syntax and status levels. Help is accessed at the top level of commands in the existing definition.

Questions for resolution in the development of IMAIL

a. In carrying out the formal development in BNF of the OSI and applications, it is possible to identify all the unresolved terminals. This is one of the benefits of using a formal description language. Among the questions that can be raised from this are: is help available within any command?

b. Is marking an object the same as highlighting an object? If not what operations can take place with marked objects?

c. Should we also have "unmarking"?

d. Are commands available for changing the order of retrieval of messages?

e. Are lists of recipients allowed which are in files called by name?

Of course the answers to many of the syntax questions are directly related to the semantics adopted for the processes. As yet these are incompletely defined for various parts of the system.

State of development

The syntax and semantics of IMAIL have yet to be completely defined and the cross-references to the interface definition must be carried out. In particular, all those syntax elements marked as {ATOM} must be expanded where necessary. The easiest way of providing a cross-reference is by writing the SYNICS definition of the user interface in terms of extended BNF so that there terminals correspond to the ATOMS of this report. This will be done at stage two of the project.

References

Card, S.K. & Young, R. (1984). *Predictive Models of the User*. NATO Workshop Paper No. 6. Private Communication from the HCIRU, Loughborough University of Technology.

Carroll, J.M. (1983). Presentation and form in user-interface architecture. *Byte,* December 1983, pp. 113-122.

Carroll J.M. & Thomas J.C. (1982). Metaphor and the cognitive representation of computing systems. *IEEE Transactions on Systems, Man, and Cybernetics,* 12, pp. 107-116.

Clanton C. (1983). The future of metaphor in man-computer systems. *Byte,* December 1983, pp. 263-270.

Fischer G., Lemke A. & Schwab T. (1984). *Active Help Systems.* HCI84, BCS publications.

Guest S.P. (1982). Software tools for dialogue design. *International Journal of Man-Machine Systems,* 14, pp. 263-285.

Hannemyr G. (1983). Human factors standards. The design of conceptual language interfaces to open computer network application and management systems. *Behaviour and Information Technology,* 2, pp. 335-344.

Hannemyr G. & Innocent P.R. (1985). A network user interface: incorporating human factors guidelines into the ISO standard for open systems interconnection. *Behaviour and Information Technology,* 4, pp. 309-326.

Houston T. (1983). The allegory of software. *Byte,* December 1983, pp. 210-214.

Moran T.P. (1981). The command language grammar: a representation for the user interface of interactive computer systems. *International Journal of Man-Machine Studies,* 15, pp. 3-50.

Muylwijk B. van, Veer G.C. van der & Waern Y. (1983). On the implications of the user variability in open systems. An overview of the little we know and of the lot we have to find out. *Behaviour and Information Technology,* 2, pp. 313-326.

Norman D.A. (1983). Some observations on mental models. In A.L. Stevens & D. Gentner (Eds.), *Mental Models.* Hillsdale, N.J.: Erlbaum.

Payne S.J. (1985). *Task Action Grammars: The Mental Representation of Task Languages in Human-Computer Interaction.* Unpublished PhD thesis, University of Sheffield.

Pfaff G. (Ed.) (1983). *User Interface Management Systems.* Eurographic Series, Heidelberg - Berlin - New York: Springer Verlag.

Rich E. (1983). User are individuals: individualising user models. *International Journal of Man-Machine Studies,* 18, pp. 199-214.

Rumelhart D.E. & Norman D.A. (1983). Analogical processes in learning. In J.R. Anderson (Ed.), *Cognitive Skills and their Acquisition.* Cambridge, Mass.: Harvard University Press.

Shneiderman B. (1980). *Software Psychology.* Winthrop Computer Science Series, New York: Winthrop.

Shneiderman B. (1982). Multiparty Grammars and related features for defining interactive systems. *IEEE Transactions on Systems, Man, and Cybernetics,* Vol. SMC-12, No 2, pp. 148-155.

Tauber M.J. (1985). Top down design of human-computer systems. *Proceedings of the IEEE Workshop on Languages for Automation,* Palma de Mallorca, June 1985, Silver Spring.

Tauber M.J. (1987). The Heidelberg Interface Description Method. In *Progress Report on the Working Group Human Factors in Telematic Systems.* Cost-11 ter, E.E.C. Brussels.

Veer G.C. van der & Felt M.A.M. (1988). Development of mental models of an office system. In G.C. van der Veer and B. Mulder (Eds.), *Human-Computer Interaction - Psychonomic Aspects.* Heidelberg: Springer Verlag.

Veer G.C. van der & Muylwijk B. Van (1984). Human-computer interaction: individual differences and adaptation In J.C.P. Bus & P.Th.J. Ploeger (Eds.), *NGI-SION 1984 Informatica Symposium - State of the Art.* Nederlands Genootschap voor Informatica, Amsterdam.

Veer G.C. van der, Tauber M.J., Waern Y. & Muylwijk B. van (1985). On the interaction between system and user characteristics. *Behaviour Information Technology,* 4, pp. 289-308.

Wheeler T. & Innocent P. (1983). Human factors in and requirements of the OSI environment. *Behaviour & Information Technology,* **2**, pp. 335-344.

Waern Y. (1986). Understanding learning problems in computer aided tasks. In F. Klix and H. Wandke (Eds.), *Macinter I.* Amsterdam: North Holland.

Mental Models and Human-Computer Interaction 1
D. Ackermann and M.J. Tauber (Editors)

GNEWS: RESULTS OF AN EXPERIMENT ON THE REINFORCEMENT OF A MENTAL COMMUNICATION MODEL BY A VISUAL INTERFACE

Michael L. Begeman

Software Technology Program, MCC, Austin, Texas

ABSTRACT

It has been widely claimed that visual interfaces are "better" than linguistically-based interfaces for many applications. Most experiments investigating this claim have focused on users' performance at some particular task, such as editing a document. This paper demonstrates that a visual interface which reinforces its users' mental model of a communication paradigm can aid their ability to effectively express that model via machine-mediated conversations.

Introduction

Much effort has been spent over the past decade developing a science of interface design. In one corner, we have had people working on optimal methods of presenting graphical information (Benbasat et al. 1986, Dickson et al. 1986) providing basic insights into the effective use of color, shape and texture. In another, we have those who develop models of human-computer interaction from a psychological or linguistic point of view (Norman and Draper 1986, Ortony 1979), providing us with the understanding to make effective use of interaction styles such as direct manipulation, as well as insight into techniques such as rules on the use of metaphorical interfaces. In yet another, we find those practitioners who have produced hosts of visual languages, visual programming or design environments, and visual simulation systems (Glinert and Tanimoto 1984, Duisberg 1986, Reiss 1985, Melamed and

Morris 1985). Rarely, however, have studies been reported on the impact which the introduction of such a tool or technique has on the environment into which it was introduced. This paper presents the results of such an analysis.

Problem background

The members of MCC's Software Technology Program use an in-house electronic bulletin board system to post notices of general interest and to hold machine-mediated group discussions (i.e. informal group meetings which are neither cotemporally nor cospatially located (Eveland and Bikson 1986, Malone et al. 1986)). This bulletin board is implemented as a set of local newsgroups *) using the UNIX† USENET news network software (Horton and Adams, 1986). In this environment, a discussion begins when one user of the system submits (or "posts") an article to a newsgroup. Over a period ranging from a few hours to a period of days, other users will read the article and perhaps reply to it in the form of a "followup" article (an article which contains a symbolic reference to the original posting). Other users can also reply to the original posting, or may reply directly to other followups as they wish. The sequence of postings is completely unrestricted by the syntax of the system.

Figure 1 shows the abbreviated header information for five articles and the resulting logical structure. The original article, 1016, is responded to by two followup articles, 1017 and 1019 (notice that articles are linked via the "Message-ID" and "References" fields using unique, system-supplied message identifiers). Followup article 1019 itself has two followups, 1025 and 1054, and so on. In this and subsequent graphs, the numeric article identifier represents a temporal ordering of the articles based upon creation time.

While the underlying representation of the articles preserves the referential links among them, none of the existing news reading programs took advantage of these links to order the presentation of

---

* A newsgroup is a collection of individual articles, often grouped according to a particular topic (e.g. philosophy, woodworking, etc.)

† UNIX is a trademark of Bell Laboratories.

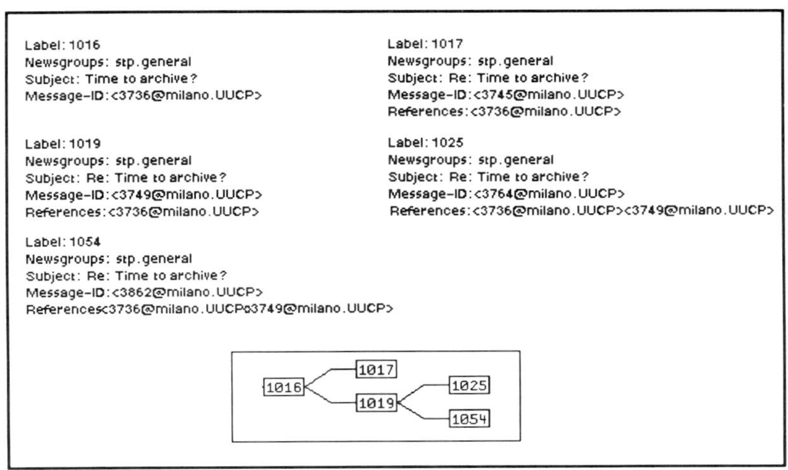

Figure 1. A discussion consisting of 5 articles

articles; they were always presented in the order in which they were submitted. If, for example, a user posted 3 articles (A1, A2, A3) to the newsgroup, and another user later responded to A1 with followup F1, a subsequent reader of the newsgroup would be led through the articles in the temporal order A1, A2, A3, F1. That is, the link which binds (A1, F1) into a discussion would be ignored, and the reader, after reading A1, would have to read the irrelevant articles A2 and A3 before being presented with the article semantically closest to A1, namely F1.

This leads us to the actual experiment: we hypothesized that providing a visual presentation of the articles which clustered them into conversational units would significantly enhance people's ability to use the USENET news network as a mechanism for holding machine-mediated group discussions. There is suggestive evidence for this hypothesis from the hypertext community (Halasz et al. 1987, Conklin 1986). Researchers in that field have consistently claimed that people's ability to navigate through nonlinear text spaces is greatly enhanced by the addition of a browser, a tool which provides a graphical presentation of the structure of the data. We therefore felt that the addition of such a browser would allow the subjects to use the USENET news network more effectively as a conversational medium.

Thus, we set out to build our experimental vehicle, gnews: a graphical browser for the USENET news network. There are several design criteria which were important to us: first, the tool needed to provide a visual indication of the articles and the links which tie a followup to its parent article **). Secondly, the articles must be spatially arranged so that articles which have been referentially linked are spatially close to one another as well. Third, the tool's interpretation of "Next Article" needed to mean "next" in the newly-constructed referential space, not the "next" in the temporal space of the old news reading programs. Lastly, to reinforce the graphical presentation of the semantic space, followups must be constructible as well as viewable via direct interaction with the article graph itself.

Figure 2 shows the tool interface with the graph of a newsgroup's articles loaded into it. The tool interface consists of four major areas: a graphical article browser (left), a subject index window (top right), a control panel (middle right), and a window for reading the contents of articles (bottom right). For a more detailed description of the tool, refer to Appendix A.

Experimental approach

Our experimental population consisted of 62 subjects who had access to the local newsgroups of the USENET news network. Of the subjects, 58 were existing users of the local newsgroups (4 people didn't read news articles for a variety of reasons). Additionally, 7 people did not have access to the new gnews interface because of hardware limitations. This left a population of 51 subjects who were candidates for "conversion" to gnews. We collected 8 months of baseline newsgroup data for each of 17 newsgroups, introduced gnews, and collected 8 more months of data to compare with the baseline. In addition, we collected 5 months of detailed by-user usage data on the tool itself.

Selected subjects were interviewed by the author during the 8-month period after the tool's introduction. These interviews are the basis for the nonnumeric conclusions described in the section

** An article which references a set of articles is physically linked to only the last element of that set.

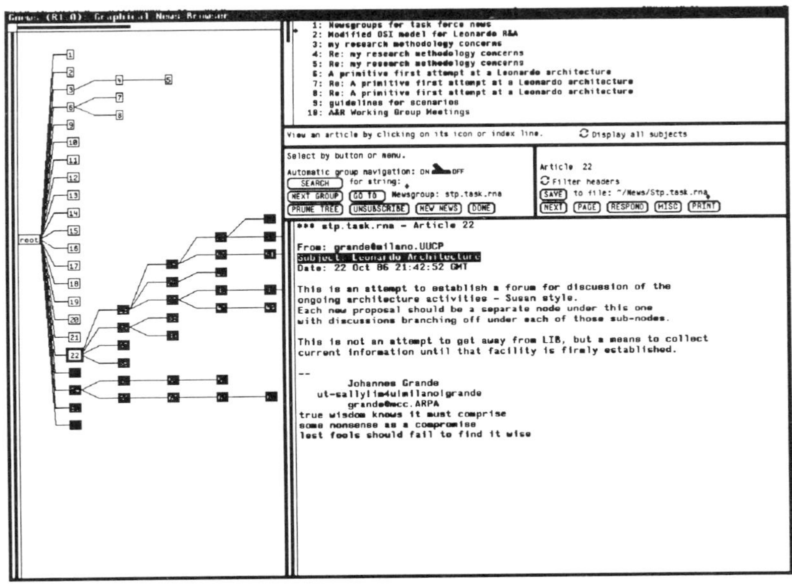

Figure 2. The gnews interface (also see Appendix A.)

"Discussion". The significance of the structural changes to the newsgroups which gnews facilitated were analyzed using standard parametric statistics as described in the next section.

Results

Usage data

The most striking immediate result of releasing the tool was its rapid acceptance by the population. Gnews was simply made available to the population; there was no coercion to switch from their "old favorite" news reading program (users already had three news reading programs from which to choose before the introduction of gnews). Figure 3 shows that close to 90% of the subjects voluntarily chose gnews as their primary news reading program by the end of the 5-month usage study.

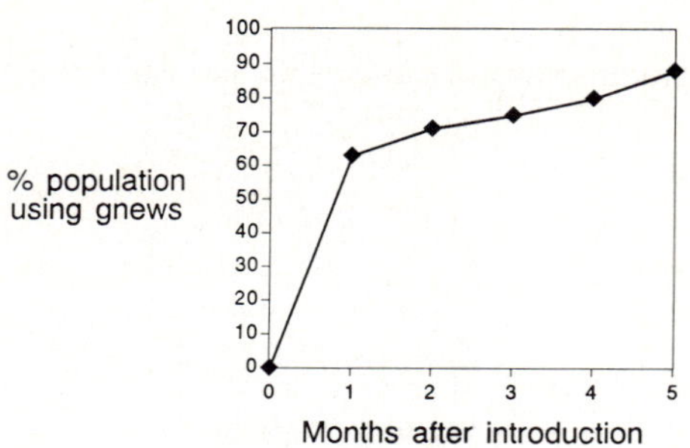

Figure 3. Rate at which users spontaneously converted to gnews

In interviews, the 2 primary reasons given by users for their acceptance of gnews were the clustering of semantically related articles, and the addition of the graphical browser which let them "see" the discussions which were occurring. More will be said about this in section "Discussion".

Structural effects

In comparing the pre- and post-gnews structural data, we had to define the term "conversation". One can see in figure 2 that many of the articles submitted have no followups, others have a few followups, and others are the root of large discussions. After looking at the content of these articles, we chose to define a conversation as a set of more than 3 nodes which are bound by followup links. Clearly, singleton articles (those with no followup) do not qualify as conversations. We also found that most of the 2-3 node clusters were simply requests for clarification or some other simple response, and thus should not be considered conversational per se. As we begin to analyze the contents of the articles to see if the tool affected the quality of the conversations, we may be able to define conversations qualitatively rather than by the current quantitative method.

Conversationality of a group

Certain groups tended to lend themselves to containing conversations. Of the 17 newsgroups studied, 10 contained no conversations either before or after the introduction of gnews. These tended to be groups which either had very low traffic to begin with (i.e. relatively low interest groups), or groups which were primarily informational (e.g. used for reporting software bugs and tracking fixes) and therefore did not seem to inspire extended conversations.

The remaining seven newsgroups which contained conversations split themselves into two classes, high and low conversationality. The five high conversationality groups (> 50% of the articles participated in a conversation) were quite narrow in the scope of their subject, and thus lent themselves to focused discussion and debate. The two remaining groups were much more general and informational in nature, and thus showed a lower proportion of conversation nodes to the total.

The remaining analysis of conversational characteristics is limited to the 7 groups in which conversations occurred.

Effect on the measure of a group's conversationality

After the introduction of gnews, subjects began producing followup responses much more than before the introduction. The number of followup articles (as a percentage of total articles) across all newsgroups rose from a pre-gnews level of 35% to a post-gnews level of 58%. Further, a t-Test for related measures showed the effect to be weakly significant across the groups ($p = 0.1$). This effect extends across both conversational and non-conversational article groupings, and suggests that the users considered responding via the newsgroups to be a more adequate method for response after gnews' introduction than before.

The percentage of conversational articles (i.e. those articles involved in a conversation as defined above) similarly rose from 27% to 49%, indicating the subjects' increased perception of newsgroups as a place to hold conversations. Again, this effect was shown significant ($p = 0.1$) across the groups.

Figure 4 shows a compressed structure map for four of the seven conversational newsgroups (note that the right-center graph of figure 4 is a compressed version of the graph in figure 2). The horizontal lines passing through each graph indicate the time in each newsgroup's history at which gnews was introduced. One can visually detect a difference in the structure of the pre- and post-gnews halves, reinforcing the results just described.

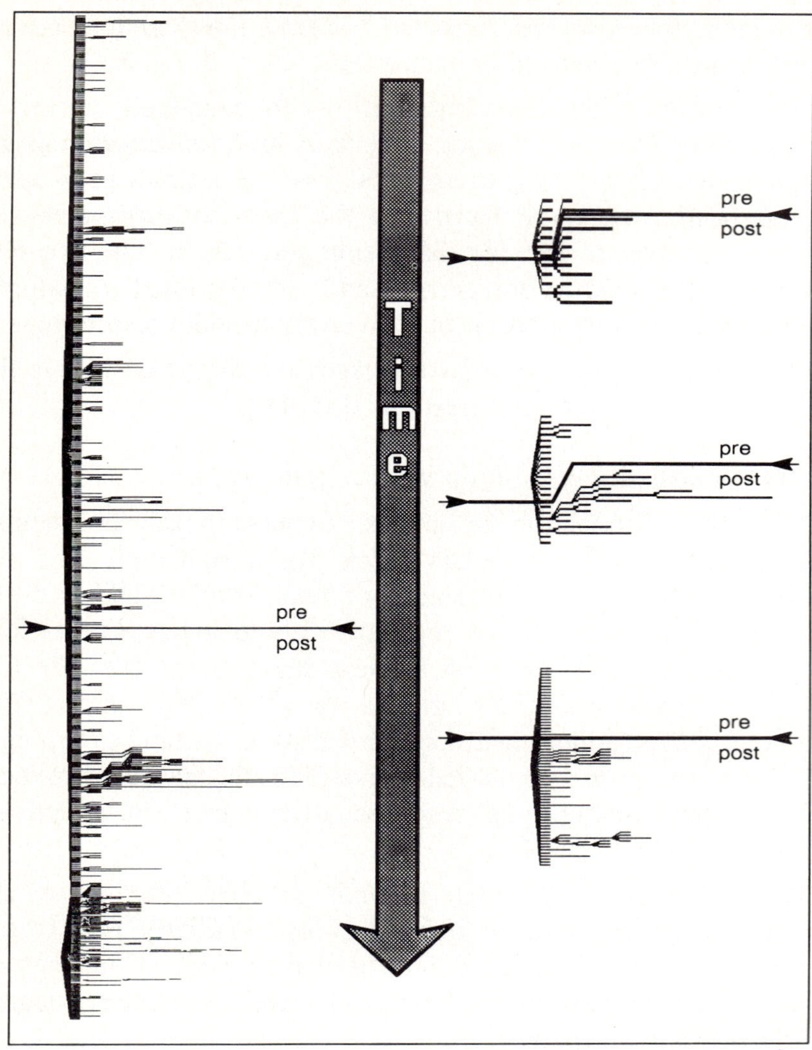

Figure 4. Structure graph of 4 newsgroups. Line indicated by → ← corresponds to the introduction of gnews.

Effect on individual conversations

Gnews' availability correlates positively with a change in the internal structure and size of individual conversations as well. The maximum size of a conversation (number of articles involved) across the newsgroups almost tripled ($p = 0.025$), and the maximum depth (greatest path length through the tree) almost doubled ($p = 0.1$), suggesting that gnews gave the subjects the ability to construct and work with larger, more complex conversational structures.

We believe this is primarily attributable to the visual component of the tool: subjects were able to physically see the structure graph of a conversation, and this in turn gave them a greater ability to manage its structural complexity. Additionally, the graph was a constant reminder of a newsgroup's conversational potential - it reinforced the concept of conversation by making it visually apparent, and this presumably contributed to the effect.

Effect on the organization using it

Perhaps most interesting are two organizational changes which corresponded to gnews' release. As soon as gnews was introduced, some of the staff members wanted to use it as the vehicle for capturing conversations about a particular topic - that is, they wanted a private newsgroup established for the explicit purpose of holding focused conversations on a single topic. Since then, we have created nine such special-purpose groups for the discussion of design issues related to particular ongoing tasks in the organization.

Figure 5 shows the graph resulting from the first such effort. Clearly, the tool gave its users the mechanism for holding a machine-mediated conversation of unprecedented size (64 articles, 4 times the pre-gnews maxim). It must be noted, however, that the term "conversation" is qualitatively defined in this context and we therefore did not include these group's numbers in the structural analysis above.

Secondly, gnews was influential in raising the organizational awareness of the importance of conversation per se. The Software Technology Program is now looking into ways to capture particular conversational formalisms such as "conversations for possibility" (Winograd and Flores 1986) and "issue-based" conversations (Rittel and Kunz 1970).

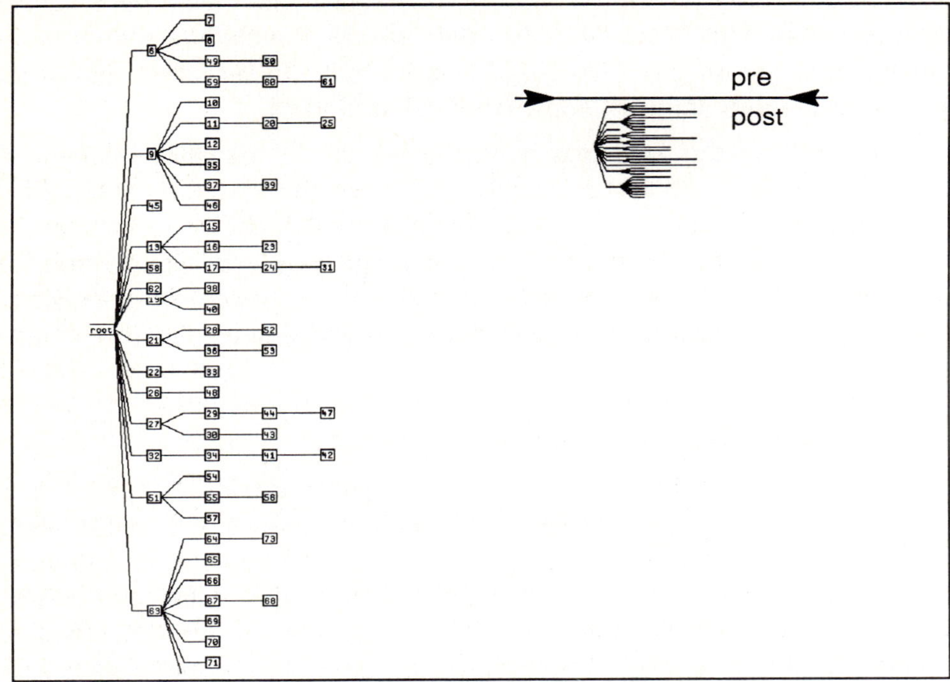

Figure 5. Structure of a newsgroup created explicitly for conversation.

Discussion

We have seen that the introduction of gnews is associated with a significant change in the structure of machine-mediated conversations. A number of factors might help to explain this.

First, gnews provides the user with a view of the structure of a conversation. While users think of news as a collection of conversations (where a conversation is made up of a root article, followups to the root, followups to the followups and so forth), the existing news interfaces largely ignored this. The gnews interface, however, presents a visual model of the information which closely matches a canonical mental model of this conversation space, and this match appears to result in more effective use of the available structure.

Secondly, the tool groups articles into conversational units so that users can deal with information which is highly related without having to filter extraneous articles and constantly switch cognitive contexts. By providing users with this strong sense of context, they not only know what is in the discussion, but where they are in the conversation as well. (Some subjects have admitted that they read an article more closely if they can see that it has spawned a number of followups.) In a sense, gnews has exploited the concept of "locality of reference" to reduce cognitive thrashing in the same way that Operating System paging algorithms and DBMS buffer management algorithms have exploited the concept to reduce thrashing in their domains.

Third, gnews' visual feedback was associated with an increase in the conversationality of the newsgroups. This visual feedback gives subjects the ability to see their contribution, and to know how it fits into the conversational structure. It also gives articles a new sense of permanence: other news reading programs give no indication of the presence of articles which have been read, but with gnews the articles remain visible over time. It seems likely that people are more apt to contribute to a permanent conversation than to one which is perceived to disappear after being read.

We cannot say, however, that gnews caused the observed changes because there exists a major confounding variable which was not controlled: the sociology of the subject group. Gnews' acceptance was concomitant with an emerging research interest in holding and capturing formal, structured conversations. We cannot separate out how much that interest influenced the way people used gnews, nor conversely how much the introduction of gnews helped to demonstrate the value of and sell the concept of structured conversations. Nevertheless, the simultaneous occurrence of gnews' acceptance and the development of a richer structure in news conversations suggests that gnews facilitated the changes which have been described.

While the quantitative data also do not allow us to separate the effects of the visual browser from those of the semantic clustering, interviews reveal large individual differences in the importance of these two components to the subjects. Some reported that they "almost never" look at the graph and that the reason they switched to gnews was because of the article clustering. Others said that they refer to the graph "all the time", often directly selecting an article based upon its tree position (parent, sibling, ...) relative to the current article. This widely varied feedback invokes the right-brain/left-brain, verbal/visual and linguistic/graphic distinctions which have been popularized, and suggest that the designers of future interfaces must begin providing multiple alternate presentations of the same data to accommodate these strong individual differences (see Reiss (1985) for another example of how this has been done).

Lastly, the author wishes to discuss the significance of these findings in the light of performing ex post facto analysis of data from field experiments. From a classical experimental point of view, this experiment raises more questions than it answers. One is challenged with many queries: what is the interaction between the tool and the group's interest in conversation as a topic for study? What is the independent effect of the browser? The clustering? The subject index? The direct manipulation interface? Is the tool's effect primarily attributable to one of these factors or would we find that it is the result of many small effects?

In this field experiment there were few controls. The subject population varied somewhat during the 16 months, the conversational topics varied in quality (some claim that we had "better" topics after gnews' introduction), the tool itself varied (some new features were added after introduction), and of course subject's familiarity with the USENET news mechanism itself increased. What can legitimately be claimed from such an uncontrolled enterprise? First, that an observable phenomenon did indeed take place: post-gnews news conversations became more the norm, and they tended to be broader and deeper than before. Secondly, that these results are dependent upon our definition of conversation, and may not be generalizable to qualitatively defined conversations or to specific types of conversation (Winograd and Flores 1986). And lastly, that the phenomenon took place within the particular context of an organizational interest in machine-mediated conversation, and that duplicating that sociological factor may be necessary to replicate these findings.

Suggested future research

While there is evidence that gnews impacted the structure of conversations, an obvious question left open is whether the content of the discussions was significantly altered. Determining methods to reliably assess conversational quality is a difficult problem, but is a necessary step so that conversations can be qualitatively defined and assessed.

This leads to the research issue of conversational techniques. In certain domains, we feel that the introduction of specific conversational techniques (Rittel and Kunz 1970, Dehlinger and Protzen 1972, Winograd and Flores 1986) can help propel a desired process. Searching for sociological, rather than technological solutions to some of our process breakdowns appears to be a largely overlooked opportunity with promising potential. To this end, we have begun research into defining a taxonomy of conversational elements which are intended to facilitate the formal capture of design decisions and the design rationale.

As discussed above, it is debatable whether the structural changes which we have observed are caused by the gnews tool itself, or rather are due to cognitive and sociological changes in which gnews participated. Some evidence exists that complex machine-mediated conversations can indeed exist without the visual feedback of a browser. An interesting area to pursue is the tool-sociology interaction: Is the tool alone sufficient to effect these changes? Is sociology? What is the incremental benefit of introducing a tool along with sociological motivators? The answers to these questions may result in more effective techniques for the introduction of new technologies into existing organizations, and thus have important implications in the field of Technology Transfer.

References

Benbasat, I., Dexter, A. & Todd, P. (1986). An experimental program investigating color-enhanced and graphical information presentation: an integration of the findings. *Comm. ACM,* (29) 11.

Conklin, J. (1987). Hypertext: an introduction and survey. *IEEE Computer,* (20) 9.

Dehlinger, H. & Protzen, J. (1972). *Debate and Argumentation in Planning: An Inquiry into Appropriate Rules and Procedures.* Working paper #178. Institut für Grundlagen der Planung I.A. University of Stuttgart.

Dickson, G.W., DeSanctis, G. & McBride, D.J. (1986). Understanding the effectiveness of computer graphics for decision support: a cumulative experimental approach. *Comm. ACM,* (29) 1.

Duisberg, R. (1986). Animated graphical interfaces using temporal constraints. *Proc. ACM CHI'86: Human Factors in Computing Systems.*

Eveland, J. & Bikson, T. (1986). Evolving electronic communication networks: an empirical assessment. *Proc. CSCW'86: MCC/ACM conference on computer-supported cooperative work.*

Glinert, E. & Tanimoto, S. (1985). Pict: an interactive graphical programming environment. *IEEE Computer,* (17) 11.

Halasz, F., Moran, T. & Trigg, R. (1987). NoteCards in a nutshell. *Proc. ACM CHI'87: Human Factors in Computing Systems.*

Horton, M. & Adams, R. (1986). (Center for Seismic Studies, Arlington, Va.). *How to Read the Network News.* Distributed by Mr. Adams quarterly over the USENET news network.

Malone, T., Grant, K., Lai, K., Rao, R. & Rosenblitt, D. (1986). Semi-structured messages are surprisingly useful for computer-supported cooperation. *Proc. CSCW'86: MCC/ACM conference on computer-supported cooperative work.*

Melamed, B. & Morris, R. (1985). Visual simulation: the performance analysis workstation. *IEEE Computer,* (18) 8.

Norman, D.A. & Draper, S. W. (Ed.) (1986). *User Centered System Design.* Hillsdale, New Jersey: Lawrence Erlbaum Associates.

Ortony, Anthony (Ed.) (1979). *Metaphor and Thought.* Cambridge: Cambridge University Press.

Reiss, S. (1985). PECAN: Program development systems that support multiple views. *IEEE Trans. Software Eng.,* (SE-11) 3.

Rittel, H. & Kunz, W. (1970). *Issues as Elements of Information Systems.* Working paper #131. Institut für Grundlagen der Planung I.A. University of Stuttgart.

Winograd, T. & Flores, F. (1986). *Understanding Computers and Cognition: A New Foundation for Design.* Norwood: Ablex Publishing Corp.

Appendix A: gnews interface description

gnews Frame

Figure A-1 shows the gnews frame. The frame contains six windows that either display information or contain function buttons for performing gnews operations.

1) The Graph Display window contains a graph of the articles in the current newsgroup. Articles in the group are shown vertically on the graph; follow-ups are shown as horizontal branches on the graph. Unread articles appear as solid boxes, while articles that have already been read appear as outlined boxes. The current article is shown as a heavy-outlined box. This window can be used to examine the group structure and to directly select articles.
2) The Graph Control window controls group search and navigation functions. This window can be used to perform operations on newsgroups and sets of articles (NEXT GROUP, UNSUBSCRIBE, and so on).
3) The Subject Display window lists articles in the current group by number and by subject line. This window can be used to determine article contents and to select an article for inspection.
4) The Subject Control window contains a toggle that controls which articles are displayed in the Subject Display window.
5) The Article Control window provides functions that apply to articles such as NEXT and PRINT. This window can be used to navigate within a newsgroup and to perform operations on individual articles.
6) The Article Display window shows the contents of the current article.

Article tree structure

As can be seen in the Graph Display window (Figure A-1, 1) articles in a newsgroup are arranged in a tree structure. The root of the tree is the newsgroup itself; each article posted directly to the newsgroup is displayed as a branch from the root. However, articles that are posted as follow-ups to an article are attached to the article that they follow. For example, Figure A-1 shows article number 22 as a branch from the root. Article 22 has four follow-ups, numbered 23, 24, 35 and 36. Article 24 has two followups (33, 34), and so on.

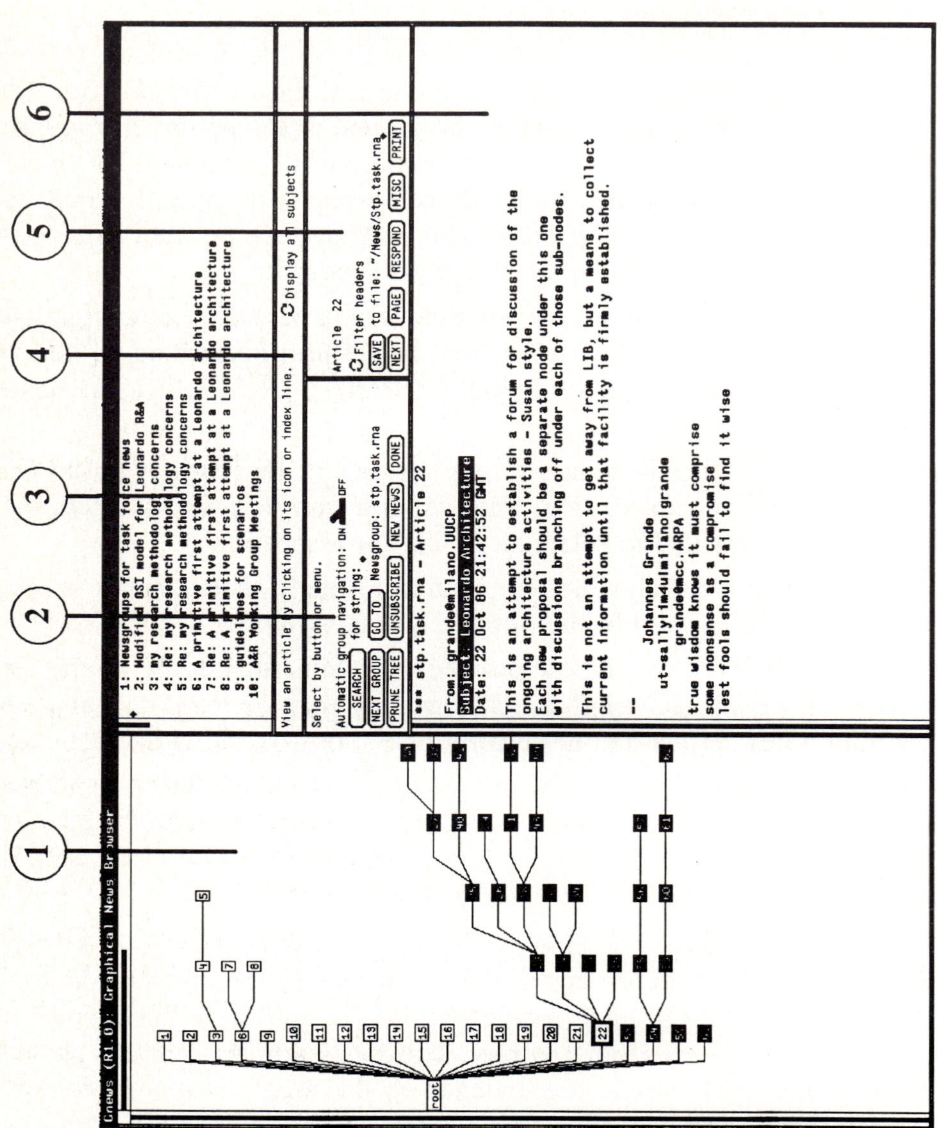

Figure A-1. The gnews frame

Mental Models and Human-Computer Interaction 1
D. Ackermann and M.J. Tauber (Editors)
Elsevier Science Publishers B.V. (North-Holland), 1990

MENTAL CONCEPTS AND DIRECT MANIPULATION: DRAFTING A DIRECT MANIPULATION QUERY LANGUAGE

Gabriele Rohr

IBM Science Center Heidelberg, FRG

ABSTRACT

Some preliminaries to be considered when designing a direct manipulation query language are discussed. There are the rules of what can be represented graphically in which form, and the different aspects of operation and task characteristics at different levels of the overall query application. Additionally, some first analyses are done on what is going on in people's mind when asking questions. By means of these analyses and considerations a rough draft of a direct manipulation database user interface is proposed.

Introduction

What means direct manipulation?

Graphical user interfaces with direct manipulation of graphically represented system objects are nowadays assumed to be useful in imparting the software system's structure to the user. Henceforth, this approach is widely used for generating user interfaces with more or less success. A clear definition of what direct manipulation really means is lacking, but seems to be important hence there is still a lot of confusion about what it is and what it is not, i.e., either a collection of pictures to be picked up or the use of windows and pop-up menus. Our first concern were attempts to make this point more clear.

Direct manipulation is always defined as working on graphical objects, i.e., also in text editing, text is regarded as a graphical object whose graphical properties (font, size, thickness, place, etc.) can directly and visibly be changed. Generally, graphical objects and their arrangement in space are supposed to express system components (objects) and their relations (space) (see also Tauber 1987). The graphical representation can be more abstract showing mainly spatial relations (see figure 1) or more concrete (picture like) using necessarily metaphors to describe the semantics of the system's components (see figure 2).

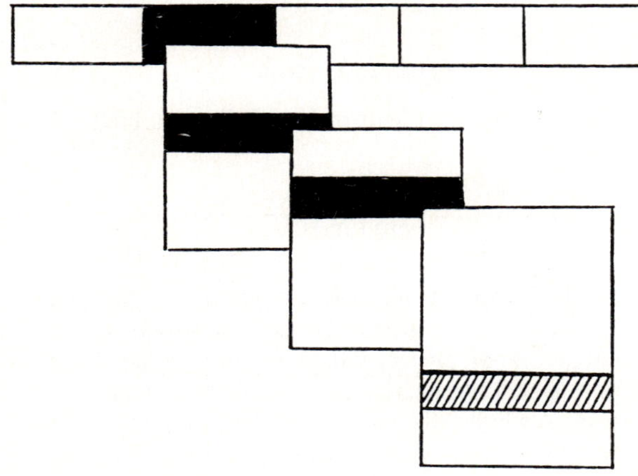

Figure 1. Abstract spatial relations as used to express menu dependencies

Consequently, one of the most important ease of use problems is to find the adequate metaphor expressing clearly the semantics of these objects.

Operations are defined by pointing at these objects arranged in space or at locations of a spatial structure and initiating an action by a special klicking event. Objects or entities pointed at and klicked will then change parameters as color and shape or may be 'dragged' around which means the implementation of some kind of animation. Those graphical 'events' have to be clearly and consistently related to system's operation semantics.

Because nearly everything will take place in space and on objects it is important to make all functionally relevant components of the software system visible. Furthermore, all changes of the system state have to be seen immediately in a graphical way (direct event). This stands in direct contrast to control statements which initiate a chain of events where only the final result might be visible.

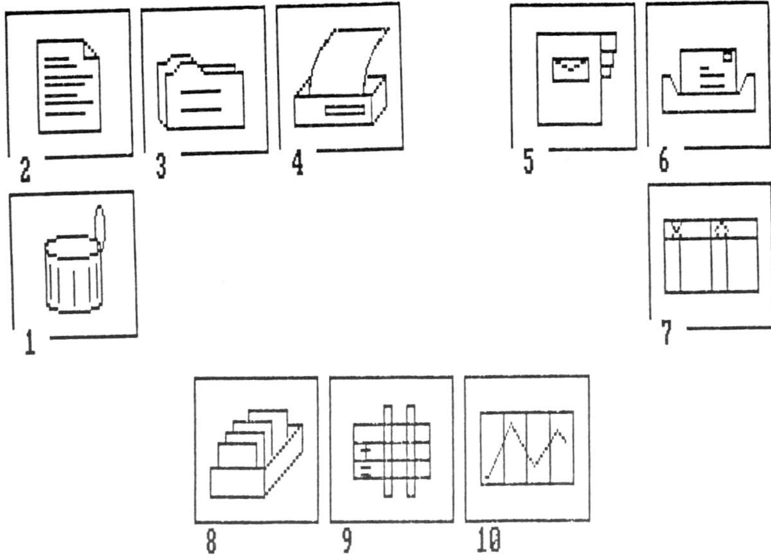

Figure 2. Pictures in desk-top metaphor for an integrated application: pictures express system objects and functions. E.g., picture 1 (trash-can) is a metaphor for the erase procedure. Each file (text: picture 2, graphics: picture 10) picked up and dragged upon picture 1 will be erased.

To use direct manipulation, however, certain requirements have to be met. Mainly, technical and conceptual requirements can be distinguished. The technical requirements can be easily described. Needed is a medium to high resolution screen either black and white with different grey levels or a color screen allowing different color levels to be generated by means of different 'red', 'green', 'blue' values. Also necessary is the existence of a pointing device like a mouse with at least two buttons. There might be applications where a touchscreen is adequate. However, this allows only very rough pointing accuracy.

The conceptual requirements are still a concern of research now. In order not to confuse the user by a lot of graphics, the semantics of graphical representations and concepts at the user's side have to be clearly and unambiguously mapped to the semantics of the software system. This means that the semantics of the interface has to be formally defined by means of an adequate specification language. It requires also a great deal of detailed investigations on users' understanding of graphical concepts. The software ergonomics group at the IBM Science Center Heidelberg concentrates on these questions, especially, with respect to complex database applications.

When direct manipulation will be useful?

The first thing that has to be considered in deciding for direct manipulation or for other kinds of interface representations is the characteristic of the task that has to be performed, and the characteristics of the single operations within the tasks. Derived from results of human memory research, especially on the limitations of working memory, the information representation strategies used to overcome these limitations, and the kind of information which can be handled by each of these strategies (see Rohr 1987), assumptions can be made about which task needs which kind of information and has then, consequently, to be represented in which manner. This can be called task characteristic. Gerstendörfer and Rohr (Gerstendörfer & Rohr, 1987) proved these assumptions on task characteristics.

Three global areas of task characteristics can be distinguished:

1) *different views on different parts of an overall structure,*
2) *control of sequences of operations,*
3) *the allocation or relocation of data sets to distinct classes and their computation.*

The second area, control of sequences, can be furthermore split into two aspects:

1) *the control of a linear sequence of operations,*
2) *the reconstruction of a sequence from randomly ordered elements.*

An experiment has been set up to clarify their interaction with the representation mode. Three different tasks varying in their characteristics (structural views, sequential procedure, and manipulating sets of data or events) were given to subjects in three representation forms each (picture, text, and formal table). Times to learn and to perform the tasks were taken separately. The three individual problem solving types (visualisers, verbalisers, and formalisers) were balanced within groups.

Gerstendörfer and Rohr (Gerstendörfer & Rohr, 1987) found out that independent of the individually preferred problem solving strategy (visualising, verbalising, formalising) tasks requiring different views on an overall structure were best performed when represented by means of a picture, and tasks requiring allocating and relocating data sets to distinct classes and conducting computations on them within and between classes, were best performed when represented by means of a formal table (see figure 3). The reconstruction of operation sequences was first assumed by them to go best with natural language (text) but came out as the worst condition at all, and going best with pictures for formalisers and with formal tables for visualisers. This seems to support a more formal graphics representation to be best for this kind of task characteristics. In a later experiment they found out that natural language was going best with the control of linear operation sequences. Also important, is the finding that individual differences vanish when the best representation form is met.

While the task characteristics determine in some way the global best representation strategy, the operation characteristics determine how this is worked out in the detail. There are two general kinds of operations: spatial operations and existential operations (Rohr 1986). Spatial operations are defined by the existence of an object which is moved in some way from one place to another in a certain direction. These kinds of operations will be best performed when represented as pictures of objects which will be directly manipulated.

Existential operations are defined by state transformations of objects and the formulation of their condition. These kinds of operations will be performed best when formulated as words.

If one has decided to represent system application objects as graphical entities to be operated on, the question arises how they will be best represented, i.e. as

- *concrete complex "metaphorical" objects*
- *more abstract objects differing in their global structure with*
  - *either meaningful features*
  - *or arbitrary features*
- *abstract objects differing only in naming*

In elaboration of a first experiment by Arend, Muthig, and Wandmacher (Arend, Muthig & Wandmacher, 1987) an investigation was done by Arend and Rohr (in preparation) to clarify these questions.

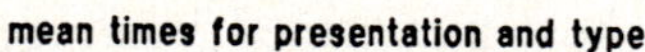

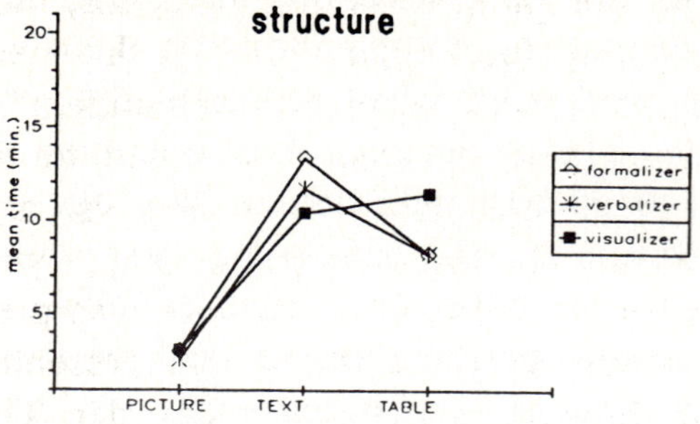

mean times for presentation and type

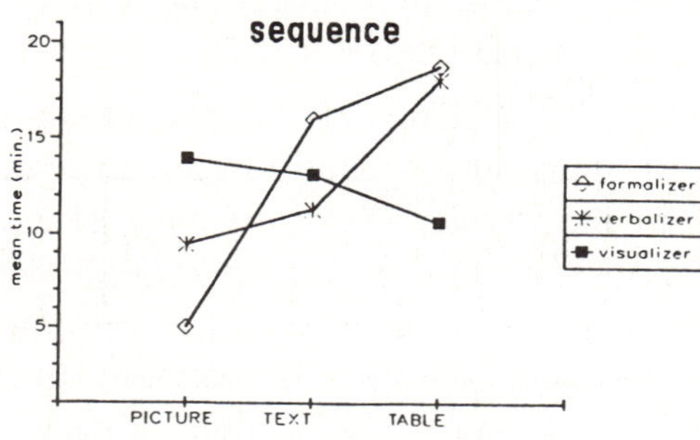

mean times for presentation and type

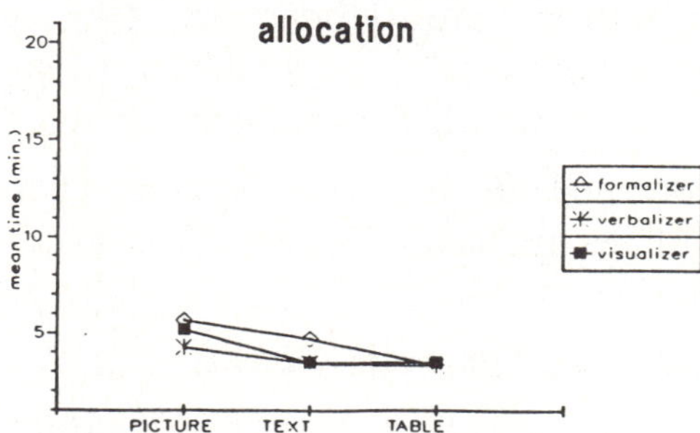

Figure 3. Task characteristics, representation mode, and individual problem solving style: mean times of performance for each individual problem solving group (formalizers, verbalizers, visualizers) under each presentation and task condition.

Three sets of 10 icons each (global structure meaningful, global structure arbitrary, complex desktop metaphor, squares containing words) were compared (see figure 4). Tasks were taken from a hypothetical "integrated working place environment". Always a complete set of 10 icons was repeatedly presented to the test subject in different spatial orders (meaningful grouping vs. arbitrary grouping). Before the presentation the task was given (e.g., "you want to draw a graphic"). In the easy task condition, one task was presented at once, in the difficult task condition, three tasks were presented at once, which meant to select the three icons in the correct order. The time to perform each task was recorded.

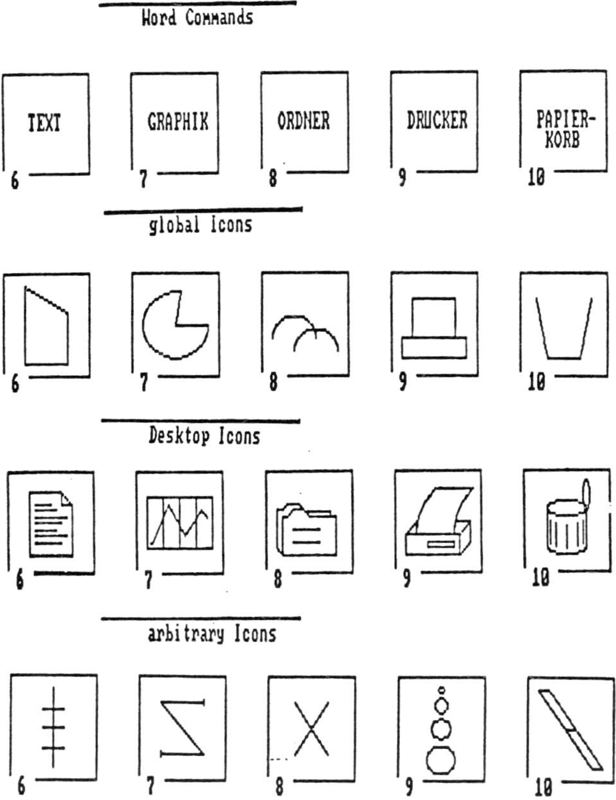

Figure 4. The tested different icon sets for integrated applications: example of five icons out of ten for each set condition.

Global meaningful icons were constructed according to the principle of using few elements, good distinctiveness, and a small relatedness to the command. Desktop icons were constructed as simple objects according to a desktop metaphor. Arbitrary icons were similar in construction to global meaningful icons, but showed no relationship at all to the meaning of the command. Word icons were constructed as one word, object oriented commands.

The results showed a strong advantage of global icons over all other groups, especially the meaningful ones in the difficult task condition (see figure 5). In addition, the effect of meaningful vs. arbitrary spatial grouping of the icons was evaluated. Here, it came out that meaningful grouping brings again better performance.

When deciding for a graphical interface and direct manipulation these aspects have to be regarded. An application which main task characteristic consists of views on structures and where the main operations are spatial operations, is best suited by a graphical user interface with direct manipulation in contrary to one where the main task characteristic is the control of linéar operation sequences and where the main operations are existential ones.

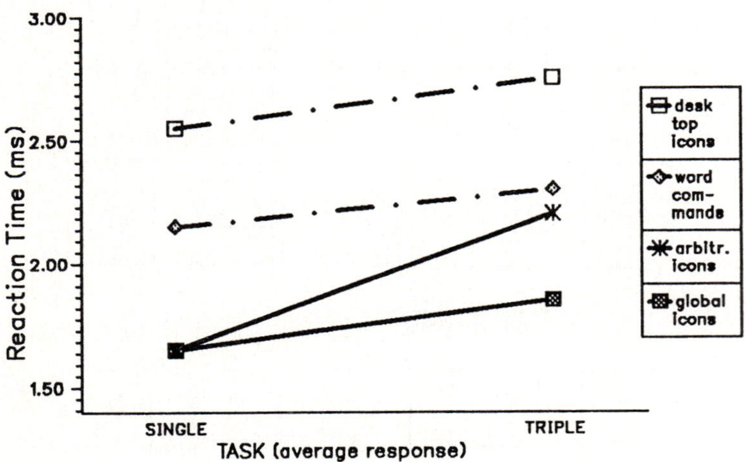

Figure 5. The results of the different icon sets (reaction times)

Analysing databases

In databases we first have to distinguish three operation levels which have to be analysed separately with respect to task and operation characteristics. The first level is the selection of parts of a database to be operated on. The second level is concerned with defining a substructure within the part, aiming at a special result (query). The third level is concerned with operations on the query result.

The first level can be regarded as a kind of zoom on the database, i.e. a selected view. The main operation has a spatial characteristic, i.e. take parts from a whole structure. Consequently the first level will be best suited by a graphical representation with a kind of direct manipulation. In the second level the view on the structural relations and dependencies of the data sets becomes important. The main operations are: creating different views on these relations according to the intended query result which is a spatial operation (i.e. restructuring in space), and defining conditions for the view of the final result which is an existential operation. Here, graphics, is also the best representation form of the structure showing the dependencies. Direct manipulation must allow to show the structural dependencies from different chosen points, where it also must be allowed to enter conditions into the structure by means of words. Figure 6 shows an example of such a solution for a 'department' database. The figure above is the first view showing the dependencies from the department number, multiple sheets indicating one to many relations. The figure beneath shows the same database structure from another point of view and also conditions entered into the structure.

The third level is mainly determined by the purpose of the result. Either it means again analysing structured relations, consequently, it has to be represented graphically, or it means the computation of the elements. In the latter case a formal table format of the data will be most suitable. The operations can be different. One operation might be to shift the elements around which is a spatial operation and best represented by direct manipulation. The more frequent operation will be to condense sets of elements, i.e. compute them, which is an existential operation. This could be done by entering the function in the respective table field.

As could be shown, it is very important to analyse an application very carefully before deciding where to introduce direct manipulation.

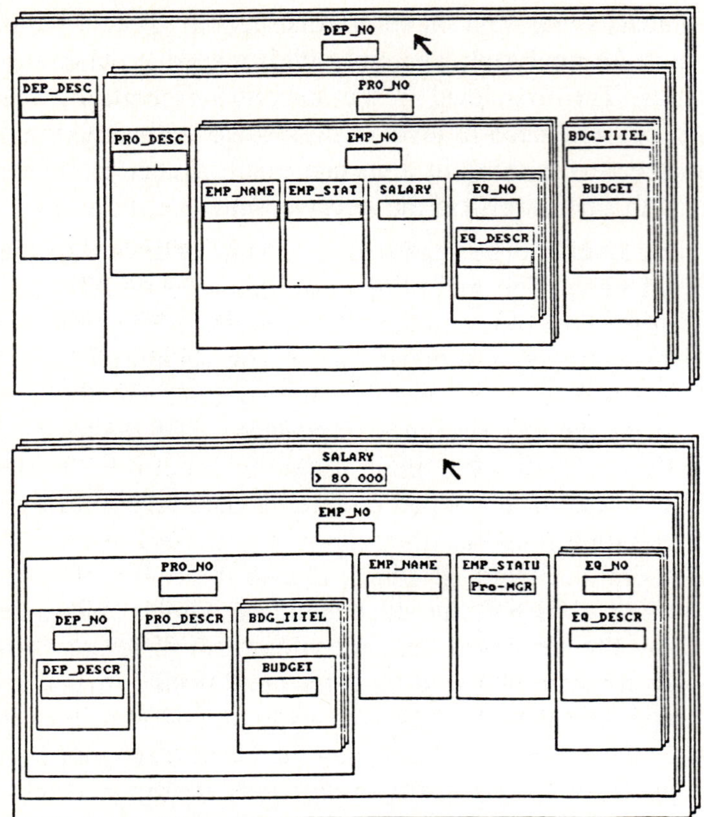

Figure 6. Changing views on a database structure

A direct manipulation query language: a conceptual frame

In defining direct manipulation it could be shown that there are various possibilities in representing objects, relationships and operations which have to be mapped to the user's understanding of the underlying semantics. Some of them are very clear now, like pointing and klicking meaning to select something, or writing into a structure meaning to define something, or shifting a structure to show dependencies. Some of the expression possibilities are very unclear yet, i.e., if choosing concrete symbols for a representation of system entities which metaphor will be adequate. It can be assumed that this is very application dependent and still needs a lot of user investigations.

The only thing which can be decided now is when to use more concrete or more abstract, spatial graphics representations. The decision is again related to the operation levels. With concrete symbols used in a consistent metaphor one can show natural relationships between objects and by this, it will help in the quick search for entities to be selected. This is the main purpose in level one. With abstract spatially arranged graphics one can show functional dependencies expressed as spatial relations and some additional graphical cues. Here, one cannot show natural relationships, as one cannot show functional dependencies in the former case. The view of functional dependencies however, is the main purpose of level two. Because of the distinct purposes of the two levels they have to be clearly separated, but because of their purpose both have in common, i.e. to keep an overview on the overall structure, they have to be presented simultaneously. This can only be done by a windowing technique. Figure 7 shows an example for an 'environment' database (with a window containing a concrete super-icon for the search level, the overall-structure and the chosen relations to be operated on, for the query level). These findings of users' switching between levels have been widely discussed in Rasmussen (1986).

In a first step we concentrated on the investigation of a direct manipulation query language in connection with the structural representation of the database. The main task is to find out what happens when people ask questions. As we know from investigations on three-step order problems (i.e. *a > b, b > c: which is the greatest/smallest*) the existence of a conceptual end-anchor (e.g., *a > b, c < b* where "*b*" is the reference), the correspondence of logical and grammatical subject (i.e., *b > a, b < c*, which means b is between a and c, and is logical *subject*), and the linearity of the presented order (i.e., *a > b, b > c* and *not a > b, c < b*) are important factors for answering questions more easily (for an overview see Groner, 1978).

It is not is known yet if these parameters will also hold for other then order problems, e.g., inclusion or possession. With the possession function (Jackendoff 1983) conceptual dependencies can be expressed metaphorically in the human's mind: thing A has (possess) thing B, thing B belongs (is possessed by) to thing A. This can also be a metaphor to express dependencies in databases. Employees belong to a

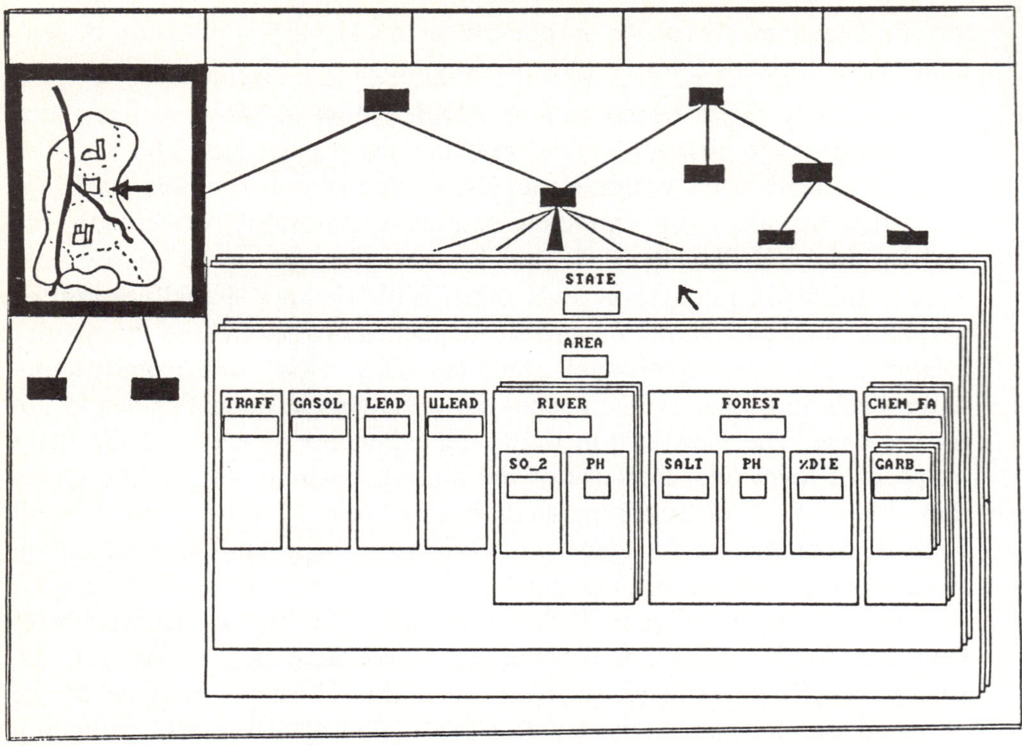

Figure 7. Changing views on a database structure

project leader, and employees possess a salary. If the project leader is the fixed point (known subject: Miller) to determine the employee names and their salary which will be asked for, the question arises how the question will most easily be structured.

1. With the *conceptual end-anchor*
   Miller possesses which employees, which salary belongs to them?
2. with the correspondence of *logical / grammatical subject*
   Which employees belong to Miller and possess which salary?
3. with the *linearity* of the possession function
   Miller possess which employees with which salary?

This analysis is important when defining the semantics of a special view on the graphical database structure (i.e., which thing has to be placed on the top to express what?). E.g., if the third parameter holds in question asking, "Miller" has to be placed on top, otherwise for the second parameter it will be "employees".

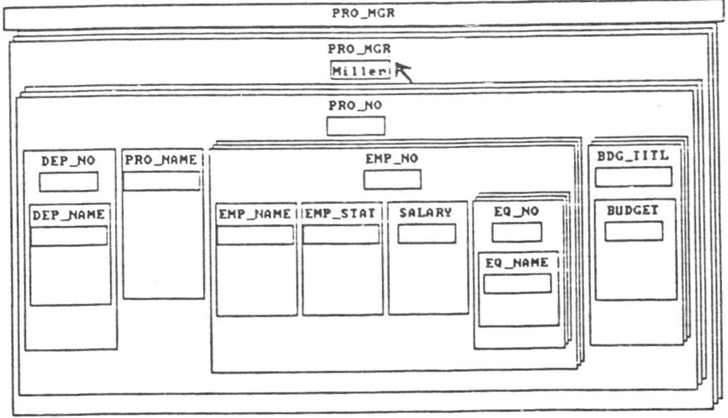

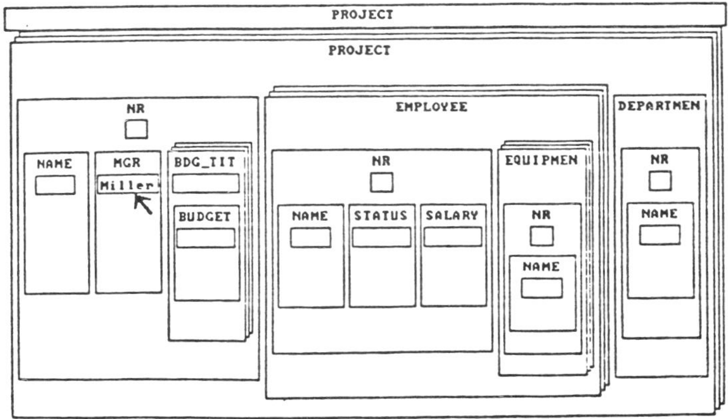

Figure 8. The different operating levels in a database: the super-icon in the upper left corner shows all database entities in a natural relationship. Each graphical object can be highlighted separately and determines the entities chosen from the overall database. In the window behind is the chosen selection of the database structure to be operated on for query formulation.

A second question is, how people structure their knowledge space they ask on. Do they see object entities with attributes and relate the objects over the attributes, or do they first create an object in mind with specified attributes they ask for? Let us take as an example the question of Miller and his employees with their salary. In the first case the object "project" with its specified attribute "leader" will be related to the object "employee" with its attributes "name" and "salary". In the second case, the defined object "Miller" as a project leader will be asked for its attributes "employee names" with their attributes "salary". These different mental operations have different implications for their graphical representation when question asking should be aided by graphics. Figure 8 shows the different graphical solutions.

The spatial metaphor used to describe these semantic concepts is derived by means of formal mental semantics descriptions of Jackendoff (1983) which allow to transform "type" concept descriptions into "possession" concept and "place" concept descriptions. See the following example:

<THING TYPE A> IS INSTANCE OF <THING TYPE B>
<THING A> PLACEFUNCTION(ON) <THING B>

and

<THING TYPE A> IS EXEMPLIFIED BY <THING TOKEN a>
<THING a> PLACEFUNCTION(IN) <THING A>

This formal specification of user semantics allows also to describe database semantics and is therefore useful for a formal interface description between the users' semantics expressed at the screen and the respective database semantics. First modelling approaches mapping the two user semantic models to the semantics of a relational data model have been developed (see Rohr, in preparation).

References

Arend, U., Muthig, K.-P., & Wandmacher, J. (1987). Evidence for global feature superiority in menu selection by icons. *Behavior and Information Technology,* 6(4)

Gerstendörfer, M. & Rohr, G. (1987). Which task in which representation on what kind of interface? In H.J. Bullinger & B. Shackel (Eds.), *Human-Computer Interaction - INTERACT '87.* Amsterdam: North Holland.

Groner, R.(1978). *Hypothesen im Denkprozeß.* Bern: Hans Huber.

Jackendoff, R. (1983). *Semantics and Cognition.* Cambridge, Mass.: MIT Press.

Rasmussen, J. (1986). *Information Processing and Human - Machine Interaction.* Amsterdam: North Holland.

Rohr, G. (1986). Using visual concepts. In S.K. Chang et al. (Eds.), *Visual Languages.* New York: Plenum Press.

G. Rohr (1987). How people comprehend unknown system structures: conceptual primitives in systems' surface representations. In P. Gorny & M.J. Tauber (Eds.), *Visualization in Programming.* Lecture Notes in Computer Science, Vol.282, Berlin - Heidelberg - New York: Springer.

Rohr, G. (in preparation). What happens when people ask for information? Cognitive analysis and experimental design in database interface research. In A.M. Pejtersen & J. Rasmussen (Eds.), *Proceedings of the EFISS 1987.* London: Academic Press.

Schlager, M.S. & Ogden, W.C. (1986). A cognitive model of database querying: a tool for novice instruction. *Proceedings of the CHI 1986,* ACM SIGCHI, Boston (Mass).

Tauber, M.J. (1987). On visual interfaces and their conceptual analysis. In P. Gorny & M.J. Tauber (Eds.), *Visualization in Programming.* Lecture Notes in Computer Science, Vol.282, Berlin - Heidelberg - New York: Springer.

Widdel, H. & Kaster, J. (1986). Transparency of a dialogue through pictorial presentation of the dialogue structure. In H.P. Willumeit (Ed.), *Human Decision Making and Manual Control - 5th EAM, 1985.* Amsterdam: North Holland.

Mental Models and Human-Computer Interaction 1
D. Ackermann and M.J. Tauber (Editors)

MENTAL MODELS AND THE DESIGN OF USER MANUALS

Walter Rupietta

TA Triumph-Adler AG, Nürnberg, FRG

ABSTRACT

This paper deals with the role the idea of mental models plays for the designer of user manuals describing software systems. It is proposed that one purpose of a manual is to induce a suitable mental model in its user in order to enable him to effectively use the system. This aspect must be considered in the design of user manuals by introducing a system model which is supposed to make up a suitable mental model. This is called a descriptional model and is the basis for descriptions in a user manual. A user manual presents to its users an underlying descriptional model which comprises only aspects and features relevant to the user.

Introduction

The concept of a mental model is a means to explain how humans deal with computer systems (and, of course, other systems too). Today the operation of computer systems is largely determined by software systems, so the latter term will be preferred in this paper. User manuals are intended to provide the necessary information to operate software systems. Both mental models and user manuals are connected with the use of software systems: they guide a user in operating systems and planning their use.

This paper discusses the role of mental models in the design of user manuals for software systems. The first part introduces the idea of a user's mental model and takes into account the view of the software designer by considering his conceptual model of the software system. Some basic features of user manuals are discussed and related to mental models.

In the second part the development process for user manuals, especially the design step is explained. The discussion of manual design is based upon the proposition that one main purpose of a user manual is to induce a mental model in its user. It is explained how this purpose is taken into account during the design of a manual by designing a model of the software system that captures those aspects which concern the user.

The role of mental models for the design of user manuals

This section discusses the user's mental model, the software designer's conceptual model of a software system and some basic features of user manuals for software systems. The significance of mental models for the development of user manuals is determined.

The user's mental model

A *model* is an image of an object or a state of affairs representing only those aspects of the object or state of affairs that are considered relevant in a given context. It is an abstraction from the real object or state of affairs.

Using a software system, a user adopts his own mental image on construction and operation of the system. This image is called the *user's mental model* of the system (synonyms are *mental model* (Norman, 1983), *cognitive model* (Saja, 1985), *operative image system* (Hacker, 1987)). A user's mental model of a complex software system is his internal private representation of that system in his memory.

Mental models are often incomplete and do not necessarily reflect a technically correct image of the target system (Norman, 1983). In fact, sometimes users are not even aware of having such a model, their mental model is only partially represented in conceptual structures. Mental models may comprise structural knowledge about the system, rules and procedural knowledge (e.g. on how to perform some operations). They capture only aspects relevant to the user.

Mental models serve to explain and predict the system's behaviour. A mental model helps a user to explain, why certain steps are necessary to carry out some procedure. If a user has some task to solve, he "consults" his mental model of the system to decide how this can be accomplished. Thus the user predicts how the system will behave. Based on these explanations and predictions, the user may plan action sequences and project future use of the systems.

To attain this goal the user's mental model must be consistent with the real system, otherwise the system's behaviour is not predictable and the user will not be able to plan future use of the system. For this purpose it is not necessary to represent every system detail in a mental model, it must only contain relevant information that enables the user to use a software system. A mental model is sufficient if it allows to solve problems with the system and to perceive its limits.

Users acquire and expand their mental model by observing the system's behaviour in course of its use, by training, instruction and documentation. The mental model is also expanded by deduction based on the existing model and is influenced by experiences with other systems.

There is no way to directly access users' mental models. All aspects presented so far can only be inferred by observing the user's behaviour and his utterances. To some extent, researchers infer their statements on mental models from personal experience.

The software designer's conceptual model

During the design and development of a software system the designer adopts a model of the system in terms which are appropriate for his task. This model is called the *software designer's conceptual model* of the system. It is a representation of the system on a conceptual level depending on the specific view of the designer. See Streitz (Streitz, 1985) for a detailed discussion of conceptual models. The term "*user's virtual machine*" (Tauber, 1985) corresponds roughly to a conceptual model.

A designer's conceptual model represents functions or constituent parts of the system and their mutual relations. It leaves out details that are of no concern for the designer's point of view. The designer's conceptual model is an image of the implemented system on a certain level of abstraction suitable to the designer. This means the model comprises aspects of system construction (system components and their relations) and implementation (technical constraints, algorithms) as well as aspects of system operation (based on anticipation of how the system will be used).

In general, it may be supposed to be correct and complete on the given level of abstraction and consistent with the implemented system, but often implementations deviate from the design. (For example the designer may not be the programmer.) So the designer's conceptual model may differ from the implemented system, thus they must be distinguished. (We will not consider an additional underlying function principle as the intended target system, see (Streitz, 1985).)

One purpose of the designers conceptual model is communication on the system in question. This is a purpose which may also be attributed to a user manual for a system. The designer has to communicate his ideas to other people concerned. In his system design, he describes his conceptual model of the system as a basis for the implementation and further developments. Only aspects of interest and not all details are presented.

The acquisition of a conceptual model by the software designer is explicitly considered as part of the software development process. The model is a conceptualization of the designer's ideas. Initial ideas are gradually refined, specified and conceptualized.

User manuals for software systems

User manuals for software systems are defined to represent information on the use of the system to distinguish them from other types of system documentation (Rupietta, 1983). This definition is also valid for representations contained in the system's user interface, such as prompts, messages, online help etc., which are a kind of user documentation too. Various types of manuals serve different purposes. Two main purposes or functions can be distinguished: introduction and reference.

- An *introduction manual* instructs the reader how to perform certain tasks with the underlying system. In general it does not introduce every system detail.
- A *reference manual* contains exact and complete descriptions of certain system features for explicit lookup.

Most user manuals try to combine the introductory function and the reference function, in fact every real manual will contain both types of descriptions. Manuals are often composed of introductory and reference parts or by adding a reference card to an introduction manual.

User manuals are external representations meant to explain and predict system behaviour and to allow planning of action sequences. Users' mental models are internal representations which serve the same purposes. By procuring the related information, user manuals are involved in the acquisition of a mental model. But mental models are also involved in the design of user manuals. This holds for both introduction and reference manuals because both must take existing mental models into account.

- For introductory manuals the existence of a mental model (of the manual's target system) may not be presupposed. This means that introductory manuals should instruct the user and thereby *establish a useful mental model* of the system which in turn enables further use of the system without the manual.

It is not necessary to represent every system detail in a manual, because the mental model must only enable the user to use a software system and to perceive its limits. Problems may arise if a previously existing mental model is incompatible with the model procured by a manual.

- A reference manual presumes the existence of a partial mental model as part of the user's previous knowledge. The contents of a reference manual must be consistent both with the described system and the user's mental model of the system to serve its purpose. Here, the anticipated model of the user is considered in the design of the reference manual.

Reference manuals add to the user's mental model because it may be assumed that a user looking up something in a reference manual gains some knowledge and thus updates or expands his mental model of the system.

User manuals are external representations of information on the use of a software system. Users "internalize" this information and thereby form their mental model of the system. So we may conclude:

> *Thesis*:
> The main purpose of a user manual is to induce a suitable mental model of a system in its users.

In the design of a user manual a first approach to accomplish this goal might be to define the software designer's conceptual model as the suitable mental model for the user (see figure 1). Descriptions in the manual could then be based on this model.

This is not a favourable approach, because the purpose of the software designer's conceptual model is not compatible with the requirements of manual design. A manual designer must take into account the user's task and the intended characteristic of the manual as a reference or introduction manual, whereas a software designer must handle aspects of system construction and implementation in a given environment.

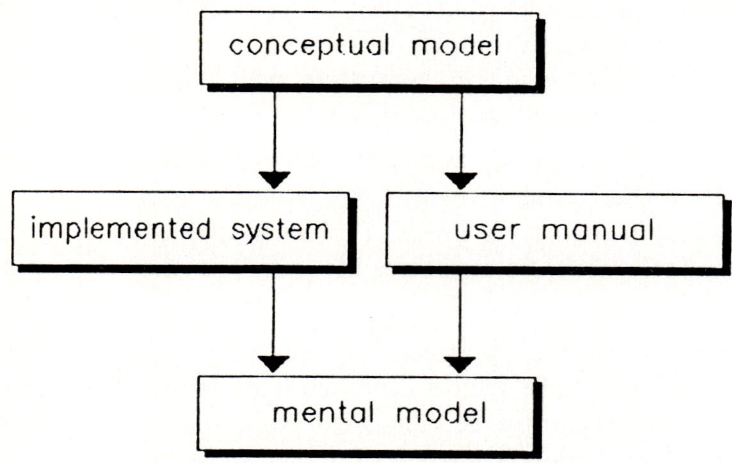

Figure 1. User manuals as presentation of the software designer's conceptual model

At this point we have to consider whether manual designer and software designer are different persons. A manual designer possesses his own mental model of the system he has to describe. Of course this model and not the software designer's conceptual model will be the basis for descriptions in the manual. At first sight, it seems quite reasonable to assume that the manual designer's model may be an appropriate mental model for a user too. But often manual designers are involved in the system development procedure and therefore are likely to have an internal model more or less identical with the software designer's conceptual model. This will especially be true when the software designer is also the manual designer. In this case our argumentation holds.

Designing user manuals

This section describes how user manuals are developed and in which way mental models are considered during the development process. At first the development process for user manuals is explained. Mental models are considered during the design step, so this step is examined more closely.

The development of user manuals

The development process for user manuals consists of the following steps (see for example, Duffy, 1981; Rupietta, 1987):

- specification of requirements,
- design,
- draft,
- review and revision,
- production and distribution of the manual.

This process is roughly analogous to the process of software development.

The *specification of requirements* defines the purpose of a manual, the audience and the system to be described. All the necessary information for writing a manual is collected. In the context of mental models the consideration of users is of special importance.

Different types of users have to be considered in the development of software systems. The first approaches to take users into account consisted of dividing users into several (mostly two) classes according to their prior experience, e.g. novice and expert users were distinguished.

Recent investigations take more dimensions into account and are aimed at modeling individual users, not classes of users (Möller & Rosenow, 1987). The purpose of such *user models* is to optimize ease of use. User models are constructed and consulted during system operation to adapt the mode of operation to individual users and thus have to be dynamic.

To design a user manual, information on the audience is also needed, so a user model might be appropriate. In contrast to user models for online consultance, there is no possibility to adapt a manual dynamically to individual users. Users are classified during the specification of requirements for a manual, not while using the manual.

In consequence, there is no need for dynamic user models.

Nevertheless users are classified to more than one dimension for purposes of manual design. Rupietta (1983), for example, classifies users according to their previous knowledge and their task in connection with the software system to be documented. The tasks determine which components of the system the user comes in contact with and has to know about. The user's previous knowledge defines what is already known and to which detail. The previous knowledge comprises the user's actual (maybe empty) mental model of the system.

Based on this collection of information a *design of a manual* is developed which specifies the exact contents and the structure of the manual in a design document. The role of a manual design maybe compared with that of a functional specification for a software system. It may also determine the manner of representation to be used in the manual.

The design is then transformed into a first *draft* of the manual. The manual is written according to the design and all figures are drawn. The draft is reviewed and revised (sometimes a second draft is produced, reviewed and revised) and at last the manual is produced and distributed.

The design step

In a *manual design document* the manual designer determines how the manual will look like. He determines what will be described in the manual and in which sequence. He also fixes the manner in which the descriptions will be presented to the user. Before this can be done, the system to be documented must be regarded more closely and the user must be taken into account.

We may suppose that the system to be documented and the software designer's conceptual model of the system are available to the manual designer. Thus a model of the users (stemming from the specification of requirements) and a model of the system (the software designer's conceptual model) are the basis for designing a user manual.

The main purpose of a manual is to induce a suitable mental model in its user, so the first step of manual design must be to decide how such a suitable and useful model might look. Such a model must

- abstract from system details that are not necessary to fulfil the user's tasks,
- comprise all components and relations the user has to be aware of,
- be consistent with the real system.

We have already concluded that the software designer's conceptual model is not the best choice, so we have to look for a better model.

From the conceptual model all components and the construction of the system are known. From the user model the user's tasks are known. Both models are used as a filter to find out, what the user has to know about the system and to which detail:

- The user's tasks determine which system components must be explained to the user.
- The procedures the user has to carry out to fulfil his tasks with the system determine which specific relations between system features the user must know.
- The tasks and the user's previous knowledge determine to which detail the user has to know about the system features and their mutual relations.

Thus by a filtering process the existing conceptual model of the system may be tailored to a model that describes exactly the level of detail the user must know and hides anything that is not necessary. We will call this a *descriptional model* and maintain that it is suitable as a user's mental model. It captures those system concepts which concern the user.

This model must still be checked against the implemented system, because the system image (Norman, 1983) may not reflect the conceptual model and thus be inconsistent with the model just constructed. In most cases there will be such inconsistencies (resulting for example from later corrections and expansions; whether they make a better system or not shall not be discussed here) and the manual designer cannot eliminate them by changing the system image. So the descriptional model just constructed has to be adapted in order to be consistent with the system image the user will see when using the system.

Example:
In an office system the screen representation of a document may be either an icon or a text in an editor window. Looking

closer we may observe that the document is stored in a UNIX† file system as a subdirectory containing the text file and a format file.

Considering a manual for office clerks, a descriptional model might talk about documents as units that are either closed and represented as icons or opened and represented as text in an editor window. Considering a manual for system engineers, a descriptional model will in addition refer to the document's implementation in the Unix file system.

Sometimes software systems establish themselves *metaphors* (like the desktop metaphor) which can be seen as a kind of descriptional model for the user. The purpose of these metaphors is to utilize the user's previous knowledge transferring it to the operation of the system in question. This knowledge transfer may be regarded as the establishment of a mental model for the system by deriving it from an already existing mental model. Metaphors can also be used to construct descriptional models for software systems even if the system itself does not establish an explicit metaphor. The description must then connect the metaphor to the real system image.

In this way from the available information on the users and the system a suitable descriptional model of the system may be structured. The descriptional model determines the contents of the manual by specifying what the user must know about the system (see figure 2). This contents has still to be constructed. The structure depends on the purpose of the manual.

A reference manual is in most cases structured according to the descriptional model which reflects the structure of the system. Such a structure assumes that the user knows about the procedures to fulfil his tasks with the system and only needs exact descriptions of details. The user may then by consulting his (partial) mental model (which we assume to be consistent with the descriptional model) find out where the information he is looking for is located in the manual.

An introductory manual may be structured according to (some of) the procedures the user has to carry out in fulfilling his tasks. As users' tasks may vary there will always be a restricted number of standard

† UNIX is a trademark of Bell Laboratories.

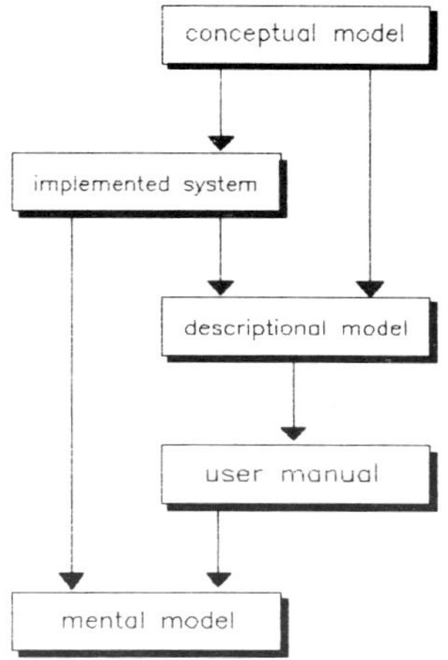

Figure 2. User manuals as presentation of a descriptional model.

tasks that are described. The description is centered around the descriptional model to enable the user to acquire a compatible mental model that enables him to find out how to carry out other tasks than those explicitly described.

The first draft of a manual is based on the design document and has to carry on the reference to the descriptional model. The vocabulary used in the draft has to be consistent with the descriptional model and of course with the implemented system. Therefore it is necessary, to specify the descriptional model explicitly in the design document.

It should be clear from the discussion of the design step that the descriptional model is not the only input for the development of a user manual. Other factors like a user model, the purposes of the manual etc. influence the user manual either directly or by consideration in the descriptional model.

Concluding remarks and open questions

The concept of a descriptional model is introduced to make explicit what manual designers have always done: find some level of abstraction (or level of detailedness) suitable for the users and their tasks and maintain this level throughout a manual, regardless whether it is an introduction or reference manual. So we will conclude with the following

> *Proposition*:
> If a user manual presents a suitable descriptional model of a system to its users, we may expect the users to acquire a compatible mental model of the system.

The descriptional model explicitly connects the idea of a user's mental model to the design of a user manual. It compels manual designers to

- conceptualize and express their own knowledge on the system,
- reflect on the qualification of their own and of the software designer's system models as users' mental models.

The existence of a (good) descriptional model does not guarantee a good user manual, there are other factors still to consider.

A first question concerns the representation of descriptional models. Most user manuals give informal descriptions of systems based on a decomposition of a system into related functional units. This representation yields a structure whose components are functional units linked by different types of relations. Often the set of functional units is divided into active units (actors) and information carrying units (media) linking the actors. Is this kind of representation always appropriate?

The descriptional model of a system is the basis for a manual draft, so it must be explicitly specified. If we want to verify, if a user of a manual based on such a model has indeed adopted a compatible mental model of the system, we must have an explicit representation of the descriptional model for reference. What kind of representation mechanism is appropriate for representing descriptional models?

Of course it is only a hypothesis that we can induce an intended mental model by describing a suitable descriptional model to our users. To verify this hypothesis, it would be necessary to check actual mental models of users against the descriptional model used to instruct the users. Unfortunately there is no possibility to directly access mental models, so we can only infer a user's mental model by observing his behaviour and his utterances. Are there methods to decide if a user's mental model is consistent with a descriptional model we wanted to induce (provided the descriptional model is explicitly specified)?

Even if we suppose our hypothesis to be true, it is quite easy to state that a manual describes some descriptional model of a system. But does the user understand the description in the way the manual author has intended? From our experience we know that descriptions can be ambiguous or incomprehensible because of various other reasons. So, how can we produce comprehensible descriptions?

In many cases the user does only see parts of the whole software system - the system image (Norman, 1983; Streitz, 1985) which is presented to him. The system image contains representations of objects present in the system. The user has to know the meaning of these representations and he has to know the operations he may apply. If the objects change then the representations must also change to preserve *consistency* between the representation and the real objects.

Those parts the user may not directly observe must be presented in other ways - for example by manuals or online help facilities. Here we have also the problem of consistency between an external representation (the manual or the online help information) and system internal procedures or objects. If a system feature is changed, how can we guarantee that the related external description is also changed and still a valid representation?

For printed manuals there will be no guarantee, but for online help there may be means to check consistency. Online help and system implementation could be based on the same internal representation of system features. Such a uniform representation together with a pair of interpretation mechanisms (one for implementing the system and one for generating explanations; i.e. external representations) could guarantee consistency of online help and system implementation.

Another idea might then be to apply the concept of a descriptional model to the internal system representation to adapt the system's online help to different user groups. Online help could be generated by considering a descriptional model derived from the system representation and not the system representation itself. This approach would allow to use a detailed system representation for implementation and to filter out the features relevant for explanations by means of a descriptional model. Thus the level of detailedness in online explanations would be independent of the implementation level and could be tailored to a specific group of users.

References

Duffy, T.M. (1981). Organizing and utilizing document design options. *Information Design Journal,* Vol. 2, No. 3&4, 1981, pp. 256-266.

Hacker, W. (1978). *Allgemeine Arbeits- und Ingenieurpsychologie.* Bern: Huber.

Möller, H. & Rosenow, E. (1987). Benutzermodellierung für wissensbasierte Mensch-Computer-Schnittstellen. In W. Schönpflug & M. Wittstock (Eds.), *Software-Ergonomie' 87.* Berichte des German Chapter of the ACM Bd. 29, Stuttgart: Teubner.

Norman, D.A. (1983). Some observations on mental models. In D. Gentner & A.L. Stevens (Eds.), *Mental Models.* (pp. 7-14). Hillsdale, N.J.: Lawrence Erlbaum Associates.

Rupietta, W. (1983). Dokumentation als Aspekt der Software-Ergonomie. In H. Balzert (Ed.), *Software-Ergonomie* (pp. 147-158). Berichte des German Chapter of the ACM Bd. 14, Stuttgart: Teubner.

Rupietta, W. (1987). *Benutzerdokumentation für Softwareprodukte.* Mannheim: Bibliographisches Institut.

Saja, A.D. (1985). The cognitive model: an approach to designing the human-computer interface. *SIGCHI Bulletin* 16, 3 (January 1985), 36-40.

Streitz, N.A. (1985). Die Rolle von mentalen und konzeptuellen Modellen in der Mensch-Computer-Interaktion: Konsequenzen für die Software-Ergonomie? In H.-J. Bullinger (Ed.). *Software-Ergonomie '85 Mensch - Computer - Interaktion* (pp. 280-292). Berichte des German Chapter of the ACM, Bd. 24, Stuttgart: Teubner.

Tauber, M.J. (1985). Mentale Modelle als zentrale Fragestellung der kognitiven Ergonomie. Theoretische Überlegungen und einige empirische Ergebnisse. In H.-J. Bullinger (Ed.), *Software-Ergonomie '85 Mensch - Computer - Interaktion* (pp. 293-302). Berichte des German Chapter of the ACM Bd.24, Stuttgart: Teubner.

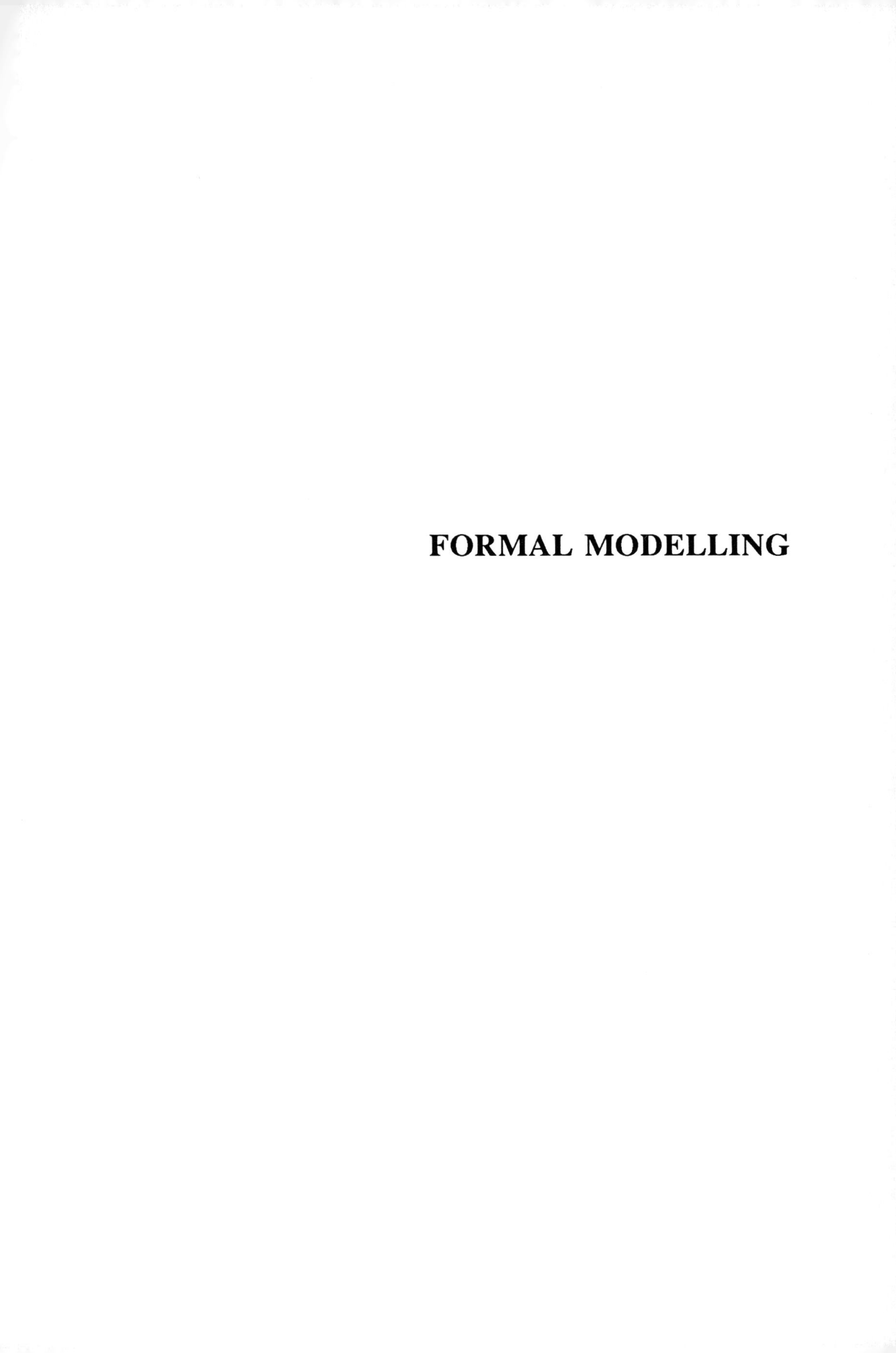

FORMAL MODELLING

Mental Models and Human-Computer Interaction 1
D. Ackermann and M.J. Tauber (Editors)

USER MODELLING FOR A TEXT-EDITOR COACH

Michel C. Desmarais, Luc Giroux and Serge Larochelle

Departement de psychologie and Departement de communication,
Universite de Montreal
Canadian Workplace Automation Research Center (CWARC)

ABSTRACT

The architecture of an advice-giving system generally includes a module for the analysis of user actions and another module that is often called "user module". We describe a formalism for the representation and the inference of a user's state of knowledge which serves as a basis for the user module of a text-editing coach. We show that with a knowledge structure defined with this formalism it is possible to infer user knowledge from the analysis of behaviour in terms of goals, methods, and primitive actions. Moreover, a method is proposed to automatically construct the knowledge structure from data on a number of individual's knowledge state.

The structure of a text-editor coach

A text-editor coach is a type of intelligent tutoring system that monitors the user's actions and suggests, when appropriate, new commands and methods to improve performance. Contrary to an "active" tutoring system, the coach does not control the user's task, but lets the user proceed with his/her work. It makes corrections and suggestions after having previously diagnosed erroneous or inefficient methods of editing. Such a system thus has, first, to identify which method is being used for doing what. Second, it has to judge whether the method used is appropriate. If not, then it has to determine what to teach the user next, according to the current knowledge he or she has. Each of these two sub-tasks has a dedicated module. One is for the representation and recognition of the user's actions and underlying goals. The second one is for the evaluation of the method used, the assessment of the user's current knowledge, and for determining what to suggest. This latter module is the user modelling module.

We will describe the overall structure of the coach and its underlying modules in the next section. In the subsequent sections we will focus on the user modelling module, and more specifically on the knowledge assessment process. A representational scheme for knowledge assessment will be presented, followed by a discussion on its implementation and an evaluation of its validity.

The module for the representation and recognition of expertise

The knowledge of text-editing, like many domains, is characterized by a great deal of "procedural knowledge", that is, competences which are manifest in users' actions. For that reason, it is possible to get a clear idea of someone's knowledge simply by observing this person working on a text-editing task. A tutor can then act as a coach, sitting apparently idle until a proper moment arises to teach the pupil something he/she has not learned yet. This constitutes an advantage in the sense that the pupil can learn from the tutor (coach) without going through a formal learning session, but it burdens the tutor with the tasks of identifying the goal behind the pupil's sequence of actions, and of making a knowledge assessment without the help of a question-answering process.

An adequate formalism is thus needed for the representation and identification of the procedural knowledge. For this purpose, we use a *procedural network*. This formalism is similar to Sacerdoti's own procedural network (1977) for planning systems. It differs in its role which is to *recognize* the goals behind actions instead of *planning* actions to satisfy some goals.

Figure 1 illustrates a simple procedural network (PN) composed of two goals. Each node in a PN is either (1) an *observable action*, (2) a *goal* that can be further decomposed in other goals (sub-goals) or in observable actions, or (3) a control node which determines disjunctions of paths in the network or iterations over a path, etc. The goals are in capital letters while the control nodes are in bold, and the observable actions are in standard characters. The three goals are linked together in a hierarchical structure to satisfy the top goal of moving some text segment to a new position. At the top level we find a single goal, "move <text> <pos>". This goal is decomposed at the second level in a structure composed of another goal, "select <text>", and of a more complex sub-structure delimited by two control nodes, "XOR" and "JOIN".

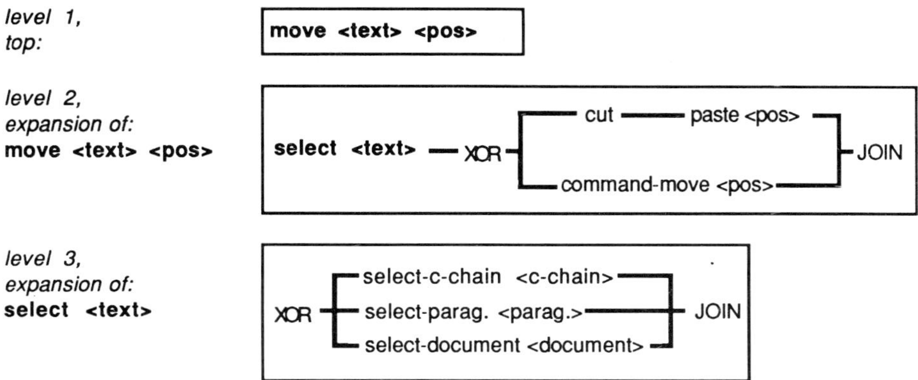

Figure 1. Simple procedural network composed of two goals. These goals are decomposed to form a hierarchical structure.

Essentially, the second level means that the goal of moving text to a position can be satisfied by first selecting the text to be moved, and then, using either a method commonly named "cut and paste" in the desktop metaphor, or using an alternative method which consists of a single command dedicated specifically to moving text. Hence, the nodes XOR ("exclusive or") and JOIN ("join paths") serve the purpose of representing alternative methods of achieving some goal. We find these nodes again at level three, where we have a structure made out of three methods for decomposing the goal of selecting text. Notice that the methods differ in the *objects* to which the actions apply. Indeed, there is a general method for selecting character-chain, which can be anything from a single character to the whole document. There are also two *specialized methods* for selecting a paragraph and the whole document. Usually, as it is the case here, the methods delimited by XOR and JOIN differ in their degree of efficiency and generality. Specialized methods are more efficient but less general, and vice-versa.

The PN is thus a formalism that represents all possible means for achieving given goals. Associated with it is a process that *parses* a user's actions into a goal hierarchy. Figure 2 illustrates two goal hierarchies which could be the result of the parsing process from figure 1's PN. This result yields information as to what goal is behind the actions and, when many alternatives are available, which method is chosen for achieving the goal. This is the core information needed by the user

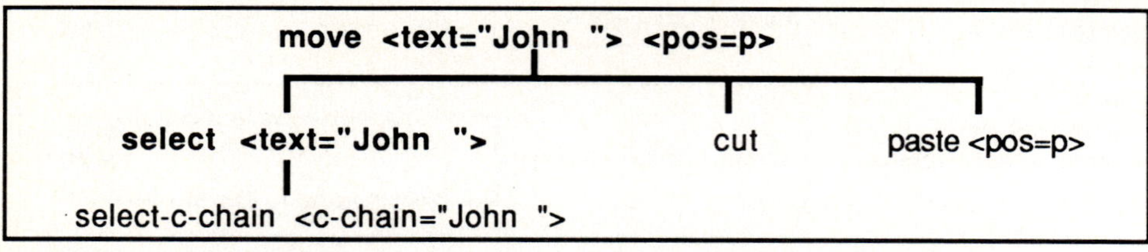

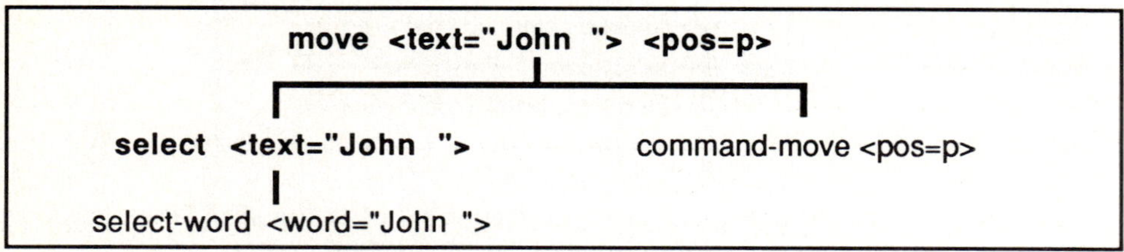

Figure 2. Two examples of goal structures which could be generated by figure 1's PN.

modelling module to assess the user's knowledge, or the user's *knowledge state*. The module will then evaluate if the user needs assistance, and what to teach, if anything, from this knowledge state. Furthermore, it will indicate which actions and methods are likely to be observed by the PN module. The interaction between the PN module and the user modelling module is summerized in figure 3.

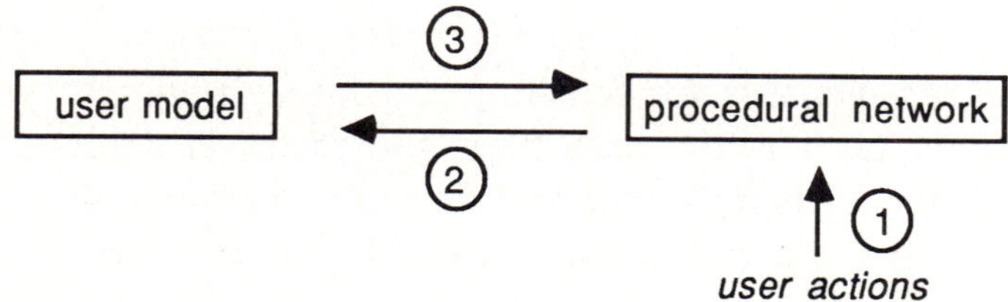

Figure 3. Flow of information between the system's modules and the user.

First, the PN module identifies goals and methods in the user actions. Second, this information is used for making a knowledge assessment. And third, the knowledge assessment feeds information back to the PN module in terms of what is likely to be observed or not according to the user's knowledge state. This process is repeated for each new observation.

The user modelling module

Essentially, the user modelling module contains all the knowledge directly related to the task-domain in the form of a set of discrete knowledge items, which we call the *complete knowledge set* (CKS). To each node of the PN corresponds a single knowledge item in the CKS. Methods in the PN are also represented by knowledge items. We use the term *competence* to designate that type of knowledge (actions, goals and methods). The CKS also contains another type of knowledge which is not procedural but *conceptual*, and which includes notions about "text-filling", "paragraph", "paragraph property", etc. Such notions are also represented as a discrete element of the CKS.

A user's *knowledge state* is represented as a sub-set of the CKS. This knowledge state indicates which actions and methods the user is able to perform, which goals (tasks) he/she is able to achieve, and which concepts he/she knows. It is based, as mentioned, on the observation of a user's actions. Indeed, some observations can tell a lot about the user's knowledge state and much goes on after a single observation to complete the knowledge assessment process. For instance, the usage of the method "select-document <document>" is a specialized method to rapidly select the whole document and is generally only used by regular users. The knowledge assessment process will infer from its observation that the user probably knows the more general methods of selection, like "select-c-chain <c-chain>", and all the basics of the task domain, like the "cut and paste" method.

In fact, the CKS is highly structured and the possible knowledge states, which are sub-sets of the whole CKS, are greatly constrained by the interdependencies among the knowledge items. In the rest of this paper we will look at the different types of relations with which we can model the structure of the expertise. Although our discussion is framed within the context of the text-editing task and for a coach-type system, it is by no means intended to be limited to this context and can be extended to other tasks and applications.

The structure of expertise

The structure of knowledge, which we termed here the structure of expertise to differentiate it from "semantic knowledge" or "episodic knowledge", can be modelled by a limited set of relations which bear interesting properties for the knowledge assessment process. For instance, in the example above we inferred that the ability to perform the "cut and paste" method was surmised from that of performing the action "select-document <document>", because it is generally learned before "select-document" is. The learning order of competences and concepts, or "C/C's", determines a "surmise" relation from the latest C/C's to the earlier ones. It is at the core of the knowledge assessment process. It defines a type of structure called partial order in graph theory. Doignon and Falmagne (1985) present the formal properties and assumptions of this type of knowledge structure and of AND/OR graph structures in the context of knowledge assessment. We will review this theory briefly, along with structures containing other types of relations like conditional probabilities and XOR relations.

Partial order

A partial order is a directed graph defined by a reflexive, antisymmetric, and transitive relation like the "surmise" relation above. The previous example illustrates this relation between two competences ("select-document <document>" surmises the "cut and paste" method). Whenever two C/C have a constant learning order we find a surmise relation between both. This is generally the case for two C/C's which have a logical precedence. For instance, the concept of "paragraph" logically precedes that of a "sequence of paragraph". Every method involving a paragraph will then be learned before those involving a sequence of paragraph (eg. changing the paragraphs format properties of a single paragraph will be learned before changing a sequence of paragraphs' properties).

The generalization of the surmise relation over a whole CKS is that whenever the C/C's are learned in a constant and systematic order, we find that all the possible knowledge states can be totally described by a partial order. More formally, a set of knowledge states that is closed under union and intersection can be totally described by a partial order (see Doignon and Falmagne, 1985, for a demonstration of this theorem). That is, if we have a domain knowledge in which the *intersection* as well as the *union* of two people's knowledge state is always someone else's knowledge state, then we will find a one to one correspondence between each person's knowledge state and a knowledge state defined by a partial order.

This is demonstrated in the following schema which defines all the possible knowledge states for the CKS including the C/C's discussed in the previous example:

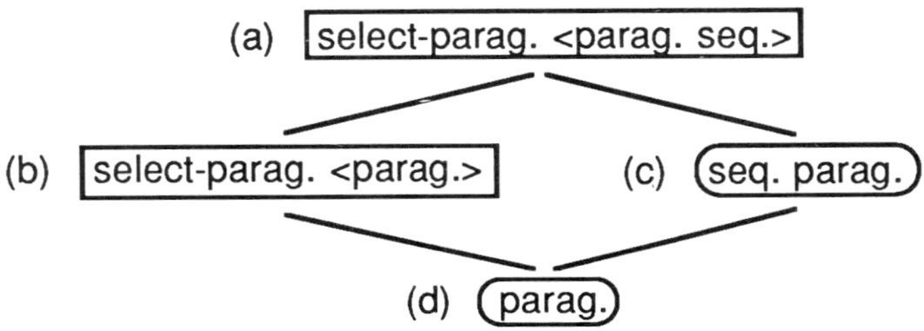

Figure 4. Partial order representing logical precedence among C/C's.

Logical precedence from a bottom node to a top node is indicated by a binary relation between two C/C's, which can also be interpreted as a logical implication relation from a top node to a bottom node. This schema defines the possible knowledge states as: {{}, {d}, {b, d}, {c, d}, {a, b, c, d}}. Indeed, any other knowledge state is incompatible with the interdependencies of the C/C's involved in this example.

A partial order can formally represent the totality of the possible knowledge states if and only if the CKS meets the closure under the assumptions of union and intersection. If, for instance, the learning order is not constant, or if a C/C can be preceded by only one of many C/C's, then these assumptions are violated and the partial order will not constitute a proper formalism for *completely* representing the structural dependencies between knowledge items (although it will represent some of them). This can be seen in the PN of figure 1. Suppose we were to find that the ability to move text to another position implies, first, the ability to select text, and, second, the ability to use either the "cut and paste" method or the "command-move" method. This would be impossible to represent directly with a partial order. Indeed, it is represented in the PN with the use of an XOR node and there is no equivalent provision in a partial order.

AND/OR diagrams

To represent a disjunction of precedence of C/C, we need to include in the knowledge structure an OR relation. For instance, suppose we want to represent the fact that the ability to select a paragraph implies either the ability of using "select-chain <parag.>" or "select-parag. <parag.>". We can modify figure 4's schema by adding the appropriate nodes and relation:

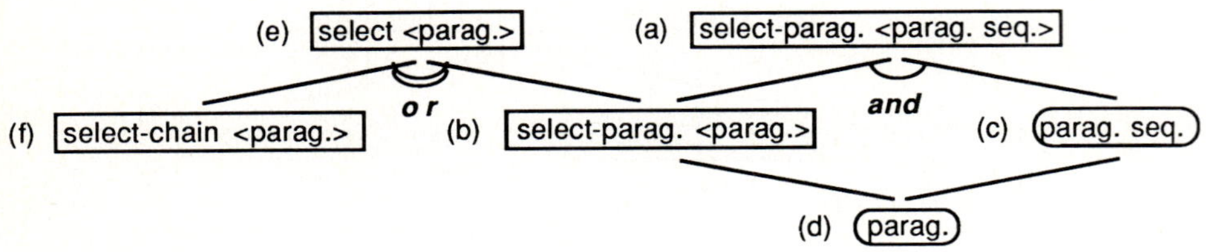

Figure 5. AND/OR graph representing a disjunction and a conjunction of precedence.

This type of diagram is called an AND/OR graph. The modification of the original schema, with the addition of the "e" and "f" nodes, and of an OR relation, defines the following knowledge states as also possible: {{e, f}, {e, b, d}}.

Although the OR relation is fairly useful to represent text-editing expertise, it usually applies to disjunctions of methods and is isomorphic to the XOR-JOIN sub-structures in the PN. Moreover, the hierarchical goal decomposition of the PN also tends to be redundant with the AND relation between competence nodes of the knowledge structure. For instance, the "cut and paste" method implies a conjunction of the "cut" and "paste <pos.>" actions. In other words, unless concepts are involved, an AND/OR graph structure is fairly redundant with the PN structure. On the other hand, this is not always the case when there are concepts involved or other types of relations as we will see below.

XOR relations

Sometimes, the usage of a method indicates that some notions are *not* known. This is the case of the "break line" method. This method is typical of users who transpose their knowledge of a typewriter to text-editing. They tend to always type a "return" at the end of each line instead of letting the text-editor do the text-filling automatically, as it should be done with WYSIWYG-type editors. The "return" character is a paragraph delimitor, thus, usage of this character to break lines shows that the user does not know the notion of "paragraph" in the text-editing sense. The relationship between the "break line" method and the "paragraph" concept is indicated by an XOR relation between 'g' and 'd' in figure 6.

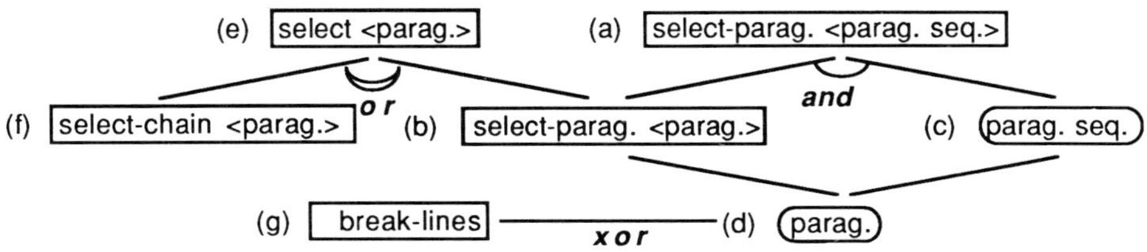

Figure 6. AND/OR graph supplemented by an xor relation representing an "exclusive or" between two C/C's.

Following the observation of the "break-lines" method, we can logically deduce that the node "parag" (d) will be absent from the user's knowledge state. Furthermore, we can deduce from the logical structure of the diagram that the C/C's in the set {d, b, c, a} will not be contained in the knowledge state of this user, for the absence of 'd' means that every C/C which implies 'd' directly or by transitivity will also be absent ({b, c, a}).

It should be noted that it is abusive here to talk of *knowledge* state, since the knowledge of the concept "paragraph" does not necessarily imply that a user does not *know* the "break-lines" method, but simply that he will not *use* it because it is an inadequate method for text-editing. Thus, we should distinguish between *usage* and *knowledge* of procedural knowledge. Such distinction is even more important for methods accomplishing the same goal but with varying degree of efficiency. This is the case between "select-c-chain <parag.>" and "select-parag. <parag.>". When the selection is a paragraph, it is generally more efficient to use "select-parag." than "select-c-chain". For that reason, they should be linked together with an XOR relation, since usage of the less efficient method probably means that the user does not *know* the more efficient one, and usage of the more efficient one means that the user will probably not *use* the less efficient one, even though he surely knows it.

To complicate matters a little more, usage of the less efficient method, if only slightly less efficient than the alternative one, might still be preferred by a user because it means fewer things to remember, or because in certain contexts it is not more efficient, or simply by preference. Hence, the difference in *cost* of using a method vs. another should be taken into account, especially for pedagogical purposes: we would like to insist on teaching methods that conveys significant cost difference and let the user free to use whatever method suits him/her best when the difference is small. The *cost difference* between two methods could then be represented in the knowledge structure by a weighted and ordered relation, where the weight indicates the difference.

Unfortunately, we lack empirical data to evaluate the importance of the distinction, within the context of a text-editor coach, between usage and knowledge of C/C, and of the problem of cost difference between methods. They are mentioned here as possible extensions to the formalism for a representation of a knowledge structure.

Conditional probabilities

Another problem of the partial order as a representation scheme for knowledge structures is that there might be a surmise relation between two C/C's, and yet, there might be some exceptions to the normal learning order. This is especially true when the surmise relation is not based on a logical precedence but on other factors, like the fact that general C/C's are learned before specialized ones. This is the case for the surmise relation from the action "select-document <document>" to the "cut and paste" method that was mentioned earlier. Although unlikely, it could happen that someone learns the former before the latter and, thus, knows "select-document" but not the "cut and paste" method. It would be more appropriate, then, to have a weight attached to each surmise relation indicating some kind of probability.

Friend (1981) developed such a probabilistic approach within a Bayesian framework. Each node has a probability of being "mastered". When evidence that a node is mastered, the probability of being mastered is recomputed for every other node.

Although Friend's scheme seems quite performant in evaluating knowledge, as she demonstrates with a Monte Carlo simulation, the computation relies on a number of simplifying assumptions. The most important of these assumptions is that the conditional probability must be a constant value for every computation of the new probabilities given evidence. This means that the "relevance" of a surmise relation must be uniform all over the network, a rather strong assumption.

Another probabilistic approach, developed within the framework of expert systems for making inferences from multiple evidence, could be applied to our context. For instance, Kadesh (1986) developed an approach to inference from multiple evidence based on a Bayesian scheme. He introduced the concept of "relevance" between two items, which could take the place of the value of a relation between two C/C's. Although it does not suffer from any of Friend's simplifying assumptions, it is much too costly computationally. A computationally feasible version is available, but here again, limiting assumptions have to be introduced which could invalidate the approach. Unfortunately, we do not have empirical data to assess its validity under these assumptions at the present time.

The elaboration and implementation of knowledge structures

We have talked so far about the formalism needed to represent and assess user knowledge. We now turn the problem of constructing the knowledge structures with the formalism presented.

Automatic construction of knowledge structures with surmise relations

A surmise relation is characterized by a simple distribution of user knowledge. That is, if a knowledge item A is surmised by knowledge item B, then we find (1) users who know A and B, (2) users who know A but not B, and (3) users who don't know both (in fact, we can always assume there exist people who don't know both). However, we should never find people who know B but not A, for if we can surmise A from B, it means A must be known when B is.

This distribution of user knowledge can be readily exploited by an algorithm to construct a knowledge structure composed of surmise relations. Indeed, we need only check for pairs of knowledge items bearing a distribution like the one described above. First, that involves compiling, for a number of users, each user's knowledge of a pair of knowledge items into one of four possibilities:

(1) item A known, item B known
(2) item A known, item B unknown
(3) item A unknown, item B known
(4) item A unknown, item B unknown

Second, this compiling process is repeated for each pair of knowledge items of the knowledge set. Finally, if we find item pairs that have users in conditions (1), (3) and (4) only, then we indicate a surmise relation from A to B; and if we get users in conditions (1), (2) and (4) only, then we indicate a surmise relation from B to A.

Automatic construction of knowledge structures by observation of competence

With the use of the algorithm above and the module for the recognition of competence, it becomes possible to set up a system that would construct a knowledge structure comprised of the competences observed.

This experience was tried with the knowledge of UNIX† commands (Pavel and Desmarais, 1986). The usage of 126 UNIX commands by 51 users was monitored for a month. From this data, a knowledge structure was constructed with the algorithm above. The knowledge structure obtained contained over 500 relations, once all relations that could be inferred from transitivity were removed to form a minimal *digraph*. A preliminary evaluation of a system using this knowledge structure for the assessment of user knowledge shows that it makes a fairly accurate assessment, in the sense that few commands that were reported by the system as known by a user were actually not known (around 15%). It did indicate, however, that making a

† UNIX is a trademark of Bell Laboratories.

knowledge assessment by the observation of competence, as is the case in a computer coach, is limited by the fact that the use of competences that tell a lot about a user's knowledge state do not occur as frequently as competences that are more elementary. Thus, a coach might have to wait awhile before making a reliable assessment. These conclusions should be taken with care though, since they are based on preliminary results and within a different context.

Nevertheless, the experience with UNIX clearly demonstrated two limits of the construction of knowledge structures in the manner described above. The first one is that, by using a deterministic scheme instead of a probabilistic one, we end up leaving a lot of information aside. For instance, if we only find one or two people that, say, know item A and not B, and many people in the other three conditions, should we still consider that there is no surmise relation from A to B? Doing so would leave out a probable, though not absolute, surmise relation. The second problem with the above scheme for knowledge structure construction is that, although we can be fairly confident that if someone manifests a competence then he/she probably masters this competence, we cannot be sure that the absence of manifestation of this competence is a clear indication of non-mastery. We can, however, compute the probability that someone masters a competence given it was not used on a given number occasions, based on competence manifestation statistics. But it remains a probability which would lose informative value if integrated into a deterministic scheme, whereas it could be directly integrated in a probabilistic scheme.

The construction of complex knowledge structures

The current limits of automatic construction of knowledge structures become even more obvious when we need to integrate concepts and the other types of relations presented in the second section. Concepts cannot be directly observed like competences can and, consequently, their assessment must go through a formal testing, which rules out the observation scheme. Moreover, concepts are not as obvious to identify as competences are, and thus need to be well thought out.

As for the other relations, although the XOR relation can be identified algorithmically by a knowledge distribution in the same manner the surmise relation can, the OR relation (of an AND/OR graph, not the logical OR) is much more complex to identify since it is not a binary relation but it involves at least three C/C. Fortunately, the OR relation is already defined for procedural knowledge by the PN.

Conclusion

We have presented a formalism for the representation and assessment of user knowledge in the context of a text-editor coach. User knowledge is represented as a sub-set of the CKS (complete knowledge set). A small number of relation types are included in the CKS to assist the knowledge assessment. These relations are, in fact, logical relations from which we can make various types of inferences. They include the surmise relation which forms partial orders, the OR relation of AND/OR graphs, and finally the XOR relation. Together, they can adequately represent most of the interdependencies among concepts and competences we find in a domain like text-editing.

There remains a number of empirical questions regarding the usefulness of each type of relations relative to each other in the knowledge assessment process. In spite of the few experiment we carried out with the knowledge of UNIX commands, much more has to be done to evaluate the accuracy of the knowledge assessment, and to explore its role in a coach-type tutoring system. We are presently building a coach-like system for text-editing and carrying out some experiments to construct a knowledge structure for this system. This work should yield some interesting results for the evaluation and improvements of the user knowledge assessment scheme presented here.

References

Doignon, Jean-Paul, & Falmagne, Jean-Claude (1985). Spaces for the assessment of knowledge. *International Journal of Man-Machine Studies,* 23, pp. 175-196.

Friend, Jamesine E. (1981). *Domain referenced adaptive testing.* Research report no. cis-10 (ssl-81-3). Palo Alto, CA: Xerox Parc, Cognitive and Instructional Sciences.

Kadesh, R.R. (1986). Subjective inference with multiple evidence. *Journal of Artificial Intelligence,* 28, pp. 333-341.

Pavel, Michael & Desmarais, Michel C. (1985). *UNIX knowledge assessment.* Psychology Department, Stanford University.

Sacerdoti, Earl D. (1977). *A Structure for Plans and Behavior.* New York: Elsevier.

Mental Models and Human-Computer Interaction 1
D. Ackermann and M.J. Tauber (Editors)
Elsevier Science Publishers B.V. (North-Holland), 1990

A GRAMMAR-BASED APPROACH TO UNIFYING TASK-ORIENTED AND SYSTEM-ORIENTED INTERFACE DESCRIPTIONS

Heinz Ulrich Hoppe

GMD - Institute for Integrated Publication and Information Systems
Darmstadt, FRG

ABSTRACT

Formal descriptions of human-computer interaction can roughly be classified as either user-oriented (e.g. simulation models of user behavior) or system-oriented (e.g. technical specifications of interface components). At present, an explicit conceptualization of tasks is only provided by user-oriented approaches. On the other hand, there are several possible applications of making tasks explicit on the side of the system, e.g. automatic protocolling on the task level, intelligent tutoring, context dependent help, or macro generation. The method of *task-oriented parsing* is introduced as a basic technique in order to realize applications of this type. In contrast to solutions which have emerged from the field of artificial intelligence, this approach is based on a notion of tasks compatible with current user-oriented models like task-action grammars. Task-oriented parsing essentially inverts the process of task-action mapping as realized by several psychologically motivated approaches to modeling human-computer interaction. On the practical side, it is shown how task-oriented parsing as well as task-action mapping can be achieved with one bidirectional Prolog program.

Formal descriptions of user interfaces: methods and purposes

There is a growing interest in applying formal description techniques to human-computer interaction (HCI), caused by the practical promises of user interface management systems (UIMS's) and generating tools on the one side, and the obvious advantages of using analytic methods in order to evaluate usability characteristics of systems on the other side. As an introduction to the problem domain to be discussed here, it is adequate to refine the rough distinction between system-oriented and user-oriented models and give a more detailled classification of different approaches to formally describing HCI. The following five categories of models ranging from the user-oriented to the system-oriented end of the spectrum will be compared:

(I) Modelling cognitive processes of the user when interacting with a system (the user-oriented approach);

(II) Modelling the knowledge required to be able to operate a certain system in order to execute a certain class of tasks (the task-oriented approach);

(III) Formal specification of an interaction language (the language-oriented approach);

(IV) Specification of the interface as a system component at different levels (e.g. I/O, syntactic, semantic - the interface-oriented approach);

(V) Using formal descriptions as source code for interface generators (the implementation-oriented approach).

The different categories are related to different stages of information processing in HCI. These relations may be illustrated using an extension of Norman's *stages of user activities* (Norman, 1986) as a reference scheme (cf. figure 1). Figure 1 describes typical sub-processes in the flow of information between user and system. In contrast to Norman's view, there is an explicit description of what is happening inside the system. The term *functional specification of actions,* which has been introduced here, should be understood in the sense of the functional + argument levels of a GOMS model (Card, Moran & Newell, 1983). On these levels, the functions to be invoked are specified and supplied with arguments, but the production of keystrokes is still left to the lowest level.

Models of type (I) describe processes inside the *user* box. GOMS models or production systems, developed in the framework of cognitive complexity theory (Kieras & Polson, 1985), are typical representatives of this category. Most of the current work is concerned with the generation of input actions (namely keystrokes) from given task descriptions and toplevel goals. This coincides with steps (1)-(3) in the reference scheme. As analytic models of external representation and related perception phenomena are still missing, steps (7)-(10) are only treated globally as a black box.

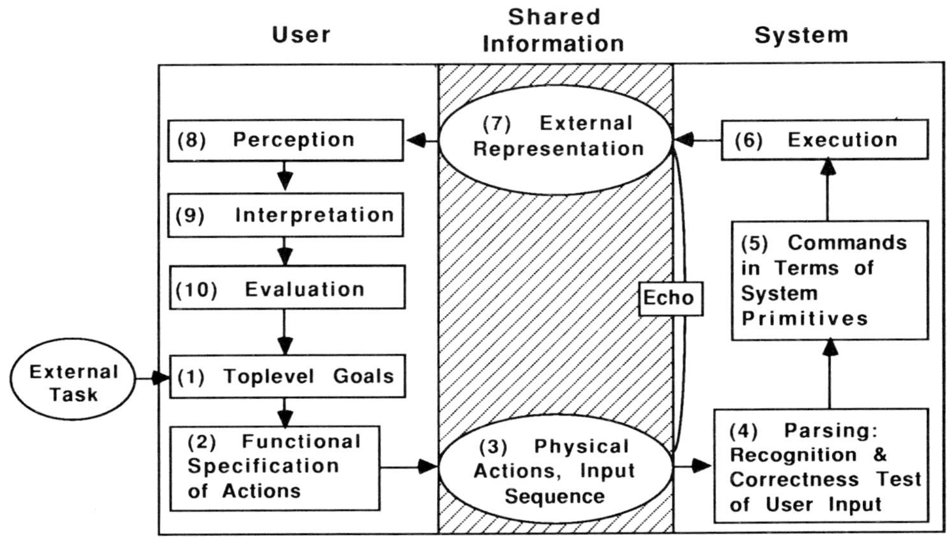

Figure 1. Stages of information processing in HCI

The models contained in category (II) refer to the knowledge underlying and governing the human information processing in HCI. In comparison to process models (I), these have been characterized as *competence models* (Green, Schiele & Payne, 1988). Competence models, e.g. those formulated as task-action grammars or TAGs (Payne & Green, 1986), have a limited scope in that the stages of information processing described are confined to (2) and (3). On the other hand, they may yield valuable insight into the internal structure and representation of the user's knowledge.

Language-oriented model (III) describe the structure and content of interaction languages. Again, as for the first category the present applications are mostly limited to input languages, either covering (2) and (3) in the case of user-oriented descriptions or (3) and (4) if system-oriented. Although it is a very common view to describe external interfaces in terms of the input and output languages, precisely formalized representation systems for the output language are still missing. Language-oriented models have been constructed for analytic use, e.g. Reisner's formal grammars (Reisner, 1981). Another application lies in synthesizing interfaces based on grammatical descriptions of input languages to be processed by generators such as the UNIX tools LEX and YACC.

Type (IV) and (V) models either specify (IV) or actually define (V) mechanisms for parsing, translation, or evaluation of input on the system side. Interface generation tools may also allow a complete description of the surface representation. Models from these categories are located somewhere between (3) and (7). Typical instances of these categories are layered models of the interface (e.g. the ISO-OSI reference model) or source descriptions for interface generators. An overview of such models is provided in Hoppe et al. (1986).

The reference scheme (figure 1) shows that the information which is explicitly shared between the user and the machine is selective, local and low-level (as far as the degree of abstraction is concerned). As for the input channel, the expressions of the user are physically linked to the system via keystrokes/key-codes, mouse events or even acoustic signals in a strictly sequential process. The simplicity is not so obvious for the external representation of pictorial, *direct manipulation* interfaces. Pictorial output languages can indeed provide a lot of information about the actual state of the system in terms of objects and functions available. But usually, this information is not explicitly contained in the system's representation of the output (pixels, graphics primitives etc.). And even if higher-level constructs are represented in the system, e.g. in an object-oriented manner, we do not understand analytically how users perceive and evaluate the information provided.

In addition to the information actually and explicitly shared between user and system, virtually shared information has also to be considered. Virtually shared information is a projection used by one dialogue partner to anticipate what is happening "on the other side". Projections of the machine made by the user are referred to as *mental models* (Norman, 1983), metaphors or *user's virtual machines* (Tauber, 1985) on the user's side. If, on the other hand, the system had such a virtual image of the user, we would call this a user model (i.e. a model of the user).

This article will not follow the already popular lines of discussions about mental models or user models, but is focussed on the representation of knowledge about tasks on the system side. The notion of task plays a central role in type (I) and (II) models, but it is not explicit inside the system. A system with a user interface based on a complete formal description of the input language will still accept input sequences which do not correspond to any meaningful task. (Of course, tasks can be defined at different levels of aggregation, and this influences our understanding of what a *meaningful* task is. This question has to be clarified - and hopefully will be - in the next section.)

Based on a preliminary, intuitive understanding of what is considered to be a task, it is already possible to anticipate the advantages of introducing the task as an explicit concept on the system side. First of all, it would mean another extension of the channel of virtually shared information. Although this is not an advantage per se, the additional information could be used for different purposes. Obvious fields of application are intelligent tutoring and context dependent help, where the user's goals and intentions could be identified via the recognition of task patterns. Task-oriented protocolling could also be very helpful for evaluation purposes and thus facilitate empirical studies.

The notion of task in cognitive psychology and theories of Human-Computer Interaction

The meaning of *task* is usually defined as goal-directed activity to transform some given initial state (of a general system or "world") into a goal state. A state transformation is produced by applying an operator to the actual state. Tasks and the so-called *interpolation problems* (Dörner, 1976) have in common that the set of applicable operators is well-known. (This is, of course, a subjective criterion.) The conceptual difference between a task and a problem lies in the availability of fixed strategies or *methods* for producing a solution. Problems are characterized by the absence of such methods, so that a solution has to be constructed by finding a correct sequence of operators. The Towers of Hanoi puzzle, for instance, defines a problem only for those persons who do not know a solution strategy.

Task execution generally requires less cognitive effort in terms of processing time and STM capacity than problem solving. On the other hand, this "local" advantage has to be paid for by installing some appropriate method in LTM, i.e. the method must be learned. For being globally efficient, a method learned should apply to a whole class of conditions (i.e. initial states).

As the invariant characteristic of a task is the associated method and not a special initial state, state-oriented descriptions are not adequate for tasks. Instead of this, it is reasonable to characterize a task in terms of its method. A procedural description of a method specifies how this method is constructed of sub-methods and primitive operators including the representation of control structure and parameter constraints. Methods in this sense are decomposition rules for complex tasks. For instance, a *replace* task may be broken down into a *delete* operation applied to some object X followed by a *move* with some object Y where the target location of *move(Y)* has to be identical with the original location of X. Concrete instances of tasks are then described by means of the task type instantiated by the name of the respective method, and further feature-symbol/feature-value pairs (more technical details are given in section 3).

The understanding of tasks outlined so far is very close to the task-action grammar approach developed by Green & Payne (Payne & Green, 1986; Green, Schiele & Payne, 1988). Figure 2 demonstrates an example of a TAG description modelling *copy* and *move* operations for the Macintosh desktop (document and file handling). In this context two aspects are essential: the use of feature/value lists for the description of tasks and the notion of *simple tasks*. As far as the replacement rules (*rule schemas* and *subtask rules*) are concerned, it is sufficient to know that they represent methods for task completion in terms of a hierarchical decomposition. As the use of features for task description has already been explained, what remains is to have a closer look at the simple tasks:

> "In brief, a Task-Action Grammar rewrites 'simple tasks' into action sequences. 'Simple' tasks are those which can be accomplished with no problem solving component or control structure; they may be at a very low level, for novices, or may be composed into larger grouping with experience. ... simple tasks are determined primarily by the characteristics of the device itself. If the device has no direct way of handling paragraphs, the user may still form a simple task at the paragraph level - but only if the execution of that task requires no problem-solving and no control actions." (Green, Schiele & Payne, 1988)

The concept of simple tasks reveals some problems inherent with TAG models. The dictionary of simple tasks defines the conceptually relevant task units on the top level. What the conceptually relevant units are may be depending on the type of user to be modelled. But once defined, it is not within the scope of TAG to go beyond this

List of Features	*Possible Values*
Object	folder, document, paper basket
Position, Target_Pos	(a pair of coordinates)
Effect	copies, moves

Dictionary of 'Simple Tasks'

copy_object :: Object = ONE-OF {folder,document}, Position = ANY, Target_Pos = ANY, Effect = copies .

move_object :: Object = ANY, Position = ANY, Target_Pos = ANY, Effect = moves .

Rule Schemas

Task [Object = ONE-OF {folder,document}, Position = ANY,
Target_Pos = ANY, Effect = copies]
::= duplicate [Object, Position] + drag [Target_Pos] .

Task [Object = ANY, Position = ANY, Target_Pos = ANY, Effect = moves]
::= select [Object, Position] + drag [Target_Pos] .

Subtask Rules

duplicate [Object = ONE-OF {folder,document}, Position = ANY]
::= select [Object, Position] + PRESS-KEY('X'+'D') .

select [Object = ANY, Position inside Object]
::= MOVE-MOUSE-TO(Position) + CLICK-MOUSE-BUTTON .

drag [Target_Pos = ANY] ::= PRESS-MOUSE-BUTTON +
MOVE-MOUSE-TO(Target_Pos) + RELEASE-MOUSE-BUTTON .

Action Primitives

Keystrokes: PRESS-KEY(...)

Mouse Actions: MOVE-MOUSE-TO(Position), PRESS_MOUSE_BUTTON, RELEASE_MOUSE_BUTTON, CLICK_MOUSE_BUTTON .

Figure 2. A TAG description of *copy/move* for the Macintosh desktop

border and introduce higher level units into the same model. This is a strong restriction because simple tasks are not recursively nested. Although there is no formal reason for excluding nested simple tasks, this would be inconsistent with the understanding of simple tasks as maximal control-free units of user behaviour.

The TAG approach is a representative of category (II) in so far as it yields competence models. Nevertheless, there is an interesting analogy between the TAG concept of simple tasks and the so-called *unit tasks* in process-oriented GOMS models:

> " ... the task (of manuscript editing) is structured as a set of separate modifications. However, it is up to the user to decide how to organize these modifications into a series of unit tasks. ... the unit task is not given by the task environment, but results from the interaction of the task structure with the control problems faced by the user." (Card, Moran & Newell, 1983, pp. 386f)

In a GOMS model, the top level control structure is essentially a repetition of the steps *acquire next unit task* and *execute unit task*. The unit tasks appearing on this level are equivalent to the simple tasks of a corresponding TAG description. The internal structure of a unit task in GOMS is described by a method which is invoked by a specific start goal (e.g. GOAL DELETE OBJECT <Name>). A method contains the necessary control information about the serial composition of steps and the decomposition into sub-methods to be called. In GOMS, it is possible that a unit task A "calls" another unit task B by establishing the start goal for B and thus invoking the associated method (e.g. *replace* could be a unit task containing *delete* and *move* subtasks despite *delete* and *move* being proper unit tasks).

For the purposes of introducing the concept of tasks into the dialogue processor of the system, it is reasonable to be as flexible as possible concerning the grain size of the task units to be recognized. Especially, assumptions about the user cannot be fixed. So, mechanisms to deal with task units at different levels of refinement including a nesting mechanism have to be provided. Indeed the elementary task units to be recognized will correspond to *simple* or unit tasks for novices, but these may be accumulated to build up higher level task constructs.

TOP - a task-oriented parser based on attribute grammars

The use of grammars for modelling HCI

Grammars are a well-understood formalism for the description of language syntax and semantics. They have already often been used to describe input languages in HCI, either in the sense of the user's *grammar in the head* (Payne & Green, 1983), or as formal specifications of input recognition modules (parsers). An important quality of most of the grammar notations is that there are tools available for generating a parser from a given description automatically (parser generators - e.g. the UNIX tool YACC).

The basic problems arising with the use of grammars for the formal description of languages are the following:

Parsing: For a given sentence, decide whether it may be derived from a certain grammar. Parsing is often combined with translation or evaluation of sentences.

Generation: Generate the set of well-formed sentences for a given grammar. Often this problem is specialized to generating a subset of all possible sentences which comply with certain constraints.

Grammar induction: Given a set of sentences, find a grammar generating these sentences.

A grammar defined by a set of context-free productions, e.g. in BNF notation, gives a mere syntactic description of a language. In other words: if such grammar describes semantic aspects, then the semantic constraints must be implicitly contained in the syntax rules. If semantic aspects of a language shall be expressed explicitly, more powerful meta-languages like attribute grammars (Knuth, 1968) or two-level grammars (van Wijngaarden, 1966) have to be used. Context-sensitivity for these notation systems is achieved by associating variable parameters (attributes or meta-symbols) as well as constraints on these parameters with the context-free syntax rules.

There are different ways of expressing semantics by means of grammars. In the field of programming languages, Pagan (1981) distinguishes the *translational approach* and the *interpretive approach*. The translational approach is characterized by translating correct sentences written in some higher-level language into some other language which is closer to the *semantics of the machine*. This is the typical job of a compiler. The task-oriented parser (TOP) to be described here is based on the interpretive approach and therefore this approach will be considered in more detail:

> "The philosophy on which this technique rests is that the 'meaning' of a program should be described essentially in terms of the correspondence it defines between its input data and its output data and that a formal system therefore constitutes a complete semantic formalization if it generates triples consisting of (a) a syntactically valid program, (b) an input file, and (c) an output file such that the execution of the program with the input file produces the output file." (Pagan, 1981, p. 99)

A bit more formally, we could say: an interpretive semantic parser is a mapping

$$\sigma : S \times E \rightarrow E, \qquad (1)$$

where E denotes the set of possible *environments* or system states, and S denotes the set of all syntactically correct sequences of statements. In the context of HCI, we will - for obvious reasons - replace the term *syntactically correct sequences of statements* by *syntactically correct input sequences* (in terms of some input primitives).

The example given in figure 3 shows how the toplevel rules for such a parser can be expressed in attribute grammar notation (cf. Watt & Madsen, 1983) and how this grammar is translated into Prolog in a one-to-one way. A short and concise introduction to the use of attribute grammars (AGs) for modelling purposes is provided in a survey report on formal modelling techniques in HCI (Hoppe, Tauber & Ziegler, 1986). As there are presumably more people familiar with Prolog than with attribute grammars, I will further use this programming language as notation system (cf. Clocksin & Mellish, 1981).

The idea of task-oriented parsing

The work reported here started with writing AG-parsers for modelling and simulating different user interfaces. Such a parser may not only be regarded as a device model but also as a model for the competence of a skilled user. According to the latter view, the grammar-based models should also be usable for generating input sequences for given changes of the environment. This problem is equivalent to finding solutions for the equation

$$\sigma\ (X, E_1) = E_2, \qquad (2)$$

(AG)

```
[session >ENV <NEW]        ::=   [operation >ENV <NEW1] +
                                 [session >NEW1 <NEW].

[operation >ENV <NEW]      ::=   [selection >ENV <NEW1] +
                                 [operation >NEW1 <NEW].
[operation > ENV <NEW]     ::=   [function >ENV <NEW]

[selection >ENV <NEW]      ::=   [mouseclick <POS],
                                 where POS = position(first(NEW)),
                                 applicable("select", first(NEW)).
```

(Prolog)

```
session([],Out_List,Env,Env).
session(In_List,Out_List,Env,New_Env) :-
                    operation(In_List,Out1,Env,New1),
                    session(Out1,Out_List,New1,New_Env).
operation([],Out_List,Env,Env).
operation(In_List,Out_List,Env,Env_New) :-
                    selection(In_List,Out1,Env,New1),!,
                    operation(Out1,Out_List,New1,New_Env).
operation(In_List,Out_List,Env,New_Env) :-
                    function(In_List,Out_List,Env,New_Env).
selection([mouseklick,Pos|Rest],Rest,Env,New_Env) :-
                    position(Pos,Obj,Env),
                    applicable(Obj,select),
                    make_first(Obj,Env,New_env).
```

Figure 3. Toplevel of an interaction parser as AG and in Prolog (from: Hoppe, Tauber & Ziegler, 1986)

where E_1 and E_2 stand for the given initial and goal environments. Of course, normally there is an infinite number of solutions for X but only a few of these are not redundant in the sense that no part of the sequence may be omitted. Excluding redundant solutions and finding the *simple* ones requires a typical backtracking search procedure. This is easy to realize in Prolog, but my experience is that it cannot be achieved by simply using the original parser in the inverse way. Instead, I had to provide additional control structures and heuristic rules for the choice of operators. These extensions led to what I called a *semantic planner,* but were of no use for the parsing application.

The task-oriented approach was developed as another extension of the semantic parser-interpreter. It yields interesting new features for both parsing and generation. A task-oriented parser may formally be described as a mapping

$$\tau\colon S \times E \rightarrow E \times T, \tag{3}$$

where T denotes the set of all finite sequences of tasks <t1, ... , tn> . A task can be represented as a list of task features with associated feature values (just like property lists in LISP). This may be illustrated by the following example:

```
example_task = ( (function MOVE)
                 (object folder_1)
                 (source_pos 1)
                 (target_pos 4) ) .
```

For a given system, possible combinations of features (task-patterns) have to be defined. Domain restrictions for the feature values could be defined explicitly in the data base or implicitly with the parsing rules. Instantiated task-patterns form the basis of the entire task space of the system. This basis may be extended by applying certain operators for the construction of new tasks. Possible operations are task composition (a binary operation) and task specialization (value restriction for one task). Provided the basis of elementary tasks and the construction operators have been specified, the set T is completely defined. The next section will show how this can be realized with a Prolog database.

The inversion problem is now better determined, as expressed by the following equation replacing (2):

$$\tau\,(X,E_1) = (E_2,T_0)\ , \tag{5}$$

i.e. for given environments E_1, E_2 and given task list, find an input sequence X producing (E_2,T_0) from (X,E_1). Here, the task parameter provides additional information.

The next section describes a Prolog implementation of such a task-oriented parser (called TOP) which is still based on the AG-approach. It turns out that the introduction of a task-parameter makes generation and parsing feasible with the same predicates.

TOP - a task-oriented parser implemented in Prolog

TOP is a task-oriented parser realizing the principles described above. It is implemented as a Prolog program with the following modular components (cf. figure 4):

- general (toplevel) parsing predicates,
- a system-specific part with basic and derived task descriptions,
- general (low level) utility predicates, e.g. special operations on feature lists.

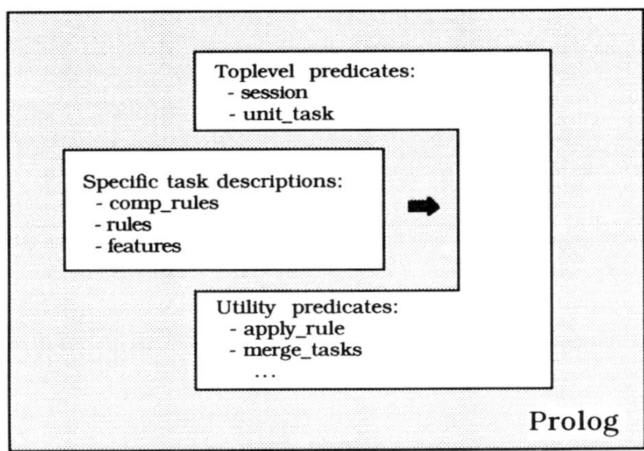

Figure 4. The modular structure of TOP

The parsing mechanism is invoked by formulating a query using the toplevel predicates *unit_task* or *session* with the following parameters:

Input_Sequence (IS) -
a complete list of input actions on the keystroke level, each separate action represented as one element;

Remaining_Sequence (RS) -
the rest of the input list not reduced by the parser - normally specified as the empty list;

Input_Environment (IE) -
the initial state of the system to be modeled;

Output_Environment (OE) -
the final state of the system;

Task or Task_List (T) -
a single task described as a list of feature/value pairs for the *unit_task* predicate, or a sequence (list) of task descriptions for *session.*

Using the toplevel predicates in *parsing mode,* IS, IE, and optionally RS are specified and the remaining parameters will be computed. In *generating mode,* IE and T have to be provided, RS is specified as the empty list, and a solution in terms of IS and OE will be determined. In comparison to equation (5), this is even more general because it is not necessary to specify the output environment.

TOP may be used to model different systems by just adding the specific part of the database to an "empty" TOP-frame comprised of the toplevel and utility predicates. As, in this context, the internal mechanisms of the invariant components are not of interest, only the structure of the system specific database will be explained.

Figure 5 shows the description of some basic tasks for an imaginary forms filling system. In this example, three elementary tasks *(select, fill, quit)* and one composite task *(sel_fill = select + fill)* are defined. The *features* clauses are Prolog facts representing elementary tasks with the associated lists of feature names. They correspond to the *dictionary of simple tasks* in a TAG. For every elementary task another fact (the *rule* clause) has to be provided. The *rule* predicate has four arguments: the task name <task>, a triggering input sequence (eventually containing variables denoted by names beginning with a capital letter - e.g. [mc,N] denotes a mouseclick at position N), and two references to subordinate predicates (normally named do_<task> and <task>_tf).

The do_<task> predicate specifies the changes produced in the environment, i.e. it describes the side effects of that task. It takes the trigger, the incoming and the outcoming environment as arguments. The <task>_tf rule determines how the feature list is instantiated. Therefore it is supplied with the triggering sequence, the incoming environment, and a task pattern (the feature list). The instantiation of the task pattern is achieved by successively applying the *add_feature* predicate starting with an empty feature list. The instantiation mechanism also works in the reverse direction, i.e. it can extract feature values out of given feature lists. This is necessary for using TOP in generating mode. Finally, the *applicable* clauses tell what functions are applicable to which objects. In this special case, *applicable* is always true.

```
comp_rule(sel_fill,[select,[field]],[fill,[field],[text]]).

features(select,[function,field]).
features(fill,[function,field,text]).
features(quit,[function]).

rule(quit,[press_Q],do_quit,quit_tf).
rule(fill,[[type,S],press_ENTER],do_fill,fill_tf).
rule(select,[[mc,N]],do_select,select_tf).


do_select([[mc,N]],Env,Env1) :-
            el([N,Str],Env),
            applicable([N,Str],select),
            make_first([N,Str],Env,Env1).
select_tf([[mc,N]],[F1|R],T) :-
            el([N,_],R),
            add_feature(function,select,[],Tx),
            add_feature(field,N,Tx,T).


do_quit([press_Q],Env,Env).
quit_tf([press_Q],Env,[[function,quit]]).
do_fill([[type,S],_],[[N,S1]|R],[[N,S]|R]) :-
            applicable([N,S1],fill).
fill_tf([[type,S],_],[[N,_]|Rest],T) :-
            add_feature(function,fill,[],Tx),
            add_feature(field,N,Tx,Ty),
            add_feature(text,S,Ty,T).

applicable(Obj,Fn).
```

Figure 5. Specific predicates for an imaginary forms system

Dealing with side effects and extracting feature values from the actual environment requires an adequate (symbolic) representation of the system states. This representation is not predefined and has to be specified for the system to be modelled. The structure of this representation is implicitly contained in the do_<task> or <task>_tf clauses. In the example, it is simply a list of fields, a field being represented as a pair of field-id (a number) and field-value (a text). When using a TOP-like parsing facility together with a real system, the environment parameters could be treated as global variables external to the parser.

The *compose* predicate allows the definition of new tasks as compositions of two tasks already defined. In this case, *sel_fill* is defined as a combination of *select and fill.* The first argument of *compose* is the new task name, the second and third arguments are lists comprised of a subtask name in first position and the features *exported* to the new task in the following positions. So, the feature list for the new task is the union of all the exported features. Features are identified by name, i.e. in the example the select-field and the fill-field have to be identical. The exported features are enclosed in brackets, because in some cases it is necessary to specify a second name to be used with the new task replacing the original name (an example will be given later).

```
?-  session([[type,1987],press_ENTER,
            [mc,3],[type,'OCG/GBT'],press_ENTER,
            press_Q],[],
            [[2,1986],[1,schaerding],[3,'ACM']],OE,T).
OE   = [[3,'OCG/GBT'],[2,1987],[1,schaerding]]
T    = [[[function,fill],[field,2],[text,1987]],
        [[function,sel_fill],[field,3],[text,'OCG/GBT']],
        [[function,quit]]]
?-  unit_task(IS,[],
            [[2,1988],[1,toronto],[3,'ACM-SIGCHI']],OE,
            [[function,sel_fill],[field,1],[text,washington]]).
IS   = [[mc,1],[type,washington],press_ENTER]
OE   = [[1,washington],[2,1988],[3,'ACM-SIGCHI']]
?- ...
```

Figure 6. A session with TOP and the forms predicates

An example session with TOP and the forms predicates is shown in figure 6. The user query follows the system prompt "?-" and is terminated by a full stop. In the first two queries, TOP is used as a parser, and in the third as a generator.

Figure 7 provides a more complex example, modelling the desktop interaction with the Xerox Star system. The more technical details of the do_<task> and <task>_tf rules are left out here. The elementary tasks are *copy, move, rename, and delete. Select* plays a special role in so far as it has no function feature. Selection, in this model, is not considered to be itself a meaningful task, but it can be combined with any of the other functions. This avoids introducing a lot of compositions like *select* + *copy* etc. Technically, it was enabled by just adding one clause to the (toplevel) *unit_task* predicate.

It is particularly interesting to have a look at the composite tasks defined for the desktop application. Whereas *sel_fill* in the forms model does not apply any constraint on the arguments of the two subtasks

```
comp_rule(replace,[delete,[object,del_obj],[position]],
                  [move,[object,rpl_obj],[source_pos],
                      [target_pos,position]]).
comp_rule(copy_with_rename,
                  [copy,[object],[source_pos],[target_pos]],
                  [rename,[position,target_pos],[new_name]]).

features(select,[object,position]).
features(delete,[function,object,position]).
features(rename,[function,object,position,new_name]).
features(move,[function,object,source_pos,target_pos]).
features(copy,[function,object,source_pos,target_pos]).
rule(rename,[press_PROP,press_DEL,[type,N],[mc,ready]],
                        do_rename,rename_tf).
rule(copy,[press_COPY,[mc,Pos]],do_copy,copy_tf).
rule(move,[press_MOVE,[mc,Pos]],do_move,move_tf).
rule(delete,[press_DEL],do_del,del_tf).
rule(select,[[mc,Pos]],do_select,select_tf).
```

Figure 7. Elementary and composite tasks for the desktop application

```
?- session([[mc,2],press_DEL,
        [mc,4],press_COPY,
        [mc,2],press_PROP,
        press_DEL,[type,new],[mc,ready]],[],
       [[a,1],[bg,0],[b,2],[d,4]],OE,T).
OE = [[new,2],[d,4],[bg,0],[a,1]]
T  = [[[function,delete],[position,2],[object,b]],
     [[function,copy_with_rename],[object,d],
      [source_pos,4],[target_pos,2],[new_name,new]]]
?- unit_task(IS,[],
         [[a,1],[bg,0],[b,2],[d,4]],OE,
         [[function,replace],[del_obj,a],
          [position,1],[rpl_obj,d],[source_pos,4]]).
IS = [press_DEL,[mc,4],press_MOVE,[mc,1]]
OE = [[d,1],[bg,0],[b,2]]
?- ...
```

Figure 8. An example session with the desktop model

being composed, *replace* in the desktop model shows how such constraints may be expressed: a *replace* task involves two objects which are not identical, the object to be deleted (*del_obj*) and the replacing object (*rpl_obj*). Furthermore there is a constraint that the target position where the *rpl_obj* is moved to must be the original position of *del_obj*. This is expressed by giving the features to be linked identical names (schema: [<old name>, <new name>]).

The composition operator also allows the definition of recursive task structures, e.g. the following clauses could be added to the forms database:

```
comp_rule(fill_form,[sel_fill],[quit]).
comp_rule(fill_form,[sel_fill],[fill_form]).
```

By this definition, any sequence of *select* + *fill* operations followed by *quit* would be recognized as a *fill_form* task. On the other hand, this definition is too general to associate *fill_form* with semantic features exported by the subtasks.

Generally speaking, TOP provides facilities for representing the task space of a system in a constructive way: first, the elementary tasks are defined as the *atoms* of the task and then more and more complex *molecules* may be constructed by means of task composition. The atomic units of the task space usually are very close to the primitive functions of the system, whereas the composite tasks represent higher level concepts in the user's representation of the task space.

Conclusions and perspectives

The idea and realization of TOP has been strongly influenced by the TAG approach conceptually, and by attribute grammars on the formal level. Indeed, the basic idea was introducing a task parameter into an interaction parser based on AGs. I was astonished to discover another parallel after having written the system: the mechanism of task construction, particularly the treatment of features and constraints is similar to a modern approach in linguistics - the Lexical Functional Grammar or LFG (Kaplan & Bresnan, 1982). In LFG, attributes like gender, number, etc. are associated with phrases and the attribute values are unified in the parsing process. Obviously, phrases correspond with tasks and features with attributes. This concordance gives a plausible argument confirming the choice of the formalism for TOP.

The outcome of this first attempt to task-oriented parsing should be evaluated with regard to the aspects of functionality and representation. As far as the functionality is concerned, we have seen that TOP models may be used for parsing and generation purposes including a simulation of the system on an abstract level. For the online use with a real system, it is not appropriate to replace the single-command-oriented parsing mechanism by a task-oriented parser, because the user needs the normal feedback to all his input actions - not only to those constituting meaningful tasks. So, task-oriented parsing is thought as an additional mechanism essentially for monitoring the user and recognizing what he is doing in terms of tasks.

It should not be concealed that this can be problematic in professional situations in so far as it allows much more hidden supervision of the user than for instance counting of keystrokes. In the applications I have in mind, this mechanism will not be hidden. I have already mentioned protocolling and tutoring as well as the generation of (task-) context-dependent help. Provided with a mechanism for rule induction, a task-oriented parser could also be used for macro generation by identifying frequently repeated combinations of tasks.

The TOP approach is also interesting with regard to the representation of tasks: whereas TAG and GOMS are based on the analytic approach of task decomposition, what we do with TOP is task construction. Both approaches are complementary in so far as the elementary tasks in TOP correspond to the smallest unit- or simple tasks (for novices). There are three levels of task complexity represented in a TOP model:

- the keystroke complexity,
  which is simply the number of elements in the trigger list for the elementary tasks;
- the semantic complexity,
  determined by the number of features a task has;
- the hierarchic complexity,
  i.e. the number of *compose*-operations necessary to define a certain task.

It seems promising to use these complexity parameters for predicting usability characteristics of the system modelled. In this respect, task-oriented parsing could be a multi-purpose tool to be used by system designers and implementers, as well as evaluators. In the spectrum of methods and purposes of formally modeling HCI, TOP fits in with categories (II), (III), and - when forming part of an adaptive interface - even (IV) and (V). Therefore it can be seen as a synthesis of task- and system-oriented interface descriptions.

References

Card, S.K., Moran, T.P. & Newell, A. (1983). *The Psychology of Human-Computer Interaction.* Hillsdale, NJ: Lawrence Erlbaum Associates.

Clocksin, W.F. & Mellish, C.S. (1981). *Programming in Prolog.* Berlin - Heidelberg - New York: Springer Verlag.

Dörner, D. (1976). *Problemlösen als Informationsverarbeitung.* Stuttgart: Kohlhammer.

Green, T.R.G., Schiele, F. & Payne, S.J. (1988). *Formalizable models of user knowledge in human-computer interaction.* In G.C. van der Veer, T.R.G. Green, J.M. Hoc & D. Murray (Eds.), *Working with Computers: Theory versus Outcomes.* London: Academic Press.

Hoppe, H.U., Tauber, M.J. & Ziegler, J.E. (1986). *A Survey of Models and Formal Description Methods in HCI with Example Applications.* ESPRIT Project HUFIT, Report B3.2a.

Kaplan, R.M. & Bresnan, J. (1982). Lexical-functional grammar - A formal system for grammatical representation. In J. Bresnan (Eds.), *The Mental Representation of Grammatical Relations.* Cambridge, Mass: MIT Press.

Kieras, D.E. & Polson, P. (1985). An approach to the formal analysis of user complexity. *Int. J. Man-Machine Studies,* 22, pp. 365-394.

Knuth, D.E. (1968). Semantics of context-free languages. *Math. Systems Theory,* 2, pp. 127-145.

Norman, D.A. (1983). Some observations on mental models. In D. Gentner & L.A. Stevens (Eds.), *Mental Models.* Hillsdale, NJ: Lawrence Erlbaum Associates.

Norman, D.A. (1986). Cognitive engineering. In D.A. Norman & S. Draper (Eds.), *User Centered System Design.* Hillsdale, NJ: Lawrence Erlbaum Associates.

Pagan, F.G. (1981). *Formal Specification of Programming Languages - A Panoramic Primer.* Englewood Cliffs, NJ: Prentice-Hall.

Payne, S.J. & Green, T.R.G. (1983). The user's perception of the interaction language: a two-level model. *Proceedings CHI' 1983.* Boston (Mass.), Dec. 1983, pp. 202-206.

Payne, S.J. & Green, T.R.G. (1986). Task-Action Grammars - A model of the mental representation of task languages. *Human-Computer Interaction,* Vol. 2, pp. 93-133.

Reisner, P. (1981). Formal grammar and human factors design of graphic system. *IEEE Transactions on Software Engineering,* Vol. SE-7/2, 229 - 240.

Tauber, M.J. (1985). Top down Design of human-computer systems from the demands of human cognition to the virtual machine - An interdisciplinary approach to model interfaces. *Proceedings IEEE Workshop on Languages for Automation.* Palma de Mallorca, June 1985, pp. 132-140.

Watt, D.A. & Madsen, O.L. (1983). Extended attribute grammars. *The Computer Journal,* Vol. 26, No. 2/83, pp. 142-153.

Wijngarden, van A. (1966). Recursive definitions of syntax and semantics. In T.B. Steel (Ed.), *Formal Description Languages for Programming.* North-Holland: Amsterdam.

AUTHOR INDEX

I

J

K

L

M

N

O

P

R

S

T

U

V

W

Y

Z

SUBJECT INDEX

V

Y